P9-DMC-285

Human Rights and
Development in Africa

K
3238
.A1
H85
1984

Human Rights and Development in Africa

Edited by

CLAUDE E. WELCH, JR.

and

RONALD I. MELTZER

State University of New York, Buffalo

State University of New York Press
ALBANY

Tennessee Tech. Library
Cookeville, Tenn.

357364

Published by
State University of New York Press, Albany
© 1984 State University of New York
All rights reserved
Printed in the United States of America
No part of this book may be used or reproduced in any manner whatsoever without
written permission except in the case of brief quotations embodied in critical articles
and reviews.
For information, address State University of New York Press, State University Plaza,
Albany, N.Y., 12246

Library of Congress Cataloging in Publication Data
Main entry under title:

Human rights and development in Africa.

Includes index.
1. Civil rights—Africa. 2. Africa—Economic
conditions—1945- . I. Welch, Claude Emerson, Jr.
II. Meltzer, Ronald I.
LAW   323.4'096   83-24122
ISBN 0-87395-836-5
ISBN 0-87395-837-3 (pbk.)

10 9 8 7 6 5 4 3 2

To our children — Lisa, Sarah, Martha, and Chris;
and Molly, Sarah, and Alicia

Contents

Preface

Global interest in human rights has increased markedly since World War II. The 1948 adoption of the Universal Declaration of Human Rights provided a framework within which, over twenty-five years later, International Covenants came into force for Civil and Political Rights, and for Economic, Social, and Cultural Rights. Establishment of the European Court of Human Rights, and steps toward a similar court for the Americas, gave individual citizens the opportunity to use international channels to challenge their governments' policies. The Helsinki accords on security in Europe attempted to provide standards for human rights for the continent as a whole. Human rights policy initiatives by the Carter administration indicated greater United States interest in the subject; Congress mandated the State Department to provide annual reports on human rights practices of other states; U.S. aid to other governments became increasingly linked to their protection of individual liberties. International nongovernmental organizations, such as Amnesty International, the International Commission of Jurists, and the Commission to Study the Organization of Peace, provided publicity about infringements on rights, and proposed more satisfactory mechanisms through which promotion and protection of basic liberties could be pursued. The 1970s was thus a period of markedly increased international awareness of human rights issues by individual governments, international organizations, and nongovernmental organizations.

Greater interest does not necessarily mean greater protection, however. The rights to be protected are themselves in some dispute. Enforcement depends on states that, in ratifying international treaties, agree to accept certain limitations on their sovereignty as well. Governments can also be the major threat to maintaining basic liberties—not just the necessary agents for achieving them. A delicate

1

balance thus exists. States have traditionally been unwilling to bind themselves to external definitions and reviews of their actions. They have been chary of definitions of rights that appear to them to be biased or partial; they seek to defend their domestic sovereignty. Accordingly, the enunciation of basic liberties, and even the ratification of international agreements, cannot be translated, directly and automatically, into more extensive safeguards of human rights than the domestic law of individual states might provide.

Africa presents particularly interesting human rights questions. South Africa exhibits one of the world's most blatant and systematic denials of rights. Race serves as the basic determinant of individuals' civil, political, cultural, and social rights. Despite numerous international resolutions about apartheid, and even a United Nations covenant against its practices, little dent has been made in the panoply of restrictive laws and regulations affecting the overwhelming majority of South Africa's inhabitants.

But apartheid is only one of several practices affecting human rights in Africa. This book looks at less well known, but perhaps more typical and therefore highly significant, human rights issues on the continent as a whole. Most African states achieved independence within the past twenty-five years. They confront serious domestic problems, such as manifestations of "tribalism," that have been cited to justify suppression of cultural and political rights. Many government leaders have seized power by unconstitutional means—and, once in power, have used brutal tactics to maintain their positions. Pervasive economic underdevelopment has affected governmental priorities. Nongovernmental organizations that traditionally have promoted awareness of rights, such as lawyers' associations or national branches of entities such as Amnesty International, have few members, and even less influence. Popular awareness remains constrained by ethnicity, regionalism, limited educational opportunities, and even more limited economic development. Despite occasional references in national constitutions to the Universal Declaration of Human Rights or similar documents, the promotion and protection of human rights by individual governments remain restricted. The existing conditions, it would appear, offer scant support for optimism about human rights in Africa.

As just suggested, economic factors influence the recognition and protection of basic liberties. Human rights and development are, indeed, fundamental problems in contemporary world politics. A great deal of attention has been given to both areas, although with seemingly meager results. What is important to note are the growing ties seen by political leaders between economic and social development and the advancement of human rights. In effect, each is a conditioning factor for the other, as well as an aspect of the other's realization. Despite their extensive interconnections, however, institutional and political developments in these areas have not kept pace with evolving formulations and requirements. The reason lies in the extensive legal, organizational, and political obstacles to the joint realization of human rights and development objectives. Indeed, attempts to draw such links in current international deliberations have resulted in widespread politicization. The "right to development," for example, has become an issue symbolizing the major contrasts between the industrialized states of the "North" and the developing states of the "South," including Africa.

A major purpose of this book, *Human Rights and Development in Africa*, is to clarify the connections that exist between levels of development and local standards and practices of human rights. Should it be argued, for example, that greater protection of basic liberties could occur within individual states only with a major restructuring of international economic relations? Are the rights that have been defined by the United Nations, or by constitutions based substantially on European models, in fact appropriate for the conditions of contemporary Africa? What external and internal factors influence the ways in which African political leaders view human rights and development?

To answer broad questions of this sort, it is advisable to work at three levels of analysis—domestic, regional, and international—which reflect the various ways in which human rights and development are defined and pursued, and to give detailed attention to traditions of human rights, to conflicts between differing conceptions, and to political leaders' goals with respect to those rights. At the domestic level, for example, various "traditional" societies within particular states manifest their own definite ideas about the liberties and obligations of their members. Further, each government is directed in its actions by leaders whose priorities may or may not include vigorous pursuit of human rights or of economic development. Attention to the regional level—that is to say, Africa as a whole—allows us to focus, for example, on recent steps by the Organization of African Unity, such as the 1981 adoption of the Banjul Charter of Human and Peoples' Rights, which opens the way for eventual establishment of a regional commission on human rights. Finally, at the international level there can be broader consideration of the wider framework within which human rights and development are situated. The legacy of colonialism and underdevelopment; the growing influence of Third World countries in international forums; the demands of poor states for greater recognition of their conditions of impoverishment and their unfavorable position in world trade: Factors of this sort, most appropriately analyzed in global terms, are vital to understanding the constraints upon and opportunities for human rights and development in Africa.

Human Rights and Development in Africa touches upon many different actors in the quest for both development and human rights: individual governments; nongovernmental organizations; regional entities such as the Organization of African Unity and the European Community; international bodies such as the UN Commission on Human Rights and the UN General Assembly. Nation-states cannot be considered the sole agents for protecting human rights and achieving development. In fact, in many societies the governments themselves are among the main obstacles to both.

This book does not attempt to be exhaustive; were it to be so, many more pages would have to be added. For example, the long-standing problem of apartheid—examined in dozens of other volumes—receives limited attention in the pages that follow. Although refugees in Africa suffer great personal tragedies, and symbolize major political issues, they are not discussed. No systematic survey is made of "traditional" conceptions of human rights in Africa, although attention is given to selected areas of concern. The case studies of individual countries that appear below are restricted in range; no attention is given to states of North Africa, for example, although attention is given to selected areas of concern. The case studies of individual countries that appear below are restricted in time, space, and expertise; however, the editors and the eleven authors have attempted to draw appropriately broad implications from their particular contributions.

The chapters in this volume were initially presented in May 1982 at a conference at the State University of New York at Buffalo (SUNY/Buffalo). The editors acknowledge, with deep thanks, the financial support of several entities: the National Endowment for the Humanities; the "Conversations in the Disciplines" program of the State University of New York; the "Conferences in the Disciplines" program and the Research Development Funds of SUNY/Buffalo; the New York Council on the Humanities; the University at Buffalo Foundation; and the Department of Political Science, SUNY/Buffalo. The editors, of course, bear full responsibility for the content of the book as a whole.

The research assistance provided by Vicki Kraft and Robert Wigton both eased completion of the manuscript and enhanced its academic accuracy. The comments of Professors Carl G. Rosberg and Vernon Van Dyke on an earlier draft were extremely helpful. Major help in administering the details of both the conference and the manuscript came from Betty Balcom and Margaret Kasprzyk. Our spouses—Jeannette Ludwig and Carol Frank—endured with grace the time and attention we took for this book. We give our special thanks to them, and to the so many others whom space precludes us from mentioning.

I

Roots and Implications of Human Rights in Africa

INTRODUCTION

A serious division of opinion exists with respect to human rights in "traditional" Africa. One school of thought argues that, prior to the colonial takeover and installation of "Western" constitutional forms and norms, human rights were inadequately recognized and protected. They were embedded in collective settings—in the "traditional" milieu of clan, age-set, ethnic group, or similar ascriptive groupings—and were not inherent in individuals' situations. Under such conditions, proponents of this view suggest,[1] key rights, such as safety of the person, were protected only within particular contexts. Human rights were not applicable to all individuals under these conditions; although concepts of human "dignity" existed, they did not adhere to the criteria of universality deemed necessary by adherents of this first viewpoint.

By contrast, a second school of thought extolls the recognition and protection of human rights found in "traditional" societies in Africa. The imposition of European rule abridged rather than widened such rights, since colonialism was inherently authoritarian. Whether the rulers were British, French, Belgian, or some other nationality, they relied ultimately on coercion, and were interested in African colonies primarily as economic resources. Contrasting the abridgement of liberties under colonial rule with their expression in pre-colonial Africa prior to the late nineteenth century, such authors[2] are sharply critical of any claim that European rule enhanced human rights. Far more attuned to the needs of Africa, they claim, were the "traditional" means of defining and safeguarding individual and group liberties.

Bald contrasts of this sort are challenged by the five chapters that follow. The simple before-and-after dichotomies suggested by the two schools of thought fail to recognize historical and cultural reality.

7

"Traditional" African societies were by no means devoid of practices intended to protect human rights; on the other hand, such practices could not be separated from their various social milieus, notably their ethnic groups. Colonialism introduced different legal definitions of human rights, including court systems that in many respects superseded indigenous systems of justice; however, the provision of political rights, especially self-determination, came only late in the period of European rule. Summing up the chapters that follow, the following general points emerge:

1. Individuals in "traditional" African societies existed within social contexts that recognized and protected a variety of human rights;
2. rights accordingly were expressed in ways that varied with the particular settings;
3. so-called "traditional" societies were not static, but subject to significant alteration over time; equally, "traditional" beliefs could be, and were, changed in response to different pressures;
4. constitutional and legal forms for recognizing and protecting rights have shortcomings that result from the continuing influence of "traditional" definitions and practices, meaning that human rights in contemporary Africa may best be supported by relying on, and gradually changing, the "traditional" definitions and practices of rights.

In the first chapter, Claude Welch comments upon the political, social, and economic factors that influence the ways in which Africans perceive human rights. He gives particular emphasis to political leaders, finding them primarily concerned with economic development and national unity. These two concerns, he argues, affect many civil and political rights: They are viewed as less important than the need for rapid economic advance in a world marked by manifest global inequalities.

Welch sets forth three problems in human rights in Africa. The "problem of arena" involves the level at which such rights most effectively can be defined and protected. Paradoxically, it is at the national level that most abuses by governments occur, and where most protection can be afforded. The international level has been, until recently, the one on which African leaders have been most active, notably in the attempt to eliminate apartheid and colonialism. But it is the regional level, the continent of Africa, that is becoming increasingly significant. The decision of the Organization of African Unity to adopt the Banjul Charter of Human and Peoples' Rights marks a new step. The "problem of definition" involves basic questions regarding what rights are to be protected, and which means ought to be used. The Banjul Charter introduces many elements of a so-called "third generation" of human rights. Among these rights is the claim to a "right to development," examined in Welch's chapter as a third area, the "problem of development."

The importance of "traditional" definitions and means of protecting human rights emerges in Lakshman Marasinghe's case study of the Yoruba. In Western Nigeria, he finds, the right to family membership, freedom of thought, speech, beliefs, and association, and the right to enjoy private property are fundamental. Marasinghe criticizes scholars who assert that African societies lacked conceptions of human rights prior to the imposition of colonialism; in this respect, Marasinghe takes direct issue with Jack Donnelly, in Chapter 12. Most presumed violations of human rights in Africa, Marasinghe argues, refer to conceptions recognized and guaranteed by essentially external documents, notably national constitutions. Hence, attention must be given to indigenous ideas about freedoms and responsibilities. Empirical research into internalized conceptions of human rights in a traditional society, Marasinghe concludes, would lead to "enormous satisfaction as to the basic democratic way in which the society protects its own human values."

In Chapter 3, Rhoda Howard uses the 1979 UN Convention on the Elimination of All Forms of Discrimination against Women to assess women's rights in seven English-speaking countries of tropical Africa. It should come as no surprise that females in these states lack many human rights. Three sets of factors—international inequality and neocolonialism, internal class inequality, and indigenous sexual inequality reinforced by custom and culture—provide a multicausal explanation. Attention must be given the historical and sociological context for human rights. Howard, like Marasinghe, stresses that legislative action without adequate understanding of this broader context leads to unsatisfactory results. She gives detailed attention to issues such as polygyny, inheritance, and genital operations to illustrate the interplay between indigenous custom and Western-inspired laws.

Islam is the most rapidly growing religion in Africa; its influence obviously shapes the ways in which rights are perceived and protected in Muslim societies. Abdullahi Ahmed El Naiem argues a controversial point in Chapter 4. He suggests that, although certain aspects of traditional Islamic law are inconsistent with universal human rights, Islam as a whole can in fact help achieve such rights. The need, he argues, is for fundamental reform of Islam. Left for further consideration is whether fundamental change of the sort El Naiem recommends can in fact be achieved. Religions are intimately interwoven with their particular milieus. Yet a Sudanese Muslim leader has proposed radical reform; such basic updating would be necessary to ensure the realization of the originality and individuality of each and every person—in El Naiem's view, the "ultimate" human right.

Finally, Richard Weisfelder turns in detail to a section of Africa in which human rights issues—including self-determination on the basis of majority rule—have raised a variety of problems. The independent states of southern Africa display a variety of governmental human rights practices, even though all are embedded in a regional context dominated by the Republic of South Africa. By considering the intensity, extensiveness, duration, and deliberateness of violations of human rights, Weisfelder provides a detailed picture of the complexities of protecting these rights.

The chapters in this section by no means exhaust all that could—and should—be written about conceptions of human rights in Africa. The authors do make clear, however, the urgent need for detailed research on the fundamental bases of African societies; only in this fashion can the relationship between indigenous ideas and external definitions be clearly established, and the most appropriate strategies for promoting and protecting human rights devised.

NOTES

1. See, for example, Jack Donnelly, "Human Rights and Human Dignity," *American Political Science Review* 72, no. 2 (June 1982), pp. 303–16, and his chapter later in this book.

2. Latif O. Adegbite, "African Attitudes to the International Protection of Human Rights," in Asbjorn Eide and August Schou, eds., *International Protection of Human Rights* (New York: Interscience Publishers, 1968), pp. 69–81, and Dunstan M. Wai, "Human Rights in Sub-Saharan Africa," in Adamantia Pollis and Peter Schwab, eds., *Human Rights: Cultural and Ideological Perspectives* (New York: Praeger, 1979), pp. 115–44.

CHAPTER ONE

Human Rights as a Problem in Contemporary Africa

CLAUDE E. WELCH, JR.

Africa presents a paradoxical picture in the study of contemporary international human rights. More acted upon than actor in international human rights issues, Africa as a whole has been affected by conflicting perceptions about precisely what are human rights, how they can best be achieved, and where the needs are greatest.

Recognition and protection of human rights certainly existed in the precolonial period. African definitions of human rights differed in key respects, however, from those prevalent in the West. The context of family, clan, and ethnic solidarity—in short, the web of kinship—provided the frameworks within which individuals exercised their economic, political, and social liberties and duties. With the imposition of external rule, Africans lost most opportunity to define and control such rights. Conflicts emerged between indigenous and European conceptions. The "redomestication" of human rights in Africa, adapting and adopting rights appropriate to existing circumstances, required both political independence and growing domestic awareness of the issues involved.

When colonialism was overturned, high aspirations existed, both in Africa and in the international commuinity as a whole. Without the deadening weight of colonialism, so the general belief ran, individuals' standards of living would rise, political freedoms and opportunities would increase, cultural development would occur unskewed by external constraints, and the "authentic" African personality could flower. Obviously, the higher the initial expectations, the more caustic the subsequent judgments.

That the hopes of independence were unrealistically high needs little elaboration. Later chapters in this book provide details about abuses of human rights in several African states. The end of colonialism did not automatically usher in a new era, a dawn of basic liberties, nor did it bring marked or immediate economic affluence. As Rupert Emerson wrote, "What is unhappily not established, and cannot be, is that the desired rights and freedoms spring to life automatically when the alien ruler is banished."[1] The widespread popular political mobilization of the late colonial period has disappeared. Competitive party systems have been transformed into single-party or no-party systems; military juntas have seized control and themselves frequently been subject to violent overthrow. Open trials, independence of the judiciary, and procedural rights have been abused. Leaders of political opposition groups have been liable to imprisonment, "disappearance," or execution after abbreviated trials; members of certain ethnic groups have suffered from gross violations of their most basic right, the right to life. The country reports submitted by the U.S. Department of State on rights in individual states generally describe declining opportunities for citizens to exercise democratic choice.[2] Thus, in terms of basic civil and political rights, accomplishments have remained far short of expectations.

The record seems as dismal economically and socially as it does politically. With the exception of a few oil-exporting states, economic growth has rarely outpaced population increases; the gap in living standards between urban and rural areas has frequently widened; conflict between "ethnic" and "national" identity has remained and in several respects intensified. Various economic development strategies, such as import substitution or collective self-reliance, have had scant effect on the pervasive conditions of underdevelopment. States of the industrialized "North" continue to dominate world markets. One result, discussed in the chapters by Ronald Meltzer and Timothy Shaw, is that the developing states of the "South" have little leverage to transform the inequalities of development. The toll of natural events such as drought has been compounded by government inefficiencies and continued dependence on the export of primary products. In many African countries, the standard of living has actually decreased.

With more than a score of years since most African states achieved self-government, and with the Organization of African Unity itself reaching its twentieth anniversary, it is an appropriate time to take stock to assess the background to and position of human rights in Africa. Thus, this chapter sets out to achieve three goals:

1. to sketch, in broad terms, the political, economic, cultural and social framework of contemporary Africa, in order better to illustrate the context in which human rights are exercised:
2. to elaborate on the major problems involved in the choice among conflicting rights and among strategies to achieve them, with par-

ticular emphasis on the dilemma of choice between "liberty" and "development"; and

3. to suggest major areas in which further research is essential.

BASES FOR HUMAN RIGHTS IN CONTEMPORARY AFRICA

Political Factors

Of the major continents of the world, Africa endured the most recent and widespread colonialism. A number of political constraints on the exercise of human rights in Africa can be attributed directly to the imposition of external rule.

First, the basic shape of the states themselves was the consequence of European administrative convenience or imperial competition. What African nationalist leaders widely condemned as "artificial" frontiers stemmed from imperial rivalries and compromises. Colonialism created states in which the promotion of self-government was, at most, a minor priority for the ruling powers until the last years of the colonial interlude. Little opportunity existed after independence for redrawing boundaries,[3] helping to set the stage for later attempts at secession.

Second, an authoritarian framework for local administration was installed, reducing most indigenous rulers to relatively minor cogs in the administrative machinery, and leaving until the terminal days of colonialism the creation of a veneer of democratization.

Third, European law codes were introduced and widely applied, notably in urban areas, while "traditional" legal precepts were incompletely codified and relegated to an inferior position in civil law, notably in rural areas. One result was widespread confusion over applicable standards; a second consequence was the creation of dual legal systems with areas of overlap between them and limited standardization within them; a third effect, discussed in greater detail below and in the chapters by Marasinghe and Howard, was significant alteration of and reduction in the rights that individual Africans enjoyed.

Fourth, constitutional recognition and protection of rights were belated, with the constitution created at independence being in many cases the first significant expression of them. Specific provisions dealing with human rights tended to be most elaborate in African states in which large European expatriate populations lived, and tended further to protect minority rights far more than advance majority rights.

Fifth, initial constitutional provisions were drawn overwhelmingly from patterns familiar to the departing colonial power, hence reflecting assumptions far more common in the metropole than in particular African societies; being externally imposed, these constitutions lacked popular support and legitimacy.

Many Africans have argued, with eloquence and rationale, that the period of colonial administration provided scant encouragement for respecting and protecting human rights; after all, it was a time of authoritarian rule. On the other hand, apologists for the past have suggested that the European powers, carrying out their *mission civilisatrice*, introduced new, appropriate human rights norms. Where, more precisely, may one strike the balance?

That the physical boundaries and initial constitutions of individual African states were bequeathed by colonialism cannot be denied. However, the rhetoric of colonial administration—the justification to the effect that Africans were being prepared for the "strenuous conditions of the modern world," to quote a noted phrase from the Covenant of the League of Nations—considerably overstated the reality. What apprenticeship may have been served was in large measure irrelevant; it certainly was belatedly encouraged. The period of European rule was one in which the right to vote and to participate in "modern" political institutions scarcely existed. Colonial policies placed indigenous institutions in subordinate positions. Means of popular consultation and participation in the "traditional" setting—for example, councils—lost much of their significance. Chiefs and other leaders became far more responsive to pressures from above (the colonial administration) than from below (the populace). Institutions and values were in essence imposed; "real" adoption required subsequent adaptation, which could be meaningfully undertaken only after independence.

On the other hand, precolonial African societies lacked numerous civil and political rights familiar to the colonizing powers, and desired now by African leaders. For example, as Abdullahi Ahmed El Naiem points out in a later chapter of this book, traditional Islamic law (Shari'a) did not recognize universal suffrage, organized political opposition, independence of the judiciary, separation of powers, or the right of women and persons of different religious backgrounds to participate in political matters.

On balance, European administration undercut precolonial norms and expectations of political rights. Such rights, however, had rarely been exercised on an equal basis among all adult members of particular African societies. The frameworks brought by colonialism reflected Western liberal assumptions; "traditional" expectations, such as those about the responsibilities of chiefs or the nature of judicial settlement, were jeopardized. The overall effect was one of weakening the effectiveness of indigenous standards and traditional institutions without firmly implanting new ideas. The impact of European norms was most marked on the small segment of the populace that benefited from extensive education and opportunities (along with many frustrations) to participate in the political institutions created by the colonial masters. For the great majority of the population, however, the colonial period was a time during which various rights defined within existing groups were abridged, without corresponding advances in establishing and maintaining individual political liberties.

Social Factors

The precolonial roots of contemporary African states remain highly relevant for understanding conceptions of human rights. Although the formal legal and political frameworks of the early years of independence reflected colonial models far more than indigenous sources, the *context* in which rights were defined and exercised owed, and continues to owe, much to existing local norms. What may best characterize contemporary Africa is a richness, or confusion, of norms: expectations imposed during the colonial period, presuppositions inherited from earlier periods, and new ideas developed since independence.

The roles and responsibilities of individuals were not static in precolonial Africa. Several factors, including migration, the osmosis of new ideas and religions, and the effects of conflict, influenced the ways in which social rights were perceived and expressed prior to the colonial interlude.

The imposition of external rule introduced new complexities: the European colonizers changed many existing indigenous practices. When collective and individual expression came into conflict, the values of the colonizing powers were presumed to be superior to those indigenous to African societies. European rulers thus had both the inclination and the strength to impose new procedures and values.

Perhaps this point becomes clearer through brief reference to certain problem areas. Several matrilineal African societies had practices of inheritance by which property passed from father to nephew, rather than from father to son; colonial legal codes, based on different assumptions, assaulted this belief by stressing inheritance through direct descent. Polygyny was accepted in many, if not most, groups in Africa; European powers, encouraged by missionaries, tried to eliminate this practice, although with indifferent success. Rights existed in the context of the extended family; they were not inherent in individuals, but latent in ascriptive groups. The social context was thus of paramount importance, emphasizing collective or communal rights. "The concept of human rights in Africa," according to Chris Mojekwu, "was fundamentally based on ascribed status . . . . One who had lost his membership in a social unit or one who did not belong—an outcast or a stranger—lived outside the range of human rights protection by the social unit."[4] Or, to cite Latif Adegbite, "the indigene in traditional Africa enjoyed greater freedom than his modern counterpart. Admittedly, his rights were not guaranteed by the state such that he could, at his own instance, enforce them against the whole world. He had to rely on his intimate group, the extended family or the clan, to manipulate the political and social forces to secure his rights."[5] Similar arguments are advanced by Lakshman Marasinghe, in the following chapter.

"Traditional" African societies recognized six major sets of rights: the right to life, the right to education, the right to freedom of movement, the right to receive justice, the right to work, and the right to participate in the benefits and decision making of the community.[6] All these rights existed within collective contexts, and were frequently expressed in ways unfamiliar to Europeans. Ignorance of African norms, and a firm belief in the superiority of European practices, led colonial powers to abridge many rights that had been protected prior to colonialism. What Marasinghe documents for Yoruba society in Nigeria was thus typical of Africa as a whole: changes in the right of association, as well as in the rights of thought, speech, and belief occurred as a result of external rule, often to their detriment.

Information of this sort contradicts what has been paraded as gospel. For many years colonial rule was rationalized as improving the conditions of life and the rights of Africans. The *Pax Britannica* was justified in part by the claim that precolonial African societies had unduly restricted individual liberties. For example, the "bridewealth" given for marriageable daughters was interpreted by Europeans as more akin to purchase of unwilling females than to insurance and protection through the extended family. Chiefs, who drew on advice of elders and who could be deposed if they "violated the laws of the land and disregarded the rights of the people,"[7] were portrayed by colonizing powers as despotic—and were in fact made so by colonial policies.

Accordingly a basic difference in emphasis existed. European conceptions, notably of political and civil rights, stressed *individual protection*; African conceptions emphasized *collective expression*. The former was based upon a set of assumptions about the rights of persons, particularly vis-à-vis governments; the latter was founded on kinship roles and village groups, in which legal, political, and social institutions were intertwined. The notion of a legal system and a political system embodied in distinct institutions was central to what Europeans considered appropriate, or "civilized." "Traditional" African societies were characterized by unified institutions. In the jargon of social science, functional differentiation was limited. But did these contrasting expectations mean that human rights did not exist in precolonial Africa? The answer, obviously, is no. However, expression of such rights could not readily be abstracted from the context in which they were recognized and protected. Such liberties were applicable within cultural boundaries where kinship played a paramount role; they did not exist in the abstract, as rights inherent in *all* human beings. For this reason, some analysts have been unwilling to view "traditional" conceptions as embodying human rights as classically defined.[8]

Economic Factors

The right to life and the right to work were widely recognized in "traditional" Africa, as already noted. Both these rights depended on the most fundamental economic resource, land—for, without an area to cultivate, or year-round access to pasture, a family would lack fundamental security. Problems of landlessness appear to have been relatively rare in "traditional" Africa. Shifting bush fallow (abandonment of fields that were declining in fertility to permit regeneration) was the basic method of agriculture. General control of land was vested collectively, with individual heads of household enjoying the right to cultivate. Alienation of land from the group could not occur, in general, without the concurrence of the entire group.

One need have only a fragmentary knowledge of Africa to recognize that land problems resulted from the imposition of European rule, especially in areas of white settlement. South Africa, Kenya, Algeria, Zimbabwe: All faced major protests from Africans as a result of indigenous lands being seized by outsiders. But several other economic issues resulted from colonialism, as well. The imposition of direct taxes frequently ran counter to accepted practices. Mining disrupted many regions. Colonial governments viewed promotion of commercial agriculture as an appropriate means of pursuing and justifying their "civilizing mission" and of funding administrative costs; hence, establishment of plantations, compulsory cultivation of cash crops, and European settlement were encouraged in many areas. During the colonial period, accordingly, the central government came to exercise a direct economic role qualitatively distinct from precolonial periods.

Turning to the present situation, one can distinguish four sets of economic factors influencing the recognition and application of human rights in Africa: (1) low levels of economic development; (2)

uneven but readily politicized expectations regarding the distribution of economic benefits, notably in the waning days of colonialism; (3) the expectation of African leaders that the postindependence state should take a major role in economic leadership; and (4) the further desire of African leaders for substantial change in international economic relations. The first and fourth factors will be analysed in the section dealing with the issue of development; the others merit attention at this point.

What became a bandwagon of anticolonial feeling owed much to unequal distribution of economic resources. It has been generally argued that "traditional" African societies were characterized by a basically egalitarian economic structure, although this conventional wisdom is subject to increasing attack.[9] Not open to dispute, however, is the fact that even greater economic disparities opened up as a result of colonialism. The differences between living standards that widened as a direct consequence of European rule gave aspirant politicians a ready issue to mobilize support—and meant, in many cases, that the chief question after independence was a reslicing of the economic pie.

This widespread popular concern for economic redistribution interacted with the desire of African leaders to carry out major economic improvement. Confronted simultaneously with preindependence norms of relative egalitarianism and with colonial patterns of skewed income distributions, nationalist spokesmen saw political action as the most appropriate vehicle for development. Improvement would be sought through government. Although the colonial period had been one in which administrative actions had often increased disparities in income levels, the independence epoch would be one in which political leaders would achieve the betterment of all. Leaders' desires thus reinforced public pressures. The upshot was a set of expectations that gave governments a significant agenda for economic and social action.

How did these varied views influence perceptions of human rights? To prefigure a conclusion of this chapter, significant emphasis was placed on *collective* achievement *through government*. Carried over from "traditional" societies was a sense that mutual efforts were necessary; added from the colonial interlude was a belief that what governmental actions had failed to accomplish under European auspices could be achieved under African leadership. Recent African perceptions of human rights thus came to be heavily influenced by the desire and the political need to enhance living standards. Widespread economic improvement became a *sine qua non* for leaders, both domestically and internationally. The emphasis became increasingly collective, economic, and oriented toward "peoples" with the achievement of independence. In the process, what had been considered as rights prior to the imposition of colonial rule, and what were defined as rights in a series of post-World War II international documents, became subject to reinterpretation in African states.

PROBLEMS OF CHOICE

A basic problem lies at the heart of human rights: are they best pursued through proclamation and promotion—relying on international publicity and standards—or through enforcement that, necessarily, must be carried out by and within individual states? As will be illustrated in this section, the question of *what* rights exist and *how* they can best be achieved is of crucial importance. Attention must be given to three specific areas: *arena* (international, regional, and national settings within which rights can be promoted and protected); *definition* (specification of the rights to be protected, and the means to be used); and *development* (the relationship between claims for economic growth and human rights policies pursued by individual governments).

The Problem of Arena: International, Regional, and Domestic Settings

To understand the problems of choice—choice among potentially conflicting rights, choice among potentially conflicting strategies for achieving those rights—it is appropriate to take note first of the political and institutional avenues African leaders have utilized with respect to human rights.

Like other developing countries, African states have used the UN General Assembly as their chosen forum to manifest their primary international policy objectives. UN Declarations and Conventions since 1960 have given a clear indication of African priorities. Issues relevant to Africa, and to other parts of the Third World, have absorbed an increasing portion of the UN's attention. The major areas of human rights concern for African states include apartheid, colonialism, development, independence, racism and racial discrimination, and self-determination. As relatively new members of the UN, African states have been fundamentally concerned with translating international resolutions into effective action.

During the 1960s and early 1970s, the Organization of African Unity (OAU) was still in a relatively early phase of its development. Its annual conferences of heads of state and government were devoted far more to discussions of lingering colonialism in Africa than to investigations of human rights issues within member states. Their primary concern remained safeguarding the newly acquired independence of their countries. Few, if any, human rights problems other than apartheid and self-determination for colonial territories were examined. Practically no attention was given within the OAU to internal repression or illegal changes of government within member states, these being considered items of unchallengeable domestic jurisdiction. The lack of attention within the OAU was paralled by lack of attention by other bodies. For example, with the exceptions of the January 1961 Lagos conference of the African Bar Association, the February 1966 Dakar seminar on human rights in developing countries, and the September 1969 Cairo seminar on regional human rights groups sponsored by the United Nations, no major conference held in Africa focused on human rights during the 1960s.

By the late 1970s, however, the relative quiescence of human rights issues in the preceding decade had changed. For historic reasons examined in the chapter by Edward Kannyo, African states gave increasing attention to human rights abuses within particular states. In addition, several regional meetings were held to consider ways of better protecting civil and political liberties. The impetus for convening such conferences (a list of which appears as Appendix III) came from several sources: non-governmental organizations such as the World Council of Churches and the International Commission of Jurists; the United Nations through its Secretariat and the Commission on Human Rights; the OAU; and groupings of individual states. An increasingly important theme was that of drafting a charter of human rights designed specifically for African conditions. As Kannyo points out, this approach was based on increased willingness to use a regional as contrasted with a global forum to examine the major issues. By the end of the 1970s, conditions were ripe for the OAU to turn specifically and directly to proposals for promoting and protecting human rights.

The Problem of Definition: Rights to Be Protected

The 1979 session of the Assembly of Heads of State and Government (as the supreme body of the OAU is formally known) unanimously approved a resolution introduced by Senegal and the Gambia, calling upon experts to prepare a draft charter on human rights in Africa. The specialists assembled in Dakar in December 1979, three months after a UN-sponsored seminar had met in Monrovia and had proposed establishing a regional commission for human rights in Africa. The activities of both groups of specialists merit brief review.

The Monrovia experts had decided not to prepare a distinct set of rights for Africa. Most of their efforts were devoted to suggesting operating procedures for a proposed African regional commission on human rights, modeled in some measure after the Inter-American Commission on Human Rights. As discussed in the subsequent chapters by Kannyo and Richard Gittleman, the draftsmen at Monrovia recommended that existing international documents serve as standards for promoting and protecting human rights in Africa (Appendix 2 provides a concordance among these documents). But the experts at Dakar, assembled under OAU auspices, opted for a dramatically different type of document than had the Monrovia specialists, assembled under UN auspices. Their proposed "African Charter of Human and Peoples' Rights" gave detailed attention to specific rights. Twenty-nine of the sixty-eight articles were devoted to rights and freedoms that applied to "every person and every people . . . ." Three areas—the role of the populace in selecting government leaders, "third generation" rights, and "clawback" clauses—merit brief review in the form they took at the two conferences at Banjul in the Gambia in 1980 and 1981.

Consonant with the International Covenant on Civil and Political Rights, the Banjul Charter (the text which is given in Appendix 1) states, "Every citizen shall have the right to freely participate in the government of his country, either directly or through freely chosen representatives." Perhaps relying solely on the words "freely chosen," however, the African specialists did not indicate the means to be used. The UN Universal Declaration and the International Covenant, by contrast, make specific reference to secret ballot on the basis of universal, equal suffrage.

The Banjul Charter, in comparison with its major forebears, asserts a series of rights that, as examined in greater detail by Jack Donnelly, belong to a "third generation" of human rights. Among those mentioned are the "right to information," to "a generally satisfactory environment," to "the unquestionable and inalienable right to self-determination," to "freely dispose of their wealth and natural resources," to "economic, social, and cultural development," and to "national and international peace and security." "Colonized or oppressed peoples," the Banjul Charter states, "shall have the right to free themselves from the bonds of domination by resorting to any means recognized by the international community."

A third striking feature of the Banjul Charter is the insertion of several "clawback" clauses that, as shown in the subsequent chapter by Gittleman, limit the application and protection of rights to what is provided by domestic law. Such clauses seriously weaken the protection of specific rights, and would appear to offer little effective challenge to the political authoritarianism that marks many contemporary African states. As the chapter by Harry Scoble makes apparent, several other changes were made from the initial to the final version, almost all of which reduced the authority of the proposed regional commission. Consequently, the document adopted at the 1981 Nairobi summit was weaker in crucial respects than the prior Dakar draft. Protection of "liberty" was seemingly subordinated to maintenance of existing systems. It is clear that the laws and practices of individual African states can potentially override the liberties the Banjul Charter is intended to define, promote, and protect.

The Problem of Government Power: Conflicts of Liberty and Development

That African states are poor and their governments limited in their ability to bring about dramatic change needs little elaboration. The potential effects of economic impoverishment on the recognition and protection of human rights require detailed attention, however.

Africa's record in bolstering living standards in rural areas and in achieving substantial economic growth has been mixed, at best. The limited results cannot be attributed to lack of desire, nor to an absence of internal and international initiatives. On the global level, UN-endorsed development decades have come and gone without significant transformation of the international economic system. Third World countries issue periodic manifestos on the need for restructuring global economic relations; the UN General Assembly has held special sessions devoted to the call for a New International Economic Order; various UN agencies have increasingly stressed development programs and the satisfaction of basic needs. On the domestic level, individual states have adopted ambitious development plans, strategies of import substitution, industrialization, self-reliance, deficit financing, the like.

Despite these initiatives, the gap between affluent and impoverished states has widened. While in the 1950–1980 period industrialized countries enjoyed an annual growth in per capita Gross National Product (GNP) of 3.1 percent, low-income countries achieved a rate of only 1.3 percent. As a consequence, during those thirty years, citizens of industrialized states saw annual per capita GNP increase from $3,841 to $9,684; those in agricultural states witnessed a meager increase from $145 to $245. Economic impoverishment remains particularly acute south of the Sahara, most notably for non-oil-producing nations. Of the thirty-nine countries listed in a recent World Bank study as having GNPs per capita below $365 (1978 base), twenty-five were located in Africa.[10] Thirty-four of the sixty-nine states in which annual GNP per capita fell under $850 were African. Indeed, for the continent as a whole, only countries at the geographic extremes—Algeria, Tunisia and South Africa—exhibited GNPs over

$850; the figure for South Africa masked marked differences by race.[11]

Economic figures by themselves have no necessarily direct relevance to human rights, however; impoverishment cannot by itself predict whether or not respect for human rights characterizes individual states. As is well known, governments noted for their recognition and protection of civil and political rights have ruled over some of the poorest states in the entire continent, a point stressed in the chapter by Richard Weisfelder. Low levels of economic development, in other words, may impede but do not preclude vigorous government efforts to protect civil and political rights. On the other hand, it is frequently asserted that such low levels seriously affect the achievement of basic needs, and of economic and social goals.

Western scholars, particularly those of liberal background, distinguish between civil and political rights, on the one hand, and economic, social and cultural rights, on the other. African leaders, in common with other Third World spokesmen, have placed increasing emphasis on the latter set, and in many instances assert that economic betterment should precede enhancement of political liberties.

Political and civil rights refer primarily to protection of citizens' rights against government infringements. They are designed to preclude arbitrary government intrusion into private affairs. Phraseology tends to be negative, placing limits on official actions. States are mandated, under the International Covenant on Political and Civil Rights, to respect and ensure, for *all* individuals within their territories or under their jurisdictions, the rights set forth in the Covenant "without distinction of any kind, such as race, colour, sex, language, religion, political or other opinion, national or social origin, property, birth, or other status." Such recognition of the "equal and inalienable rights of all members of the human family" is derived from the "inherent dignity of the human person." In other words, an individual is endowed from birth with specific civil and political rights. Even in times of public emergency, many of these cannot be weakened or derogated from, for example, the right to life, freedom from torture and cruel, inhuman or degrading treatment, freedom from slavery or servitude, freedom from imprisonment merely on grounds of inability to fulfil a contractual obligation, freedom from retroactive criminal legislation, the right to recognition "as a person before the law," and freedom of thought, conscience, and religion. Governments are obliged both to adopt legislation to "give effect" to the stipulated political and civil rights, and to provide "effective remedy" to persons whose rights are violated.

Unlike civil and political rights, which limit government actions, the implementation of economic, social, and cultural rights requires affirmative government action. As a consequence, these rights tend to be positively defined as "rights to" rather than "freedoms from." For example, states that are party to the International Covenant on Economic, Social and Cultural Rights "undertake to take steps . . . *with a view to achieving progressively* the full realization of the rights recognized in the present Covenant *by all appropriate means*, including the adoption of legislative measures." (Emphasis added.) All the rights listed (e.g., to social security, to the "highest attainable standard of physical and mental health," to an "adequate standard of living," to education "that shall enable all persons to participate effectively in a free society") are thus subject to the constraints of finance—as well as to constraints of political will.

The framers of the Universal Declaration of Human Rights, on the basis of which the two International Covenants were drafted, viewed the two sets of rights as interdependent. They believed that the achievement of civil and political rights should not be accorded higher priority than the achievement of economic, social and cultural rights. "Liberty" and "development" were linked. However, African leaders—like many other leaders in the Third World—have increasingly stressed "development" as a need to be satisfied prior to the implementation of full civil and political rights.

In contemporary Africa, economic development is viewed as both a collective right and a primary objective of government policy. The Banjul Charter makes this explicit, its wording including both rights enjoyed by individuals and rights exercised collectively by peoples. For example, "Every individual shall have the right to enjoy the best attainable state of physical and mental health"; "Every individual shall have the right to education"; "The State shall have the duty to assist the family which is the custodian of morals and traditional values recognized by the community"; "All peoples shall have the right to their economic, social, and cultural development with due regard to their freedom and identity. . . . States shall have the duty, individually or collectively, to ensure the exercise of the right to development." However, neither the Banjul Charter nor the International Covenant on Economic, Social and Cultural Rights includes target dates or precise goals. Both recognize the progressive nature of achieving change. One should ask, more appropriately, whether contemporary definitions of development contained in these documents accord with the real needs of contemporary Africa and reflect the basic concerns of Africans.

In instances of conflict between "liberty" and "development," African leaders appear, through their actions, to favor the latter. They appear to believe that strong government is essential for achieving national goals. As a result, they are prone to reject political activity likely to challenge their authority. As James S. Coleman and Carl Rosberg suggested, the "political culture" of African heads of state encourages them to restrict political participation. They "confronted a situation that was not only conducive to the consolidation of one-party dominance, but also made strong government attractive, if not necessary."[12] Many African presidents have seemed inclined to follow the sentiments expressed by Kwame Nkrumah in his autobiography:

> The economic independence that should follow and maintain political independence demands every effort from the people, a total mobilization of brain and manpower resources. What other countries have taken three hundred years or more to achieve, a once dependent territory must try to accomplish in a generation if it is to survive. . . . Even a system based on social justice and a democratic constitution may need backing up, during the period following independence, by emergency measures of a totalitarian kind.[13]

How have views of this sort been expressed in international settings? To answer this question, it is appropriate to turn to the "right to development," as it has been enunciated in international forums.

It has been largely through the efforts of Africans—and especially through the efforts of the eminent Senegalese jurist Keba M'Baye—that a "right to development" has been articulated within international forums.[14] M'Baye, formerly his country's representative to the United Nations Commission on Human Rights and now a judge of the International Court of Justice, expressed a widespread feeling throughout Africa: a sense of deep resentment against the economic backwardness of much of the continent, the consequence, as many saw it, of colonialism and the "development of underdevelopment."

That the right to development has become highly politicized requires little elaboration. It has been enunciated, particularly since 1977, in an international arena characterized by growing regional disparities—and, more important, by greater realization of these differences. The debates within the UN Commission on Human Rights, like those in the special sessions of the General Assembly devoted to the NIEO (New International Economic Order), make clear that economic redistribution is perceived by developing countries as not merely desirable, but as essential. A claim based on a recognized right would obviously strengthen the position of developing countries in bargaining for financial assistance, better terms of trade, agreements for stabilization of commodity and raw materials prices, and price indexing. Clearly, much of the debate over human rights in the Third World is fueled by lingering resentment over colonialism, and by continuing concern over neocolonialism, unequal terms of trade, different levels of industrialization, and the like. In short, the politically charged atmosphere of North-South relations influences any discussion of what rights should take primacy in instances of conflict, as illustrated by Ronald Meltzer in his analysis of relations between the industrialized members of the European Community and the largely agricultural associate members.

The "right to development" became prominent on the world stage fairly recently. It forms part of a new emphasis in international human rights, which has been termed the "third generation" of human rights foci. The first generation stressed civil and political rights, notably *liberty* against governmental intrusions on individuals. The second generation emphasized economic, social, and cultural rights, by which *equality* rather than liberty was the watchword, and for which governments were to pursue collective achievement of betterment. Third generation rights, by contrast, involve *solidarity*, both among developing states as a group, and among all states in general. The right to development, along with the rights to peace, to a healthy environment, and to sharing a common heritage, form part of this third generation of rights. That the Banjul Charter incorporates such an emphasis should come as no surprise.

Most human rights issues that African states have focused upon remain unachieved. Apartheid has not been significantly modified, despite scores of resolutions from the UN and other international bodies; economic development remains uneven, marked by extraordinary disparities and the unfulfilled promises of NIEO. Self-determination has yet to be achieved for Namibia, and, as George Shepherd indicates in Chapter 11, international constraints make full independence nearly impossible.

What must be underscored, however, is the intensity of African concern over the perpetuation of racism and the continuation of underdevelopment. That which colonialism appeared to create historically, and that which existing patterns of neocolonialism appear to maintain, are global inequities. Proponents of human rights in Africa—and most particularly African governments—link all three generations of rights, the rights of liberty, equality, and solidarity. They are far less inclined than Western advocates and political leaders to stress liberty over the others; by contrast, many are prepared to deny certain civil and political rights in their own countries in their desire to enhance economic growth and cultural unity. External pressure to foster recognition and protection of basic rights arouses concern about unwarranted interference, as illustrated in the abortive effort to include these in the treaty of association between the European Community and the African-Caribbean-Pacific states.

QUESTIONS FOR RESEARCH

The key questions future research must be directed toward answering include the following: Most fundamentally, are there rights that Africans deem more important than do citizens of other geographic areas? Do attitudes exist, among the populace in general or among political leaders in particular, that give the promotion and protection of human rights in Africa aspects not confronted on other continents? To what extent, and in what fashion, should research emphasize national environments, regional considerations directed to Africa as a whole, or the overall international setting?

African leaders appear intent on proclaiming a set of rights and means of enforcement uniquely suited to the continent. They are influenced by the mixed heritage of colonialism, which brought authoritarian and bureaucratic forms of government as well as constitutional and legal frameworks with which rights could be protected. They rely in differing degrees on "tradition." They respond in varying ways to the imperatives of economic, social, and political development and decolonization. They act, as do leaders everywhere, to protect what they perceive as both the national interest of their states and the personal interests they hold in office.

Analysis of the Banjul Charter makes clear that its drafters both added new features not found in major prior international human rights documents and weakened some protections. The Banjul Charter built upon the Universal Declaration and the International Covenants, but added several peoples' rights, the recognition of "any means recognized by the international community" in the struggle for self-determination, a delineation of duties of individuals, and a stress on "third generation" rights to development, information, and a healthful environment. Some weakening of protection of individuals against the state resulted from the addition of "clawback" clauses. The nascent regional commission, which would be established when a majority of OAU members ratify the Banjul Charter, would be empowered to proceed in a fashion generally similar to those followed by the Inter-American Commission—which significantly expanded its activity over time. In content as well as procedure, accordingly, the Banjul Charter builds in most respects on prior documents.

Definition of an African concept of human rights appears to come most readily through what the Charter defines as "applicable principles." These include, as subsidiary measures, "African practices consistent with international norms on human and peoples' rights . . . ." Precisely what might these be? The first significant area for research, it appears, are the relevant traditions that might fall within the Banjul Charter's purview. The problems for investigation are immense. The sources of these practices, and their presuppositions, are diverse and occasionally contradictory. Take, for example, women's rights. Many groups expect women to enjoy relative economic independence—as witness the "market mammies" in coastal Ghana and Nigeria. By contrast, many other groups (especially in areas of Islamic influence or practice) subordinate wives to economic dependency upon their husbands. Marriage and family obligations, as Howard and Marasinghe illustrate in their chapters, often involve links between lineages, and thus constitute far more than acts by individuals. What appears as "the right to the respect of the dignity inherent in a human being and to the recognition of his [sic] legal status" will be affected by the cultural milieu. The centrality of the family—in the words of the Banjul Charter, "the custodian of morals and traditional values recognized by the community"—may well come into conflict with the goal that immediately follows, namely "the elimination of every discrimination against women . . ."; the chapter by Howard probes these issues. A conscious, informed effort must be made to discern and apply "tradition," lest it be forced into a twilight zone of popular expectation but legal unenforceability. Such work might best be carried out by teams of national experts, seeking through their codification and reform gradually to enhance the scope of applicable human rights norms. Unification of laws with customs, expectations, and practices will require time, dedication, and careful research.

The commitment of individual leaders to human rights is clearly a second area for comparative research, as illustrated in this volume in the chapter by Weisfelder. Given the extent to which power has been centralized in African states, the outlook of the president or prime minister would appear to be the primary factor in setting national policies. Some have built reputations as effective proponents of both personal freedoms and economic development, such as Dauda Jawara, President of the Gambia; others such as Idi Amin, Jean Bedel Bokassa, and Macias Nguema gained notoriety because of their consistent, gross violations of basic liberties. What different leaders believe, and how they implement their views, require analysis. On the other hand, awareness of an individual head's of state commitment (or non-commitment) to human rights should not be pressed to an extreme. Personalistic factors cannot explain all significant state practices; national emphases exist. For example, Nigeria, a country that has had both military and civilian governments, has pressed consistently for OAU sponsorship of a regional human rights commission. The predilections of leaders may explain much, but they cannot explain all.

Affecting government actions from "below," as it were, are institutions and popular perceptions. The promotion and protection of human rights are directly influenced by non-governmental organizations, both domestic and international. Without active, informed individuals and organizations, one can suppose that the protection and promotion of human rights would fall on officials' shoulders—and it is precisely certain actions of government officers that human rights efforts are designed to preclude. Judging by the information presented in the chapter by Scoble, African non-governmental organizations that might protect individual liberties are few in number, uncertain in their impact, and intermittent in their functioning. Whether existing values indeed permit such groups to flourish equally must be probed. Does, for example, a presumed "revolution of rising expectations" mean citizens of a particular society willingly forego certain civil or political liberties in the interest of collective economic advancement? Information is scanty, and popular pressures may in fact be negligible—with the result that leaders are given freer rein in following their own intentions. But such a presupposition by no means erases the need for careful research on the fundamental popular basis.

Fourthly, regional norms within Africa influence the definition and expansion of human rights. All through this chapter, what is distinctly African—and what is not—has been stressed. The key point in this regard is that the Organization of African Unity has become the vehicle through which the proposed African Commission on Human Rights will operate. The assumptions and values of the OAU, plus its organizational efficiencies and inefficiencies, will directly affect what occurs. Central to the OAU for at least its first decade was unwillingness to probe the domestic affairs of member states. Violent changes of government, for example, were viewed as internal matters; rare indeed was the African leader who cited a coup d'état as pretext for denying international recognition.[15] The Organization of African Unity is a collection of states, inadequately funded, with a limited track record to date in the field of human rights—with the obvious exception of denouncing South Africa. As an entity, the OAU is not now prepared to take on major responsibilities in human rights enforcement; steps, if any, will depend on the proposed regional commission, whose efficiency in turn will be affected by funding, staffing, utilization, and cope of recognized, legitimate activity.

Perhaps most fundamental, however, is the international context within which human rights in Africa are protected and promoted. Do the existing and foreseeable world system provide any basis for optimism? Shaw's assessment suggests that national leaders enjoy limited room for maneuver. Although certain "capitalist" states may seek to protect civil and political rights at home and abroad, they may scarcely be able to affect certain economic, social, and cultural rights because of the deeply rooted problems of the current international economic system. The "right to development" is an obvious case in point. Article 22 of the Banjul Charter, as noted earlier in this chapter, places an obligation on states to "ensure the exercise of the right to development" on behalf of "all peoples." With the gap between developed and developing states widening rather than narrowing, and with the terms of trade and other international economic trends increasingly turning to the disadvantage of African countries, the global context appears to be one in which further research will uncover little that is encouraging.

In the final analysis, however, the responsibility for the definition, protection, and promotion of human rights in Africa rests upon Africans. The leaders of African governments, responsive in varying ways to traditional perceptions of human rights, to the regional and international definitions of liberties and duties, and to what they perceive as the best interests of their respective states, play the fundamental role. It may be a truism to affirm that respect for liberties cannot be imposed; it must grow from within. Whether this is occurring now in Africa will require further studies beyond the scope of this book.

NOTES

1. Rupert Emerson, "The Fate of Human Rights in the Third World," *World Politics* 27, no. 2 (January 1975), p. 205.

2. U.S. Dept. of State, *Country Reports on Human Rights Practices, Report Submitted to the Committee on Foreign Affairs, U.S. House of Representatives, and Committee on Foreign Relations, U.S. Senate* (Washington, D.C.: U.S. Government Printing Office, annual).

3. According to Mojekwu, "Because the U.N. sponsored self-determination for colonial peoples of Africa meant that the colonial boundaries in Africa, that had been drawn by the imperial powers, were the ones that decided the unit that was to be 'self-determined,' the peoples and ethnic nations within each colonial administrative boundary forever lost that 'freedom to choose.' 'Self-determination' thus became a 'once and for all' exercise in colonial territories, not chosen by the 'self' but by external powers." Chris C. Mojekwu, "International Human Rights: The African Perspective," in Jack L. Nelson and Vera M. Green, *International Human Rights: Contemporary Issues* (Stanfordville, N.Y.: Human Rights Publishing Group, 1980), p. 90. For illustrations from West Africa of problems in implementing self-determination,

see Claude E. Welch, Jr., *Dream of Unity: Pan-Africanism and Political Unification in West Africa* (Ithaca, N.Y.: Cornell University Press, 1966).

4. Mojekwu, "The African Perspective," p. 91.

5. Latif O. Adegbite, "African Attitudes to the International Protection of Human Rights," in Asbjorn Eide and August Schou, eds., *International Protection of Human Rights* (New York: Interscience Publishers, 1968), p. 69.

6. Hurst Hannum, "The Butare Colloquium on Human Rights and Economic Development in Francophone Africa: A Summary and Analysis," *Universal Human Rights* 1, no. 2 (April-June 1979), p. 64.

7. Adegbite, "African Attitudes," p. 70.

8. Jack Donnelly, "Human Rights and Human Dignity: An Analytic Critique of Non-Western Conceptions of Human Rights," *American Political Science Review* 76, no. 2 (June 1982), pp. 303-16.

9. For a criticism of such views, see Irving Leonard Markovitz, *Power and Class in Africa* (Englewood Cliffs, N.J.: Prentice-Hall, 1977), pp. 99-197.

10. World Bank, *Poverty and Human Development* (New York: Oxford University Press, 1980), pp. 2, 68-69. It should be noted that several small, poor African states (e.g., Equatorial Guinea; the Gambia; Sao Tome) are omitted from the tables.

11. Annual per capita income of South African Blacks ranges between R200 and R250 ($200); for whites around R2,500 ($2000). Study Commission on U.S. Policy toward Southern Africa, *South Africa: Time Running Out* (Berkeley and Los Angeles: University of California Press, 1981), p. 133.

12. James S. Coleman and Carl G. Rosberg, Jr., *Political Parties and National Integration in Tropical Africa* (Berkeley and Los Angeles: University of California Press, 1964), p. 655.

13. Kwame Nkrumah, *Ghana: The Autobiography of Kwame Nkrumah* (Edinburgh: Thomas Nelson, 1957), p. x. It should be noted that the wording was modified in subsequent editions.

14. Keba M'Baye, "Le droit au développement comme un droit de l'homme," *Revue des droits de l'homme* 5 (1972), pp. 505-34; Keba M'Baye, "Emergence of the 'Right to Development' as a Human Right in the Context of a New International Economic Order," UNESCO Doc. SS-78/CONF.630/8, 16 July 1979.

15. Claude E. Welch, Jr., "The OAU and International Recognition Questions: Lessons from Uganda," in Yassin El-Ayouty, ed., *The Organization of African Unity after Ten Years: Comparative Perspectives* (New York: Praeger, 1975), pp. 103-17.

CHAPTER TWO

Traditional Conceptions of Human Rights in Africa

LAKSHMAN MARASINGHE

The reality that one witnesses in contemporary Africa differs greatly from that envisaged by the departing colonial powers. They expected that constitutional provisions and a Western-trained judiciary would protect human rights, as these had been defined, determined, and delineated in the constitutions left behind at independence. Either through coups d'etat or proclamation of states of emergency or siege, however, constitutional protections, and often whole constitutions, have been abrogated, annulled, or amended so as to subvert the human rights that had been made sacrosanct in the constitutions of various African nations. It is important, therefore, to examine the alternatives that are available in African countries for the protection of human rights under traditional customs and systems of law.

These systems of law and custom are underpinned by social forces peculiar to each society and are not the creations of colonial constitutions. The abrogation itself of a constitution will therefore have no effect on the traditional concepts of human rights that are peculiar to each African society. The best guarantees of human rights in Africa are to be found by preserving conceptions of human rights recognized by each society's law and custom. Such conceptions of human rights are so closely associated with the traditions of an African society that their strict observance becomes a basic concern for its members. The cohesion and the stability of that society are considered to be dependent upon the preservation of such traditions. Furthermore, these traditions are closely connected with the maintenance of the individual as a human being and as a member of that society. To that extent the underlying guarantees for the preservation of human rights in a traditional society may be considered to be well rooted and are not the subject of change, except with the general consensus of its members.

There is, however, a point of difference that one might detect between traditional conceptions of human rights and conceptions of human rights fostered in modern societies. In the latter, human rights are considered universalistic in nature and therefore applicable to all human beings irrespective of their geographic location; in the former, by contrast, human rights exist within the context of particular groups.

In modern legal theory, the universalistic notion of human rights has been strengthened by reference to Stammler's theory of "Natural Law with a variable content." Stammler stressed two principles of respect for humans: the content of a person's volition must not depend upon the arbitrary will of another; and every legal demand can only be maintained in such a way that the person may remain a fellow creature.[1] Stammler added two principles of human participation in his community: A person lawfully obligated must not be arbitrarily excluded from the community, and every lawful power of decision may exclude the person affected by it from the community only to the extent that the person may remain a fellow creature.[2] These principles of "respect" and of "participation" provide a general basis for the traditional concepts and, in particular, of the rights to family membership, to freedom of thought, speech, beliefs, and association, and the freedom to enjoy property as discussed in this chapter.

The conceptions of human rights considered here are not sanctioned by a normative system deriving its validity from a constitutional base or a *Grundnorm* but by a set of social values ingrained as a set of basic principles espoused by at least a substantial majority of a given society. The durability of these rights is guaranteed by the fact that they symbolize some of the basic elements which hold that society together. The right to membership, the freedom of thought, speech, belief, and association, and the right to enjoy property have all been recognized by most traditional societies as fundamental human rights.

In most traditional societies, the control of membership vitally affects its cohesion. The power to exclude becomes a powerful instrument of coercion in the hands of the members of a traditional society. It is this that makes "membership" a human right in most traditional societies. Equally appropriate is the recognition of the freedoms of thought, speech, beliefs, and association. Coextensive with these are factors that contribute towards maintaining the esprit de corps of a traditional society. The ability to freely exchange ideas and beliefs is essential for social cohesion. It provides a useful escape valve for pent-up feelings and, to that extent, helps to neutralize the forces of disruption. The right to enjoy property is basic for any traditional society. Finally, the right of association has important implications for marriage and raising children. It is, therefore, appropriate to suggest that these fundamental human rights have a wide and general application in most traditional societies, particularly in Africa.

THE RIGHT TO FAMILY MEMBERSHIP

In traditional Yoruba society, the extended family is considered as having a distinct legal personality. Membership in it provides its members with a number of rights. The right of succession to family property is held in common. The right to be supported in times of scarcity, the right to claim societal and psychological help at moments of need, and similar rights are provided within the extended family. In modern societies, the problems associated with old age, infirmity, widowhood, and being orphaned generally fall within the social welfarfe underwritten by the state. In the context of a traditional society, by contrast, these problems are generally the concern of the members of an extended family.

At the outset it must be emphasized that, within the context of a traditional society, membership in an extended family is itself regarded as a fundamental human right. Any unlawful attempt to exclude a person from the membership of an extended family is considered in Nigeria, for example, as a violation of human rights guaranteed under Section 22 of the Federal Republican Constitution.[3] Although the reasons and the justifications for excluding a person from his membership in an extended family may be found in the native laws and customs of every tribe, the Nigerian Constitution provides for the judicial review of such a step.

The case law suggests that the traditional grounds for the expulsion of a member from his extended family will no longer be considered sufficient by the Nigerian courts. Under native laws and customs an incorrigible rogue, a willful murderer, a coward in war, a traitor to the other members of his extended family, and persons guilty of incestuous relations have all been liable to expulsion from the extended family. A decision to expel is always considered to have grave implications, both for the person expelled and for the family from which he is being expelled. The decision, therefore, is taken either by the family council (to be discussed later) or at a general meeting of as many members of the family as can be assembled for that purpose.[4]

A problem, however, arises if the expelled makes an application to the courts for an injunction to prevent his expulsion. The courts have consistently held the view that where the basis for a person's expulsion constitutes a criminal offense under the Nigerian Criminal Code, then the sanction decreed under that code will have exclusive application. This thus negates the decision which the family council or a general meeting of the members of the extended family may have taken to expel the individual. On the other hand, if the particular act or event that the family council or the general meeting of the members considers as justifying expulsion is one of mere social disgrace to the family, or is an offense considered to be criminal only under native law and custom and not under the Criminal Code, the Supreme Court of Nigeria will be only too willing to reverse the order to expel. One of the leading cases in this area that has come before the Nigerian courts is *Aoko versus Fagbemi and D.P.P.*[5] The applicant was found to have committed adultery, which was a criminal offense under the native law and custom. The Family Council decided to expel her from her extended family. She applied to the Nigerian courts for an injunction. The court allowed her application on the grounds that adultery was not an offense under the Nigerian Criminal Code, and therefore her expulsion constituted a violation of her fundamental rights under Article 22(10) of the Federal Constitution.

A wide gap accordingly exists between the Nigerian courts and native law and custom regarding the basis upon which a person can be expelled from an extended family. Using the provisions in the Nigerian Constitution that protect human rights, the courts through the use of injunctions have consistently protected members of extended families from expulsion orders issued by their peers. This, however, has not provided the members with the relief that they have sought. In the well-known village of Ishogba court injunctions to stop a number of expulsions have in reality proved to be of no effect. The expelled have found themselves quarantined by their own families and, therefore, within a very short period of time have been compelled to leave the tribal homeland for other locations, usually urban centers, to make a new life. In other cases the expelled have come to terms with their family and have paid handsome reparation to its members in order to gain readmission. The power to expel has often been used as a whip, to force the deviants back into conformity. The family councils have often readmitted a much-chastened member back into the fold. The price extracted for readmission, both in monetary and human terms, varies with the extent of culpability and whether the expelled has taken his family to court in an attempt to obtain an injunction. For this reason, the number of expulsions that have gone before the courts has been very low. As a rule, the issues leading up to an expulsion go before a family council for mediation.

A family council is composed of the heads of each of the branches that comprise the extended family. The eldest member of this group acts as its president. Among the Yoruba, women have been recognized as having the capacity to act as family heads and therefore family councils among the Yoruba are mixed assemblies of both sexes. A decision taken at a council which could affect a particular family branch is not binding upon it, unless the head of that family has had sufficient notice of the meeting at which matters concerning his family were to be discussed. When there has been sufficient notice, the head of the family branch is bound by the Council's decision, whether or not he was present at the meeting.

The family council is competent to make rules and guide the several branches of the extended family in both spiritual and temporal matters. The council sets out limitations on the rights of the members of each extended family, including the conditions for their exclusion; it has the power to levy contributions from members for such things as funeral expenses; and it helps determine "bride-wealth" for younger members of marriageable age. In addition, the council finds the necessary finances to aid victims of trade depression, bad harvest, fire, or theft, settles disputes between its members, including husbands and wives engaged in domestic battles, provides funding for the education and advancement of its members, takes an active interest in the management and control of the family property including inspecting and attending to repairs, drainage, and erosion control, and, finally, has access to all property belonging to the extended family because this is considered to be held in common. In traditional Nigerian society the family council, therefore, "was an important, plenipotential organ which might be described as a miniature local government council, improvement society, Court of Law and Privy Council rolled into one."[6]

Against this background, it becomes necessary to emphasize that the nature and character of rights emanating from the fundamental human right to remain a member of an extended family depend largely on the composition of the family council. The right to free speech, the freedom of association, the right to follow one's beliefs, and the right to own property are fundamental only in the abstract; in fact they are limited according to the needs of each extended family, as determined by the collective wisdom of its family council.

FREEDOM OF THOUGHT, SPEECH, AND BELIEFS

These freedoms are considered by modern societies as interrelated and equal. The freedoms to think and to believe are considered as of no value unless they are buttressed by the freedom to speak and to associate with one another.

In a traditional society, particularly among the Yoruba, the freedom to speak has always been regarded as a common, communal right. It is subject, however, to a very real limitation, namely, the "principle of respect." The "principle of respect" is not peculiar to the traditional societies in Nigeria or West Africa.⁷ Respect is more in the nature of a custom backed by strong social sanctions than a notion of religious significance. The principle of respect involves respect for both oneself and others. With reference to respect for oneself, the notion rests on one's showing pride—the pride of being a member of a particular extended family. The respect for others raises a notion of stratification along a hierarchy of respect determined within each social unit. The hierarchy of respect for parents, for elders closely related by blood, for elders belonging to the same extended family, and finally for the head of the whole family, provides a classic paradigm.

Respect as determined and made manifest by the social and moral forces of an extended family provides a particular limitation upon the freedom of speech. Respect when expounded in this way does not fall within the normative structure of the non-traditional legal system. Modern societies would proclaim this aspect entirely the product of the respective mores of each society. This is equally correct among traditional societies. But in traditional societies, as Deng points out, the level of respect due from one to another is determined by the society (or extended family) in question. Further, it determines the extent to which one is free to speak about another. "The defamation of a person higher in status, such as a Chief, is a very serious offence which often calls for heavy compensatory payment."⁸ The principle of respect in traditional societies is thus a part of its normative system and thus aids in determining to what extent the freedom of speech may be enjoyed; the Yoruba are no exception to this rule.

The principle of respect and the question of "family status" in Yoruba society are essentially the products of a social morality generated by the tribal society to which the extended family in question belongs. The limitation introduced by the principle of respect and the need to leave most slanders and libels to mediation and conciliation through family councils as matters affecting "family status" must be viewed as indicative of the fundamental belief that all freedoms are ultimately limited by the need to preserve the traditional society. Viewed in that way, the limitations placed upon the freedom of speech by a modern society appear not to be different from those imposed by a traditional society. The difference lies in the fact that the freedom of speech in a modern society is largely controlled by a normative system which could be manipulated by a ruling elite which controls its legislative machinery. In a traditional society, manipulation of the freedom of speech is internalized and therefore becomes a part of the common weal of the traditional society.

Yoruba society is highly politicized and well organized, especially at the level of the "chief." Each extended family includes several branch families. In each branch family a head represents it within the family council. The eldest among the heads of the branch families usually becomes the "chief" of the extended family. At each of these two levels the heads play a highly politicized role, for they are essentially answerable to their constituents—the members of their own branch. The choice of a head of a branch family and thereafter the selection of a "chief" of that extended family are matters of great importance.

Among many tribes in Nigeria, including the Yoruba, the head of an extended family is normally referred to as a "chief," which raises serious issues. Non-traditional law—i.e., English law—conceives of a chief very differently. The chief of an entire tribe is the only chieftaincy which the non-traditional courts entertain. In *Adanji versus Hunvoo* the full court of the Nigerian Supreme Court declined jurisdiction regarding a dispute concerning the "chieftaincy" of a Yoruba extended family. The court sent the matter back to the family council for determination according to its native law and custom. Acting Chief Justice Speed called chieftaincy "a mere dignity, a position of honour, of primacy among a particular section of the native community," with the result that the court had no jurisdiction to decide upon it.[9] The main point of this decision is that the selection of the "chief" of the particular extended family was not a legal but a political question, and as such should have been determined at the level of the extended family rather than through the judicial system. By leaving such matters to the extended family, the decision becomes highly politicized, making the expression of the choice of its members an outcome of the political process.

In sum, it must be said that the freedom of belief, on both the religious and the political plane, is very wide. As was the case with the freedom of speech, traditional society internalizes the limits on the freedom to believe and express beliefs. The very nature of the society requires the broadest interpretation of these freedoms. Such interpretation is, in my opinion, almost always commensurate with the needs and the traditions of that society.

FREEDOM OF ASSOCIATION

The first indication of a limitation on rights of association appears when one considers the rights of widows. Aside from this single area, the freedom of association among the traditional societies is significantly wide. Not only is there a right to associate freely with one's own kin within an extended family, but there is also a right to intertribal associations, including marriages. However, as S.N.C. Obi has written, women but not men are able to assume, in effect, a new ethnic identity:

> Under customary law, a woman is a member of her husband's family— for a number of purposes, at all events—for as long as she possesses the legal status of a married woman. It is immaterial that in her unmarried state she belonged to an ethnic group different from her husband's. Thus, if a Yoruba or an Ibibio woman is married to an Ibo man, she acquires a right to take any Ibo titles open to other local housewives; she has a right to assume (and often does assume) a local Ibo name; it would be incest for a blood relation of her husband's to have sexual connection with her; and, more generally, she becomes subject to the authority of the local (customary) social and political authorities, while at the same time acquiring rights and obligations under the local customary law as if she originally belonged to that ethnic group. Now, membership of an ethnic group depends on membership [of] some family within the group, as an ethnic group is no more than the apex of a socio-political pyramid whose base comprises a large multitude of extended families. It would seem to follow, therefore, that a woman is sufficiently absorbed into her husband's family, under customary law, for her to acquire her husband's nationality as above defined. The converse, however, is not true: A husband never assumes his wife's nationality to any extent at all, not even in the matrilineal societies, and not even where he resides among her people.[10]

However, this freedom of association becomes limited in the case of widows, an issue discussed at greater length in the following chapter. In most traditional societies in Africa, the widow remains a member of the deceased husband's extended family. As a part of this right, she is obliged as a matter of duty to marry a man chosen by the head of the branch family of her deceased husband. In most cases the choice is made in favor of a brother of the deceased; failing that, a first cousin of the deceased is chosen. The justification here is that the widow should not be compelled to uproot herself from the environment into which she has been accepted and in which her children are presently growing. Besides, according to traditional beliefs, the children belong to the extended and branch families of their father as full members of a fraternity. If their widowed mother were to be allowed to marry into a different extended family, the argument goes, they would never be able to develop any firm roots and would disintegrate as valuable human beings. Children of the widowed mother could never be accepted by the new extended family into which their mother might enter by a fresh betrothal because membership, even in a matrilineal society, can only be claimed through the deceased father and not through the remarried mother.

Against this social setting the Nigerian courts were asked to settle a dispute concerning the children of a widow in *Loromeke versus Nekegho and Ayo*. To summarize this complex case, the defendant, Nekegho, was the widow of an Urhobo man; the plaintiff, Loromeke, was the brother of the defendant's deceased husband. The head of his extended family had nominated the plaintiff to marry the defendant. The defendant refused, left with her children, and returned to her own family and parents. The plaintiff sought an order from the court ordering her either to marry the plaintiff or to return half the "brideprice" paid her family at the time of her marriage, and to return the children of her marriage to her deceased husband's family. The plaintiff established to the trial court's satisfaction that all three claims were based on Urhobo native law and custom. Upon appeal, however, the Urhobo native law and custom was held repugnant to "natural justice, equity, and good conscience,"[11] Such a rejection of the customary law concerning matrimonial rights could have incalculable social consequences, a point discussed in greater detail in the following chapter by Rhoda Howard.

In my view, the limitation on widows' freedom of association could be justified upon the grounds of a deeply felt social need to protect the widow and the children of a traditional marriage. As mentioned before, the alternative to this arrangement is social welfare underwritten by the State and the tax-paying general public. The latter, I believe, are a poor psychological substitute for the former. In a traditional society, the former is more honorable than a life spent living on handouts received from the State. The latter help may end due to fiscal constraints, while the former is guaranteed to continue until the end of an extended family.

FREEDOM TO ENJOY PROPERTY

The Nigerian Federal Constitution has declared the freedom to enjoy property as a fundamental human right. This right is linked to a carefully worded "due process of law" clause adopted from the United States Constitution. However, numerous decisions have recently indicated the weakness of this constitutional protection.[12] The protection against any unlawful incursions into the right to hold movable property under native law and custom is an absolute one.

The problem, however, arises particularly in immovable property, primarily land.

Rights Concerning Immovables

Here the focus is on land. Under the traditional system, Yoruba family land is not subject to private ownership. In fact, where a member renounces his rights and interests in the family property or establishes a homestead on land which he owns privately, then under the native law and custom he ceases to be a member of his extended family.[13] A member could have two homesteads, one within his extended family property and another in the capital city or elsewhere. In such a situation, however, he does not cease to be a member of his extended family.

The fact that family property is considered to be communal property is basic to property rights as conceived by most traditional societies in Africa. Any act of alienation of such property requires the consent of all members of the extended family. I shall cite one example, showing some limitations on this principle. In *Aganran versus Olushi,*[14] land belonging to the Esan family was sold by the head of that family, Chief Afopo. Although most of the members of that family had consented to the sale, the plaintiff Aganran was not consulted. He, however, accepted five pounds as his share of the proceeds from the Chief but subsequently returned the money and maintained his opposition to the sale. Aganran then sued to have the purchaser, Olushi, evicted on the grounds that the sale of the communal land had not received the consent of all its co-owners. This action was brought after the defendant, Olushi, had constructed a house upon it. The Nigerian Supreme Court upheld Aganran's right to void the sale under native law and custom. But the enforcement of this right was denied to him on the grounds that the plaintiff had delayed bringing this action until the defendant had erected a house upon the property, a situation that created equities in the defendant's favor.

The limitation upon the freedom to own immovable property is a recognized principle among most traditional societies in Africa, justified principally upon the grounds that land and the extended family are inseparable and therefore any parceling of the family's land which may eventually lead to the incursions of other extended families into the domain of the first, could begin the process of social decay. An extended family without family land has been likened to "a building without pillars or walls."

Judicial views have now been clearly stated for West Africa that family land is not owned by any member of the family, including its chief, and no member has any right to sell such land, without the consent of every adult member of the family. This was decided by the West African Court of Appeal (which had jurisdiction over all former British West African colonies) in the Yoruba case of *Adedubu versus Makanjuola*.[15] There the chief of the Mogaji family sold family land to the defendant without the consent of all its members. The West African Court of Appeal, reversing an earlier decision of the Nigerian Supreme Court, invalidated, and therefore set aside the sale. In *Onasanya versus Shiwoniku*[16] the court set aside a partitioning of family property between two Yoruba families on the grounds that all members of one family had not been consulted and therefore had not consented to the act.

This requirement to obtain the consent of all applies to all land transactions, including leasing, mortgaging, and the determination of boundaries. Admittedly, this slows down any urgent and pressing reorganizing of family holdings. But the wisdom of the ancients in all traditional societies was that the preservation of family land for the use of its members is a supreme task which should not be lightly considered or set aside. The right to collectively own family property and thus exclude individual ownership is a dependent right, arising out of membership in a Yoruba family. This is true not only in Yoruba native law and custom but also in all other African native laws and customs.

CONCLUSIONS

It is a popular myth to assume that traditional societies of Africa are devoid of any conception of human rights and that when one refers to human rights the modern societies of the West are the exclusive custodians of this universal concept. Many writers claim that freedom of speech, of thought, of association and of property are basic human rights which no civilized nation should impugn. While saying that, a finger of accusation is directed at most traditional societies in Asia and Africa as arch enemies of human rights, as conceived from a Western Judeo-Christian standpoint. In this line of accusation one avoids inquiring into the conceptions of human rights espoused by traditional societies of Asia and Africa, for their concepts are considered not to be "rights" at all but mere "privileges" granted by a ruling elite. Jack Donnelly expresses this view strongly, declaring that "most non-Western cultural and political traditions lack not only the practice of human rights but the very concept. As a matter of historical fact, the concept of human rights is an artifact of modern Western Civilization."[17]

Human rights, to be effective and to be meaningful, must be considered within the parameters drawn by a system of laws. In any system of laws—both traditional and non-traditional—human rights are not "rights" as properly conceived but "powers." The "power holder," by exercising his powers to speak openly, associate freely, or use such other powers possessed in a given society, places his "co-relative"—the State or an individual—under a "liability" that keeps them from preventing the "power holder" from exercising that power. Once that liability is created in the co-relative, then the latter is automatically recognized as a person who is under a duty to carry out that liability. Once the law finds a legal duty in the holder of that liability, the original power holder acquires a right to have his power enforced. Human rights, therefore, remain always as a power in the human being. In this form, "human rights" exist in all civilized systems and most certainly in the Soviet Union, in Islamic and Hindu law, and in all traditional societies in Asia and Africa.

The problem, however, surfaces when the enforcement of these powers in the nature of a right—transformed to that position in the manner outlined above—occurs. In some non-traditional legal systems, such issues as procedural difficulties, constitutional limitations, economic restrictions, or rules of evidence excluding certain types of proofs of the violation, may prevent the "power holder" from obtaining his remedy. Such sophisticated limitations on access to justice are not found in most traditional legal systems. Empirical research has shown that there is a greater possibility of success in enforcing human rights violations in traditional societies than in non-traditional societies.[18] The reality is in fact the precise opposite of what Professor Donnelly finds in his research.

Constitutions protecting human rights can be ended, suspended, or amended. The extended family, on the other hand, is a permanent institution which must exist as long as the individuals who form a part of it exist. To that extent the vulnerability of the traditional conceptions of human rights is minimized. When one speaks of the violation of human rights in Africa, one refers mainly to the violation of human rights as guaranteed by the externalized constitution or by the *Grundnorm*. But if one were to conduct empirical research into the internalized conceptions of human rights recognized by a traditional society, one would find enormous satisfaction as to the basically democratic way in which the society protects its own human values. As shown in this chapter, it is important to recognize that the values we embody within our own conceptions of human rights are identical with the value sytem which traditional societies endeavor to protect through their conceptions of human rights. But there is one difference: While our conceptions are guaranteed to the extent to which our rulers guarantee them through tightly drafted constitutional documents, theirs become institutionalized as an essential part of their own social organization which guarantees their existence in society. This makes their conceptions of rights less vulnerable and more permanent than ours.

NOTES

1. Rudolf Stammler, *Theory of Justice*, trans. Isaac Husik, Modern Legal Philosophy Series (New York: 1925), p. 161.

2. Ibid., p. 163.

3. It can safely be concluded, therefore, that the family no longer possesses the right to expel any of its members by physical force. It is also submitted that it can no longer expel a member in the sense of disowning him and denying him the right to participate in its social life. Such participation is an important aspect of a person's civil rights. If this be so, it would be a violation of one of the fundamental human rights guaranteed by section 22 of the 1963 Federal Republican Constitution, for the family to interfere with that right in any way other than by the normal process of legal action. According to section 22(1),

> "In the determination of his civil rights and obligations a person shall be entitled to a fair hearing within a reasonable time by a court or other tribunal established by law and constituted in such manner as to secure its impartiality."

S.N.C. Obi, *Modern Family Law in Nigeria* (London: Sweet and Maxwell, 1966), p. 38.

4. Ibid., p. 36.

5. *All Nigerian Law Reports* 1 (Lagos: Ministry of Justice, 1961), p. 400.

6. Obi, *Modern Family Law*, p. 32.

7. Francis M. Deng, *Tradition and Modernization: A Challenge for Law among The Dinka of the Sudan* (New Haven: Yale University Press, 1971), pp. 29–26.

8. Ibid., p. 226.

9. *Nigerian Law Reports* 1 (1908), p. 78.

10. Obi, *Modern Family Law*, p. 206.

11. *West African Law Reports* 1957, p. 308.

12. Nigerian Supreme Court 58/69 (unreported). See also *International and Comparative Law Quarterly* 20 (1971), pp. 117–36.

13. Obi, *Modern Family Law*, p. 35.

14. *Nigerian Law Reports* 1, p. 69.

15. *West African Court of Appeal* 10 (1944), p. 33. This decision has been followed in several later decisions. See also *Adewuyin v. Ishola* (1958), *Western Region Nigerian Law Reports* 110; *Esan v. Faro* (1947), *West African Court of Appeal* 12, p. 135; *Onasanya v. Shiwoniku* (1960), *Western Region Nigerian Law Reports* 166; and *Buraimo v. Gbamgvoye* (1940), *Nigerian Law Reports* 15, p. 139. Note the first two decisions concern Yoruba land.

16. *Western Region Nigerian Law Reports* 166 (1960).

17. Jack Donnelly, "Human Rights and Human Dignity: An Analytic Critique of Non-Western Conceptions of Human Rights," *American Political Science Review* 76 (1982), 303.

18. M.L. Marasinghe, "The Relationship between the Social Infrastructure and the Working of the Legal System: A Case Study on Access to Justice in Northern Nigeria," *Verfassung und Recht in Ubersee* 14 (Hamburg: Forschungstelle fur Volkerrecht und auslandisches öffentliches Recht, 1981), pp. 3–21.

CHAPTER THREE

Women's Rights in English-speaking Sub-Saharan Africa

RHODA HOWARD

THE SOCIOLOGICAL CONTEXT

Discussion of women's rights in underdeveloped countries, including the seven African countries—Ghana, Kenya, Malawi, Nigeria, Sierra Leone, Tanzania, and Zambia—under consideration in this chapter, is often linked with debate as to whether or not the concern with women's rights or women's "liberation" is merely a latter-day form of Western ideological imperialism. I take the position that women's rights are not merely a Western concern. While the provision of women's rights cannot be separated from the attempt to develop sub-Saharan African countries, neither can women's rights be put aside until such a Utopian time as the government of a newly developed society sees fit to grant them.

Macrosocial global inequalities do not render inequalities between men and women within specific African societies irrelevant, nor are such gender inequalities merely the result of ideological control by colonial powers. In indigenous social structures in sub-Saharan Africa, women's rights and duties differed from men's, and in many cases rendered women unequal in family, lineage, and state affairs. Such differences have been elaborated upon in the colonial and postcolonial eras to create substantial legal, social, political, and material inequalities between the two sexes. In the postcolonial period, capitalist competition and social stratification have further widened the gap betwen the two sexes. Moreover, whatever their ideals when they first take office, those who are in power tend to consolidate that power in their own interests: Hence women's rights are likely to be shunted aside by the men in power, who have a *material* as well as an ideological interest in continuing women's subordination.

Thus the African woman of today is not merely a member of her indigenous primary group; she is also a citizen of a nation-state which has undergone five centuries of change as a result of its incorporation into the capitalist world economy. "Modernization" and colonialism have altered the status of women in Africa to such an extent that perhaps only "modern" ideologies of women's liberation can provide the intellectual organization necessary in the struggle for equality for women. African societies may be rooted in traditionalism and communitarianism, but they also contain strong competitive traits. Urban society, and increasingly rural society, too, is divided into social classes, primarily distinguished by differing levels of wealth. Elites (usually male) usurp both socioeconomic resources and political privilege. The status of women is determined as much by their class as by their sexual positions, and analyses of gender relations must be made in tandem with analyses of political economy and social stratification in African societies.

My thesis, then, is very simple: The political economy, comprised of the three elements of international inequality and (neo) colonialism, internal class inequality, and indigenous sexual inequality reinforced by custom and culture, explains the absence of many human rights for women in English-speaking sub-Saharan Africa—and, by extension, in other parts of Africa.

UNITED NATIONS AND ORGANIZATION OF AFRICAN UNITY PROVISIONS REGARDING WOMEN

A number of major conventions pertaining to women's rights have been adopted by the United Nations, the International Labor Organization (ILO), and UNESCO for ratification by member states of these organizations. All of these agreements spring originally from the Universal Declaration of Human Rights (1948). The two basic conventions are the International Covenant on Civil and Political Rights (1966) and the International Covenant on Economic, Social and Cultural Rights (1966), both ratified by only Kenya and Tanzania of the seven countries under consideration in this chapter.[1] The former guarantees most of the political and legal rights familiar to persons living under British parliamentary regimes, while the latter guarantees a number of essentially "welfare" rights. Both contain explicit provision against discrimination on the grounds of sex.

Two Conventions pertain quite specifically to indigenous African marriage customs. The Supplementary Convention on the Abolition of Slavery, the Slave Trade and Practices similar to Slavery, adopted in 1956 and ratified by all of the countries under consideration except Kenya, contains two clauses especially applicable to sub-Saharan Africa, namely, that countries ratifying the Convention must prohibit bridewealth and inheritance of a widow by her late husband's relative, both practiced with some frequency in sub-Saharan English-speaking Africa.

The Convention on Consent to Marriage, Minimum Age for Marriage and Registration of Marriages (1962), not yet ratified by any of the seven countries under discussion, also contains a number of clauses directly pertinent to "traditional" African marriage practices, seeking both to insure freedom of marital choice, and to eliminate betrothal of young girls before the age of puberty. In these cases, the United Nations "sets international standards"[2] that are more aspiration than reality.

Two other Conventions pertain to women's political rights. The Convention on the Political Rights of Women (1952) has been ratified by all seven states here under consideration except Kenya. It provides that women have equal rights with men to vote, to stand for and hold office, and to have access to the public service. The Convention on the Nationality of Married Women (1957), of the seven countries not ratified by Kenya and Nigeria, deals with problems arising from "provisions concerning the loss or acquisition of nationality by women as a result of marriage, of its dissolution or of the change of nationality by the husband during marriage" (Preamble).

Three ILO and UNESCO Conventions deal with equality of work and education for women and men. The purpose of the ILO Convention (No. 100) Concerning Equal Remuneration for Men and Women Workers for Work of Equal Value (1951, not ratified by Kenya and Tanzania) is self-evident, as is the purpose of the Convention (No. 111) concerning Discrimination in Respect of Employment and Occupation (1958, ratified by Ghana and Malawi). It is important to note that Article 5 of the latter Convention states that "Special measures of protection or assistance . . . designed to meet the particular requirements of persons who for reasons such as sex . . . are generally recognized to require special protection or assistance, shall not be deemed to be discrimination." Such measures are usually interpreted to mean protection of the health of pregnant or fertile women, maternity leave, and special provisions at work for nursing mothers. Finally, the 1960 UNESCO Convention against Discrimination in Education (ratified only by Nigeria) includes sex as one of the inadmissible criteria of distinction in education, and provides for equality of access to and content of education (Article 1), with the proviso (Article 2) that "the establishment or maintenance of separate educational systems or institutions for pupils of the two sexes . . . shall not be deemed to constitute discrimination."

All of the above rights, along with many more, are included in the omnibus Convention on the Elimination of All Forms of Discrimination against Women (1979), ratified by Ghana, Tanzania, and Malawi.[3] The 1979 Convention reflects the new influence of the underdeveloped countries in the United Nations with their concern for world economic reform, the provision of basic human needs, and the elimination of all forms of colonialism.[4] In addition, the proposed Banjul Charter on Human and Peoples' Rights prohibits discrimination on the basis of sex, provides for respect to "the integrity of the person," and calls upon states "to ensure the elimination of every discrimination against women." Some potential issues arise, however, with clauses specifying "the family" as the "natural unit and basis of society," while the state is to protect and promote "morals and traditional values recognized by the community."

POLITICAL RIGHTS OF WOMEN

Women do not suffer more extreme political disabilities as compared with men in sub-Saharan Africa in the formal, legal sense. With regard to rights of nationality, for example, only Kenya and Nigeria of the seven countries under discussion have not yet ratified the convention on the rights of married women. Such rights are important insofar as they define a woman's right to become and remain a citizen of the country of which her husband is a citizen, or not to become such a citizen; and conversely either to retain or to give up her citizenship of birth upon marriage; from such a right flows the right to participate as a citizen in politics. Ratification of the Convention, however, does not mean immediate legal equality of males and females regarding citizenship rights. The 1980 Ghana constitution, for example, specifies that a woman can attain Ghanaian nationality upon marriage to a Ghanaian male, but she would lose it should she divorce; a man can attain citizenship through his wife if the marriage is monogamous or has lasted five years, but he does not appear to lose it upon divorce.[5]

Once a woman is acknowledged to be a citizen of any of the seven countries under discussion, she enjoys equal political rights with men. In almost all of these countries women have enjoyed such rights since independence or before. In colonial Ghana women were granted the right to vote (in the Gold Coast in 1950 and in 1955 in Togoland); in Kenya in 1963 and in Malawi in 1964, at independence; in pre-independence Nigeria in 1954 in the Eastern Region, in 1958 in the Western Region and in 1976 in the Northern Region; in Sierra Leone in 1961 and in Zambia in 1964, at independence.[6] Women were also permitted to hold office and stand for election on the same basis as men. The single geographical area in which women have not always enjoyed equal political rights with men was the former Northern Region of Nigeria. Until the constitutional revision of 1976, women could neither vote nor stand for or hold office. Northern Nigeria is a predominantly Muslim area in which Muslim law had been entrenched through centralized state rule, and the independent government of Nigeria, following colonial British practice, originally preferred not to disturb the indigenous legal structure.

There is now no discrimination against women's formal political rights in the seven states. The problems faced by women are by and large those also faced by men, namely, the irrelevance of formal political right in times of military or one-party rule. However, formal political equality does not mean that there are no contrary cultural norms. In many African societies, the indigenous custom was for men to hold political office as chiefs, while women could be influential only in advisory capabilities. This indigenous tendency against political leadership by women was reinforced by British legal and cultural practice during the colonial period and even more by subsequent military rule.

The granting of formal political rights upon independence masks the adverse effects that colonialism had on women's political rights in their indigenous societies. In 1970, ten of 146 prominent chiefs (in effect local administrators) in Sierra Leone were women; this was not a "modern" development but a continuation of a traditional pattern.[7] Oral histories in West Africa recount stories of women chiefs' forming small states, such as Mampong, Wenchi, and Juaben in Ghana, and receiving tribute (as did Queen Amina of Katsina, in Nigeria, in the early fifteenth century) from other powerful chiefs.[8] Among the Igbo of Midwestern Nigeria, a "dual-sex" political system existed, in which "each sex manage[d] its own affairs, and women's interests [were] represented at all levels".[9] The best-known example of female political action in the British colonies was the 1929 "Woman's War," in which tens of thousands of Igbo women attacked "warrant" chiefs (appointed by the British) and the so-called Native Courts: at least 50 women died after being fired upon by police and troops.[10] In part, the women were protesting against abrogation of their own traditional power.

The point of recounting such information is to indicate that although in the postcolonial period women in English-speaking Africa have more formal political rights than they (or men) had under colonialism, their situation is not necessarily better than it would have been had there never been a colonial interlude. The effect of the introduction of Western ideology and the consolidation of nation-states along the Western model has been to deprive women of the political influence they seem to have had in many indigenous African societies. Formally legislated equality cannot compensate for the erosion of such influence.

WOMEN AND THE POLITICAL ECONOMY

Rural Women

Discussion of human rights in the international arena includes agreement that the right to a basic living standard is as important as the right to civil and political freedom. Article 14 of the omnibus 1979 Convention on women's rights specifies what such rights to "basic needs" should (in part) entail. These include the right to work, training and education, adequate living conditions and health care facilities (including family planning), equal treatment in land and agrarian reform, and participation in development planning.

African women would benefit substantially from the "welfare" human rights elaborated in this Article. When the infant mortality rate is as high as 185 per thousand, as it was in Tanzania in 1978,[11] when female life expectancy varies between 37 years (Nigeria) and 51 years (Kenya),[12] and when the literacy rate varies between 15 percent (Sierra Leone) and 66 percent (Tanzania)[13] (keeping in mind that women always constitute the majority of illiterates), economic development to raise the standard of living is absolutely necessary to the dignity of human beings.

The delegates to the 1980 International Women's Year conference at Copenhagen placed responsibility for impoverishment of women in underdeveloped countries clearly on the West. ". . . This impoverishment is due mainly to the consequences of colonialism and neo-colonialism, inequitable international relations and the aftermath of uncontrolled industrialization and urbanization."[14] This perspective implies that economic underdevelopment is the key to understanding the position of women in poor countries, and that economic development is the solution to their problems. In large measure such a perspective is correct. Nevertheless, while economic development would certainly alleviate many of the problems that women face, it is not a complete solution. The analysis of the status of women cannot be separated, even in the poorest of countries, from class analysis. Their continued subordination is as contingent upon the differentiation of formerly homogeneous "tribal" societies (and already stratified state societies) into rich and poor as it is upon the economic effects of the world economic system. Furthermore, women as a group suffer more from poverty than men as a group, and this is directly contingent upon their sexual status. The perpetuation of poverty is in the material interests of the wealthy; the perpetuation of inequitable access to productive resources and of inequitable work loads between males and females is in the material interests of men.

Clearly all rural Africans, male and female, suffer from economic underdevelopment. Clean water, for example, is necessary for good health, yet in 1970, it was estimated that only 7½ per cent of rural Africans had access to it.[15] But what water there is, safe or unsafe, is provided primarily by women, who can spend "as much as one-third of their work day locating and transporting water for drinking, agriculture, food production and preparation, and family hygiene."[16] There is no particular reason linked to world political economy why women, not men, should perform such labor.

All the evidence suggests that in sub-Saharan Africa, women have a dual load of productive and domestic labor, while men have the single load of productive labor only. According to the UN Economic Commission for Africa, in the area of production, supply, and distribution of food, water, and fuel, women do at least 70 per cent of every major chore except food storage and animal husbandry, and a greater proportion of most chores. Moreover, they do all the child-rearing, cooking, and cleaning, and most of the "community self-help work". Of all subsistence activities, only in house-building do men do more work than women.[17] A typical Zambian woman, for example, works for fifteen hours a day during the planting season;[18] moreover, during much of her adult life (typically ending at age 48) she is pregnant, lactating, and/or carrying a baby on her back. Malnutrition affects women and children more severely than men. With their extremely heavy work load, women may literally not have the time to prepare proper meals and serve them to their children.[19] Overworked, poor women also tend to eat irregularly or skip meals, contributing to their own malnutrition. Taboos against eating certain foods exacerbate the problem. So does the cultural practice, evident in some ethnic groups, of always allowing the male head of household to eat first and eat most, leaving children and (pregnant and nursing) mothers to eat what is left over.[20]

In this context, the provision of "appropriate technology" for women such as small grinding mills for flour, clothes lines, and small power saws for fuel preparation could substantially reduce their workload.[21] Another suggestion is that day-care centers be provided, although the real problems may be mothers' overwork generally, not child care specifically.[23] This problem is exacerbated by the increased incidence of female-headed households in rural areas in sub-Saharan Africa, as a result of male rural-urban migration in search of employment. In Kenya in 1975, for example, it was estimated that a third of rural households were headed by women.[24]

The normal expectation in most indigenous sub-Saharan African societies is that women will contribute substantially to their own and their children's support, through agricultural work, marketing, or wage labor. Sixty to 80 percent of agricultural labor in Africa is women's work.[25] Of course, Article 14 of the Convention on the Elimination of Discrimination against Women provides for "equal treatment in land and agrarian reform as well as in land resettlement schemes." Yet although women must perform the bulk of the subsistence agricultural labor, women's access to land in contemporary Africa is rapidly declining. In large part, the loss of land by women has been a result of the integration of Africa into the world trade system, particularly as a consequence of the introduction of cash crops. In Tsito, Ghana, for example, once men started to grow cocoa for cash, they both increased women's labor load and also took over the better land for cocoa. As a result, the women of Tsito started to grow the nutritionally less adequate cassava, because it could grow on poorer land and took less labor to cultivate than yams, their former staple crop. When the cocoa cash income became less reliable and Tsito men began to migrate to the towns for work, the women became even more economically marginalized.[26] Undoubtedly, the colonial organization of the cocoa economy contributed in large part to the impoverishment of rural Ghanaians.[27] But the additional impoverishment of women was a consequence of indigenous cultural patterns regarding male control of land allocation.

A similar situation is occurring among the Luo women of Kenya. As a result of the pressures upon the land due to the land reserves system of the British administration, men began to usurp the customary land use rights of women. In addition, the British introduced formal land registration in the names of individual, not lineage, titleholders; because of their own cultural biases, the British registered land only in men's names. The independent Kenyan government chose to continue this practice, with the result that Luo women can now find themselves landless as their sons sell their land out from under them to finance their own migrations to the city.[28]

Even in Tanzania, which purports to base its economy on "African socialism" with roots in the indigenous organization of society, women are losing land rights. In some new "ujamaa villages" in matrilineal areas, women settlers, who were used to having clearly defined land-use rights in their original communities, suddenly found themselves without any land-use rights in the new society; widows, for example, were expected to quit the land they had helped their husbands to settle.[29] In 1975 Tanzanian law was revised to give women in ujamaa villages the right to receive half the land to which men were entitled.[30]

The problem of land access is also a problem of access to agricultural credit and extension services. In Kenya, women provide 80 per cent of the "self-help" labor which is vital to such projects as construction of roads, schools, and village community centers.[31] Yet despite the combined evidence of male out-migration, women's farming, and female "manual" labor on such projects, in the "education of farmers in the use of the modern farming and stock raising methods. . . . it seems to be assumed . . . that Kenyan farmers are men".[32] Kenyan extension officers are more likely to visit male farmers than female; since their services include assistance in filling out applications for farm credit, such a differential actively hinders female success in farming.[33]

Whatever the original colonial impetus, therefore, to disorganize African societies by depriving women of their lineage-based land rights, male African administrators have continued the practice in the independence period. It may perhaps be the case that African administrators, trained as they are in Eurocentric educational establishments, have adopted European ideological models of male-female relations which they rather unthinkingly apply to their own land and development programs.[34] On the other hand, such European biases regarding women's role may merely reinforce indigenous cultural beliefs that women, whatever their productive role, should be under men's authority.

Education

Article 10 of the 1979 Convention on discrimination against women contains a number of provisions regarding women's education, most guaranteeing a similar type of education to males and females, and similar access to education for both sexes; in particular, article 10(f) proposes "the reduction of female student drop-out rates and the organization of programmes for girls and women who have left school prematurely."

Much remains to be done in English-speaking Africa to translate these goals into reality. With regard to access to education, in 1975 between 27 per cent (Sierra Leone) and 92 percent (Kenya) of girls aged 6–11 were enrolled in school. For those 12–17 years of age, the percentage enrolled ranged from 14 (Nigeria) to 42 (Zambia). Of those 18 through 23 years of age (senior secondary and postsecondary level), only between 1 and 4 percent were enrolled. Extremely few women have access to the technical and scientific training so important to future economic development.[35] The vast majority of women over 15 are illiterate; moreover, more women than men are illiterate.

To compound the problem, educational policies based on the British model result in girls' being offered education which is unsuitable to the economic realities of African women. In 1975, the Economic Commission for Africa estimated that over 50 per cent of mass education for girls consisted of so-called "domestic science".[36] As for elites, much of the education at one elite Ghana girls' secondary school in the late 1960s actually consisted of learning how to behave like Europeans; how to "cut out European style dresses with the use of patterns . . . to produce fancy English cakes and biscuits".[37] Insofar as girls receive separate education from boys, it would seem, they are being trained in obsolete and irrelevant British knowledge and customs.

Even such obsolete and irrelevant education, however, teaches basic literacy and arithmetic knowledge which is less easily obtained by females than by males. There are many reasons why African parents, with limited resources for school fees, would prefer to educate boys. Girls are required at home to assist their mothers in their numerous productive, household, and child-rearing chores, while boys are more easily spared. Parents may lose bride price if their daughters fail to marry at an early age;[38] in any case, when daughters marry into another lineage their parents' investment in their education is lost. Girls may also be obliged to drop out of school should they become pregnant; this is a common problem in Zambia, even though the indigenous culture does not stress premarital chastity.[39] In short, the loss of a young girl's labor time is more costly to her parents than the loss of a boy's, while the returns to her education, from the parents' point of view, are lower.[40]

Uneducated girls become uneducated women. Female adult illiterates find more difficulty in attending adult literacy classes than do male adult illiterates.[41] Nevertheless the evidence suggests that women will attend adult literacy classes when given the chance; the proportion of such classes which is female (43 percent in Ghana, almost 75 percent in Malawi, and 65 percent in Tanzania in 1968, as against only 16 percent in Sierra Leone) suggests that government policies may also be a factor affecting women's education.[42]

Urban Women

The sections on rural women and women's education have touched upon the division of women into social classes. Whatever the differential between men's and women's labor in rural sub-Saharan Africa, the wife of a rich peasant will probably have more economic resources at her command than the wife of a landless or quasi-landless proletarian. Similarly, rich peasants may be able to afford to invest in girls' education, whereas poor peasants will not. In the urban environment, the educated, professional woman will have many more opportunities open to her than the illiterate market trader or wageworker. In this connection, then, development issues and analyses of possibilities for human rights cannot be separated from an analysis of social stratification. For the purposes of this discussion, I wil use occupation as an indicator of women's class position.

Fewer African women are in elite occupational positions than women in developed countries. African women do have good access to professions such as law or medicine, but they have very little access to administrative and managerial positions, either in the private or the government sector.[43] These are the powerful positions, especially in economies dominated by a combination of multinational corporations and state monopolies. The picture for elite women, therefore, seems to be one of differential access to high-status positions. This violates article 11, 1 (b) of the 1979 Convention, which specifies that women should have the same employment opportunities as men. It would seem, however, that once elite women obtain a job, they are likely to obtain the equal remuneration and benefits specified in article 11, 1 (d); indeed, scattered evidence suggests that such women are probably more likely to obtain such benefits as maternity leave (article 11, 2 (b)) than their counterparts in the West.[44]

For elite women, then, the situation in English-speaking sub-Saharan Africa is one which approximates that of their counterparts in the West. Discrimination against women in elite occupations certainly exists, but such women have better access to the basic amenities of existence, and more resources to fight for their rights, than do the mass of women who work for wages or in trade in the cities.

Opportunities to work for salary are limited. There are far fewer women in the clerical or service occupations in sub-Saharan English-speaking Africa than in the West. Women constituted between 7 (Ghana) and 21 (Zambia) percent of such workers in 1968.[48] Clerical occupations, implying literacy and the status of being engaged in a non-manual occupation, are dominated by men in Africa.[46] Formal domestic service also tends to be a male occupational category. The chief occupation for women in the urban areas, in West Africa in particular, is in trade.

There is a pleasant fiction in the minds of many analysts of the West African urban scene that the "market mammy" controlling vast fortunes in cloth or soap or food, is typical of the West African woman trader.[47] But most women traders are engaged in a very marginal,

day-to-day existence, selling tiny quantities of one or two commodities such as steel wool or cigarettes, or preparing food to sell to
male workers on the streets. Even the wealthier women traders have
to contend with the problem that the more they make, the less money
their husbands may be willing to give them as a contribution to famly
support.[48] In the past, Accra women traders were obliged to give one-
half to two-thirds of their profits to their husbands.[49]

Many women traders are more accurately called hawkers. While
their economic activity is clearly crucial to the circulation of goods in
underdeveloped economies with limited "modern" wholesaling,
retailing, and transportation establishments, their long-term survival,
both as a group and as individuals, is precarious. As a group they are
likely to be pushed out of trade as more (male-dominated) formal
trading establishments are organized, either privately or by the
state.[50] As individuals, their opportunities are blocked; urban trade in
the "bazaar" sector is not an intermediate step between rural village
life and the "modern" sector, as Ester Boserup contends:[51] rather it is
the only opportunity available for women whose occupational
choices are limited both by their sex and by the general economic
underdevelopment of their societies.[52]

Nor do African women have many opportunities in the industrial
sector. As in the Western world, so in Africa the vast majority of jobs
in this sector are held by men. Women are likely, if they are fortunate
enough in the first place to be able to engage in wage labor, to be
hired part-time and at lower wages than males. In Tanzania, "There
are no laws guaranteeing equal job opportunities and . . . sexual
discrimination is rampant."[53] In northern Nigeria, Hausa women
working on a European-owned farm growing vegetables for the European market earned only about 15 per cent of male workers' wages in
the late 1970s.[54]

The "public" role of women as active producers in rural
agricultural societies, therefore, has not served to guard them against
inequitable conditions in the "modern" sector. Rather, their pattern
follows the European: from productive but subordinate rural worker,
to subordinate and exploited female proletarian, to subordinate and
economically dependent wife of the westernized elite male. Robertson notes that "Central Accra women tend to equate financial
dependence on a husband with high-status marriage".[55] "Modernization" for the elite woman thus can have the contradictory effect
of raising her material well-being while reinforcing her indigenous
cultural subordination with the Western ideology of female economic
dependence, privatization, and confinement to the home as a
decorative symbol of her husband's prosperity. The elite African
woman may prefer to brave the cultural stigma of being unmarried as

an alternative to this stifling life.[56] To understand why African women are confronted with such choices, we must turn to an analysis of the cultural expectations regarding relationships between women and men.

LAW AND CUSTOM: WOMEN'S RIGHTS IN THE PERSONAL SPHERE

Marriage and the Family

The rights of women in marriage and family matters are central to their rights as individuals. Insofar as women's lives are affected far more profoundly than are men's by their reproductive roles, lack of rights in this area can effectively mean that women cannot exercise any rights they may formally have in other areas. Nevertheless, the assurance of rights for women in this most personal of spheres is a complex matter, given that all societies value the preservation of the family as much as they purport to value individual freedom. If woman is the linchpin of the family, can her rights then be considered more important than those of the larger group?

In sub-Saharan English-speaking Africa, where extended families predominate and marriages are usually a matter of lineage concern, this question is even more pressing than it is in areas where the nuclear family prevails. The customs of child betrothal, arranged marriage, bridewealth, and inheritance of a relative's widow, all of which contravene United Nations' provisions for human rights, are central to the organization of society. Marriages based on these principles are generally contracted in good faith, and the people who arrange the marriages are attempting to obtain a satisfactory outcome both for the individuals concerned and for the lineages allied by the particular marriage.[57]

In this connection any advocacy of immediate implementation in sub-Saharan Africa of laws which conform to United Nations provisions for women's rights in the sphere of marriage and the family could be interpreted as an imposition of a secularized, individualistic view of human relations upon Africa. Different cultures have different norms of individual versus social needs. While socioeconomic rights embodied in the "basic human needs" approach, and even rights of civil and political freedom, seem to be accepted as universal, rights impinging on "custom" can be seen as more relative. On the other hand, there is almost universal evidence that marriage customs are based on the subordination of women as a group to men as a group. Customs are neither immutable in time, nor neutral in their impact.

Three principles regarding culture can serve as a guide in understanding the difficulties in implementing women's rights in English-speaking sub-Saharan Africa. First, people value customs even when they seem to be "irrational" to an outsider. The symbolic value is a real personal value. Secondly, culture and customs can change *endogenously*, not merely as a result of colonialism or contact with Westernization or urbanization. As Luckham remarks regarding the codification of "customary" law in Ghana into written law, "the static conception of the law which resulted was wholly alien to the flexible and adaptive nature of custom."[58] Finally, just as those who attempt to modify or change customs may have personal interests in that change, so also do those who attempt to preserve customs. Again regarding Ghana, Luckham states that "customary law tended to be systematized from the start by people who had a personal and class interest in its operation."[59] The preservation of custom can mask real conflicts over economic or political resources.

The discussion of cultural relativity is even more pertinent in former British Africa than elsewhere, because of the continued existence, in all of the countries under consideration except Tanzania, of more than one code of law. The British chose to formally codify "customary" law in their African colonies. Codification of customary law is complicated by the fact that each ethnic group has its own legal system, so that conflicts can occur, for example, when two people of different ethnic groups marry. In the urbanized areas British law was introduced in order to serve Europeans and "modernized" Africans. In most sub-Saharan English-speaking countries, then, there is a customary sector and a formal legal sector, the latter being exemplified in the case of marriage law by the Marriage Ordinance. In addition, some countries provide separate laws for Muslims, and Kenya also has a separate Hindu law for its citizens of Asian origin. Reform of legislation involving human rights thus also implies unification of the law, as recommended, for example, by the Economic Commission for Africa.[60]

In this connection Tanzania's recent decision to adopt a unified marriage law, with such new provisions as the rights of the child being paramount in custody cases, is of particular interest. By abolishing legal pluralism, it puts all marriages on an equal footing. It also subordinates customs, including Islamic custom, to a secular, legal framework.[61] Interestingly, the Tanzanian law is based upon a proposed reform of Kenyan law which did not get through the Kenyan Parliament. The Kenyan Law Reform Commission had been instructed to frame a uniform law of marriage, paying "particular attention to the status of women." The principles underlying the comission's report are of special interest. *"Uniform law must be founded in the African way of life"*; traditional rites and customs "should not be codified, as to do so would impede natural and gradual change"; and such law "must be based upon a recognition of human dignity, regardless of sex."[62] (emphasis in original). Despite these principles, objections to the Bill, from members of Parliament as well as others, included the claims that the Bill was "un-African," and that it gave too many rights to women. Accordingly it can by no means be taken for granted that the men in power in sub-Saharan Africa will willingly grant women equal rights. In the culturally sancrosanct family, men retain a material, sexual, and moral dominance that many are unwilling to relinquish.

The custom of polygyny, which is permitted by both customary and Islamic law in English-speaking sub-Saharan Africa (including Tanzania, where unification of the law nevertheless has not prohibited polygyny), is often cited as an example of male dominance. But there is no provision in any United Nations or Organization of African Unity convention, nor indeed in any International Women's Year recommendations, that polygyny should be abolished. Nevertheless its continuance is a matter of debate among Africans. The Economic Commission for Africa, for example, has advocated its abolition, although not by changes in the law.[63]

The case against polygyny seems to be that it is considered demeaning for one man to "own" several wives, and that it is impossible, in a multiple-wife situation, for the (Western) ideal of a companionate marriage based upon love, trust, and mutual respect to be realized. From the wives' point of view, polygyny also means that they must share their husband sexually, and their children must share his material and emotional resources; that they will be plagued by rivalry; and that senior wives will fear younger, prettier wives while junior wives will live under the senior wives' authority.[64]

The case for polygyny, from the man's point of view, is that it allows him to accrue economic resources of female labor power, and that it ensures him the status and long-term material security of large numbers of children.[65] From the woman's point of view, polygyny provides other women to share in child rearing, husband care, and possible economic ventures such as marketing; it provides companionship; and it ensures her the right to postpartum celibacy so that she can space her children.[66]

The assumption among most women is that husbands are necessarily unfaithful; the Christian ideal of monogamy, on which many non-Africans' and "modernized" Africans' objections to polygyny are based, is seen as unrealistic. While men married under the Marriage Ordinance are not legally permitted to take customary wives as well, they often do so. This results in a situation in which the Ordinance wife has legal rights while the customary wives do not. The trend, therefore, in African legal reform circles is not to advocate that polygyny be abolished, but rather to ensure that marriages (and wives of all types) be on an equal legal footing.[67]

Polygyny is in fact related to a complex of customs in "traditional" African societies which violate United Nations norms: These include bridewealth, arranged marriages, child betrothal, and inheritance of widows. Certainly to those who believe in the individual's right to choose her spouse, the ideas of child betrothal, arranged marriage in return for a monetary consideration, or the "inheritance" of a widow by her deceased husband's relative, are abhorrent. Yet these practices are far from abhorrent in a society which regards marriage as an alliance between lineages, which believes that young people are incapable of making reasoned decisions regarding their future spouses, and which wishes to protect widows by providing them with a new male guardian on the death of their spouses.

There are contradictory indications, for example, as to whether or not bridewealth means that a daughter is subject to "sale" by her father. Writing in the early 1960s, Izzert noted that among the Yoruba, "acceptance [of bridewealth by the father] indicates approval of the marriage and a willingness to render assistance if the bride's husband dies or turns out to be unreliable, the assistance being given to the bride and her children."[68] In the past, then, bridewealth served as a form of insurance. A man who divorced his wife without cause permanently forfeited his bride price, which could then be used to support his wife and children; similarly, a wife who left her husband without cause would know that her family would be obliged to return the bride price. Nowadays, there are signs that "Fathers [are] tempted to hold up their daughters to the highest bidder";[69] however, among the more "modernized" population, "there is [also] a growing tendency among educated parents . . . to refuse all money payments, saying their daughter is not for sale."[70]

Exchange of bridewealth is practiced extensively in sub-Saharan Africa. An attempt to abolish it by legislation could well interfere with traditional means of protecting a woman from abuse by her husband. It would seem that among the elite population the practice will die out in any case, as a new ideology of women's autonomy takes hold. The sensible legal course to take would probably be not to abolish the practice outright, but merely to ensure the right of any woman not to be subjected to the practice if she chooses otherwise.

The same principle should probably be applied to arranged marriages and child betrothal. No one should be forced against her or his will to enter a marriage. Registration of all marriages, and the enforcement of a rule that marriages can only be formalized after the age of majority has been reached, would ensure a mechanism to ascertain whether or not both spouses agreed to the marriage. Parental pressure, however, would still influence a young woman's decision.[71] Legislation cannot control how decisions to marry are made; it can provide a means by which a young woman who wishes to escape from traditional family controls can do so. It can also embody a new ideology as an impetus towards future relaxation of community norms.

A similar analysis can be applied to the custom of inheritance of widows. Sagay discusses the case of a succeeding Yoruba *Oba* (chief) who inherited fifty "palace wives": The issue at hand was whether he could actually marry these fifty women under customary law, given that he had already married one woman under the monogomous Marriage Ordinance. One solution posited that as long as the women were merely "institutional wives" and the marriages were not consummated, they would be legal. Such a solution suggests that widow inheritance is actually a form of protection for women.[72] By being formally affiliated to a man from their husband's lineage, they maintain their residence rights and (limited) rights to support. Sagay notes that, "In modern times, an Oba's widow who does not wish to become the wife of her husband's successor may move out of the palace."[73] However, in practice such a choice may not be tenable, as in many parts of Africa, a woman who is not a wife is a woman without any rights to her children or property.[74]

Economic Rights of Women in Marriage

Just as it is necessary for women to have real economic rights in marriage, the same is true at its dissolution by divorce or death. In this sense, inequitable access to divorce constitutes a discriminatory liability under which women suffer. Article 16, 1 (c) of the 1979 Covenant against discrimination guarantees women and men "the same rights and responsibilities during marriage and at its dissolution." But this right is not necessarily guaranteed to all women in English-speaking sub-Saharan Africa. Muslim women are under the greatest legal disability in all seven states. In Kenya and Sierra Leone, a husband can divorce his wife by repudiation, and even in Tanzania, a husband's repudiation can be taken as evidence of irreparable marriage breakdown.[75] Customary law seems to guarantee the most rights for women in divorce; marriage breakdowns are matters for negotiation between the two families. However, custom can discriminate against women. For example, a husband can divorce a woman for "barrenness" or adultery, whereas she cannot leave him for the same reasons. Family negotiation, in addition, may leave the woman dependent upon decisions and advice from male elders of her own lineage, with whom she may not agree.

Moreover a divorced wife may not have rights to maintenance for herself or her children, or even to retain property acquired during marriage. This is hardly surprising. In "traditional" societies, wives are expected to provide much of their own and their children's support through agricultural and marketing activities; the divorced wife presumably can return to her own lineage and acquire land use rights there, so that she is not in need of maintenance. Unfortunately, the urban wife does not have the same resources at her command. The "modern" wife married under the Ordinance, moreover, is subject to discriminatory provisions of British law which assume that a wife's housework is not an economic contribution to the household, and which provide very weak sanctions against husbands who default on maintenance payments.

Article 16, 1 (h) of the 1979 Convention against discrimination guarantees women and men "the same rights for both spouses in respect of the ownership, acquisition, management, administration, enjoyment and disposition of property. . . ." This provision is acknowledged in some court decisions in English-speaking Africa, so that educated urban women, who have the resources to avail themselves of the courts, have some recourse against ex-husbands who default or do not offer maintenance payments. In other cases, even educated women have no such recourse; in 1969 Kenya repealed its Affiliation Act, which obliged fathers of children born out of wedlock to pay for their support.[76] In the customary sector the wife seems to be dependent upon family negotiations and the goodwill of the two parties. For women living in "detribalized" urban settings, or married outside of their own ethnic groups, such provisions are of limited use. With regard to both inheritance and maintenance rights, many women in English-speaking Africa still suffer severe legal disabilities.

The final matter in which women suffer legal discrimination is in the matter of custody law. Article 16, 1 (d) of the 1979 Covenant specifies that women and men shall have "the same rights and responsibilities as parents, irrespective of their marital status, in matters relating to their children; in all cases the interests of the children shall be paramount." However, the countries under discussion do not necessarily guarantee women equal rights with men regarding their own children; indeed, the presumption seems to be that fathers' rights to custody are paramount, even in supposedly matrilineal societies. For example, although the interests of the child are supposedly paramount in Kenya, in practice "some judges insist on using the traditional concepts which considered the father as the 'owner' of the child".[77] Schuster reported that some of the mothers she interviewed in Lusaka (Zambia) did not want to accept badly needed maintenance payments from the fathers, since the father would then claim he had the right to custody of the children when they were older.[78] In many instances, as in Sierra Leone, the mother bears the full burden of raising the child until it is about seven; the child is then removed from her.[79] Aside from whatever "maternal" feelings a mother may have for a child she has raised for seven years, when she loses a child she loses a valuable economic resource, both for assistance in her day-to-day chores and as security for her old age.[80]

There are two themes running through the above discussion of women's rights in marriage. First, although many women may prefer to live under those customs with which they are most familiar even though the customs deny them personal freedom, international human rights legislation, as well as some of the legislation of the countries concerned, requires that women be able to remove themselves from the control of these customs should they so desire. Second, formal economic rights of women in marriage are becoming increasingly necessary as customary means for providing for women and children within the lineage break down.

"New" Rights of Women

A third comment which can be made regarding women's rights in the marriage and family sphere in Africa is that a number of the concerns of "Western" feminists, namely the sharing of domestic responsibilities, the issue of violence against women, and rights of women to control their own reproductive systems, have been inadequately addressed in the United Nations and in the individual African countries.

To ignore these concerns under the pretense that they are indications of Western bias is to show disregard of the true nature of relationships between men and women in Africa. Regarding "household" chores, the section above on political economy has clearly demonstrated that women do an inordinate share of productive and domestic labor. The provision of article 16, 1 (d) of the Convention opposing discrimination against women that both men and women share "the same rights and responsibilities as parents" may be interpreted to mean that men should share in day-to-day child-rearing chores; however, there is no mention or discussion of this possibility in the literature on human rights.

With regard to violence against women, there is no specific mention of this problem in the various UN covenants, although the 1980 International Women's Year conference did recommend that "legislation should . . . be enacted and implemented in order to prevent domestic and sexual violence against women."[81] In Africa, the problem of violence against women seems to be one of wife-beating, rather than of rape. Even here, however, the evidence is not clear. Schuster reports of her "sub-elite" sample in Lusaka that "nearly everyone has submitted to sexual relations out of fear of the consequences of refusing."[82] Izzert reported of her Yoruba sample that "married women often complain of physical cruelty—usually of frequent beatings without any justification."[83] In a high percentage of Nigerian divorce cases cruelty is cited as the reason for the divorce.[84] A number of cultures in East Africa give positive sanction to wife-beating.[85]

The problem of violence against women seems to be partly exacerbated by women's increasing tendency to step out of their presumptive roles, especially in urban areas. Mushanga explains wife-murder partly by the fact that many men believe that women should "remain subservient" to their husbands, and that they become enraged when their wives are not.[86] Men seem to use violence as a form of social control when communal norms break down and women assume new freedom. The "single" woman of the city, who defies convention by living independently of a man, is especially likely to incite male hostility; presumably the assumption is that she is a "loose woman," and this can be used as a justification for attacking her, as sporadic assaults against women in miniskirts in Malawi, Tanzania, and Kenya testify.[87] "Men are angry at women because they are no longer subservient",[88] but to defend oneself against violence from men by the assumption of a subservient role seems faint protection. Cultural beliefs of this sort may call for legislation, in conformity with the provision of the Organization of African Unity Declaration on human rights that "human beings are inviolable."

Finally, the provisions for women's right to control their own reproductive powers are ambiguous. The 1979 Convention reflects most UN documents in its provision (article 16, 1, (3)) that women and men have "the same rights to decide freely and responsibly on the number and spacing of their children and to have access to the information, education, and means to enable them to exercise these rights." This statement ignores the reality that the burden of childbearing falls only on women, and of child rearing disproportionately on women. Moreover, there are differences between husbands and wives regarding the desired number of children. For example, a study of nine rural Yoruba couples revealed that the husbands' ideal number of children was eleven, while the wives' was six.[89] The men in this small sample, as in many other cases, also preferred boys, so that wives can be compelled to bear children until they produce the requisite number of sons. Given the cultural domination of men in decision making, combined with their physical capacity to impose sexual relations on their wives, the reality of the matter is that men usually have the last word on family size, as the Economic Commission for Africa has recognized.[90] Moreover, the "means to enable" the right to determine the number and spacing of children are denied to women insofar as abortion is denied by legislation, as in Kenya and Ghana.[91] Akingba found that "while Nigerian men still contend that all pregnancies are welcome, the incidence of unwanted pregnancies, and hence abortions, in both single and married women is a major problem."[92]

Female Genital Operations

The question of control by women over their own bodies raises the issue of female genital operations, a matter which has received much attention in the Western press and among Western feminists since about 1979, largely as a result of the work of Fran Hosken.[93] Circumcision, both male and female, has been cited in Christian Europe for centuries as evidence that not only Africans but also Australian aborigines and indeed European Jews are a lesser form of being.[94] Hence in discussing the practice of female genital mutilation, it is important to keep in mind the ideological context in which previous discussions have been couched. To avoid discussion of the practice altogether, however, or to interpret it, as anthropological functionalists have done in the past, as merely an integrative indigenous custom,[95] is to avoid confronting its detrimental effects on women. It should be noted that I use the term "female genital operations" rather than the inaccurate term "female circumcision."

"Several tens of millions of women"[96] are estimated to have undergone genital operations in Africa as a whole, yet there is overwhelming medical evidence that even the mildest form of genital operation can have very serious consequences.[97] There is absolutely no evidence that female genital mutilation contributes to hygiene, as is often claimed in its justification; on the contrary, retention of urine or menstrual flow as a result of excision or infibulation is extremely unhygienic.

The operation also has the consequence of interfering with basic physiological responses to sexual stimulation; indeed, this is fully acknowledged by the many Africans who claim (somewhat erroneously) as justification for the practice, that it will control promiscuity in young women. Some Western feminists, among them Hosken, therefore view female genital mutilation as a deliberate form of "sexual castration," an example of "contempt for the female of the species."[98]

Attributing the practice to gross misogyny seems unwarranted, and its functions are obscure. It may represent an attempt by males to control female sexuality or reproductive powers, or to remove the "female" parts of males and the "male" parts of females. Other informants assume that female genital operations are required under Islam—a misinterpretation of Islamic teachings.[99] In addition, women say that they perform genital operations on their daughters, or undergo them themselves, as otherwise they or their daughters would be unmarriageable.

While generally it is educated African women who have spoken out against female genital operations, there are adult, educated women who have voluntarily undergone them. These cases serve as evidence for the proposition that people value cultural practices even when they seem to be "irrational." As Jomo Kenyatta argued in the 1930s for the Gikuyu, at a time when British missionaries were trying to suppress female genital operations,[100] such practices may be central to the entire symbolic and age-grading organization of society.[101]

Defenders of female genital operations argue that the custom is so culturally central that to abolish it would be to destroy the very fabric of society. Yet cultures change, and people can learn new ways to express their ethnic identity. For example, one female member of Parliament in Kenya suggested "the expansion of girls' education as an alternative means of achieving self-identity."[102] Changes in one custom can be compensated for by adjustments in another; an ethnic group can identify itself by its language or its territory, rather than by its ritual.[103]

What, then, ought to be done with regard to this practice, which is clearly detrimental to women's and children's health, and as such clearly violates a number of UN and OAU principles regarding basic human rights?[104]

In 1979, the Economic Commission for Africa condemned "infibulation and other female sexual mutilations." It called for a campaign of education and government assistance to attempt to eradicate these practices, while at the same time it condemned international campaigns on the subject which "do not take into account the complexity of the African situation."[105] For the moment at least, an educational campaign, directed particularly at health professionals, schoolgirls, and patients in maternity clinics, would be the most appropriate way to begin eliminating the custom. Legislation banning female genital operations might merely drive the operators underground, as it appears to have done in the Sudan.[106] Legislation might be considered which permits the operation only with the consent of the woman or girl who is to undergo it, but such legislation would not solve the problems of performing genital operations upon minor females under the age of informed consent. Clearly, operations upon adult females without their consent could be made illegal. With regard to this and other cultural practices such as bride price, a useful reconciliation of social norms with individual rights could be obtained through a provision that the state would uphold the right of an individual woman to refuse to subject herself to such customs.

CONCLUSION

The human rights of women in English-speaking sub-Saharan Africa cannot be adequately analysed, nor can realistic recommendations be made for their improvement, without an understanding of their historical and sociological context. Mere legislative imposition of such rights fails to recognize the influence of culture and tradition, not only on how men view women, but on how women view themselves; it also fails to recognize the complicating factors of economic underdevelopment.

The effective implementation of women's rights in English-speaking sub-Saharan Africa is dependent, in this author's view, on a three-fold change. First, economic development, to ensure not only that the gross national product of these countries rises but also that there is an equitable sharing of resources, is absolutely essential not only for assuring basic human needs, but also so that women have comparative "leisure" to devote to assuring other rights. Civil and political freedoms must be implemented and maintained, so that women can organize in pursuit of their own interests and so that there can be rational discussion of the sometimes antithetical interests of men and women. Finally, carefully constructed legislation can assure to women the right to opt out of those customs and norms which they, as individuals, find constraining.

There is no guarantee, however, that such changes will occur. It should not be assumed that Africa is engaged in a process of "modernization" which will inevitably result in vastly increased economic wealth and the development and protection of personal and political freedoms. Instead, African economies may stagnate or regress. Military or civilian dictatorships may retain power indefinitely. For general economic and political reasons, as well as for reasons to do with the power of the individual male in the home, women's rights may continue to take second place or be relegated to a Utopian future when all other human rights problems will have been solved. For the women of Africa, as for women in the developed Western world, eternal vigilance in defence of their rights would seem an appropriate stance.

NOTES

For their helpful comments on earlier drafts of this paper, I would like to thank Omega Bula, Bruce Curtis, Roberta Ann Dunbar, Graham Knight, Michael Levin, Meg Luxton, Harriet Lyons, Claire Robertson, Vivienne Walters, and Audrey Wipper. I also owe thanks to various members of the staff of McMaster University, especially Mr. David Cook and other reference librarians in Mills Library, Ms. Barbara Freeze and the staff of the Inter-Library Loan Service, and Ms. Karen Poxon and the staff of the word-processing center. This paper is part of a larger project on human rights in English-speaking Sub-Saharan Africa, summarized in Rhoda Howard, "The Dilemma of Human Rights in Sub-Saharan Africa", *International Journal* 35, no. 4 (1980), pp. 724–47.

1. Information on this and all other treaty ratifications was found in (a) "Multilateral Treaties in Respect of Which the Secretary-General Performs Depositary Functions: List of Signatures, Ratifications, Accessions, etc., as at 31 December 1979" (New York: United Nations, 1980) UN Doc. ST/LEG/SER/D/13; (b) *UN Monthly Chronicle*, January 1980-May 1982; (c) *World Treaty Index* 2 (Santa Barbara: American Bibliographical Center-Clio) (1974); (d) *Yearbook on Human Rights* (New York: United Nations, annual), volumes for 1968, 1969, 1972, and 1973–74; (e) UN General Assembly, 35th Session, Item 83, "Status of the Convention on the Elimination of Discrimination against Women," UN Doc. A/35/428, 9 September 1980. Ratifications have been checked up to May 1982.

2. Margaret K. Bruce, "An Account of United Nations Actions to Advance the Status of Women," *Annals of the American Academy of Political and Social Science*, 375 (January 1968), p. 163, for discussion of the difficulties of gaining compliance with UN conventions.

3. See UN General Assembly, Resolution 2263 (XXII), 7 November 1967, for an earlier "Declaration" on this subject.

4. See Articles 4, 16, 17, and 18 of the Charter, all of which could be construed to protect women's rights.

5. Chapters 5, 15, 3, and 4 of the Constitution of the Republic of Ghana, in A.K.P. Kludze, "Ghana," in *Constitutions of the Countries of the World* (Dobbs Ferry, N.Y.: Oceana Publications, 1980).

6. UN Commission on the Status of Women, *Report of the Secretary-General*, "Constitutions, Electoral Laws and Other Legal Instruments Relating to the Political Rights of Women" (New York: United Nations, 1968), UN Doc. A/6447/Rev. 1, table 4, pp. 121–35. This source does not mention Tanzania; however I assume women were granted political rights equal to men's in Tanzania at independence.

7. Carol P. Hoffer, "Mende and Sherbro Women in High Office," *Canadian Journal of African Studies* 6, no. 2 (1972), p. 151.

8. Annie M.D. Lebeuf, "The Role of Women in the Political Organization of African Societies," in Denise Paulme, ed., *Women of Tropical Africa* (Berkeley and Los Angeles: University of California Press, 1971), pp. 95–96.

9. Kamene Okonjo, "The Dual-Sex Political System in Operation: Igbo Women and Community Politics in Midwestern Nigeria," in Nancy J. Hafkin and Edna G. Bay, eds., *Women in Africa* (Stanford: Stanford University Press, 1976), p. 45.

10. Judith Van Allen, "Aba Riots or the Igbo Women's War?—Ideology, Stratification, and the Invisibility of Women," *Ufahamu* 6, no. 1 (1975), pp. 11–12.

11. World Bank, *Poverty and Human Development* (New York: Oxford University Press, 1980), p. 78.

12. United Nations, *Statistical Yearbook* (31st Issue) (New York: UN, 1981), pp. 79–80.

13. World Bank, *Poverty and Human Development*, p. 68.

14. "Report of the World Conference of the United Nations Decade for Women: Equality, Development and Peace," Copenhagen, 14–30 July 1980, UN Doc. A/CONF.94/35, p. 90. (Hereafter referred to as IWY 1980.)

15. UN Economic Commission for Africa, "The Role of Women in African Development," prepared for the World Conference of the International Women's Year, Mexico City, UN Doc. E/CONF.66/BP/8-8/Add. 1, 10 April 1975, p. 23. (Hereafter referred to as ECA 1975.)

16. IWY 1980, pp. 87–88.

17. ECA 1975, p. 10.

18. UN Economic Commission for Africa, "Report on Five Workshops in Home Economics and Other Family-oriented Fields" (1973), quoted in ECA 1975, p. 7.

19. Suellen Huntington, "Issues in Women's Role in Economic Development: Critique and Alternatives," *Journal of Marriage and the Family* 37 (November 1975), p. 1007.

20. "Report of the Regional Preparatory Meeting of the United Nations Economic Commission for Africa, Second Regional Conference for the Integration of Women in Development," prepared for IWY 1980, UN Doc. A/CONF. 94/17, p. 10. (Hereafter referred to as ECA 1980.)

21. ECA 1975, pp. 23–25.

22. Ibid., p. 25.

23. These observations regarding day-care needs were brought to my attention by Omega Bula.

24. ECA 1975, p. 17.

25. Ibid., p. 5.

26. Jette Bukh, *The Village Woman in Ghana* (Uppsala: Scandinavian Institute of African Studies, 1979).

27. Rhoda Howard, *Colonialism and Underdevelopment in Ghana* (London: Croom Helm, 1978).

28. Achola Pala Okeyo, "Daughters of the Lakes and Rivers: Colonization and the Land Rights of Luo Women," in Mona Etienne and Eleanor Leacock, eds., *Women and Colonization: Anthropological Perspectives* (New York: Praeger, 1980), p. 206.

29. James L. Brain. "Less Than Second-Class: Women in Rural Settlement Schemes in Tanzania," in Hafkin and Bay, *Women in Africa*, p. 278.

30. James L. Brain, personal communication.

31. ECA 1975, p. 9.

32. Susan Abbott, "Women's Importance for Kenyan Rural Development," *Community Development Journal* 10, no. 3 (1975), pp. 179–80.

33. Kathleen A. Staudt, "Administrative Resources, Political Patrons and Redressing Sex Inequities: A Case from Western Kenya," *Journal of Developing Areas* 12 (July 1978), pp. 407–8.

34. Abbott, "Women's Importance," p. 180.

35. Figures from IWY 1980, Addendum to *Report of the Secretary-General*, "Status and Role of Women in Education and in the Economic and Social Fields," UN Doc. A/34/577/Add.1/Rev.1, 23 May 1980, p. 3, "Principal indicators of women's condition and participation in development" (Indicators 8–12).

36. ECA 1975, p. 19.

37. Vandra Masemann, "The 'Hidden Curriculum' of a West African Girls' Boarding School," *Canadian Journal of African Studies* 8, no. 3 (1974), p. 484.

38. UN Center for Economic and Social Information, "The Situation and Status of Women Today: Some Essential Facts," UN Doc. OPI/CESI/NOTE IWY/15, December 1974, p. 4.

39. Ilsa M. Glazer Schuster, *New Women of Lusaka* (Palo Alto, Calif.: Mayfield, 1979), p. 44.

40. ECA 1980, pp. 10, 12.

41. UN Doc. OPI/CESI/NOTE IWY/15, p. 4.

42. Elise Boulding, Shirley A. Nuss, Dorothy Lee Carson and Michael E. Greenstein, *Handbook of International Data on Women* (New York: Wiley, 1976), p. 139.

43. ECA 1975, p. 16.

44. See for example Carmel Dinan, "Pragmatists or Feminists? The Professional 'Single' Women of Accra, Ghana," *Cahiers d'études africaines* 17, no. 1 (1977), p. 160.

45. Boulding et al., *Handbook*, p. 100.

46. Ester Boserup, *Women's Role in Economic Development* (New York: St. Martin's Press, 1970), p. 133.

47. See for example Mudiaga Odje, "Human Rights of African Women" (unpublished, presented to the African Bar Association, Fourth Conference, Nairobi, Kenya, 1981), p. 8.

48. Claire Robertson, "Ga Women and Socioeconomic Change in Accra, Ghana" in Hafkin and Bay, eds., *Women in Africa*, p. 120.

49. Dinan, "Pragmatists or Feminists?" p. 161.

50. Dorothy Remy, "Underdevelopment and the Experience of Women: A

Nigerian Case Study," in Rayna R. Reiter, ed., *Toward an Anthropology of Women* (New York: Monthly Review Press, 1975), p. 370.

51. Boserup, *Women's Role in Economic Development*, p. 178.

52. Huntington, "Issues in Woman's Role in Economic Development," p. 1006.

53. Deborah Fahy Bryceson, "The Proletarianization of Women in Tanzania," *Review of African Political Economy* 17 (January-April 1980), p. 20.

54. Sam Jackson. "Hausa Women on Strike," *Review of African Political Economy* 13 (May-August 1978), p. 24.

55. Robertson, "Ga Women," p. 125.

56. Dinan, "Pragmatists or Feminists?" p. 164.

57. Yaa Luckham, "Law and the Status of Women in Ghana," *Columbia Human Rights Law Review* 8, no. 1, (Spring-Summer 1976), p. 69.

58. Ibid., p. 71.

59. Ibid., p. 74.

60. ECA 1980, p. 32.

61. Roberta Ann Dunbar, "Legislative Reform and Muslim Family Law: Effects upon Women's Rights in Africa South of the Sahara," paper presented at the African Studies Association, Philadelphia, October 1980, p. 28.

62. "Notes and News: The Rejection of the Marriage Bill in Kenya," *Journal of African Law* 23, no. 2 (1979), p. 111.

63. ECA 1980, p. 33.

64. Helen Ware, "Polygyny: Women's Views in a Transitional Society, Nigeria 1975," *Journal of Marriage and the Family* 41 (February 1979), pp. 185–95.

65. Felix K. Ekechi, "African Polygamy and Western Christian Ethnocentrism," *Journal of African Studies* 3 (August 1976), p. 331.

66. Ware, "Polygyny"; Huntington, "Issues in Woman's Role in Economic Development"; and A. Izzert, "Family Life among the Yoruba in Lagos, Nigeria" in Aidan Southall, ed., *Social Change in Modern Africa* (London: Oxford University Press, 1961).

67. "Notes and News: Rejection," p. 112; Luckham, "Ghana," p. 93; and C.E. Donegan, "Marriage and Divorce Law in Sierra Leone: A Microcosm of African Legal Problems," *Cornell International Law Journal* 5, no. 1 (1972), p. 63.

68. Izzert, "Family Life," p. 309.

69. Aidan Southall, "Problems of the New Morality," *Journal of African Studies* 1 (Winter 1974), p. 384.

70. Izzert, "Family Life," p. 308.

71. Rose Maina, V.W. Muchai, and S.B.O. Gutto, "Law and the Status of Women in Kenya," *Columbia Human Rights Law Review* 8, no. 1 (Spring-Summer 1976), p. 189.

72. Lakshman Marasinghe in this volume also interprets widow inheritance as a form of protection for women.

73. Itse Sagay, "Widow Inheritance versus Monogamous Marriage: the Oba's Dilemma," *Journal of African Law* 18, no. 2 (August 1974), p. 169, n. 3.

74. A.N. Allott, "The Legal Status of Women in Africa," *Journal of African Law* 5 (1961), p. 128.

75. Dunbar, "Legislative Reform," p. 31.

76. S.B.O. Gutto, "The Status of Women in Kenya," Discussion Paper no. 235, Institute for Development Studies, University of Nairobi (April 1976), p. 30.

77. Maina et al., "Kenya," p. 194.

78. Schuster, *New Women of Lusaka*, p. 137.

79. Donegan, "Sierra Leone," p. 73.

80. I owe this point to Harriet Lyons.

81. IWY 1980, p. 13.

82. Schuster, *New Woman of Lusaka*, p. 93.

83. Izzert, "Family Life," p. 315.

84. Delores E. Mack, "Husbands and Wives in Lagos: The Effects of Socioeconomic Status on the Pattern of Family Living," *Journal of Marriage and the Family* 40, no. 4 (November 1978), p. 815.

85. Tibamanya M. Mushanga, "Wife Victimization in East and Central Africa," *Victimology* 2, nos. 3–4 (1977–78), pp. 479–85.

86. Ibid., p. 484.

87. Audrey Wipper, "African Women, Fashion and Scapegoating," *Canadian Journal of African Studies* 6, no. 2 (1972) (special issue on African women, ed. Audrey Wipper), pp. 329–49.

88. Southall, "New Morality," p. 371.

89. Mack, "Husbands and Wives," p. 809.

90. ECA 1980, p. 29.

91. Maina et al., "Kenya," p. 200, Luckham "Ghana," p. 90.

92. J. B. Akingba, *The Problem of Unwanted Pregnancies in Nigeria Today* (Lagos: University of Lagos Press, 1971), quoted in Mack, "Husbands and Wives," p. 808.

93. Fran P. Hosken, *The Hosken Report: Genital and Sexual Mutilation of Females* (Lexington, Mass.: Women's International Network News, 1979).

94. Harriet Lyons, "Anthropologists, Moralities and Relativities: The Problem of Genital Mutilations," *Canadian Review of Sociology and Anthropology* 18, no. 4 (November 1981), pp. 499–518.

95. Ibid., p. 507.

96. Scilla McLean, ed., *Female Circumcision, Excision, and Infibulation: The Facts and Proposals for Change* (London: Minority Rights Group, 1980), p. 3. This short, accurate, and unbiased summary, prepared in consultation with many African women experts, is the best single source on female genital operations.

97. Esther Ogunmodende, "Female Circumcision in Nigeria," quoted in Hosken, *Report*, p. 8.

98. Hosken, *Report*, p. 1.

99. McLean et al., *Female Circumcision*, p. 7.

100. Jocelyn Murray, "The Church Missionary Society and the 'Female Circumcision' Issue in Kenya 1929–1932," *Journal of Religion in Africa* 8, no. 2 (1976), pp. 92–104.

101. Jomo Kenyatta, *Facing Mount Kenya* (London: Heinemann, 1979, 1st ed. 1938), pp. 131–35.

102. McLean et al., *Female Circumcision,* p. 17.
103. I owe this last suggestion to Omega Bula.
104. McLean et al., *Female Circumcision,* p. 10.
105. ECA 1980, pp. 43–44.
106. McLean et al., *Female Circumcision,* p. 19.

A Modern Approach to Human Rights in Islam: Foundations and Implications for Africa

Abdullahi Ahmed El Naiem

Islam remains one of the main determinants of political and social developments in many parts of Africa, south as well as north of the Sahara. Although the Muslim population in tropical Africa is more widely dispersed and less contiguous, and although fewer states in this region are formally constituted as Islamic states than in north Africa and the Middle East, this region may still be regarded as one of the major Islamic regions in the world.[1] It is therefore important to consider the position of human rights in Islam because it directly affects individual attitudes, social norms and institutions, and legal principles pertaining to human rights in Africa.

Islam in Africa is a vast and extremely rich subject that may be approached from historical, political, sociological, anthropological, or legal perspectives. The question of human rights is also complex, and interdisciplinary. It is not possible, therefore, to exhaust even a single aspect of the subject of human rights in Islam in one chapter. It may be possible, however, to consider the basic compatibility of Islam and contemporary universal standards of human rights. Although it can easily be shown that certain aspects of Shari'a, traditional Islamic law, are inconsistent with some universal human rights, the purpose of this chapter is to illustrate that Islam itself can be consistent with and conducive to the achievement of, not only the present universal standards, but also the ultimate human right, namely the realization of the originality and individuality of each and every person.

THE ISLAMIC HUMAN RIGHTS DILEMMA

Some aspects of traditional Islamic Shari'a, as understood and practiced by all shades of traditional opinion, and which are binding on all Muslims regardless of local social and cultural variations, are clearly inconsistent with modern universal standards of human rights. These aspects, moreover, cannot be reformed within the traditional framework, as will be explained below. The choice facing the modern Muslim, therefore, is either to insist on enforcing the totality of Shari'a regardless of standards of human rights, or to seek a radical reform within Islam that will reconcile the Shari'a with present-day human rights requirements and expectations.

The horns of the dilemma for modern Muslims may be described as follows: On the one hand, there is the fundamental religious obligation to implement the totality of Islamic law, a comprehensive and intricate body of rules governing every aspect of public and private life. Yet, on the other hand, as can well be expected with a legal system established fourteen hundred years ago, some basic aspects of Islamic law as manifested in the Shari'a are simply unworkable today. More important, these same aspects seem to be inconsistent with the fundamental nature and essence of Islam itself. The clear options open to a modern Muslim with regard to this dilemma have so far been limited to two: either adhere to all aspects of traditional Islamic Shari'a law, in accordance with the religious imperative, regardless of the consequences; or make a clear break and opt for a secular solution in response to the demands of modern life.

Some contemporary Muslim states appear to have opted for one extreme or the other, but the majority have so far been too ambivalent to make a definite choice. Even the extreme examples of Turkey and Iran are not conclusive. The secular solution was imposed in Turkey by an authoritarian dictatorship that maintained its choice by force, and may have thereby created new conditions negating the Islamic option altogether. The Iranian alleged fundamentalist choice of total conformity to Shari'a is not conclusive either. For one thing, it has not yet implemented the Shari'a fully and conclusively in all spheres. In fact, the policies of brutal oppression and summary executions the Iranian Muslim Republic has pursued over its first four years are most un-Islamic in form as well as substance. Moreover, judging by political events in that country, the whole exercise seems to be headed towards total failure. In any case, the peculiarities of Shi'ite theology that prompted the Iranian situation are not prevalent enough anywhere else to make a repetition of the Iranian revolution likely.

Despite the apparent differences between the Turkish and the Iranian experiences, they both reflect some of the inherent problems of Muslim politics. If intelligent free popular choice is the criterion for the validity of any ideological position, such choice is hard to discover, difficult to exercise, and almost impossible to reverse subsequently in accordance with democratic theory in the context of traditional Muslim politics. There is first the long tradition of elite guardianship and manipulation of the masses where fundamental issues of social and legal policy are obscured and confused by subjective, coercive religious concepts. There is no room for argument against the will of Allah and His infinite wisdom which the religious elites claim to interpret and enforce. Thus, it is difficult to discover what was or would have been the rational free choice of the masses if they had the necessary information and means of exercising such free choice. Moreover, once the "choice" is made, whether by the masses or on their behalf, there is no provision for peaceful and orderly basic ideological change by the same or any subsequent generation. Once Shari'a rule is installed, even the expression of the desire to change, it is *ridah*, repudiation of the faith, punishable by death.

The assessment of the desirability and workability of the secular option is outside the scope of this paper. It must be noted, however, that such a choice is incompatible with the religious obligation of all Muslims to implement Islamic principles. As such total secularism is extremely unlikely to succeed in practice in the Muslim world. If and when a secular ideology is enforced, the community simply ceases to be a Muslim community, although some of its members may remain Muslim. This is no doubt possible, and some may even argue that secularization is the most likely direction for parts of the Muslim world; yet it is irrelevant to the question of human rights in Islam itself.

To remain within the framework of Islam, modern Muslims must therefore seek a way of resolving their dilemma. It will be argued in the following pages that the only way Muslims can retain their faith and fulfill their religious obligations without reverting to an oppressive medieval existence is to implement radical reform of Islamic Shari'a law itself. For reasons to be explained below, such reform must go beyond even the most drastic of the traditional techniques of reform and adaptation known. In proposing this revolutionary approach, one is aware of the many difficulties facing its practical implementation. Similar difficulties, however, have historically been encountered and overcome in effecting major religious reform. As will be suggested in the final part of this chapter, Muslims can and must overcome all the challenges facing this proposed solution.

TRADITIONAL ISLAMIC SHARI'A LAW

Shari'a is the comprehensive code of Islamic law, ethics, worship, practices. It is binding on every Muslim in private as well as public life. The basic sources of the Shari'a are the Qur'an and the *hadith*, that is, the traditions of the Prophet Muhammad. The totality of the Qur'an is held to be heavenly revealed, and all Qur'anic verses and *hadith* are held to be true and valid by all Muslims. In the development of the positive principles of law in Shari'a, however, some Qur'anic and *hadith* texts, usually of the earlier stage in Mecca before the migration to Medina, were deemed to have been repealed or abrogated. As will be explained below, this abrogation (*naskh*) was necessary because some of the specific verses and *hadith* of Medina were inconsistent with earlier verses and *hadith* of Mecca. Legal efficacy was attached to the texts of the Medina stage because they were more appropriate to the socioeconomic and political realities of the seventh century.

Leading companions of the Prophet charged with administering the provinces of the growing Muslim state had to provide rules for novel and practical situations without the benefit of the Prophet's presence. The Prophet authorised such innovation, known as *ijtihad*, i.e., independent juristic reasoning where there is no text of Qur'an or *hadith* applicable to the situation.[2] The exercise of *ijtihad* must have been very frequent at the beginning when leading Companions, such as provincial governors had the moral authority and the knowledge of the Qur'an and *hadith* texts to make rules with confidence despite the lack of preexisting rule. With the development of Islamic jurisprudence (*fiqh*), the practice of *ijtihad* was hedged and safeguarded by increasingly strict and elaborate rules and qualifications until it was banned altogether three centuries later under the maxim: "The door of *ijtihad* is closed."

The growing body of jurisprudence developed sophisticated rules for the interpretation of the Qur'an, the determination of *hadith* authenticity to exclude fabricated traditions, reconciliation of conflicting texts and specification of general ones. Traditions grew into separate schools of thought, each with its own sphere of influence. When the intellectual and moral vigor of Islam declined, each region or group confined itself to observing the Shari'a as interpreted by their own school. Shari'a as a living and sensitive body of law was often buried under the dead weight of tradition, where formality and blind imitation sometimes frustrated the purpose of religion and defeated the interest of society.

Islamic reformers in the modern Muslim countries have tried to break these barriers between the schools, and seek appropriate answers from all reputable jurists.[3] Still unsatisfied even with the freedom to roam all over the body of existing jurisprudence, many Muslims are now calling for the revival of the independent juridical decisions of *ijtihad* in order to achieve the necessary degree of reform of Shari'a. As will be explained below, however, even *ijtihad* will not save certain aspects of Shari'a today.

Thus, while *fiqh*, or jurisprudence, is the interpretation and elaboration of Shari'a, the Shari'a itself is not the whole of Islam but rather the body of legal principles based on some general Medina texts of the Qur'an and *hadith*.

SHARI'A AND UNIVERSAL HUMAN RIGHTS

The term "universal human rights" implies general agreement among all nations on the principles of basic human rights. An objective and readily accessible index of universality is the documents reflecting international human rights principles such as the Universal Declaration of Human Rights, 1948, the European Convention on Human Rights, 1950, the American Convention on Human Rights, 1969, and the African Charter on Human and Peoples' Rights, 1981. National constitutions may also indicate broad agreement on certain fundamental rights that are commonly consistently guaranteed in the domestic law of various nations.

There are, of course, variations in the definitions of these rights, but the Universal Declaration of Human Rights may be the most basic and widely respected of these documents.[4] The Declaration, for example, asserts the following rights:

—All human beings are born free and equal in dignity and rights, without distinction on such grounds as race, color, sex, language, or religion.

—Everyone has the right to life, liberty, and security of person, and shall not be held in slavery or servitude.

—Everyone has the right to freedom of thought, conscience, and religion, including the right to change religion.

—Men and women are entitled to equal rights in marriage.

—Everyone has the right to take part in the government of his/her country, directly or through freely elected representatives; periodic and genuine elections shall be held under universal and equal suffrage.

—Everyone has the right to social security and to the economic, social, and cultural rights indispensable for dignity and the free development of personality.

—Everyone has the right to work, to just and favorable remuneration, and to education that strengthens respect for human rights and fundamental freedoms.

Brief examination of the principles of Shari'a make clear that several contrasts exist between it and provisions of the Universal Declaration of Human Rights.

Non-Muslims

According to strict Shari'a, as distinguished from subsequent modification to suit the political and economic convenience of the Muslims, non-Muslims are divided into two classes: kitaby and non-kitaby.[5] Kitabies, or believers in one of the heavenly revealed scriptures, namely Jews, Christians, and Sabies, were allowed to remain within the Muslim state as protected communities, under compacts of dhimma. (Scholars have identified the Sabies, of Sabi'un, as gnostics concerned with ritual purification, living mainly in southern Iraq when the Qur'an was written). Under these compacts, negotiated separately with various kitaby communities, Muslims generally guaranteed the security and communal integrity of the kitaby religious group, in exchange for their allegiance and payment of jizya, a humiliating poll or tax or tribute.[6] Although members of a particular community may enjoy limited administrative independence as well as the freedom to worship and conduct their private affairs in accordance with their religious belief, the dhimmis, that is, kitabies who have a compact or dhimma with the Muslims, are subject to several drastic civil and political limitations. They are disqualified, for example, from holding general judicial or political office and from joining the army. Dhimmis lack testimonial competence in any case involving a Muslim litigant. Non-kitabies, on the other hand, are not entitled to the status of dhimmis at all. In fact, non-kitabies are liable to be killed on sight anywhere in the Muslim state because of a presumed perpetual state of war between Muslims and infidels, unless there is aman, safe-conduct, for such purposes as trade or "diplomacy."[7]

This division of the world into two dominions only—dar al-harb, the abode of war, and dar al-Islam, the abode of Islam—is of course obsolete today. To revive it is to negate the very foundation of international law and the present system of international relations. Muslims are obliged to accept the existing arrangement of national states, governed internally by their national constitutions and externally by international law. The full implications of the Shari'a law in this context are too drastic and untenable to be seriously entertained by any Muslim state, even allegedly "fundamentalist" Iran or Saudi Arabia. If Shari'a is to be applied in the Sudan, for example, it would mean that more than one-third of the population would have to be killed, or taken into slavery as infidels, if they persisted in refusing to embrace Islam. The kitabies among the Sudanese, about 10 percent, would have to be relegated to the status of second-class citizens as communities of dhimmis.

Women

Shari'a established general *qawama*, guardianship, of men over women.[8] In public law, women are legally disqualified from holding general political or judicial office,[9] while in personal law they lack the capacity to contract marriage independently or exercise unilateral divorce on equal footing with men.[10] Their inheritance rights are also usually about half the share of a male with the same degree of relationship to the deceased.[11] A husband even enjoys the right to chastise his wife to the extent of beating her lightly.[12]

Again, in the context of the modern national state, the total implementation of Shari'a would require the return of a large number of working women to the home under the requirements of *hijab*, as their going out of the home for higher education and employment is not sanctioned under Shari'a.[13] A woman is entitled to leave the home to seek employment only when she lacks all other means of subsistence, and not merely in fulfillment of personal career ambitions.

Civil Liberties

Even with respect to the only full citizens of the Islamic state, the male Muslims,[14] the Shari'a regime falls short of the expectations of the citizen of a modern state. Shari'a does not contemplate constitutional government as we know it today, since, for example, it neither recognizes the doctrine of the separation of powers, nor provides for participatory government. The *khalifa* (Caliph) is not only the head of the state and chief executive, but enjoys universal and final judicial and legislative power as well. Any person exercising any executive or judicial function anywhere in the Muslim state must derive his authority by delegation from the *khalifa*.[16]

Thus, Shari'a violates most of the crucial civil and political rights provided for by the Universal Declaration of Human Rights. Non-*kitabies*, for example, are denied the basic rights of life, liberty, and security of person since they may be killed on sight or held in slavery. A *kitaby* non-Muslim is neither "equal before the law" nor does he enjoy "the right to take part in the government of his country." Muslim women, moreover, cannot enjoy "equal rights as to marriage, during marriage, and at its dissolution."

Even the male Muslim does not have the "freedom to change his religion or belief," since *rida*, apostasy in the sense of abandoning the Islamic faith, is a capital offense. Non-Muslims, in contrast, are strongly "encouraged," if not openly coerced, to abandon their faith and embrace Islam, "The will of the people," even in the limited sense of the will of the male Muslim population, is not "the basis of the authority of government" since there is no provision in Shari'a for "periodic and genuine elections" to effect an orderly transfer of power.

The "economic, social, and cultural rights" mentioned in the Universal Declaration are not contemplated by Shari'a, although some of the underlying notions of justice and fairness are provided for with respect to male Muslims. The basic discrimination against non-Muslims and all women, however, applies in this area as well. Whatever degree of "social security" that may exist under Shari'a, it is not available to non-Muslims, who are also denied "free choice of employment," since they are disqualified on the grounds of religion from holding certain jobs, such as joining the military or holding judicial office. Women are subject to similar disqualifications with respect to employment. The principle of *hijab* and sex segregation also denies women access to higher education regardless of their personal merit. Educational programs for all within the framework of Shari'a cannot ''be directed to the full development of the human personality and to the strengthening of respect for human rights and fundamental freedoms," because Shari'a treats women and non-Muslims as inferior second-class citizens.

Regardless of their historical justification, none of the features of Shari'a outlined above is acceptable today. This may account for the ambivalence and paradox in the fundamental political dialogue in the Muslim world: Traditional Shari'a can neither be disregarded nor implemented. Each side of the "fundamentalist" versus "modernist" debate appreciates the arguments of the other. A solution imposed by an authoritarian regime, whether opting for the Turkish secularist mode or the Iranian and Pakistani "fundamentalist" approach, does not resolve the basic issue but merely postpones it. With international communism in the political and ideological arena, Muslims cannot keep postponing the issue or else it may be settled on their behalf once and for all by a Marxist take-over, as in Afghanistan.

The solution suggested here is the radical reform of Shari'a in order to overcome the shortcomings outlined above. A redefinition and restructuring of some aspects of Shari'a may win over the "modernists" while satisfying the religious convictions of the "fundamentalists." The question then is one of balance: achieving the necessary degree of reform without sacrificing the Islamic quality of the law.

THE RADICAL REFORM PERSPECTIVE

Although Muslim thinkers and "modernists" have been calling for renewal and reform for over a century, nothing concrete emerged because of a curious jurisprudential obstacle that hampers reform in precisely the areas most in need of reform. Much time was lost over the petty issues of jurisprudential allegiance to one school of thought or another, when scholars and jurists refused to consider any other views than those handed down by their own *imam* of jurisprudence and his disciples. Frustrated Muslims were led to believe that if these artificial barriers were broken, the wealth of variety in Islamic jurisprudence would give them all the answers they need. Alas, this promised way out proved to be an illusive mirage.

It is true that for centuries Shari'a has succeeded in adapting itself to changing conditions through the essential flexibility of its sources and basic principles, coupled with the ingenuity of the jurists. Muslim propagandists have therefore tended to assume that Muslims can continue today to reform Shari'a in the same way. But as suggested above, even on the bases of fresh *ijtihad*, that is, the exercise of independent juristic reasoning, such reform is inadequate because of the limitations placed by explicit texts of the Qur'an and *hadith* on all reform within the framework of traditional Shari'a. All the principles and institutions of Shari'a have been built on the bases of the operative texts, as opposed to the abrogated ones. The license of *ijtihad*, as granted by the Prophet himself and exercised by his companions and leading jurists, has been limited to questions not covered by explicit texts; it was intended to allow for filling jurisprudential gaps and not interfering with the basic classification of texts as legally operative or abrogated. As the maxim says: *La ijtihada fima fyh nass*, "there can be no *ijtihad* in any matter covered by a text." This is the reason why nowhere in Islamic jurisprudence or literature, traditional or modern, can one find the suggestion that Shari'a should be amended to remove all discrimination against women and non-Muslims or change the basic nature of the Islamic state as established by the Prophet and his four *khalifas* in Medina. The only Muslim thinker who is prepared to do precisely that, is Ustaz Mahmud Muhammad Taha, a Sudanese engineer with *Sufi* training and discipline; he proposes to break the seal of abrogation to revive and implement the original texts revealed in Mecca before the migration to Medina, thereby developing a modern Shari'a which he describes as the Shari'a of the Second Message of Islam.[17]

According to Ustaz Mahmud, Islam actually consists of two messages. The First Message was implemented as the Shari'a law of that stage, while the Second Message, then premature, had to be postponed until its proper time, the present. To implement the Second Message of Islam, he maintains, there is no need for a prophet or fresh revelation, as the Qur'an contains both messages. What is needed, however, is a fresh understanding and insight into the meaning of the Qur'an.

The existence of the two levels of texts, as indicated above, is widely known. While it has so far been generally assumed that the abrogation of the earlier texts was final and conclusive, what is new in the thinking of Ustaz Mahmud is the suggestion that the earlier texts may be revived and implemented now. As to the argument that subsequent enactments are always deemed to repeal earlier ones, since they reflect the effective legislative intention of the lawgiver, Ustaz Mahmud points to scriptural evidence and logical argument to the effect that the subsequent texts on which these aspects of Shari'a were based have transitional and not permanent legal efficacy.[18]

Once the principle of reversing the process of abrogation—in other words, to reenact what has been repealed and repeal what has been enacted—is accepted, a whole range of new possibilities for the future development of Islamic law will emerge. It must be emphasized, however, that such revival and abrogation is not an arbitrary process. Rather it is a selective and internally consistent theory, based on the rationale of the initial abrogation and the timing of this revision process. In other words, Ustaz Mahmoud argues that the proposed reversal of the abrogation of any text must be justified in terms of the reasons for the earlier ruling for changing its status now. He relates the achievement of the originality and individuality of each and every person to the primary purpose of Islam. The three problematic areas indicated above—non-Muslims, women, and civil liberties—will be reformed not only because the principles of Shari'a in these areas are inconsistent with universal human rights, but because such radical reform is required by the quest of each individual person for his or her own originality and individuality.

According to the author of the Second Message of Islam, the good society stands on three pillars of equality: political equality in democracy, economic equality in socialism, and social equality between men and women, men and men, and women and women, regardless of sex, religion, race, or color. The good society, of course, is not an end in itself but rather a most effective means to the end of enabling each and every individual person to seek to achieve his or her own originality and individuality through a religious or philosophical methodology of his or her own free choice. Islam, Christianity, or Judaism, as religions, may play their role in this internal disciplinary and guiding capacity. They would compete on equal footing with each other or with any other technique an individual may choose to adopt, as the state shall display no preference for any particular religious persuasion.

IMPLICATIONS OF THE SECOND MESSAGE OF ISLAM FOR BASIC HUMAN RIGHTS

The impact of this approach to human rights in Islam may be outlined as follows:

The primary texts of the Qur'an and *hadith* offered the fundamental and original message of Islam in Mecca for about thirteen years (610 to 622 A.D.). In that message there was no compulsion, no discrimination against women, or guardianship over men and women.[19] As the community of Muslims at that stage could not sustain a full-fledged state in Mecca, these egalitarian principles were not enacted into legally binding rules but remained applicable as moral precepts voluntarily observed by Muslims out of religious conviction, until they were overruled in the next stage in Medina.

If these earlier Mecca texts were to become legally effective, there would be several consequences. For example, *ayat al-syf*, the verse of the sword, which *ayat al-ismah*, the verses of voluntary persuasion that preceded it, would be abrogated, and the principle of *jihad*, the holy war to propagate the faith, repealed. In this way, all discrimination and legal limitations on non-Muslims, whether *kitabies* or non-*kitabies* would be removed. By lifting the seal of abrogation from the verses of voluntary persuasion, Islamic law would be placed on a new basis, consistent with prevailing standards of constitutional and international law. Muslims would no longer be in a state of war with non-Muslims; there would be no such distinction as *dar al-Islam* and *dar al-harb*, the abode of Islam and the abode of war, as is the case under traditional Shari'a law.

In the same fashion, *ayat al-gawama*, the verse of guardianship over women, and *ayat ash-shwra'*, the verse of non-binding consultation, would be abrogated, to be replaced by the primary texts of equality before the law as revealed in Mecca, making all discrimination against women illegal. The constitutional framework and political process would be fully democratic, with all the formal safeguards of separation of powers, independence of the judiciary, and the rule of law, and so forth.

None of these modern notions is to be found anywhere in traditional Shari'a law for the simple reason that Shari'a abrogated or preceded all of them. Previous Islamic civilization no doubt contributed to the development and crystalization of these principles, but it would be absurd to claim either that all of these modern principles of political theory are part of Shari'a or that Muslims have no need for anything not provided for in Shari'a. Muslims do need all these principles and practices, and they are fully entitled to draw from the totality of human experience in this regard. This outlook is in any case more in accord with basic Islamic principles.[20]

This is no doubt a radical and revolutionary approach, but this may be precisely what is needed not only to bring Shari'a into conformity with universal standards of human rights but also for the fundamental purpose and message of Islam itself. Ustaz Mahmud is not a secular intellectual, but a Muslim modernist concerned with reviving Islam as a universal and comprehensive ideology for the whole of humanity. The wider aspects of his thinking are outside the scope of this chapter, but it is necessary to emphasize the fundamental religious orientation of his whole approach.

PROBLEMS AND PROSPECTS FOR HUMAN RIGHTS IN ISLAMIC AFRICA

Calling for reform in basic Shari'a law in relation to human rights of course does not resolve by itself the problems of inertia and stagnation in the Muslim world in general, and in Africa in particular, although citing the need for reform is part of the answer. This problem is best considered in the context of each specific state or community in the light of the socioeconomic and political factors prevailing there. Some general remarks may be offered to conclude this brief discussion of some aspects of the problems of human rights in Islam.

It must first be noted that none of the modern African Muslim states is organized as an Islamic state, whether traditional or otherwise. Having gone through some degree of British or French colonization, the various African Muslim communities have emerged into independent statehood under European legal and constitutional structures, except in the sphere of personal law, which is usually governed by Shari'a, customary law, or a combination of the two.[21] Although in the modern African states the constitutions of independence have generally been superseded by local political developments, and either suspended after coups d'état or replaced by new, supposedly more indigenous documents, none of the African states with an overwhelming or significant Muslim population has adopted an Islamic regime. There is apparent agreement on the unworkability of the public law aspects and political theory of Shari'a, reflecting a deeper antagonism and political deadlock between the proponents and opponents of Shari'a in these communities.

This is most unsatisfactory from the Islamic as well as the human rights perspectives. From the Islamic point of view, government in accordance with Islamic principles is both an advantage and an obligation. Muslims believe that their temporal as well as religious interests are best served by Islam. The balance and conciliation of the various social and individual claims and interests, through public and private adherence to Islamic principles, is the best framework within which religious regulations, and techniques of worship and social relations, may be applied by each person in order to resolve his own inner conflicts and tensions. The comprehensive nature of Islamic law is therefore crucial to the attainment of its religious objectives. The present dichotomy between public and private life in the modern Muslim states, with consequenent ideological ambivalence, is therefore completely untenable from the Islamic point of view.

In the absence of a clear and well-integrated ideology, the recognition and protection of human rights are bound to suffer. The basic components of such an ideology, moreover, must be derived from the traditional beliefs and institutions of the particular community. The problem here, of course, is that some of these Islamic beliefs and institutions are in fact inconsistent with the universal standards of human rights as explained above. In the context of modern Muslim states, Islamic beliefs and norms would therefore appear to be both the problem and the solution. This paradox may be resolved, however, through the distinction herein suggested between Islam itself and its traditional Shari'a, thereby maintaining Islam while removing all incompatibility with standards of human rights. Shari'a is merely a level of Islam best suited to the needs and expectations of a previous stage of human development. It should be possible therefore, to evolve new principles of Shari'a to address the needs and expectations of this day and age.

To say this is not to underestimate the genuine difficulties facing the implementation of this formula. There is first the dead weight of tradition which historically has been cited to rationalize and uphold the vested interests of the elite male population in their continued domination and oppression of women as well as of ethnic and religious minorities. The objectionable aspects of Shari'a, moreover, are entrenched against easy change by a variety of psychological and material barriers in the minds and physical existence of the would-be beneficiaries of this change—the illiteracy and lack of political maturity of women, and the distrust and lack of credibility which tend to alienate non-Muslims. The situation is further complicated by the generally poor mass communication facilities and lack of traditions that nurture orderly and effective dialogue, especially concerning more sensitive issues.

These difficulties can be overcome, however, through a combination of Islamic argumentation and propagation in the context of an effective methodology. The proponents of this modern approach, Ustaz

Mahmud and his disciples, take meticulous care in placing every proposition they advance well within the Qur'an and *hadith*, because
their entire approach is based on the reinterpretation of the fundamental Islamic texts, rather than purely on secular reasoning. In
this way, and not withstanding its radical implications, the proposed
approach is certainly within the mainstream of Islamic jurisprudential
reform. Their methods of propagating their views also reflect the
Islamic emphasis on immediate implementation in order to present
individual and social models for their theoretical position. Thus Ustaz
Mahmud and his disciples in the Sudan combine their propagation of
theory with immediate implementation of their views as far as possible, in accordance with the Qur'anic dictate: "Oh, believers, why do
you preach what you do not practice; it is most hateful to Allah that
you preach what you are not practicing."[22] Such limited practice is used
to perfect and elaborate upon the theoretical statements of the group.
It is also utilized in the propagation of the whole approach, as it indicates its practical viability and reflects its social and individual
benefits. They continue to strive to convince more and more
Sudanese of their point of view until the time comes when they will
exercise the power to legislate and implement their views on a national scale. Then this prototype of a modern Islamic state, once
established, will be used in the regional and international propagation of their views, in the same way that individual and community
models have been used to convince Sudanese Muslims of the Islamic
authenticity and practical viability of their whole approach.

NOTES

*The first draft of this chapter was prepared during my stay as a 1981–82
Rockefeller Fellow in Human Rights, Columbia University, New York. I am
grateful to Mr. Ernest B. Johnson II of The English Language Servicing Unit,
University of Khartoum, for reading my draft and making useful comments.
My debt to my teacher, Ustaz Mahmud, is beyond all gratitude and
acknowledgement.

1. I.M. Lewis, ed., *Islam in Tropical Africa* (London: Oxford University
Press, 1966).
2. The practice is based on the well-known *hadith* which reports that when
the Prophet sent out Mu'adh ibn Jabal to the Yemen as governor, he asked
how he would decide cases. Mu'adh replied that he would apply the book of
Allah (the Qur'an). When asked, What if there was nothing in the Qur'an on
the issue?, he replied that he would apply the traditions of the Prophet. When
asked further, What if there was nothing in the traditions of the Prophet?, he
replied "I shall then exercise my own judgment without hesitation." The Prophet approved his approach and sent him off to Yemen as governor.

3. On the techniques of Islamic reform within the framework of Islamic jurisprudence, see generally J.N.D. Anderson, *Law Reform in the Muslim World* (London: Athlone Press, 1976).

4. The Universal Declaration on Human Rights is increasingly accepted as having passed into customary international law binding on all nations. See Egon Schwelb, *Human Rights and the International Community* (Chicago: Quadrangle Books, 1964), pp. 35 ff.; and Louis Henkin, ed., *The International Bill of Rights* (New York: Columbia University Press, 1981), pp. 9–11 and 38.

5. On the position of Shari'a on non-Muslims, see Majid Khadduri, *War and Peace in the Laws of Islam* (Baltimore: The Johns Hopkins Press, 1955), Chapters 4, 6, 15–17; and H.A.R. Gibb and J.H. Kramers, *Shorter Encyclopedia of Islam* (Leiden: Brill, 1953), pp. 68 and 75.

6. Qur'an, 9:29 (chapter 9, verse 29).

7. Qur'an 9:5.

8. Qur'an 4:38.

9. Gibb and Kramers, *Shorter Encyclopedia of Islam*, pp. 633 ff.

10. Ibid., pp. 447–49, 564–71.

11. Qur'an 4:11.

12. Qur'an 4:34.

13. Qur'an 33:33 and 33:53.

14. Majid Khadduri, "Human Rights in Islam," *Annals* 243 (1946), p. 79.

15. Gibb and Kramers, *Shorter Encyclopaedia of Islam*, pp. 236–41.

16. H.A.R. Gibb, "Constitutional Organization," in Majid Khadduri and H.J. Liebenssy, eds., *Law in the Middle East* (Washington, D.C.: Middle East Institute, 1955), p. 17.

17. Ustaz Mahmud Muhammad Taha has published several major books and contributed numerous articles in the Sudan over the last forty years, but unfortunately all his writings have been in Arabic. The present author has just finished translating into English Ustaz Mahmud's fundamental work, *The Second Message of Islam* (Omdurman, 1967), which still awaits publication.

18. E.g., Qur'an 16:125 and 18:29.

19. Qur'an 9:5 and 9:29.

20. Prevailing custom that is consistent with the basic purpose of religion is a recognized source of legal principles in Islam. The Qur'an cites such custom as a source of law in numerous verses, e.g., 2:228 to 234, 236, 240 and 241; 3:104, 110, and 114; 4:19, 25, and 114; 7:157; 9:67, 71, and 112; 22:41, etc.

21. J.N.D. Anderson, *Islamic Law in Africa* (London: Her Majesty's Stationery Office), 1954.

22. Qur'an 61:2 and 3.

Human Rights under Majority Rule in Southern Africa: The Mote in Thy Brother's Eye

RICHARD F. WEISFELDER

And why beholdest thou the mote that is in thy brother's eye but considerest not the beam that is in thine own eye? Or how wilt thou say to thy brother, Let me pull the mote out of thine eye; and, behold, a beam is in thine own eye?

Matthew 7:3–4

SCHOLARSHIP OR RHETORIC?

The decision to examine human rights patterns within independent black-ruled states of Southern Africa generates considerable controversy.[1] Some contend that states which must constantly cope with the harsh realities of Southern African economic and military hegemony within the region should be exempted from this sort of investigation. They regard repression within black neighbors of the Republic of South Africa as being minimal and primarily reactive, so that attention should be focused instead upon the flagrant crimes of the Pretoria regime. In their view, research of this sort plays into the hands of apologists for apartheid who are already convinced that most African states have abysmal human rights records. Identification of the motes in the eyes of South Africa's neighbors may become a spurious rationale for tolerating the enormous beam in South Africa's eye which blights human relationships within that country and throughout the region.

Introduction of an implicit double standard shielding African states from scrutiny of their human rights records seems an inappropriate method of emphasizing South Africa's monumental abuses. The opportunity to demonstrate that some countries under black, majority rule have performed quite well would be lost, permitting invalid negative stereotypes to survive unchallenged. Even where abuses

90

have occurred, careful analysis would frequently reveal the existence of indigenous concepts of free speech, equal justice, due process, and public accountability, which important segments of the society seek to augment. If the policies and actions of certain African states are portrayed exclusively as responses to South African manipulation, then the relevance and legitimacy of autonomous elements of their domestic political transactions could too easily be overlooked. Oppressive black governments claiming to be victims of South African "destabilization" should not automatically earn external acceptance as the legitimate bearers of the standard of majority rule. Situational constraints imposed on black Southern African states may alter our evaluation of their behavior, but should not provide their leaders with blanket absolution for their own policy choices and actions.

Whether or not this perspective is accepted, those who question the motivation and utility of analyzing the human rights performances of South Africa's neighbors have a strong rejoinder. Much as journalism tends to focus on crises, country studies of human rights highlight abuses. A scholar is unlikely to single out cases where his only role is to eulogize the incumbent power holders for their superb performances. Despite efforts to emphasize the situational context and complex causation of violations, an author will be remembered for dissecting unsavory elements of a preventive detention act or calling attention to some repulsive atrocity. Even if the selected country is proven to have been a relatively benign offender against human rights norms, most readers will not be equipped to make subtle distinctions about degrees of culpability. The differences between small-scale abuses of power in a black-ruled state and systematic repression within the South African police state pigmentocracy may be obscured.

Further controversy arises over the definition of basic human rights, their ranking in importance, and the standards for evaluating the seriousness of violations. This study attempts to apply and refine existing criteria rather than to engage in philosophical or legal argumentation about the validity of prevailing standards. Hence it draws upon the concepts defined in the International Covenant on Economic, Social and Cultural Rights and the Universal Declaration of Human Rights. It presumes the existence of certain inalienable rights, such as the rights to life, humane treatment, equality before the law, and protection from discrimination. A second category of civil and political rights that include freedom of speech and assembly may be limited only for brief periods of genuine emergency, with the burden of proof for the necessity of their abrogation resting upon the authority demanding such restraints. A third variety encompasses economic and social rights such as opportunities for education, work, and de-cent living conditions, which should be available insofar as the economic capabilities of a society permit.[2] These latter rights are sometimes lumped together as a "right to development" that may be claimed by entire societies shackled by entrenched dependency relationships. In such cases, blame for violations would rest on the external beneficiaries of underdevelopment as well as collaborating elites within the exploited society who perpetuate dependency and gross economic, political, and social inequalities.[3]

Four factors will be utilized to judge the seriousness of derogation of these rights, namely, intensity, extensiveness, duration, and deliberateness. Intensity refers to the level of harm to the victims, ranging from death to subtle pressures that are not life-threatening. Extensiveness deals with the percentage of the society affected by the human rights violation. Duration means the length of time that the situation persists. Deliberateness involves the degree to which violations are premeditated or the result of the chosen policies of their perpetrators, hence violations "ordered and centrally directed by the power holders" would be most culpable, those "tacitly permitted by a government" somewhat less blameworthy, and those resulting "from the breakdown or non-existence of civil order" least offensive.[4] It should be noted that the application of all of these factors is dependent on the quality of the available data. Similarly, weighting of the four criteria in a final composite judgment is bound to be controversial. The inferences to be drawn here will be primarily qualitative, utilizing the preceding analytic dimensions to evaluate the evidence presented.

The objective of this essay is to provide a comparative perspective on the human rights performances of four states, Botswana, Lesotho, Malawi, and Swaziland, which negotiated independence over a decade ago, and of three, Angola, Mozambique, and Zimbabwe, which emerged more recently after bloody revolutionary epochs. Are there similarities in the human rights records of all that can be explained by their common immersion in a regional subsystem dominated by South Africa? Can differences in their performances be attributed to varying levels of economic development, alternative patterns of colonial tutelage, divergent paths to independence, differing ideologies, special qualities of political leadership, particular types of political institutions, or underlying factors of political culture? Examination of these issues leads to a transactional perspective on human rights behavior that involves the relationships of these states with each other, with South Africa, with other African and Third World states, and with the great powers. It is hoped that this comparative perspective will assure attention to human rights successes as well as failures, and compel consideration of human rights problems as attributes of the regional political economy rather than just manifestations of local idiosyncracies.

THE HUMAN RIGHTS OF INDEPENDENT
BLACK GOVERNMENTS IN SOUTHERN AFRICA

Democratic freedoms are often perceived as luxuries affordable only by highly developed states. If true, states whose economic situations are most desperate should be especially prone to domestic instability and predisposed to repress dissent severely. When impoverished states are confronted by a regional power whose economic, social, political, and military strategies threaten their existence, the probability that at least some of them would resort to authoritarian or even paranoid expedients would seem greatly enhanced. These bleak realities are common to all of the independent black states of Southern Africa.

Lesotho, Malawi, and Mozambique fall within the twenty-five least developed economies in the world. Angola and Mozambique must cope with the ravages of South African-supported insurgent movements and have yet to surmount the legacy of anticolonial wars, including the exodus of skilled personnel. Botswana's significant economic advances are threatened by a world recession that has drastically reduced the demand and prices for her mineral output. Despite a diversified economy, Swaziland's miniscule domestic market and truncated boundaries have made the country vulnerable to South African blandishments and to global economic trends. Zimbabwe possesses the most dynamic industrial and agricultural infrastructure of the black states, but internecine strife, pent-up public demand for basic services, emigration of skilled workers, and a host of colonial economic residues place severe strains on this economic base.

All of these states, together with Tanzania, Zaire, and Zambia, fall within the scope of South African economic and military power, although the degree of impact varies considerably. Enclaves such as Lesotho and Swaziland must cope with physical envelopment, are linked to the Rand currency, and along with Botswana, belong to a South African–dominated customs union. Most of the states provide migrant labor to the Republic and are dependent upon South African industry, ports, and railways for significant portions of their trade. Recognition of the extent of their vulnerability has led nine black states to form the Southern African Development Coordination Conference (SADCC) which seeks to promote economic liberation and reduce dependence upon South Africa.[5] Moreover, South African leverage has not prevented all of the black-ruled states from harboring refugees from the Republic, committing themselves to principles of non-racism, declaring their opposition to apartheid and separate development, and associating themselves with the liberation cause in South Africa.

The devastating combination of economic privation, vulnerability to military and economic pressure, and ideological polarization would seem an ideal breeding ground for systematic incursions upon human rights in the name of national survival. But placed in a broader African, Third World, or global context, states like Botswana and Swaziland have records which have been surprisingly good. Given their special problems and endemic insurgencies, Angola, Lesotho, Mozambique, and Zimbabwe have serious human rights problems, but have avoided repressive extremes. Ironically, Malawi, the most peripheral to South African power, has an unenviable history of repression and absolutism. Further afield, Tanzania, Zaire, and Zambia have human rights records more tarnished than those of the majority of South Africa's neighbors. Hence, the case studies which follow might be prefaced with the hypothesis that close exposure to racism and exploitation under the white settler regimes of Southern Africa has tended to constrain the behavior of black successor governments and neighboring independent states.

1. Botswana

The paean of praises for the success of multi-party democracy in Botswana has reached a sufficient intensity to raise suspicions that this "Botswanaphilia" may be overdone. To quote E. Philip Morgan,

> Botswana is a regional symbol of liberal democracy, an African state with a multi-party system that has held regular open elections for successive popularly elected governments. The openness of the Botswana political process stands in sharp contrast to Swaziland and Lesotho, as well as that of Zambia, much less South Africa. It provides a refutation of the paternalistic assumptions underlying the ideology of white supremacy.[6]

Surprisingly, a close examination does little to refute these laudatory images. Due process of law is the norm; preventive detention is unknown. All ethnic groups and races have access to government; the only "free speech" that has been prosecuted are racial slurs offensive to the dignity of other human beings. Four free elections have occurred; the opposition survives. To be sure, writers like Morgan may exaggerate the contrasts between Botswana and Lesotho or Swaziland. Unlike the Basotho, the Batswana people have not

been highly politicized, nor has a well-organized, ideologically dif-
ferentiated party threatened to wrest power from the incumbent
government. In 1980 power was transferred constitutionally and
routinely to the late President Khama's chosen successor, Quett J.
Masire. Still, the underlying strength of constitutional norms has yet
to be tested by the emergence of a new generation of aspirant leaders
or the need to surrender power to distrusted political opponents after
a painful electoral setback. However, occasional threats from the ruling Botswana Democratic Party (BDP) spokesmen that irresponsible
or seditious opposition will not be tolerated are not sufficient ground
for questioning the proven commitment of Botswana's leaders to the
preservation of the basic rights and liberties entrenched in the constitution.[7]

Evaluation of Botswana's record also requires attention to a number
of latent issues, problematic incidents, and worrisome portents. For
example, the disadvantaged position of the Basarwa (Bushmen) and
other non-Tswana minorities reflects a legacy of discriminatory clientage not wholly remedied. On the other hand, the disproportionate
presence of minority Kalanga in top government posts and private-
sector jobs has spawned recrimination regarding alleged favoritism in
access to educational and employment opportunities.[8]

Growing differentials between the dynamic mining and governmental sectors of the economy and the stagnant subsistence
agricultural base reflect a process of sharpening class differentiation
with increasing potential for conflict. The Botswana government has
attempted to forestall the emergence of greater inequality by resisting
wage demands from mineworkers thought to promote still wider
disparities. However, such efforts address symptoms rather than fundamental problems and have not been applied with equal vigor to the
insatiable economic aspirations of the civil service to which the functioning of the government is hostage.

The chosen strategy of funding rural improvements through rapid
expansion of capital-intensive activities like mining has led to a
burgeoning population of foreign technicians and advisors. Resultant
delays in localization and expatriate patterns of conspicuous con-
sumption are predictable sources of friction in an economy characterized by high unemployment, migrant labor, and rates of urbanization exceeding the capacity of available social services. Increasing dependence on the world market to absorb primary mineral exports has accentuated these pressures, since the current global recession has sharply curtailed both demand and prices for Botswana's coal,
copper, and diamonds.

For many years, Botswana's open political system has been put to
the test by violence spilling over her long frontiers with Rhodesia,

Namibia, and South Africa. In 1978 a brutal assault by Rhodesian security forces upon a Botswana Defense Force (BDF) convoy within Botswana resulted in 15 deaths and instigated domestic turmoil. In the aftermath, three whites in the Tuli area were killed by a BDF patrol. When the Botswana Government decided to bring murder charges against the commander, Sergeant Tswaipe, students at the University College leapt to his defense, alleging that he had only protected the nation against white terrorists. Their demonstration turned into a full-fledged riot when nervous authorities refused to permit them to march through the Gaborone mall, and surrounded the campus with baton-wielding police well supplied with tear gas.[9] What was noteworthy about these events was not the brief period of violence nor the mass arrests of students, but that university operations were swiftly restored and all students reinstated without reprisals. Tswaipe's acquittal due to inconsistent evidence offered by his troops precluded renewed confrontation, but could not disguise the explosive potential of incidents arising from the guerrilla wars on Botswana's borders.[10]

Although the transformation of white-ruled Rhodesia into black Zimbabwe temporarily lessened these pressures, the emerging civil conflict in western Zimbabwe and the continuing struggle in Namibia are causes for concern. There have been recurrent exchanges of fire between BDF forces in the Chobe area and South African troops in the Caprivi Strip. South African military aircraft regularly intrude into Botswana's airspace. Basarwa from Botswana are recruited by South Africa for counterinsurgency operations against SWAPO's fight for Namibian independence from South Africa. Herero citizens of Botswana have been drawn into the politics of their Namibian motherland. Nevertheless, the proximity of its eastern border with South Africa to Botswana's major population centers makes this the more fundamental source of tension. The most rudimentary hints of guerrilla infiltration in 1978 led certain Western Transvaal farmers to demand hot pursuit by the South African Defense Force "to root out the problem in Botswana."[11] Given the reality of South African incursions into Angola, Lesotho, and Mozambique, President Masire voiced concern that there was some "ulterior motive" for a barrage of press reports in the Republic alleging increased Soviet influence in Botswana.[12] He feared that these might be preparing the way for operations against exiles within his country or for covert actions to weaken Botswana's commitment to economic and political liberation by destabilizing his regime. If such concerns persist, expenditure on the military and police is bound to increase, providing these coercive mechanisms and their leaders with greater power and more comprehensive roles.

Despite the rapid repatriation of thousands of Zimbabwean refugees in 1980, the presence and continuing influx of refugees from Lesotho, Namibia, South Africa, and again, recently, Zimbabwe, impose substantial financial and administrative burdens upon Botswana, and produce considerable tension. Ruling BDP politicians have long alleged that South African exiles have contributed to the radicalizing of Botswana's secondary and university students. Indeed, the only permanent victims of the 1978 University riot were two black South African faculty members who were deported due to suspicions that they had incited the students. Refugees have become scapegoats to blame for sharp increases in burglaries and violent crime in Gaborone and other burgeoning towns.

To resolve these problems, utilize available facilities, and alleviate South African suspicions, the Government has compelled many refugees to leave urban centers and relocate at the remote Dukwe camp. This compulsory resettlement causes grave problems for urban-oriented refugees lacking agricultural skills and interests. It does little to forestall crime, since Namibians, South Africans, and Zimbabweans cross the porous borders legally and illegally each day. Amnesty International expressed concern after the Botswana Government's frustration with endemic refugee problems led to the summary repatriation of several South African refugees alleged to have abused their status or to be criminal elements.[13]

A proper perspective requires emphasis upon the restraint displayed as the most salient dimension of governmental behavior. The efforts of the Botswana Defence Force have been concentrated on the national borders, not on domestic dissenters or refugees. The police do not routinely carry guns. Politically difficult situations do not automatically engender repressive limitations. Sensitive events, such as student demonstrations at the U. S. Embassy or the funeral of the assassinated leader of the opposition Pan-Africanist Congress, David Sibeko, have usually proceeded without incidents necessitating police intervention or infringement upon free expression. What is remarkable is not that there are some blemishes on Botswana's record, but that substantial regard for human rights and democratic norms has flourished throughout times of intense pressure. Indeed, the recent establishment of two independent newspapers suggests an expanded interchange of ideas, not contraction.

The problems of sustaining this record are substantial. President Masire lacks the strong popular base enjoyed by his predecessor, a fact symbolized by vigorous protests when his picture replaced Seretse Khama's on the Pula currency. Economic stringency after a period of unprecedented expansion has created conditions for social unrest. President Masire is repeatedly criticized for developmental strategies that have permitted Botswana to become more vulnerable to externally induced economic disasters.[14] To say that a crisis of legitimacy already exists would be an overstatement, but a corrosive process undermining political cohesion appears to be accelerating, with all its attendant dangers for human rights in Botswana.

2. Lesotho

In contrast to Botswana, Lesotho has developed a reputation for endemic political instability under a government willing to use all necessary means to remain in power. Although comprehensive security legislation was placed on the statute books prior to 1970, Prime Minister Leabua Jonathan's decision to ignore defeat at the polls in January of that year marked the onset of authoritarian rule and subjugation of human rights to political convenience. Beyond the suspension of the 1966 constitution with its detailed bill of rights, the new order was characterized by rule by decree and draconian legislation occasionally reminiscent of South African security laws. The most noteworthy law, the Internal Security Act of 1974, provided for indefinitely renewable sixty-day periods of detention without charge or trial, and it exempted public officials from prosecution for excesses committed in the line of duty during periods of unrest dating from 1970.

What must be emphasized is that unrestrained violence against political opponents and implementation of preventive detention have generally been restricted to periods of intense conflict which followed Chief Jonathan's failure to surrender power and the abortive opposition uprising of 1974.[16] Detainees remained in jail for extended periods, but eventually were released without being charged or were tried in proceedings where due process was respected. Not even those found guilty of treason and violent subversion were executed. By 1978, all detainees had been released and those convicted of crimes were given their freedom as their sentences expired. Repressive extremes in Lesotho have had an ad hoc character, occurring when governmental capabilities were strained to the limit by the breakdown of civil order. Security laws functioned more as deterrents than as regular mechanisms for eliminating opposition.

Since 1979, the Lesotho Liberation Army (LLA), the military wing of Ntsu Mokhehle's Basotho Congress Party (BCP), has mounted a limited, but enervating, insurgency in Lesotho. Determined to claim by force the power which the BCP had won at the ballot box in 1970, the LLA has engaged in a campaign of sabotage, bombing, and assassination.[17] What began as isolated assaults in the remote Botha-

Bothe District had by 1981 and 1982 turned into a series of attacks on political notables and highly visible public facilities. Hotels, fuel depots, water works and power installations have been bombed in Maseru, the capital. The Minister of Works, Jobo Rampeta, and Koenyama Chapela, leader of an anti-Mokhehle BCP fragment, were assassinated. In December 1982, units of the South African Defense Force entered the capital and massacred defenseless African National Congress (ANC) refugees from South Africa as well as Basotho civilians. Whether or not the LLA and South Africans are working hand in glove, as Lesotho government spokesmen claim, the inability of Lesotho's Paramilitary Force (PMF) to snuff out the insurrection or deter South African aggression encourages more desperate machinations. Rumors abound regarding the alleged murderous activities of police elements and of Koeoko, a progovernment death squad, named for a mythical monster.

Whoever is responsible, prominent personalities linked to opposition parties or King Moshoeshoe II have been cut down in a wave of brutal murders. These include Edgar Motuba, editor of the Lesotho Evangelical Church newspaper, *Leselinyana*, and O. T. Seheri, Director of the Institute for Development Management and confidant of the monarch. Internecine strife also has flared at the National University of Lesotho, where struggles between progovernment and opposition-oriented students for control of the Student's Representative Council have been conducted at gunpoint.[18] The insurrection is creating a condition of permanent emergency that frustrates government policy initiatives and overextends its security capabilities. As government supporters are put in constant political and personal jeopardy, their reactions are likely to become less improvised and to assume a sinister purposiveness.

Despite these difficulties, casual observation of daily life in towns, villages, and the countryside provides little evidence of disruption. Although less voluble than in the past, political criticism and dissent are still heard and even supporters of Ntsu Mokhehle's wing of the BCP are not precluded from political activity. Statements by the LLA have been published in *Leselinyana*. The contemporary situation bears an uncanny resemblance to the authoritarian pattern of colonial administration prior to the introduction of a popular mandate. Legislators are appointed to the Interim National Assembly and can debate crucial issues, but lack real capacity to oust cabinet ministers. Opposition fragments have been co-opted through allocation of a minority bloc of seats in the legislature and a small portion of Cabinet positions. Government operates through routinized procedures and a host of laws and regulations, but defines the rules of the game itself instead of being restrained by acknowledged constitutional norms.

Chief Jonathan wields power with the backing of the police, vestiges of his Basotho National Party (BNP), segments of the chieftainship, and elements of the civil service. Like many colonial governors, he may try to serve the public interest as he sees it, but his authority is based on central coercion, not popular legitimacy. Similarly, rural administration perpetuates the old divisions in assigning overlapping responsibilities to hereditary chiefs, civil servants, and party loyalists. Local authority emanates from the central government, not from grass-roots inputs.

Throughout the past decade, Chief Jonathan and his government have repeatedly promised a new constitutional format, renewed electoral competition, and the repeal of onerous security laws. But assertions of widespread BNP popularity have been belied by reluctance to test these claims, even when the Congress Party opposition seemed hopelessly split on questions of strategy, leadership, and probity. LLA bombs and bullets were not needed to prove that conflict in Lesotho is rooted in deep socioeconomic cleavages greatly accentuated by the realities of being an impoverished labor reserve strongly impacted by South Africa.[19]

Unfortunately the authoritarian expedients designed to sustain the BNP in power and to contain partisan infighting have become a cause of more malignant forms of conflict. Elections conducted during a state of insurgency would hardly be perceived as free or fair. In fact, the legitimacy of the government could be further undermined by a Pyrrhic victory in an election thought to be rigged. Triumph by a potentially vengeful opposition is no more likely to be tolerable to the incumbents than in 1970. As the most widely acceptable political figure in a regime lacking any heir apparent, Chief Jonathan seems confined to dilatory options which may buy time, but avoid confronting the fundamental dilemmas.

The intensifying crisis of legitimacy has had severe repercussions upon efforts to promote economic development. Even before independence, development projects were the subject of constant political infighting and were often nurtured or obstructed on partisan rather than economic grounds. Episodes of political violence have interrupted and caused longer-term setbacks to tourism, private investment, and some foreign aid programs. More important, the weak administrative capacities of government have been further undermined by declining output, competence, and morale. The reports of the Auditor General and of various departments reveal pervasive corruption reflected in the collapse of internal financial controls and the demise of accountability to Parliament.[20] Lacking constitutional legitimacy, a guiding ideology, austere standards of public service, or meaningful options for ending dependency, the government is pervaded by a live-for-today, get-rich-quick, help-your-own psychology which precludes addressing the basic needs of ordinary people.

In the countryside, the primary beneficiaries of most projects appear to be BNP stalwarts. Rural compliance does not rest upon informed consent, but on Lebotho la Khotso (The Lebotho Peace Corps), a group of BNP adherents described as "the people's village guards which have been largely instrumental in the maintenance of the present tranquility in the villages."[21] Hence competent evaluators of agricultural schemes in Lesotho have noted a pervasive inertia impeding project implementation and consolidation of preliminary gains. The enthusiasm, vitality, and creativity required to initiate rural self-help efforts is missing. Disinterest, non-compliance, and passive protest have exacted a heavy toll on the fulfillment of development goals.

Despite its weak domestic legitimacy, the Lesotho Government has gained credibility in Africa, the Soviet bloc, and the West by highlighting its precarious position vis-à-vis South Africa. After abandoning his unpopular emphasis on "bread and butter" transactions with the Republic in the wake of the 1970 electoral debacle, Chief Jonathan recognized the benefits to be gained through rhetorical confrontation with Pretoria while retaining routine working relationships. He has therefore emphasized Lesotho's role as a "behind-the-lines" state every bit as engaged in liberation support as the Front Line states. South Africa's paranoia regarding the flight of ANC saboteurs into Lesotho and predictable reaction to Lesotho's new relationships with Cuba and the Soviet Union have played into Chief Jonathan's hand. The December raid and threatening statements by South African Security Police Chief Johan Coetzee provided Chief Jonathan with all the required proof that South Africa would collaborate with dissidents to destabilize his government or intervene directly just as it was doing in Angola, Mozambique, and Zimbabwe.[22]

With the domestic causes of the LLA insurrection conveniently obscured and Mokhehle simplistically identified as a pawn of Pretoria, the canny Prime Minister could turn his troubles into assets helpful in strengthening ties with African leaders, Western aid donors, and socialist states. Moreover, South African machinations could provide a ready rationale for stringent infringements of human rights necessary to consolidate power. Lesotho had finally become enmeshed in the ebb and flow of insurgency besetting the region. That Chief Jonathan continued to conduct business as usual with South Africa and to implement agreements on agricultural assistance, water projects, and private investment seemed quite irrelevant.

3. Swaziland[23]

In 1973, King Sobhuza II of Swaziland rescinded the constitution, dismissed the parliament, proscribed opposition parties, and detained various active critics of the government without charges or trial. His action was only tangentially linked to events and trends elsewhere in Southern Africa. Rather, as Absolom Vilakazi cogently observed, the election of a tiny group of opposition politicians to Parliament had been perceived as "an illegitimate contest for power" from the traditional Swazi perspective.[24] Far from defending Swaziland against the subversion of its independence by the Pretoria regime, the Swazi traditional elite found itself pitted against urban wage earners, secondary school students, and professionals, in short, the same segments of the population most mobilized against apartheid in the Republic of South Africa. Similarly, the Swazi aristocrats have shown the same low tolerance for dissent and the "nip-it-in-the-bud" mentality which has led to heavy-handed actions in South Africa. In short, violations of human rights were largely attributable to the traditional monarch's unwillingness to make even small compromises in established structures, procedures, or prerogatives to conciliate emergent social classes.

Lest a false impression be created, it must be noted that the level of derogation of human rights in Swaziland has been minimal by any comparative standard. Violent deaths, torture, or even sweeping detention of dissidents have not occurred. Expression of dissent is possible within the traditional institutional context and a number of fairly militant former opposition politicians have been encouraged to play important roles within the King's Mbokodvo Movement. What seems anachronistic is the presumption of Swazi elites that the traditional forms can contain and conciliate the new forces emerging in Swazi society, especially now that the octogenarian monarch has died and power has passed a regency acting for his adolescent successor. The triumph of old-guard conservatives in the March 1983 "palace coup," which ousted the more flexible incumbent Prime Minister, indicates no deviation from this course.

Swaziland's rulers have felt little sense of threat from white South Africa, which, after all, seeks to buttress ethnically defined traditional authority as a barrier against the cosmopolitan forces of African nationalism. King Sobhuza's dream of incorporating all Swazi irredenta in a greater Swaziland as the crowning achievement of his long reign has proven compatible with South African notions of homeland independence. Hence both states have agreed to border adjustments which could transfer the KaNgwane Bantustan to Swaziland, provide Swaziland with a corridor to the sea at the expense of KwaZulu and make all South African Swazi into citizens of Swaziland.[25] If the agreement is eventually implemented in spite of diplomatic pressures and setbacks in the South African courts, Swaziland's population would more than double through the addition of 800,000 persons involuntarily deprived of their original citizenship and rightful claims to a share of South Africa's assets. South Africa would benefit if a greater Swaziland served as a more effective buffer, shielding densely populated areas of the Republic from ANC insurgents operating out of Mozambique. Similarly, this controversial bargain could drive a wedge between Swaziland and her SADCC partners, and draw the Kingdom into P.W. Botha's competing Constellation of Southern African States (CONSAS). Swaziland's new railway linkages to the port at Richard's Bay reinforce the pattern of economic ties to South Africa.

Although Swaziland maintains normal diplomatic and economic interchanges with Mozambique, the emergence of a militant Marxist government in Maputo has generated uneasiness in nearby Mbabane. FRELIMO influence and the presence of over fifty-five hundred South African refugees within the tiny Kingdom create unprecedented possibilities for the politicization and radicalization of hitherto quiescent rural Swazi. Past experience suggests that Swazi leaders respond vigorously to the most minimal challenges to their authority and will not hesitate to use such stringent tools as the sixty-day preventive detention law. For example, the Swaziland National Association of Teachers was disbanded in 1977 after striking teachers and students were told that confrontational tactics were "not the Swazi way."[26] The growing visibility and leverage of the Swazi army provides the coercive base to enforce stern policies and to forestall the operations of ANC insurgents in Swaziland or en route to South Africa.

It would be difficult to demonstrate that authoritarian rule in Swaziland has been detrimental to economic development. The strong executive monarchical powers exercised by King Sobhuza provided a sense of order and stability conducive to aid and foreign investment. Stern resistance to pressures from organized labor kept production costs down, made Swazi goods quite competitive in world markets, and yielded favorable trade balances. However, changes in Swazi society and neighboring Mozambique make it unlikely that traditional paternalism can sustain industrial discipline and political passivity indefinitely. Absorption of large numbers of South African Swazi without acquiring the economic wherewithal to provide for them would impose a substantial strain upon society. Even without this additional burden, there is a backlog of issues of concern to the new urban professional, middle, and working classes that have simply been ignored. Should these grievances coalesce and erupt now that monarchy is in the midst of a difficult succession, the short-run economic advantages gained through traditional paternalism could be swiftly undone.

4. Malawi[27]

His Excellency, the Ngwazi, Hastings Kamuzu Banda, Life President of Malawi, has often been described as "Africa's odd man out" and his country characterized as a "Bandastan." Malawi is a personalist regime dominated by the whims and idiosyncracies of its President. From diplomatic recognition of South Africa to disregard for the Organization of African Unity (OAU), Dr. Banda has rarely concealed his distaste for the accepted political rhetoric and rituals of African diplomacy. Similarly, he has unequivocally asserted that autocratic power alone can provide an ordered and stable basis for domestic tranquility, institution building, and prosperity in Africa. He did not flinch from amending Malawi's constitution in 1968 to permit the suspension of its broad guarantees of civil and political rights. Neither did he perceive any reason to heed court decisions that contradicted his executive orders.

Within this context Malawi has functioned as a police state where the President exercises control down to the village level through the Malawi Congress Party and the police. For sustained periods, detention without charges, trial, or time limits became commonplace. Party officials and civil servants, as well as journalists, intellectuals, and Jehovah's Witnesses, were frequent victims of detention. A marked passivity observed among released detainees testified to the effectiveness of such conditions in breaking the human spirit. Not only did Banda refuse to permit external investigation of alleged human rights violations on the ground that Malawi's situation was unique, but he also threatened reprisals against detainees adopted by Amnesty International.

Malawi's grinding poverty and commercial dependence on Mozambican ports could help to account for Banda's accommodationist tactics toward white Southern Africa prior to the end of Portuguese colonialism. But only the fulfillment of Banda's development priorities, and particularly his personal vision of a new capital at Lilongwe, can provide the key to understanding his unique stance within the region. Malawi's peripheral geographical position permitted alternative options for ties to the north, but Banda saw greater economic advantage in pursuing his South African connection.

Popular or elite reaction to Banda's atypical policies may explain part of the extensive utilization of repressive expedients. Regional, ethnic, class, and ideological cleavages in Malawi society also must be taken into account. But the style of rule adopted by the President seems to have greater explanatory power. No internal or external threat to Malawi's survival could account for the xenophobic witch-hunt known as the "Anti-Subversives Campaign" that occurred in 1975 and 1976. Virtually all the dangers perceived by Banda related to real or imagined plots against his personal power mounted by Malawi exiles sheltered in Zambia, Tanzania, and Mozambique.

In a remarkable volte-face, approximately two thousand detainees were released in 1977. Since that time there has been greater restraint in the use of the enormous arbitrary power still at the disposal of the government. This change cannot be attributed to any decline in the potential challenges to President Banda's rule. In fact, his situation had been complicated by Mozambican independence under a Marxist FRELIMO regime resentful of Malawi's obstructive role during the liberation struggle. Possibly the more militant configuration of neighboring states persuaded Banda that gratuitous repression would be counterproductive. Perhaps his personalist control of the state allowed rapid adjustment to the enhanced global emphasis on human rights during the Carter era. There may also have been some truth to the claim that the old man had not been fully aware of the excesses of certain subordinates who were abruptly removed from office. Banda's capacity to adapt to the "winds of change" can also be seen in Malawi's participation in SADCC, hosting of that organization's 1981 donor conference in Blantyre, and endorsement of its final communique which condemned South Africa's "destabilizing and aggressive policies."[28] Typically, he exacted a price from the other leaders, who acquiesced in the presence of South African representatives at the ceremonies opening the conference.

The grain of erratic puritanism in Banda's authoritarian style has sometimes been credited for the moderately high rate of economic growth that Malawi has achieved. Consistent and sound market-oriented priorities have allegedly been combined with relative honesty and efficiency of administration, achieved by fear. However, most real growth has occurred in the especially favored estate farming sector, whereas the majority of subsistence agriculturalists have experienced stagnation and even declining productivity. Moreover, competent and inventive Malawi officials have often been supplanted by loyal party hacks or expatriate experts because neither of these latter groups pose any threat to Banda. Thus what development has been achieved has bypassed most Malawians. Participation in state projects is based on fear rather than an active commitment to change reinforced by positive incentives. Labor migration to South Africa has been allowed to resume to acquire needed foreign exchange. The economy has been severely buffeted by the consequences of global recession.

President Banda's authoritarianism, repressive discipline, and links with South Africa have not given Malawi the desired head start to prosperity. Instead, this strategy has depleted the country's human resources and professional capabilities. Banda's personal authority has not been used to legitimize institutions and routine procedures for political succession or attaining national objectives. Thus future leaders of Malawi will find few established means for consolidating power beyond the repressive expedients of the founding President.

5. Zimbabwe

According to the U.S. State Department, Prime Minister Robert Mugabe and his ruling Zimbabwe African National Union (ZANU) "inherited a country with Western legal and political traditions."[29] What had existed in reality was a white settler pigmentocracy, which coated a colonial-style system of "native administration" with a veneer of democratic institutions accessible only to the white group and a tiny segment of blacks. In Ian Smith's Rhodesia, the realities of power encompassed a single-party authoritarian nightmare where the entire framework of economic, social, and security legislation had fostered the prosperity and continued dominance of the ruling elite. Hence majority rule by a popularly elected parliamentary government which included the full range of alternative viewpoints has been an altogether new experience for Zimbabweans.

The state that Robert Mugabe inherited had been scarred by a decade of war, which had exacerbated ethnic, racial, class, and ideological differences. The countryside was awash with competing groups of armed guerrilla fighters lacking requisite civilian skills and of disgruntled whites unable to accept a new order led by men regarded as Marxist terrorists. Tens of thousands of refugees requiring social support poured back into the country from exile in Botswana, Zambia, and other states. South Africa, Zimbabwe's most powerful neighbor, gave lip service to accepting the new regime, but demonstrated confusion, fear, and hostility through erratic behavior, with destabilizing consequences. To this perilous situation, Mugabe brought from exile politicians and administrators who had impressive academic credentials but little practical experience in public affairs or recent exposure to Zimbabwean realities. Placed in this context, Zimbabwe's human rights record during the initial three years of independence has been fairly good despite serious recent setbacks.

Instead of flaunting his outright parliamentary majority, Prime Minister Mugabe sought to preserve the solidarity that the Patriotic

Front had achieved during the constitutional negotiations by bringing Joshua Nkomo's Zimbabwe African People's Union (ZAPU) into a coalition government. To give effect to his policy of national reconciliation, Mugabe emphasized that basic rights entrenched in the constitution would be scrupulously respected. The socialist objectives of his movement would be attained by working through the existing economic and legal framework. He also took special pains to assure whites that their skills were valued highly and that even the leaders of the old regime would not be subjected to reprisals or deprived of their property and employment. The strategy of reconciliation so central to Mugabe's initial approach failed to stem the exodus of skilled whites and was further compromised by harrassment and detention of a few prominent whites on poorly substantiated allegations of subversive activity. It has been dealt a potentially mortal blow by the breakdown of the coalition with Nkomo and the indiscriminate violence employed by Mugabe's North Korean–trained Fifth Brigade against the equally vicious insurgency mounted by ZAPU-oriented dissidents operating in Ndebele areas.

Nevertheless, images of Zimbabwe have too often been shaped by reports focusing on atypical outbursts of violence or on politically motivated ministerial pronouncements belied by governmental behavior. Even efforts to expand human capabilities by extending opportunities and services to the majority of citizens have been misrepresented as Marxist-inspired disregard for "standards." Much publicity was devoted to former Minister of Manpower Edgar Tekere's being implicated in the brutal murder of a white farmer. Less attention was given to the fact that this key ZANU leader, like the majority of Zimbabweans under arrest, was subjected to the routine workings of independent judicial process. Moreover the Smith-era Indemnity Act which permitted his acquittal on purely technical grounds was repealed thereafter. Outbreaks of violence gain more attention than the fact that major segments of the rival guerrilla forces remain assimilated within the national army or that constitutional processes remain intact in the bulk of the country left untouched by insurgency. Much has also been made of Mugabe's announced intention to amend the independence constitution and establish a single-party state. Less is said of the skill with which Mugabe has used this threat to split the obstructive opposition of Smith's renamed Republican Front or of Mugabe's promise that a single-party state would not be implemented without a clear popular mandate in the 1985 election.[30]

There would be equal danger in perpetuating a Pollyanna-like disregard of the grave crisis that presently besets Zimbabwe. The extent of the problem is reflected in Joshua Nkomo's flight into exile and the Zimbabwean Catholic bishops' report that government troops have repeatedly committed "wanton atrocities and brutalities" during operations against dissidents in the Ndebele area.[31] Suspicion that ZAPU and its military wing, ZIPRA, were planning a coup or other destabilizing acts with South African connivance had been accentuated by the discovery of arms caches on ZAPU-owned farms, sabotage of strategic installations, attacks on ZANU facilities and personnel, and violent acts by bands of ZIPRA dissidents. Ranking ZIPRA officers in the national army were detained along with hundreds of their rank-and-file supporters, but the government has failed to substantiate its charges of conspiracy and treason in cases brought to trial.[32] To many of the Ndebele, who are ZAPU's core constituency, these events were evidence that the ZANU government, based primarily on the Shona peoples, was systematically denying the Ndbele their share of political power, economic opportunity, and basic rights. Although Mugabe and Nkomo may still back off from the abyss of civil war, the depredations of the ZIPRA dissidents and the exclusively Shona Fifth Brigade have done more to disrupt Zimbabwe than the schemes of the most clever planners in Pretoria.

The Mugabe government inherited a highly centralized governmental apparatus with extraordinary wartime controls over political and economic affairs. It has extended Ian Smith's Emergency Powers Act, which confers sweeping authority for preventive detention and other derogations of civil and political rights. Censorship has been relaxed, but newspapers formerly controlled by South African interests are now owned by the Zimbabwe government. Although theoretically run by a non-partisan media trust, they are led by editors who hew to a strongly progovernment line. The Cabinet has demonstrated limited patience with trade unionists, businessmen, politicians, and others whose attitudes or activities are thought to jeopardize economic reconstruction and development. The key point to be made, however, is that a new government confronting grave domestic problems has behaved with far more restraint than rhetoric would suggest.

As Michael Bratton has observed, a major dilemma emanating from accommodationist policies of reconciliation is the need for massive spending to fulfill mass expectations, but restraint on taxation to cultivate investor confidence and retain skilled workers.[33] One result has been unprecedented budget deficits and high inflation. Other longer-term outcomes include growing dependence on foreign assistance and some sacrificing of the sanctions-induced self-sufficiency and protected small-scale industry that were positive outcomes of long white resistance to majority rule. It is doubtful that Mr. Mugabe can indefinitely sustain his delicate balancing act without eventually having to compel some segments of society to bear the brunt of difficult policy choices. The present economic crisis triggered by drought and global recession makes this denouement more imminent.

Vulnerability to South African pressures compounds Zimbabwe's economic problems. Disruption of rail traffic by South Africa, its repatriation of migrant workers, and threats to suspend the existing preferential tariff agreement have made planning problematical and strained Zimbabwean managerial capacities. Moreover, the Pretoria regime appears determined to undermine Zimbabwe's alternative economic options in order to compel Mugabe to sustain existing links with South Africa. The disruption of Mozambican railways and ports and the sabotage of the Beira-Mutare (Umtali) oil pipeline between Mozambique and Zimbabwe by the South African–supported Mozambique National Resistance (MNR) seems too well orchestrated to be coincidental.[34]

There can be little doubt that South Africa is engaged in covert operations in Zimbabwe itself. These include routine information-gathering, sabotage of strategic military installations, political assassinations, aid to dissidents, and actual intrusions by the South African Defense Force. The external threat posed by South Africa might easily provide justification for Zimbabwean authorities to impose draconian security restrictions subversive of human rights. Thus far, Zimbabwe's leaders have not risen to the bait, but have dealt with incidents where South Africa may be involved on a case-by-case basis, relying upon routine military countermeasures, diplomatic channels, police procedures, and regular judicial processes.

6. *Angola and Mozambique*

The single-party revolutionary Marxist regimes that gained power without electoral mandates in Angola and Mozambique have implicitly limited to a considerable degree a variety of basic civil and political rights. Nevertheless, the standards of evaluation adopted in this essay do not embrace Jeane Kirkpatrick's distinction between total-itarian leftist and authoritarian rightist governments.[35] The actual behavior, not the ideology, of a government shapes the overall assessment of the intensity, extensiveness, duration, and deliberateness of any violation. Angola and Mozambique have been lumped together here in part because of the dearth of objective data available for evaluation of their human rights performances since independence.[36] The important common elements of their historical experiences and present political systems provide some additional justification for this decision.

The Portuguese colonial heritage distinguishes Angola and Mozambique from the British legacy shared by all of the other Southern African states. Key points of differentiation include the lingua franca, basic administrative and legal concepts, and underlying norms regarding appropriate relationships between the rulers and the ruled. The authoritarian character of the Portuguese political culture limited the impact of concepts of democratic participation within a representative system that were preached, if not always practiced, within the British colonial context.

Like Zimbabwe, Angola and Mozambique attained independence after protracted liberation struggles that had devastating economic and social consequences. But, in contrast to Rhodesia, the departing colonial authority was too demoralized to shape substantive constitutional arrangements or to insist that the successor governments attain a clear popular mandate. In both countries, the precipitousness of the transfer of power and apparently uncompromising character of the new governments triggered a massive and undisciplined flight of Portuguese settlers, more devastating than the gradual flow that has depleted Zimbabwe's reservoir of skilled craftsmen and workers. Both countries have had severe economic problems. Mozambique inherited one of the world's least-developed economies, while much of Angola's more established infrastructure and diversified production had been rendered inoperative. The revolutionary experience and ideological direction of both the ruling FRELIMO movement in Mozambique and of MPLA in Angola made their active support for the ongoing liberation struggles in Zimbabwe and Namibia inevitable. Geopolitical realities also meant that such involvement was unavoidable and would be enormously costly.

Angola and Mozambique have experienced the most serious direct incursions of South African troops. For Angola, these have occurred with frightening regularity, involving South African government forces as well as SWAPO guerillas and including actual occupation of segments of the country for extended periods by these invaders. Mozambique has undergone only one major attack, aimed at ANC partisans, but this military strike penetrated into the outskirts of Maputo, the national capital. Both states are beset by insurgent movements funded, armed, and at least partially directed by Pretoria. The civil war between Jonas Savimbi's UNITA movement and the MPLA government of Angola has been amply chronicled. Its scope and duration have wreaked havoc on the national economy, prevented the establishment of a single authority throughout the country, accentuated ethnic and regional differences and led to the long-term engagement of Cuban troops and other East Bloc military personnel. By contrast, the toll exacted by the MNR insurgency in Mozambique is far less well known, but includes substantial disruption of transport and communications, and the diversion of vital resources to military countermeasures. To be sure, Pretoria's role is rather more complicated than in Angola, since South Africa also utilizes Mozambican migrant labor, consumes power generated at Cabora Bassa, and provides personnel vital to the functioning of the port of Maputo.

To say that Angola and Mozambique have faced a state of economic and military siege since independence is hardly an exaggeration. There can also be little doubt that limited administrative capacities, inexperienced and undertrained personnel, and inadequate finances have consistently frustrated policies designed to meet these challenges. Governments in Africa and elsewhere have been known to lash out viciously at real and imagined enemies with far less cause. But the harshest critics of the Angolan and Mozambican regimes have not been able to pinpoint massive use of terror, widespread brutality, recurrent atrocities, or even a systematic pattern of repressive excesses. Despite restrictions on access and independent reporting, evidence of such events invariably leaks out of closed societies—even when their security apparatus is far more efficient than in these two.

Most critiques have focused on the Marxist character of these regimes or the international company they keep. Undoubtedly, political coordination of the press, trade unions, and youth and women's groups by the ruling party does circumscribe free speech and association. However, it would be unfair to ignore the variety of mechanisms, such as dynamizing groups, which FRELIMO devised to foster involvement by citizens with no tradition of participation. The high visibility of women's organizations in both countries testifies to a commitment to end entrenched discriminatory patterns. The FRELIMO and MPLA governments have been willing to admit policy failings and to substantially alter economic and political strategies that have gone awry. For example, Mozambican President Samora Machel acted to correct irregularities in reeducation camps where criminal and political offenders are detained. Those reluctant to embrace FRELIMO authority continue to suffer considerably, but the premise that such individuals should be rehabilitated rather than liquidated has been affirmed. President dos Santos' MPLA government has evinced considerable flexibility and pragmatism in interactions with Western governments and investors, but intrusive national security questions restrict the capacity to implement domestic reforms.

Until the insurgencies in Angola and Mozambique are resolved, mistreatment of prisoners, preventive detention, and other repressive excesses seem bound to recur. Already, military tribunals in Mozambique are operating outside of routine judicial processes and dispense a harsh and summary justice to captured insurgents thought to have collaborated with external forces.[37] But by and large, the most serious derogations of human rights have been limited and sporadic, occasioned by the breakdown of civil order more than purposeful centrally directed policies.

SOME INFERENCES AND HYPOTHESES

No linear relationships between levels of economic privation or external vulnerability and the degree of respect for human rights are evident in the records of the seven states. The strong human rights performance of Botswana may be a contributory factor to its rapid economic growth, despite poor beginnings. On the other hand, the desire to preserve an already sophisticated economy in Zimbabwe may have created greater sensitivity to the detrimental effects of a poor human rights record. Although Lesotho, Malawi, and Mozambique, the most impoverished of the seven states, are also among the more repressive, the origins and extent of their policies differ. Despite their poverty, none of them is a flagrant offender on a global scale of comparison.

Explanations of differing performance seem closely linked to the specific political cultures and social structures of the respective states. The capabilities and personal commitments of the initial national leader in each country also appear to have a major impact. The existence of a sense of national mission within Southern Africa seems to have conditioned the behavior of most of the seven. Finally, the actual capacity of each of the governments to cut off negative images of itself through silencing of domestic critics must be considered.

For Botswana, Lesotho, and Swaziland, independence was not only a means of self-fulfillment, but also a chance to demolish the myths of white supremacy by proving that responsible, non-racial institutions could flourish in Southern Africa under black majority rule. This shared sense of mission was a product of their pervasive exposure to apartheid, their awareness of concepts of fundamental human rights, and their indigenous traditions of political participation and toleration of diversity.

On the other hand, the emergent revolutionary states within Southern Africa had another sort of demonstration effect in mind. All saw the freedom struggle in their own country as part of an inexorable regional process of liberation. Their example would inspire and guide the oppressed majority in South Africa. Their success in establishing and consolidating their power might undermine Pretoria's morale and resolve by clearly showing the handwriting on the wall. Providing a model for change in South Africa seems to have set some constraints on what is permissible behavior at home. Malawi's policy of expanding links with South Africa did not generate an equivalent élan.

Deep social cleavages, whether ethnic, religious, or class, make adherence to human rights standards more difficult, especially when there is a high level of political mobilization around these factors. While definitely not absent in Botswana, ethnic, class, and religious divisions have had a very low political salience, requiring little intervention by government. However, in Lesotho problems emerge because a strong sense of national identity is undermined by a high level of political mobilization focused around acute religious, dynastic, and class antipathies. On the other hand, low levels of social mobilization and a strong emphasis on national unity by an effectual liberation movement help to explain why Mozambique's ethnic diversity has not become a critical problem. It is the politicization of ethnic differences during the colonial period and the liberation struggle that has created festering sources of violence in Angola and Zimbabwe. Regional and ethnic favoritism has been a major cause for grievances in Malawi. Repressive excesses are likely to become more extreme when the protagonists share few elements of common identity and regard their adversaries as aliens rather than wayward brothers.

Because the bases of legitimacy in a new state are usually inchoate, the capacity of the first leader to surmount domestic cleavages and define the parameters of acceptable political behavior is of critical importance. Seretse Khama of Botswana combined impeccable educational credentials, traditional legitimacy, and the capacity for independent action, reflected in his controversial marriage to an English woman. The synthesis of competing values in a man whose authority was unquestioned permitted Khama to build his people's commitment to new political institutions and to insist on high standards of accountability. Sobhuza II of Swaziland embodied the continuity of dominant traditional structures and values, but this stance made accommodation with new social and economic forces quite difficult. As the spokesman for conservative Catholics and junior chiefs in Lesotho, Leabua Jonathan has been unable to transcend sectional infighting and to harness strong national identity to the tasks of economic transformation. Hastings Banda's only superficial roots in Malawi, due to his long sojourn abroad, help to explain why centralized coercion became his preferred technique of dealing with domestic challenges to his authority. A decisive electoral mandate in Zimbabwe followed by unexpectedly conciliatory policies have supplemented Robert Mugabe's credentials as a revolutionary, humanist, and intellectual, but do not fully compensate for the ethnic boundaries of his popular base. Samora Machel's military successes, which eroded Portuguese power, facilitated his assumption of Eduardo Mondlane's mantle as undisputed head of FRELIMO and ultimately of all Mozambique. By contrast, Angola was torn by competing sectional movements and leadership, with none able to claim a mandate based on a decisive military or electoral triumph. Once the MPLA had become ascendent, the untimely death of President Neto made it far less likely that strong leadership would be a catalyst for ending the war and moderating deeply etched hatreds.

Penetration of the mass media of the Republic of South Africa into some of the black neighboring states serves as a further, somewhat unusual constraint on their human rights behavior. The rudimentary nature of the indigenous media and the small size of its potential market in Botswana, Lesotho, and Swaziland make it unlikely that those states would deny politically conscious elements access to the South Africa press. Countries with stronger state-controlled media, like Mozambique and Zimbabwe, would be hard pressed to block out the ubiquitous radio waves. Even if they could, migrant workers would informally transmit news of general interest. Similarly, extensive commercial interchanges with South Africa and the lucrative tourist trade make interdiction of the flow of information and rumors in both directions virtually impossible.

The government-dominated media of South Africa are only too eager to feature political crises and human rights violations in black African states. Such news reinforces Pretoria's message about the perils of majority rule and the hypocrisy of repressive African regimes that dare to criticize the apartheid system. The opposition-oriented English media can prove their "objectivity" by revealing and criticizing the political failings of neighboring states at least as thoroughly as those of the ruling party in South Africa.

Reports on violence or repressive government actions in neighboring states are frequently exaggerated, cliché-ridden, and inaccurate. Overstated stories on violence in Lesotho just before the 1979 Christmas season wreaked havoc on that state's tourist industry. A series of *Rand Daily Mail* interviews with spokesmen for the insurgent LLA were avidly read in Maseru, but may have given that organization greater credibility than it merited at that moment.[38] Not surprisingly, the Lesotho government perceives the South African press as part of a more general strategy of destabilization aimed at itself.

Nevertheless, some solid investigative reporting of alleged atrocities in 1974 undoubtedly played a constructive role in compelling Prime Minister Jonathan to rein in undisciplined police and progovernment vigilantes.[39]

The Zimbabwean media are now under local ownership and control, and tend to propagate progovernment perspectives on domestic and international affairs. Government control of the media and regulation of foreign correspondents, as well as the barrier to external communication posed by the Portuguese lingua franca, restrict the impact which South Africa can have on the Angolan and Mozambican peoples. Malawi's remoteness from South Africa, together with Hastings Banda's aversion to inquisitive journalists, limit the amount of uncomplimentary information reaching the outside world or flowing back into that country. The greater independence of these states from the South African media lessens risks of damage caused by distorted reports. However, this positive element does mean that their national leaders may avoid some of the negative consequences if they should resort to repressive actions.

HUMAN RIGHTS AND THE INTERNATIONAL TRANSACTIONS OF INDEPENDENT BLACK GOVERNMENTS IN SOUTH AFRICA

Human rights issues are usually treated on a country-by-country basis. The preceding analysis, however, not only suggests the utility of a comparative perspective, but implies that international linkages and transactions, whether bilateral, regional, or global, are essential ingredients for comprehending the human rights situation in individual states. Three illustrations have been selected to demonstrate the possibilities of this approach, namely, South Africa's strategy of "destabilization," the role of the SADCC grouping, and the impact of foreign aid donors.

1. *Destabilization*

White South Africans have generally failed to accept that the human rights records of their neighbors reflect a complex blend of achievements as well as setbacks. They continue to regard black majority rule as a catastrophic outcome leading inevitably to Stalinism or macabre personalism. While conceding that South Africa must "adapt or die," the Pretoria government considers only those options which will sustain white privilege in the face of an allegedly communist-inspired "total onslaught."[40]

South Africa's black neighbors are firmly convinced that Prime Minister P. W. Botha's "total strategy" to combat this "total onslaught'' includes aggressive acts aimed at destabilizing their countries. The communiqué of the 1982 Gaborone Summit Conference alleged that ''the object of this destabilization is to undermine the security of SADCC member states and sabotage SADCC's efforts to achieve economic liberation.''[41] Experienced observers, such as the *New York Times* correspondent Joseph Lelyveld, affirm that the destabilization hypothesis can help to explain otherwise perplexing sequences of events within the region.[42] Pretoria has a history of attempting to nip all challenges in the bud. The Botha regime has the means to initiate preemptive action intended to preserve South Africa's regional predominance, by preventing the neighboring states from individually or collectively consolidating power and building alternative economic and military options.

What is the linkage between destabilization and human rights issues? Destabilization is a deliberate policy using overt and covert forms of intervention to build up stresses on weaker governments to prompt them to desperate expedients. By disrupting economic activity, undermining political and administrative institutions, accentuating ethnic, regional, or religious antipathies, and augmenting existing fears and suspicions, destabilization contributes to political decay and inability to meet basic human needs. Within Southern Africa, ''hot pursuit'' of guerrillas across frontiers, assistance to insurgent movements in neighboring states, unilateral alteration of tariff and migrant labor arrangements, and disruption of trade and transport are but a few of the available mechanisms which derive from Pretoria's economic and military hegemony. Even without deliberate governmental action, the entrenched political economy of dependence works to produce corrosive results.

Confronted by a bewildering array of inexplicable problems taxing their limited capabilities, governments being destabilized are likely to resort to a variety of emergency measures curtailing basic liberties. Not only does the instigator deny responsibility for this sequence of events, but it blames them on the incompetence, mismanagement, unpopularity, or ideology of its beleaguered neighbors. This is precisely what South Africa is doing. Having helped to create situations conducive to its neighbors' limitation of human rights, the Botha regime uses the resulting repression to castigate the foibles of black majority rule and to justify its own repressive system. It not only ignores the Biblical caution on the evils of criticizing the motes in one's brother's eyes, but also bears at least some of the responsibility for having placed them there![43]

South Africa hotly denies that it is pursuing, or even contemplating, a strategy of destabilization. However, there can be no doubt that Pretoria regularly uses available economic and military van-tage points to pressure neighboring governments into more compliant postures. Alternatively, the Botha government offers those states willing to collaborate with the Republic membership in the vaunted "Constellation," as well as substantial economic incentives and the cessation of abrasive transactions, whatever their human rights records.

2. *Southern African Development Coordination Conference*

As the struggle for Zimbabwean independence moved toward denouement, and the focus of concern turned toward Namibia and South Africa, the Front Line Presidents felt that Lesotho, Malawi, and Swaziland needed to be drawn directly into regional processes of change.[44] More attention was required to development priorities within Southern Africa if political gains were to be consolidated. The Southern African Development Coordination Conference (SADCC), which resulted from their initiatives, was able to recruit all of the independent black states within the region as charter members regardless of their many historical and ideological differences.

Should SADCC be considered a human rights organization? Its primary objective is clearly economic, namely, reducing dependence and mobilizing regional resources for economic transformation. However, efforts such as the SADCC food security plan enable members to better provide for the most basic needs of their citizens and thereby affirm the primacy and improve the quality of life itself. SADCC exists to combat dependency in general, but more particularly to extricate the black states from the South African economic stranglehold that has made them involuntary participants in degrading features of apartheid, such as the migrant labor system. The creation of alternative economic options is not designed merely to enrich member states, but to make participation in the struggle for majority rule in South Africa more feasible.

Several members of SADCC had established records as spokesmen for human rights concerns in Africa. Botswana, Mozambique, Tanzania, and Zambia had challenged the accepted practice of the Organization of African Unity (OAU) of avoiding embarrassing human rights issues by treating them as matters of domestic jurisdiction. They attempted unsuccessfully to prevent Idi Amin from becoming OAU Chairman by leading a boycott of the 1975 OAU summit meeting in Uganda. At that time, the Tanzanian government took special note of the hypocrisy inherent in condemning and seeking to isolate South Africa while turning a blind eye to atrocities elsewhere on the continent.[45]

Violations of rights in the Republic of South Africa remain a major theme of academic conferences and media coverage in SADCC states. However, there are indications of growing awareness that the impact and credibility of these critiques will be enhanced if blended with some constructive self-criticism.[46] A research project on fundamental human rights has been commissioned at the University of Zimbabwe. It will advise the government on alternative strategies for bringing Zimbabwean law into congruence with the Universal Declaration of Human Rights and other international covenants, especially in the area of women's rights.[47] Newspaper coverage of the international conference on "Law and Human Rights in Development" held at the University College of Botswana in May 1982 emphasized deficiencies in the performance of African states.[48]

The front page prominence given in the *Botswana Daily News* to a conference paper highlighting human rights deficiencies in Lesotho illustrates the complexity of handling these issues straightforwardly.[49] SADCC's survival rests on retaining a maximum of solidarity among a very diverse membership. Active participation of all black Southern African states has been strongly solicited regardless of any pending human rights issues. Lesotho's withdrawal from active participation would be a setback for the broader objectives of regional economic liberation, which also promote human rights. Similarly, Botswana's commitment to provide sanctuary to political refugees considered subversive by the Lesotho and Zimbabwe governments has triggered recrimination potentially disruptive of SADCC solidarity.[50]

The annual summits, ministerial meetings, donor conferences, and other working group sessions of SADCC permit comprehensive and diverse exchanges of views which can defuse such altercations. They provide significant opportunities for concerned members to discuss informally any serious human rights problems and to forestall their potentially debilitating impact upon the achievement of broader SADCC objectives. For example, this sort of low-key representation might help to persuade Swazi officials of the risks of consummating the controversial land transfers with South Africa. To paraphrase Claude Welch, what SADCC provides is "a *climate* in which domestic civil, economic, political, and social rights" in Southern African states are being examined "as a result of African volition."[51]

3. Foreign Aid

Cynics might query whether donor reactions to human rights records have any effect upon recipients' subsequent behavior. Yet Botswana's positive achievements in human rights and productive use of assistance have clearly whetted donor enthusiasm. More recently, Zimbabwe's commitment to national reconciliation and superior economic potential fostered a similar surge of interest. On the other hand, Lesotho faced actual suspension of assistance following the 1970 coup, and has subsequently tried to appease donors whose decisions could devastate development programs and the entire national economy. However, the salience of threatened sanctions has been dissipated by the willingness of donors to stand by ideological allies regardless of their policies, by pressures on donors to help black states dependent upon South Africa, and by donors' acceptance of promises of reform without substantive changes in recipients' human rights performance.

What can explain lack of donor resolve in attempting to remedy human rights violations? Fears that other countries will reap advantage by taking up the slack are ever-present. Likewise, vigorous actions are easily characterized as unwarranted neoimperialist interference. However, the most compelling answers lie in the characteristics of donor programs. Assistance to any country depends only partially on its unique situation and needs. Instead, the donors' broad programmatic perspectives, involving strategic, humanitarian, ideological, economic, military, and bureaucratic interests, are decisive. Aid is better conceptualized as a complex bureaucratic organism than a simple transfer of scarce resources. Long lead times and high costs are caused by project planning, budgeting, recruitment, clearance procedures and relocation. Hence the assistance spigot is not easily turned on or off in response to local developments. At best, small adjustments in the flow of funding are feasible. Moreover, aid bureaucracies will invariably rationalize all of their projects as vital to the welfare of the poorest and neediest. Thus pressures upon repressive ruling elites are likely to be rhetorical, symbolic, and brief.

In short, the level of aid, like the intensity of diplomatic links with a region, is primarily contingent upon their perceived importance to the interests and policy objectives of the great powers. While the human rights performances of given states may make some small differences in the extent of the aid they receive, other factors will determine the overall level of assistance. The very salience of the Southern African region assures that there will be alternative donors available to make up shortfalls caused by the compunctions of any single state. Only a collective effort by a significant number of great powers willing to act in accordance with the same standards could have much impact upon the protection of basic human rights in both white- and black-ruled Southern Africa.

NOTES

This chapter is an expanded and thoroughly revised version of my article, "Human Rights in Botswana, Lesotho, Malawi, and Swaziland," *Pula: Botswana Journal of African Studies*, 2, no. 1 (February 1980), pp. 5–32. I am indebted to the University of Toledo and to the University of Botswana and Swaziland for research grants which enabled me to gather materials for this project. I alone am responsible for the contents and interpretations herein.

1. The black-ruled states of Southern Africa include Angola, Botswana, Lesotho, Malawi, Mozambique, Swaziland, Tanzania, Zambia, and Zimbabwe. Tanzania and Zambia have been excluded from the case studies in this chapter due to space constraints and their greater remoteness from South Africa. The so-called "independent homelands," Bophuthatswana, Ciskei, Transkei, and Venda, have not been included since they are regarded as illegitimate progeny of the apartheid system.

The most noteworthy contributions on the Southern African regional system include Larry W. Bowman, "The Subordinate State System of Southern Africa," *International Studies Quarterly*, 12, no. 3 (September 1968) pp. 231–61; Kenneth W. Grundy, *Confrontation and Accommodation in Southern Africa: The Limits of Independence* (Berkeley and Los Angeles: University of California Press, 1973); and Timothy M. Shaw and Kenneth A. Heard, eds., *Cooperation and Conflict in Southern Africa: Papers on a Regional Subsystem* (Washington, D.C.: University Press of America, 1976).

2. This typology derives from Joyce Howland and Warren Weinstein, "Human Rights and Economic Development: An Overview for Africa and Latin America," unpublished paper presented at the Annual Meeting of the African Studies Association, Houston, November 1977, pp. 1–3, and U.S. Dept. of State, *Report on Human Rights Practices in Countries Receiving U.S. Aid, Report Submitted to the Committee on Foreign Relations, U.S. Senate, and Committee on Foreign Affairs, U.S. House of Representatives*, February 8, 1979 (Washington, D.C.: U.S. Government Printing Office, 1979), pp. 2–3.

3. The "right to development" and its implications are the subject of extensive debate: See "The Right to Develop Not Yet Recognized," *Botswana Daily News* (Gaborone), no. 182 (May 31, 1982); Jack Donnelly's chapter below, and Claude Welch's chapter above.

4. These categories were set forth in Laurie S. Wiseberg, "Human Rights in Africa: Toward a Definition of the Problem of a Double Standard," *Issue* 6, no. 4 (Winter 1976), p. 9.

5. SADCC is discussed at length in Richard F. Weisfelder, "The Southern African Development Coordination Conference (SADCC): A New Factor in the Liberation Process," in Thomas M. Callaghy, ed., *South Africa in Southern Africa* (New York: Praeger, 1983), in press.

6. E. Philip Morgan, "Botswana: Development, Democracy, and Vulnerability," in Gwendolen M. Carter and Patrick O'Meara, eds., *Southern Africa: The Continuing Crisis*, 2nd ed. (Bloomington: Indiana University Press, 1982), p. 237.

7. "A Star of Hope on a Black Horizon," *Botswana Daily News*, no. 190

(September 30, 1978), and "Gov't May Be Forced to Ban Violent Political Parties," *Botswana Daily News*, no. 241 (December 14, 1978).

8. Andrew Sesinyi, "Motion Is Now a 'Tribal Storm'," *Botswana Daily News*, no. 63 (April 1, 1980), and "House Approves Move Deploring Discrimination," *Botswana Daily News*, no. 66 (April 8, 1980).

9. See "Botswana Students Held after Break-out from Campus," *The Star* (Johannesburg), September 13, 1978, and "Students and Police Clash in Gaborone," *Rand Daily Mail* (Johannesburg), September 12, 1978.

10. "Dramatic Tuli Block Trial Nears Showdown," *Rand Daily Mail*, November 13, 1978, and "Tuli Deaths: Soldier Acquitted on All Charges," *Rand Daily Mail*, November 14, 1978. The trial was covered also in the *Botswana Daily News* during the first two weeks of November, 1978.

11. Gherhard Pieterse, "Farmers on the War Path: Anti-Terrorist Action Urged," *Sunday Times* (Johannesburg), January 21, 1979.

12. "South Arican Press Allegations Are Geared for Something," *Botswana Daily News*, no. 242 (December 22, 1981), and "SA Intentions Still Feared in Botswana," *Botswana Daily News*, no. 62 (March 30, 1982).

13. "Irresponsible Refugees: Beware, or Else . . . ." *Botswana Daily News*, no. 11 (January 21, 1981), and "Minister Outlines Policy on SA Refugees," *Botswana Daily News*, no. 57 (March 26, 1981).

14. Mmonlwmang Madikwe, "BPP Conference Opened," *Botswana Daily News*, no. 136 (July 20, 1982).

15. More detailed background for this section can be found in Richard F. Weisfelder, "The Decline of Human Rights in Lesotho: An Evaluation of Domestic and External Determinants,' *Issue* 6, no. 4 (Winter 1976), pp. 22–33.

16. A more general discussion of these events and of recent trends appears in Richard F. Weisfelder, "Lesotho: Changing Patterns of Dependence," in Carter and O'Meara, *Southern Africa*, pp. 249–68.

17. See Brendan Nicholson, "Jonathan Warned: It's War," *The Star*, December 14, 1979, and Patrick Laurence, "The War No-one Can Win," *Rand Daily Mail*, October 3, 1981.

18. The National University of Lesotho, *Vice Chancellor's Report to the University Community on Recent Incidents on Campus* (Roma, Lesotho: December 1, 1981) (mimeographed), 17 pp.

19. An excellent set of articles detailing the labor reserve concept appears in "Focus on Lesotho," *South African Labour Bulletin* 6, no. 4 (November 1980), 90 pp.

20. Lesotho, Auditor-General, *Report on the Public Accounts of Lesotho for the Three Years Ended 31st March 1978* (Maseru: Government Printer, 1982).

21. "Dr. Jonathan: Father of National Development," *Lesotho Weekly* (Maseru) 1, no. 26 (September 24, 1977).

22. Laurence, "The War No-one Can Win," "Insurgents Will Use Lesotho More—SP," *Rand Daily Mail*, August 24, 1981; and Joseph Lelyveld, "Lesotho Sees Pretoria's Hand in Shadowy Conflict," *New York Times*, September 17, 1981; and David Forret, Norman Chandler, and Ken Slade, "SA's Biggest Mess, Says Lesotho Official," *Sunday Times* (Johannesburg), December 12, 1982.

23. Useful background on Swazi politics appears in Christian P. Potholm,

Swaziland: The Dynamics of Political Modernization, Perspectives on Southern Africa 8 (Berkeley and Los Angeles: University of California Press, 1972).

24. Absolom L. Vilakazi, "Swaziland: From Tradition to Modernity," in Carter and O'Meara, *Southern Africa,* p. 274.

25. Joseph Lelyveld, "South Africa Tells Tribe of Transfer," *New York Times,* June 18, 1982, and Patrick Laurence, "Citizenship Poser for Swaziland in Transfer," *Rand Daily Mail,* June 17, 1982.

26. Geoff Dalglish, "Swaziland Faces More Trouble," *Rand Daily Mail,* October 17, 1977.

27. A useful summary of recent trends in Malawi appears in Samuel Waterford, "Malawi: Kamuzu's Maverick Rule," *Africa Report* 25, no. 5 (September-October 1980), p. 10–14.

28. "SADCC Gets down to the Basics," *The Herald* (Harare) November 23, 1981.

29. U.S. Dept. of State, *Country Reports on Human Rights Practices for 1981, Report Submitted to the Committee on Foreign Affairs, U.S. House of Representatives, and Committee on Foreign Relations, U.S. Senate* February 1982, (joint Print), pp. 317.

30. "Mugabe Will Seek Single-Party Rule," *The Washington Post,* August 5, 1982, and "No One-Party State without Referendum," *The Herald,* May 31, 1982.

31. Joseph Lelyveld, "Catholics Report Zimbabwe Atrocities," *New York Times,* March 30, 1983, and "Nkomo Takes Exile Days after Fearing Mugabe Death Plot," *New York Times,* March 10, 1983.

32. Jay Ross, "Court Dismisses Treason Charges against 6 of 7 Nkomo Followers," *The Washington Post,* March 23, 1983.

33. Michael Bratton, "Development in Zimbabwe: Strategy and Tactics," *The Journal of Modern African Studies* 19, no. 3 (September 1981), p. 463.

34. Evidence of MNR links with South Africa appears in U.S. State Dept., *Country Reports on Human Rights Practices for 1981,* p. 186; "The MNR—S. Africa's Agents of Destruction,' *The Herald,* April 27, 1982, p. 9; and John Borrell, "South Africa's Secret Aid for Guerrillas in Mozambique Seen as Regional Threat," *The Wall Street Journal,* June 12, 1982.

35. Jeane Kirkpatrick, "Dictatorships and Double Standards," *Commentary* 68, no. 5 (1979), pp. 34–45.

36. Many of the available sources are not neutral, and either justify or condemn the country in question. The best include Gerald J. Bender, "Angola: Left, Right, and Wrong," *Foreign Policy,* no. 43 (Summer 1981) and Allen Isaacman, *A Luta Continua: Creating a New Society in Mozambique,* Southern Africa Pamphlets no. 1 (Binghamton, N.Y.: Fernand Braudel Center, 1978).

37. U.S. State Dept., *Country Reports on Human Rights Practices for 1981,* p. 177.

38. Chris Freimond, "Into the Web of Lesotho's Spiders of War," *Rand Daily Mail,* November 22, 1980; Patrick Laurence, "Photo 'Proves' Rebel Chief's Return," *Rand Daily Mail,* May 4, 1981, and "Lesotho Riled by Rebel Interview," *Rand Daily Mail,* November 20, 1980.

39. Stan Maher, "Lesotho—Land of Vanishing Freedoms," *Rand Daily Mail*, March 28, 1974, and "Document on a Ruthlessly Suppressed People," *Rand Daily Mail*, April 5, 1974; and Bill Norris, "Mapoteng Massacre Witness Speaks Out," *Rand Daily Mail*, November 23, 1974.

40. Deon Geldenhuys, *Some Foreign Policy Implications of South Africa's 'Total National Strategy'* (Braamfontein: South African Institute for International Affairs, 1981), pp. 2–10.

41. Quoted in "SADCC Communique," *Botswana Daily News*, no. 139 (July 23, 1982).

42. Joseph Lelyveld, "Pretoria Chooses among Cloaks and Daggers," *The New York Times*, December 13, 1981, and "Is South Africa Helping Mugabe to Fail?" *The New York Times*, October 4, 1981; and Anthony Lewis, "Pretoria and Neighbors," *The New York Times*, December 7, 1981.

43. More comprehensive definition and analysis of destabilization appears in Richard F. Weisfelder, "Destabilization in South Africa: Conflict Management and Conflict Accentuation," unpublished paper presented at the Annual Meeting of the African Studies Association, Washington, D. C., November 1982.

44. The Front Line States included Angola, Botswana, Mozambique, Tanzania, and Zambia; Zimbabwe became a member after independence.

45. These events are discussed at greater length in Claude E. Welch, Jr., "The O.A.U. and Human Rights: Towards a New Definition," *The Journal of Modern African Studies* 19, no. 3 (September 1981), pp. 402–8.

46. See "Human Rights Meet Opens at UCB," *Botswana Daily News*, no. 98 (May 25, 1982). Human rights problems in Lesotho received extensive coverage in Zimbabwe: See Jasper Mortimer, "Political Death Squad Murders Opponents," *The Herald*, January 27, 1982, and "Death of an Editor and No Arrests," *The Herald*, January 28, 1982.

47. "Research into Human Rights 'Top Project'," *Sunday Mail* (Harare), March 21, 1982.

48. "The Right to Develop Not Yet Recognized," *Botswana Daily News*, no. 102 (May 31, 1982); and "Human Rights Means Action," *The Herald*, June 9, 1982.

49. "Human Rights Suspended in Coup D'Etat?" *Botswana Daily News*, no. 100 (May 27, 1982).

50. "Zimbabwe Reporter Is a Liar," *Botswana Daily News*, no. 65 (April 8, 1983).

51. Welch, "The O.A.U. and Human Rights," p. 419.

II

Regional Initiatives on Human Rights in Africa

INTRODUCTION

The consideration of human rights in Africa frequently focuses upon the abuses by the Republic of South Africa. Despite numerous international attempts to change the policies of apartheid, there has been little relief gained from the restrictions and deprivations imposed upon the overwhelming majority of South Africa's inhabitants. The shadow of South Africa's violations extends widely over the continent, and poses the most compelling moral and political dilemmas. However, apartheid is only one element of the total African human rights record. The problems and constraints that other African states experience in protecting human rights have gained increased attention in recent years, particularly within a regional African context.

Two factors have given rise to this regional focus. First, despite their heterogeneity, African societies evidence many commonalities, involving economic underdevelopment, social and ethnic cleavages, and political cultures and institutions, which form the basis for considering and acting upon human rights matters within a regional framework. This regionalism is rooted in the common legacies of a colonial past and in current African efforts to chart a collective political and economic course. Second, this trend reflects the thinking and activities of various UN organizations that have sought to strengthen regional institution building and activities are vital supplements to international human rights efforts. This is particularly true in the application and enforcement of basic norms and principles among member countries.

In June 1981, the Organization of African Unity (OAU) took a major step towards developing a regional perspective and capacity to deal with human rights in Africa by adopting the Banjul Charter on Human and Peoples' Rights. This created a set of human rights principles and institutions which attempts to be responsive to African needs, traditions, and circumstances. As only the third such regional human rights system in the world today, this OAU action is an important development not only in Africa, but also for the international recognition and protection of human rights generally. However, the adoption of this Charter—not yet ratified by a majority of African states—is only a beginning step. There remain many obstacles to the full realization of the Charter's intentions—difficulties which are reflected in the document itself and in the political, economic, and institutional environment affecting its eventual implementation.

This section focuses upon the development, meaning, and prospects of the Banjul Charter for the recognition and protection of human rights in Africa. In Chapter 6, Edward Kannyo describes the political and diplomatic background to this African charter, indicating factors that influenced its development, and considerations that limited its scope and content. In particular, Kannyo identifies five major factors vital to this OAU initiative: the acceptance of the OAU as the chief regional forum for resolving African problems; the embarrassment of gross human rights violations in various African states; the controversies surrounding the Tanzanian invasion of Uganda; the encouragement by UN bodies of regional activities of this nature; and increased political receptivity to human rights issues in international relations during the 1970s. Kannyo believes that the decision of African leaders to adopt the Banjul Charter has particularly important implications for the recognition and protection of human rights on the continent, because this OAU move means that the principle of non-interference in the internal affairs of member-states can no longer provide a legitimate defense for violators of human rights in the region.

In Chapter 7, Richard Gittleman considers the Banjul Charter from a legal perspective, examining the specific provisions of this document in terms of the stated objectives of its drafters and its coincidence with other human rights standards and instruments. He looks at key legal questions raised by this Charter, including its binding nature, its "clawback" clauses, its possible permission of state derogation of rights, and the importance of the proposed African Commission on Human Rights for the Charter's implementation. Gittleman concludes with considerable caution about the Charter's eventual implementation. Much depends upon the types of authority and the leeway granted to the proposed Commission. In effect, this body will need to interpret the Charter and provide institutional support in a manner that would overcome the document's internal legal weaknesses. Only an independent Commission operating parallel to other international organizations charged with the protection of human rights can fulfill these requirements, and the establishment of such a body remains fundamentally a political question.

Harry Scoble addressses another factor important to Africa's future human rights record in Chapter 9: the activities of non-governmental organizations within the region. They play a vital role in recognizing and protecting human rights, representing an increasingly important component of the human rights networks that operate throughout various regions of the world. The nongovernmenal organizations are particularly important resources for realizing human rights objectives within developing countries. But at the same time, they have been least numerous and active in the Third World. Within Africa, the status and presence of such organizations are especially precarious. Scoble indicates that this lack of effective activity contributes to the continuation of both underdevelopment and repression in African societies. His observations underscore the importance of examining human rights not only in terms of legal documents, but also in terms of institutions capable of promoting and protecting these rights.

Scoble concludes by assessing the particular weaknesses of the Banjul Charter as a human rights initiative in the region. Three factors make the prospects for successful outcomes in Africa exceedingly dim. First, the Charter does not provide the basis for an activist Commission, especially regarding the selection of its members. Second, the Charter remains silent concerning human rights nongovernmental organizations in contrast with the UN, European, and Inter-American human rights systems. Third, revisions made between the first and final versions of the Charter reveal a significant weakening of the document by member governments, especially with regard to the evolution of indigenous organizations that might challenge the human rights records of African states. Thus, despite the importance of the Banjul Charter as a human rights initiative in Africa, additional political commitment and institutional development will be required to mount an effective human rights system in the region, and there is little indication that these conditions will be easily or quickly met in the near future.

CHAPTER SIX

The Banjul Charter on Human and Peoples' Rights: Genesis and Political Background

EDWARD KANNYO

INTRODUCTION

The decision of the Eighteenth Ordinary Assembly of Heads of State and Government of the Organization of African Unity (OAU), which met in Nairobi, Kenya, from June 24 to 28, 1981, to adopt an "African Charter on Human and Peoples' Rights," has created the conditions for a regional mechanism to promote and protect the fundamental rights of over 400 million people in Africa. If and when it is fully established, the African human rights regional system will be only the third such system in the world, alongside the European and Inter-American systems.

The decision of the OAU to create a human rights system is particularly significant because it indicates that African leaders for the first time have recognized that human rights violations in African states are a matter of concern for the international community. Until now, the principle of non-interference in the internal affairs of member states, which is set out in Article 3 (ii) of the OAU Charter, has been consistently used—explicitly or implicitly—to prevent the organization from dealing with situations within member states which threatened or actually involved grave violations of human rights.[1] Moreover, jealous defense of national sovereignty has not only hitherto hindered OAU efforts to protect human rights but has also obstructed the process of greater African regional integration.

When it was founded in 1963, the OAU did not include the protection of human rights within its member states among its goals and purposes. The main aims of the organization as envisioned by its founders were to complete the process of decolonization, combat apartheid in South Africa, prevent extra-regional foreign interference—particularly by the major powers—and promote stability and greater cooperation among African states.[2]

After eighteen years of existence, why did the OAU decide to include human rights protection in its member states as one of its goals? The answer to this question is to be found in a complex of factors deriving from developments within and outside the African continent.

In the course of the eighteen years that had elapsed between the foundation of the organization and the 1981 Summit Conference, the OAU was confronted on various occasions with political problems—some of them amounting to crises—many of which had direct or indirect human rights or humanitarian implications. With each crisis, the OAU came more and more to be accepted as the proper forum for handling African problems. It was thus natural that when African leaders felt the need to create a regional mechanism for the promotion and protection of human rights, the OAU was regarded as the proper agency to create it.

Political developments in Africa cannot, however, be examined in isolation from the politics of the broader international arena. Events arising in the latter context, combined with intra-African developments, led to the drafting of the African human rights charter. More specifically, five major factors will be considered, three of them pertaining to intra-African affairs, and two emanating from the wider international political arena.

The three principal intra-African factors are: the gradual acceptance by African leaders of the OAU as the principal forum for the resolution of African problems, including those of an essentially domestic character;[3] the embarrassment caused for the OAU and African leaders in general by the atrocities of the Amin, Bokassa, and Macias regimes in Uganda, the former Central African Empire, and Equatorial Guinea, respectively; and the acrimonious debate at the 1979 OAU Summit Conference provoked by the invasion of Uganda by Tanzanian troops and armed Ugandan exiles that led to the downfall of the Amin regime.

Internationally, the work of the United Nations in its efforts to encourage the establishment of regional human rights commissions was important to the development of the Banjul Charter. In addition, this African initiative was buttressed by the increased attention paid to reports of human rights violations in the international media by politicians, intellectuals, and the general public all over the world, beginning in the mid-1970s.

Before examining these factors in detail, let us analyze the goals and purposes, as well as the structures, of the OAU as originally envisaged from the perspective of the promotion and protection of human rights.

THE OAU CHARTER

In the preamble to the Charter of the OAU, the founders clearly stated that they were "conscious of the fact that freedom, equality, justice, and dignity are essential objectives for the achievement of the legitimate aspirations of the African peoples . . . ." They also invoked the Charter of the United Nations and the Universal Declaration of Human Rights, "to the principles of which we reaffirm our adherence."[4]

The Charter of the United Nations Article 1 (iii) states that one of the principal purposes of the organization is "To achieve international cooperation in solving international problems of an economic, social, cultural or humanitarian character, and in promoting and encouraging respect for human rights and for fundamental freedoms for all without distinction as to race, sex, language or religion . . . ." Elsewhere in the Charter, provisions for the role of the United Nations in the promotion and protection of human rights are expressly set out.[5]

In spite of the invocation of the Charter of the United Nations, the Universal Declaration of Human Rights, and the importance of freedom, equality, justice and dignity for the African peoples, however, the promotion and protection of human rights was not set as one of the goals of the OAU, and no organ was created for that purpose.

The five purposes of the OAU are set out in Article 2 (i) of the OAU Charter: (1) to promote the unity and solidarity of African states; (2) to coordinate and intensify their cooperation and efforts to achieve a better life for the peoples of Africa; (3) to defend their sovereignty, their territorial integrity, and independence; (4) to eradicate all forms of colonialism from Africa; and (5) to promote international cooperation, with regard for the Charter of the United Nations and the Universal Declaration of Human Rights. And in Article 2 (ii), the Charter states that the member states shall coordinate and harmonize their general policies, especially through cooperation in (a) political affairs and diplomacy; (b) economic activities, including transport and communications; (c) education and cultural matters; (d) health, sanitation, and nutrition; (e) science and technology; and (f) defense and security.

The eradication of colonialism is undoubtedly a major condition for the full protection of human rights. Colonial domination inherently denies the claims of equality and self-determination of all peoples. Insofar as the OAU has worked for the complete decolonization of Africa and led the international campaign against apartheid in South

Africa, it has played an important role in the promotion of human rights.

However, as the postcolonial history of Africa—and of other regions as well—has shown, the problem of human rights is not resolved by the mere acquisition of political independence. In many African states, constitutional government has been overthrown, opponents imprisoned or banished and, in some extreme cases, physically eliminated. It is significant that the overwhelming majority of refugees in Africa have fled independent states for political reasons.⁶ In the socioeconomic realm, extreme inequalities with regard to access to material and cultural resources remain a fundamental problem and are the source of a good deal of the political instability that currently afflicts the continent.

As was indicated before, the OAU Charter did not provide for any body specifically designed to deal with human rights questions within member states. The principal organs of the organization as set out in the Charter are the Assembly of Heads of State and Government, the Council of Ministers, the General Secretariat, the Specialized Commissions, the Commission of Conciliation, Mediation and Arbitration,⁷ and the Coordinating Committee for the Liberation of Africa (the Liberation Committee). The principal Specialized Commissions that were specifically mentioned in the Charter are the Economic and Social Commission, the Educational and Cultural Commission, the Health, Sanitation and Nutrition Commission, the Defense Commission, and the Scientific, Technical and Research Commission.

A development which might have been used to create a human rights protection mechanism within the framework of the organization was the addition of the Commission of African Jurists to the Specialized Commissions at the OAU Summit Conference in Cairo, Egypt, in 1964. This Commission had developed out of two meetings of African jurists held in August 1963 and January 1964 in Lagos, Nigeria. According to Article 1 of the Commission's statute, its purposes were: to promote and develop understanding among African jurists; to promote in Africa the development of the concept of justice; to consider legal problems of common interest and those which may be referred to it by any member of the OAU, and to make recommendations thereon; to encourage the study of African law, especially African customary law; and to consider and study international law in its relation to the problems of African states.

The Commission of Jurists did not last long. When the OAU approved the reorganization and reduction of the Specialized Commissions in 1968, the Commission of Jurists was simply dropped as an

OAU organ. The Organization later set up its own legal commission but it did not have the protection of human rights as part of its mandate. As for the Commission of Mediation, Conciliation and Arbitration, even before its abolition it was restricted to interstate conflicts.[8]

Thus, until 1981, the OAU had neither any Charter provision nor any constituted body to deal with charges of human rights violations within member states. This shortcoming was compounded by the principle of non-interference in the internal affairs of member states, a principle which was constantly used as a shield by violators of human rights.

THE OAU AND THE PRINCIPLE OF NON-INTERFERENCE: THEORY AND PRACTICE

The principle of non-interference has been used to prevent the OAU from dealing with charges of human rights violations in member states. Yet is has not always prevented the organization from getting involved in what were essentially domestic matters in those cases where extreme political conflict has threatened to or has resulted in foreign (usually extra-regional) intervention, or has threatened regional stability.[9]

The most notable OAU attempts to settle what were essentially domestic conflicts include the "Congo Crisis" in 1964–65, the Nigerian Civil War (1967–70), the Angolan Civil War (1975–76) and the recent Chad conflict. The OAU record in this respect, however, has not been outstanding. All four conflicts were terminated only with the military victory of one of the protagonists.[10]

Attempts have been made from time to time to involve the OAU in domestic conflicts on humanitarian grounds even when the threat of extra-regional intervention and regional instability was limited. Although these efforts have generally been unsuccessful, they have nevertheless pointed to the fact that if the protection of human rights in the African region is to be dealt with in a systematic manner, the OAU is the natural organ for this.

Soon after the foundation of the OAU in December 1963, Burundi protested to the organization about the widespread killing of the Tutsi ethnic minority in neighboring Rwanda. The killings followed attacks by exiled armed groups (the "Inyenzi") who were attempting to restore monarchical and Tutsi rule.

Nearly ten years later, in 1972, it was the turn of Rwandese leaders to protest the massacre of Hutus in Burundi following an abortive uprising in May in which up to 80,000 Hutus were systematically killed by government forces. At the June meeting of the OAU Council of Ministers in Rabat, Morocco, Rwanda raised the issue, prompting a reply from the Burundi delegation. In October, Rwanda raised the Burundi massacre outside the OAU, using the United Nations General Assembly to do so. In his address to the Assembly, the Rwandese Foreign Minister, Augustin Munyaneza, declared of his country's policy that "just as it condemns *apartheid* . . . [it] has equally no fear in denouncing racism wherever it is practiced, even if it is exercised by blacks over other blacks, as is being done in that country of black Africa where an ethnic minority is in the proces of exterminating, in the name of racism, another ethnic group which is nonetheless in the majority." He caustically suggested that it would be desirable if international jurists could succeed in defining what were the domestic affairs of another country so as not to encourage indifference by some parties to situations that violated the right to life of all human beings. He added: "The case of Burundi, where more than 200,000 innocent victims have just been massacred, and the cases of the Middle East and of South Africa would serve as examples to be used in such a study."[11] Munyaneza's address was followed by a sharp response by the Burundi delegation which, in part, attempted to lay the blame for the violence on the Rwandese authorities. The Burundi Minister of Foreign Affairs also chided Rwanda for not having confined raising the matter to the African arena, and for "interference' in Burundi's internal affairs.[12]

In the course of the 1973 OAU Summit Conference in Addis Ababa, Ethiopia, Milton Obote, then in exile in Tanzania, circulated a letter to all African leaders in which he accused Idi Amin of committing atrocities in Uganda. However, the OAU did not take any action on the letter.[13]

The execution of some fifty-seven former officials of the Ethiopian imperial regime and three members of the new Provisional Military Administrative Council (PMAC), including its Chairman, General Aman Andom, in the wake of the deposing and arrest of Emperor Haile Selassie in 1974, sent shock waves throughout Africa. Given the central role that the Emperor had played in African affairs and particularly in the foundation of the OAU, it is not surprising that there was widespread African concern for his physical safety. Following reports of impending further executions, including that of the deposed Emperor, the African Group at the United Nations made a public appeal to the new Ethiopian authorities to spare his life and those of the other detainees. In a statement to the General Assembly, Salim Ahmed Salim, Tanzania's Chief Delegate and Chairman of the African Group, pointed out that the action was being taken "in conformity with our collective concern for human life and fundamental freedom" and emphasized that "we have no desire to intervene in the domestic affairs of that brother state."[14]

The decision of the OAU to hold the 1975 Summit Conference in Kampala, Uganda, gave rise to strong protests by Tanzania, Mozambique, Zambia, and Botswana, which pointed to the atrocities which had been and were continuing to be committed by the Amin regime. The OAU held to its decision but just before the opening of the conference, the Tanzanian government put out a strong statement explaining its stand. The thrust of the Tanzanian argument was that it was wrong for African states to condemn human rights violations in Southern Africa and yet remain silent about abuses within member states of the OAU. This was in effect a strong plea for the OAU to get involved in problems of human rights violations within member states.[15]

In response to the OAU's decision to go ahead with the Kampala meeting, Tanzania, Zambia, and Botswana boycotted the conference. Mozambique participated, but its delegation was led by low-ranking officials rather than by President Samora Machel.[16] However, some twenty heads of state and government turned up in Kampala.

There have been occasional (and usually abortive) attempts to challenge within OAU forums the legitimacy of governments which have come to power through violence. The issue was first raised in connection with the assassination of President Sylvanus Olympio of Togo by mutinous troops in January 1963. The Ghanaian government was blamed for the assassination by a number of African leaders who were opposed to President Kwame Nkrumah's policies. As a result of their opposition, Togo was not represented at the founding conference of the OAU in May. Such was the strength of feelings generated by Olympio's assassination that the "unreserved condemnation, in all its forms, of political assassination as well as of subversive activities on the part of neighboring States or any other State" was inserted as one of the principles of the OAU, in Article 3 (v).

The overthrow of President Nkrumah by the Ghanaian military in 1966 led to determined attempts to deny the successor regime legitimacy within the OAU. The issue was raised during the Sixth Session of the Council of Ministers in Addis Ababa in March. So many delegations withdrew in protest at the presence of the delegation representing the new military regime that the meeting came to a hasty conclusion.

A similar crisis arose following the overthrow of the government of President Milton Obote in Uganda in January 1971. The Sixteenth Session of the Council of Ministers which met in Addis Ababa in February was forced into a difficult situation when the deposed President sent a delegation to challenge that of the military government.

Rather than choose between the two delegations, each of which had its strong backers, the meeting decided to avoid the issue by adjourning *sine die*.[17]

Following the May 1978 overthrow of the regime of the Comoros' President Ali Soilih (who was killed shortly afterwards) by a force of fifty mercenaries led by Gilbert Bourgeaud (usually known by his alias, Bob Denard), the Comorian delegation representing the successor regime was expelled from the OAU Council of Ministers meeting which preceded the 1978 Summit Conference in Khartoum, Sudan. The African leaders were disturbed by the role that the mercenaries had played in the coup and in the consolidation of the new regime. Denard, a notorious mercenary and veteran of several African conflicts, had been made commander of the Comoros' armed forces and police and a member of the interim governing directorate (he had taken the indigenous-sounding name of Moustapha Hamoudjou). To make matters worse, he had turned up in Khartoum as part of the Comorian delegation—the ultimate insult to African leaders.[18] The Comorian leaders were later persuaded to expel the mercenaries and the country was able to participate in the OAU.

The most recent occasion when a violent change of regime gave rise to serious questions concerning the legitimacy of the successor regime was the aftermath of the assassination of President William Tolbert of Liberia in April 1980. This time, the issue of legitimacy arose in an even more complicated way, since Tolbert was Chairman of the OAU when he was assassinated. In addition, the actions of the successor regime soon after the coup were extremely harsh.

Ten days after the coup, thirteen former ministers and high-ranking officials in the deposed regime were publicly executed by firing squad. This action prompted the OAU Council of Ministers, which was meeting in Lagos, to appeal to the new Liberian leader, Master Sergeant Samuel Doe, to restrain such excesses. The message sent by the ministers affirmed "the right of any member state to change its government in any way it sees fit" and recognized this right as regards Liberia. However, the ministers appealed to Liberia's new leaders to exercise restraint "on purely humanitarian grounds and [in] respect for the principles of human rights" in dealing with officials of the former government still in detention.[19]

The OAU was forced to confront the issue of succession to power in Liberia because the Organization had scheduled an Extraordinary Summit Conference in Lagos on the economic problems of Africa over which, as current Chairman of the OAU, Tolbert had been expected to preside. He was assassinated less than two weeks before the conference opened. The question arose whether Master Sergeant Doe would "inherit" the chairmanship of the OAU and preside over the meeting.

In any event, it was made clear to the new Liberian leader that he would not be welcome in Lagos. Nigeria, with the apparent approval of most other states, went further, preventing the plane carrying the Liberian delegation—headed by the Foreign Minister—from landing in Lagos. A special committee of eight states then chose President Leopold Senghor of Senegal (who was one of the five vice-chairmen of the organization) to preside over the meeting.

Following the normalizing of relations with its neighboring states, the new regime was subsequently able to participate in OAU activities, including the Seventeenth Summit Conference in Freetown, Sierra Leone, held in July 1980 under the interim chairmanship of President Senghor. However, the Liberian delegation was led by the Foreign Minister, rather than Master Sergeant Doe, who stayed away. He attended his first OAU Summit in Nairobi in 1981.

The crises in the OAU following the overthrow of the Nkrumah and Obote regimes were due essentially to partisan political factors. Opposition to the successor regimes came from governments which had been friendly with the deposed leaders or which disliked the ideological coloration of the successor regimes. No issues of human rights or humanitarian concern were involved. However, the assassination of Presidents Olympio and Tolbert raised the problem of murder as a tool of acquiring political power. To the extent that this was a major factor in the opposition of other OAU states to the successor regimes in Togo and Liberia, the possibility of OAU intervention in domestic affairs on human rights grounds was suggested.

The case of the Comoros raised a different issue. The leading role of mercenaries in the overthrow of Soilih challenged the very basis of the OAU as an organization dedicated to the promotion and protection of African independence. Mercenary activities have come to be seen as one of those factors that threaten African stability and independence. The fact that Soilih had been killed—in an act of apparently deliberate murder—was probably less significant than the suggestion of an arrogant colonial-style intrusion into African affairs.

Whatever the exact circumstances, even prior to 1981 the OAU had intervened or been called upon to intervene in its states' domestic affairs, despite the principle of non-interference. The possibility of intervention on human rights grounds implied by adherence to the African Charter on Human and Peoples' Rights was therefore not entirely without precedent.

THE OAU AND THE PROBLEM OF REFUGEES

Although not entirely absent from concern for regional stability, humanitarian considerations have been more clearly apparent in the attitude of the OAU with regard to the position of refugees than in its attitude towards other African problems.[20] The question of refugees has confronted the organization since its inception.

In the early 1960s, thousands of Tutsi refugees fleeing the sporadic warfare that had followed the revolution in Rwanda entered the neighboring states of Uganda, Zaire, Burundi, and Tanzania. They created problems of security, relief, and provision of shelter. Soon after the foundation of the OAU, the host states asked the organization to do something about the problem.

The Council of Ministers which met in February 1964 in Lagos set up a ten-nation ad hoc commission to deal with the matter. It was asked to examine the refugee problem in Africa and make recommendations about solutions, and to find ways and means of maintaining refugees in the countries of asylum. The commission was later requested to draw up a draft convention on all aspects of the problem of refugees in Africa. A decision was also made to set up a Refugee Bureau in the OAU Secretariat.

The United Nations High Commissioner for Refugees (UNHCR), the Dag Hammarskjold Foundation, and the OAU convened an international conference on the legal, economic, and social aspects of African refugees in Addis Ababa in October 1967. Shortly after in 1968, the OAU set up a bureau for the placement and education of refugees. This body was intended to be a kind of clearing house to advise refugees on possibilities of training and education and later help recruit professional cadres from among them. The bureau was integrated into the General Secretariat in June 1974.

The efforts of the OAU to deal with the problem of refugees took an important step forward when the OAU Convention Governing the Specific Aspects of Refugee Problems in Africa was signed on September 6, 1969. It came into force on June 20, 1974. In addition, the 1976 OAU Summit Conference, which met in Port Louis, Mauritius, passed a resolution requesting member states to provide more employment and educational opportunities for refugees. It also called on all states concerned to declare a general amnesty which would enable many of the refugees to return to their countries of origin.[21]

Since 1976, the number of refugees has continued to grow. The continuing conflicts in the Horn of Africa, Chad, Uganda, and the western Sahara have created acute crisis in the neighboring states. Although it has only 10 percent of the world's population, Africa now has nearly half—an estimated four to six million—of the world's refugees. The plight of these refugees is among the worst, due to their sheer numbers and the poverty-stricken conditions in which they live.[22]

In response to the continuing refugee crisis, the United Nations High Commissioner for Refugees and other UN agencies, in collaboration with the OAU, organized the International Conference on Assistance to Refugees in Africa (ICARA) in Geneva in April 1981. The objective of the conference was to mobilize resources for refugee projects in Africa and to raise international awareness of the plight of African refugees. The ninety-nine countries which participated in the conference pledged a total of $560 million to support refugee programs.

By the end of the 1970s, African leaders had come to accept the OAU as the natural agency to deal with political, humanitarian, and other issues on the continent. We now turn to one of the extra-African influences mentioned above, that is, the role of the United Nations in encouraging formation of regional human rights commissions in different parts of the world.

UNITED NATIONS ENCOURAGEMENT FOR CREATING REGIONAL HUMAN RIGHTS MECHANISMS

Since the mid-1960s, the United Nations has encouraged the creation of regional human rights commissions in those areas where they did not exist.[23] These efforts have resulted in the organization of human rights conferences in Africa and have kept the subject alive in the minds of the leaders, intellectuals, legal practitioners, and other people of Africa.

The OAU was not directly involved in the efforts of the United Nations to encourage creation of regional human rights commissions. However, Nigeria, a prominent member of the OAU, did play a leading role.

During the twenty-third Session of the United Nations Commission on Human Rights in March 1967, the Nigerian delegation introduced a resolution—co-sponsored by the Congo (Zaire), Dahomey (Benin), the Philippines, Senegal, and Tanzania—asking the United Nations to consider establishing regional human rights commissions for regions lacking them, i.e., everywhere except Western Europe and the Americas. Following the adoption of this proposal, the Commission set up an Ad Hoc Study Group of eleven members to look into the possibilities. The Group was composed of representatives of Chile, the Congo, Iraq, Jamaica, Nigeria, the Philippines, Poland, Sweden, the United Arab Republic (Egypt), the USSR, and the United States.

In the course of its work, the Study Group received documents from the Council of Europe and the Organization of American States (OAS), but none from the OAU or other intergovernmental organizations. In its report, the Study Group made no recommendations, but expressed general agreement that the initiative for setting up regional human rights commissions should be taken by states in these regions, rather than by the United Nations or some other external organization.

The report was considered at the twenty-fourth Session of the Commission, which adopted a Nigerian resolution (cosponsored by Austria) requesting the Secretary-General of the United Nations to transmit the report to member states and regional intergovernmental organizations. He was also asked to consider the possibility of arranging suitable regional seminars under the program of advisory services in the field of human rights. The Commission requested comments on the Study Group's report from governments and regional intergovernmental organizations. Comments were received from twenty-nine states and three regional organizations, but the OAU was not one of them.

As part of the activities organized in observance of the twentieth anniversary of the Universal Declaration of Human Rights in 1968, the United Nations convened an international conference on human rights in Teheran. Governments of eighty-four states, UN specialized agencies, the Council of Europe, the League of Arab States, as well as the OAU were represented at the conference. All regional organizations except the OAU presented reports about their activities. Once again, at this conference, Nigeria pushed its proposal for the establishment of regional commissions on human rights. However, the working group established to consider the proposal was unable to complete its work before the end of the conference.

Since 1968, two United Nations seminars have been organized in Africa on the specific question of the desirability and prospects for the establishment of an African human rights commission. The first was held in Cairo in September 1969. It was attended by representatives of nineteen African states. Among their conclusions, the participants requested the UN Secretary-General to communicate the report of the seminar to the OAU Secretary-General and the governments of OAU member states so that the organization might consider appropriate steps, including the convening of a preparatory committee representative of the OAU membership, with a view to establishing a regional commission on human rights for Africa. In addition, the seminar called on all governments of member states of the OAU to cooperate in establishing such a commission.[24]

In the ten-year period following the Cairo Seminar, a number of other meetings were held in various African states under the aegis of the United Nations on different aspects of human rights. (A list of these sessions appears in Appendix III) At many of these meetings, the desirability of establishing an African human rights commission or some similar body was expressed.[25] The second UN seminar devoted to the question of establishing an African regional human rights commission was convened in Monrovia, Liberia, in September 1979. It was attended by participants from thirty African states.

By the time this seminar met, the OAU Summit Conference held in Monrovia in July had passed a resolution authorizing the Secretary-General of the OAU to set in motion the process that would culminate in the creation of an African human rights program. The UN seminar therefore decided to take advantage of the momentum generated by this OAU resolution to help in the search for a structure for the proposed mechanism. The participants set up a working group to draft concrete proposals for the structure and mandate of an African human rights commission. These proposals were intended to aid the work of the OAU committee of experts called for by the resolution of the OAU Summit Conference.

In its conclusions, the seminar decided that it would be desirable to establish an African Commission on Human Rights as soon as possible. It therefore requested the Secretary-General of the United Nations to transmit the seminar's proposals to the OAU as a possible model for the proposed commission. In addition, the seminar decided that its chairman (the Liberian Minister of Justice), in collaboration with the representative of the United Nations, should inform the Chairman of the OAU (President Tolbert of Liberia) about the results of the seminar and the proposals for the African commission. Finally, the seminar suggested to the OAU that it discuss with non-governmental organizations ways they could cooperate with the proposed African Commission on Human Rights in the promotion and protection of human rights.[26] Several African human rights experts who attended the Monrovia Seminar were later to participate in the work of the OAU committee of experts which produced the initial draft of the African Charter on Human and Peoples' Rights.

Between the 1969 and 1979 seminars, increased international attention to the subject of human rights violations had been reflected in international political developments, the media, and academic circles. This was yet another extra-regional influence on the attitude of the OAU.

HUMAN RIGHTS IN INTERNATIONAL POLITICS

Partly because of the central role that United States President Jimmy Carter gave to the subject of human rights in his foreign policy and in his public rhetoric, human rights became a prominent subject in international politics in the last half of the 1970s. Politicians, journalists, academics, and others in various parts of the world paid greater attention to the problem of human rights violations.

Among the events which increased the salience of human rights in international politics was the signature of the Final Act of the Conference on Security and Cooperation in Europe, which was convened in Helsinki, Finland, in 1975. This agreement was signed by heads of state or government of thirty-three European states (all of them but Albania), as well as the United States and Canada.

The Helsinki Final Act contains two sets of provisions pertaining to human rights: Principles 7 and 8 of the "Declaration of Principles Guiding Relations between Participating States" and the section entitled "Cooperation in Humanitarian and Other Fields" which has come to be known as "Basket III." Principle 7 stipulates respect for human rights and fundamental freedoms, including freedom of thought, conscience, and religion or belief. Principle 8 calls for equality of rights and the self-determination of peoples.

Under Basket III, the participating states pledged to facilitate freer movement and contacts among persons, institutions, and organizations of the participating states, and to contribute to the solution of the humanitarian problems that arise in that connection.[27]

Human rights is merely one of the subjects dealt with in the Final Act. The document also sets out measures designed to promote greater security, and economic, cultural, and other forms of cooperation between the West and the East. However, in Western countries, particularly the United States, greater significance has been attributed to the human rights provisions of the Final Act.[28]

Since 1975, Helsinki Watch Committees have been formed in a number of countries to monitor the performance of the obligations arising out of the Final Act. Together with the Review Conference, their activities have kept the subject of human rights on the agenda of international politics.[29]

Conflicts in Southeast Asia in the 1970s also contributed to heightened international sensitivity to human rights violations. In Kampuchea, the Pol Pot regime engaged in a campaign of brutalization and murder on a scale which had rarely been seen since the Nazi atrocities. In Vietnam, the flight of thousands of people, often on fragile craft—thus creating the "Boat People"—stirred international public opinion and also focused attention to human rights.

Finally, the activities of Amnesty International, the International Commission of Jurists, and other international non-governmental bodies influenced the global climate for human rights in the late 1970s. Amnesty International's receiving the Nobel Peace Prize stands out as a key event in enhancing awareness of its activities. Publications on curtailment of human rights were given increased attention in the world press. Coupled with the Helsinki accords and the proclamations of President Carter, the work of international non-governmental organizations moved abridgement of liberties to the forefront of attention.

All these events undoubtedly had an impact in Africa. However, the final catalyst in the changing attitude of the OAU towards the subject of human rights were developments within Africa in the 1978-79 period.

THE OAU AND THE PROBLEM OF HUMAN RIGHTS IN THE CENTRAL AFRICAN EMPIRE, EQUATORIAL GUINEA, AND UGANDA

Large-scale killings of political opponents, suspected opponents, and other types of people by the regimes of Idi Amin in Uganda (1971-79) and Macias Nguema in Equatorial Guinea (1968-79), and the killings of high school students in the Central African Empire in the last year of the regime of Jean-Bedel Bokassa (1966-79) were almost certainly the most important factors in the final decision of the OAU to move toward creating a human rights protection mechanism for Africa. The transgressions of these three regimes caused revulsion in and outside Africa, and threatened to damage the image and reputation of the OAU. The organization was put in a particularly embarrassing position when Idi Amin became Chairman following the meeting of the 1975 Summit Conference in Kampala.[30]

Amin combined brutal methods of government in Uganda with a flamboyant and provocative style in international affairs.[31] His violent criticism of "zionism" and Israel during his address to the UN General Assembly in 1975 prompted Daniel Patrick Moynihan, the United States Chief Delegate, to lambast him and the OAU, claiming: "It is no accident, I fear, that this racist murderer . . . is the head of the Organization of African Unity. For Israel is a democracy and it is simply a fact that despotisms will seek whatever opportunities come to hand to destroy that which threatens them the most, which is democracy . . . ."[32]

Human rights violations in Uganda were discussed at the 1977 Commonwealth Annual Conference which assembled in London. The British government had made it clear that it would not welcome Idi Amin; despite last-minute posturing, he stayed away and Uganda was not represented. In the final communique, the conference declared:

> Cognizant of the accumulated evidence of sustained disregard
> for the sanctity of human life and of massive violation
> of basic human rights in Uganda, it was the overwhelming
> view of Commonwealth leaders that these excesses were so
> gross as to warrant the world's concern and to evoke condem-
> nation by Heads of Government in strong and unequivocal
> terms. Mindful that the people of Uganda were within the
> fraternity of Commonwealth fellowship, Heads of Government
> looked to the day when the people of Uganda would once
> more fully enjoy their basic human rights which now were be-
> ing so cruelly denied.[33]

As pointed out in the chapter below by Ronald Meltzer, Amin's dismal human rights record was in part responsible for the abortive attempt by the European Economic Community's negotiators to incorporate human rights provisions in the renewed trade and aid agreement with countries of Africa, the Caribbean, and the Pacific—the EEC-ACP Lomé II Convention—signed in October 1979.[34]

Self-styled Emperor Bokassa of the Central African Empire combined harsh repression of political opposition with bizarre and megalomaniacal extravagance. In July 1972, he published a decree designed in his own fashion to combat theft. It provided for the amputation of an ear for first offenders; the second ear for a second theft; amputation of the right arm for a third theft; and public execution for further recidivism. Shortly afterwards, Bokassa personally led a group of soldiers in beating up in a Bangui prison forty-six men convicted of theft. A number of them succumbed to the beatings, and the next day the mutilated bodies of the dead and the wounded were publicly displayed in the capital's largest square.[35]

Bokassa's regime provoked an international outcry when, in January 1979, some 400 people, including scores of high school students, were killed while demonstrating against the regime. The outrage was investigated by a Commission of Jurists which was set up by the Sixth Franco-African Summit Meeting which assembled in Kigali, Rwanda, in May. The Commission was made up of representatives of the Ivory Coast, Liberia, Rwanda, Senegal (chair), and Togo. The Commission's report, published in August, concluded that Bokassa had ordered the killings and "almost certainly" took part in them himself.[36]

In contrast to Amin and Bokassa, Macias Nguema of Equatorial Guinea shunned publicity and, throughout his eleven years in power, rarely ventured outside the country. Nevertheless, Macias presided over one of the most brutal regimes that Africa has seen. Large numbers of Equatorial Guineans were killed or driven into exile. Nor were foreigners spared: Nigerian immigrant workers were subjected to harsh treatment, including killings; when they fled the country, he dragooned the local population into virtual slavery to keep the cocoa industry—the country's economic mainstay—from collapsing.[37]

Until 1979, in spite of the international outcry, the OAU had not formally taken up the problem of human rights violations in the Central African Empire, Equatorial Guinea, or Uganda. However, the successful invasion of Uganda by Tanzanian troops and armed Ugandan exiles which led to the downfall of Idi Amin was to ensure discussion of the subject at the 1979 Summit Conference in Monrovia, Liberia.

THE IMPACT OF THE TANZANIAN INVASION OF UGANDA (1978–79)

The successful invasion of Uganda by Tanzanian troops and substantial numbers of armed Ugandan exiles was triggered by incursions into Tanzanian territory by Ugandan troops towards the end of 1978. Once they had overwhelmed the small and lightly armed Tanzanian units, Ugandan soldiers proceeded to engage in a brutal orgy of murder, looting, and wanton destruction of property. To add insult to injury, Amin formally declared that he had annexed the piece of territory that his troops had occupied and vandalized (the Kagera Salient).

The Tanzanian reaction to these outrages was determined by at least two principal factors: the fact that President Nyerere had always refused to accept the political legitimacy of the Amin regime, and his belief that the Amin regime posed a permanent threat to stability in the East African region.

From the time of the coup of January 25, 1971, which catapulted Amin into power in Uganda, President Nyerere had refused to accept the legitimacy of the new regime. He had developed a close political relationship with deposed Uganda President Milton Obote, and allowed him to settle in Tanzania where he received presidential treatment.

In the months following the 1971 coup, there were sporadic clashes between the Ugandan and Tanzanian troops on the two countries' common border. At the end of 1972, armed supporters of Obote attempted an invasion from Tanzania and succeeded in capturing an important military barracks in the south-west of Uganda before they were crushed with heavy losses. From that time onwards, Amin regarded Nyerere as a deadly enemy and took every opportunity to insult and humiliate him.

Idi Amin's threats were not confined to Tanzania. He laid claim to as much as a third of Kenya territory in 1975 but he immediately and meekly abandoned these claims when the Kenya government took a vigorous stand and halted shipments of fuel through its territory to Uganda. On several occasions, Amin threatened to invade Rwanda. Thus, when Ugandan troops invaded Tanzania, Nyerere took the opportunity to solve the "Amin problem" once and for all.

President Nyerere reacted to Amin's provocations through two basic strategies, one military and the other political. On the military side, the Tanzanian government assembled up to fifty thousand heavily armed troops which successfully threw Ugandan troops out of Tanzanian territory and pushed into Uganda. At the same time, President Nyerere encouraged the fragmented Ugandan exile opposition to unite and gave them facilities to make preparations to supplant the Amin regime.

The meeting of Ugandan political exiles in the Tanzanian town of Moshi at the beginning of 1979 (a meeting which was disguised not at all) was unprecedented in the history of inter-African relations. Here was a member state of the OAU hosting a meeting of a group plotting the overthrow of the government of another member state—a direct violation of Article 3 (ii) of the OAU Charter.

In the course of the conflict between Tanzanian and Ugandan troops, President Numeiry of Sudan (the then Chairman of the OAU), General Obasanjo of Nigeria, and President Tolbert of Liberia tried without success to mediate and bring an end to the war. President Nyerere insisted that the OAU had to condemn Amin for aggression before he could consider any peace proposals, a demand which the organization refused to meet. President Numeiry pointed out that the OAU was not in the business of condemning member states.

By the time the Sixteenth Annual Summit Conference assembled in Monrovia in July 1979, a number of events had occurred in Uganda. The Amin regime had collapsed in April under Tanzanian pressure, Amin had fled, and the political exiles had formed a new government. In June, Yusuf Lule had been replaced as head of the new government by Godfrey Binaisa, who benefitted from strong Tanzanian support.

The overthrow of the Amin regime gave rise to a heated debate at the 1979 OAU Summit Conference, with the heads of state who had attempted to mediate being especially critical. President Numeiry led the attack on President Nyerere, accusing him of having violated the principle of non-interference and respect for the territorial integrity of other member states. Numeiry was supported by General Obasanjo who condemned the precedent that would be set by the Tanzanian actions. President Tolbert, the host, was also critical. President Nyerere was vigorously defended by Ugandan President Godfrey Binaisa who not only dwelt on Idi Amin's atrocities but, going against OAU practice, launched a strong attack on the regimes of Bokassa and Macias (both of whom were overthrown later in the year) for their human rights violations.

Tanzania based its case on the right of self-defense. This, however, was not very firm ground, since Tanzanian troops had gone all the way to the Ugandan capital, overthrown the Amin regime, and fanned out all over the country mopping up resistance. It is significant that Tanzania did not attempt to strengthen its case by adding the argument of humanitarian intervention. A number of factors can be suggested for this omission. One is the ambiguity connected in theory and practice with the concept of humanitarian intervention.[38] Another problem stemmed from the fact that the defense of humanitarian intervention would have implied that Tanzania was willing to subject her own human rights record to international scrutiny. Considering that the Tanzanian political regime is fairly authoritarian, this is not a risk the leadership was willing to take. It will also be recalled that President Nyerere was embarrassed when in 1968 he recognized what turned out to be the ephemeral "Republic of Biafra" on essentially humanitarian grounds. In general, humanitarian intervention was not an argument which African leaders were likely to accept.

President Sekou Touré of Guinea—who has one of the worst human rights records in Africa—pointed to a major deficiency in the structure of the organization when he reportedly told the conference that the OAU was not "a tribunal which could sit in judgment on any member state's internal affairs."[39] It was against this background that the conference decided that the OAU should establish a mechanism for dealing with the subject of human rights. The resolution of the OAU conference on human rights called upon its Secretary-General to organize "as soon as possible in an African capital, a restricted meeting of highly qualified experts to prepare a preliminary draft of an 'African Charter on Human and Peoples' Rights' providing, *inter alia*, for the establishment of bodies to promote and protect human rights."[40]

To an important degree, the resolution can be seen as having been a means to end the controversy provoked by the violent changes in Uganda in the 1978–79 period. It could also be seen as having been an attempt to forestall similar controversies in the future and at the same time redeem the image of the OAU by indicating that it was not indifferent to human rights violations within member states.[41]

Between the 1979 and the 1981 Summit Conferences, the OAU organized three meetings to draft the proposed human rights charter. The first meeting, held in Dakar, Senegal, in 1979, brought together African human rights experts who prepared the initial draft. The second meeting, comprised of African Ministers of Justice and other legal experts met in Banjul, The Gambia, 8–15 June 1980 in order to continue and complete consideration of the draft charter.

The Council of Ministers of the OAU meeting in its Thirty-Fifth Ordinary Session in Freetown, Sierra Leone, 18–28 June 1980, requested that the Ministerial Conference reconvene in Banjul for the purpose of completing the Charter. Accordingly, a second OAU Ministerial Conference on the Draft Charter was convened in January 1981. Forty of the fifty member states of the OAU participated at the Conference, and consideration of the Draft Charter was completed on schedule. With its task completed, the Ministerial Conference passed the Charter to the OAU Council of Ministers for approval.

On June 10, 1981, Mr. Edem Kodjo, Secretary-General of the OAU, presented to the Plenary Session of the Council of Ministers the Report of the Secretary-General on the African Charter of Human and Peoples' Rights. Despite early doubts over the Charter's future, the Council of Ministers submitted the Draft Charter without amendments to the Assembly of Heads of State and Government for its consideration.

On June 17, 1981, the Eighteenth Assembly of Heads of State and Government convened to discuss the Charter. The Assembly took note of the Council of Ministers' recommendations and adopted the Charter with no amendments. As of June 1982, twelve countries (Zaire, Egypt, Gabon, Guinea, Mali, Mauritania, Rwanda, Senegal, Sierra Leone, Somalia, Tanzania, and Togo) had deposited instruments of ratification with the General Secretariat. The Charter will enter into force three months after the twenty-sixth state has deposited its instrument of ratification in Addis Ababa.

CONCLUSIONS

The decision of the 1981 OAU Summit Conference, to incorporate the promotion and protection of human rights among member states as one of the goals of the organization, marked an important stage in its history. One of the incidental consequences of this decision is the increased possibility of greater interregional political cooperation and integration in Africa.

The evolving attitude of the OAU on the subject of human rights has been influenced by several mutually reinforcing political factors.

Some of them have been limited to intra-African interstate relationships; others have emanated from the international arena.

From the point of view of intra-African politics, the gradual acceptance by African leaders of the central role of the OAU as the proper forum for dealing with African problems grew out of the need to deal with the atrocities in the Central African Empire, Equatorial Guinea, and Uganda, and with the Tanzanian invasion of Uganda and the subsequent overthrow of the regime of Idi Amin. These factors were therefore significant in the evolution of the attitude of African leaders toward the question of human rights in Africa.

There were also influences from the international political arena. Of these, the two most significant were the United Nations' encouraging creation of regional human rights commissions in the late 1960s and the 1970s, and the greater prominence given in the late 1970s to the subject of human rights protection, and the condemnation of violations everywhere.

Probably the most significant fact about the decision of the African leaders to adopt the African Charter is the implied recognition that the principle of non-interference in the internal affairs of member states can no longer provide a convincing defense for violators of human rights. This development should give hope to victims of arbitrary power and to advocates of human rights in the region.

NOTES

1. U.O. Umozurike, "The Domestic Jurisdiction Clause in the OAU Charter," *African Affairs* 78, no. 311 (April 1979), pp. 197–209.

2. V.B. Thompson, *Africa and Unity* (London: Longmans, Green, 1969); W. Scott Thompson and I. William Zartman, "The Development of Norms in the African System," in Yassin El-Ayouty, (ed.,) *The Organization of African Unity after Ten Years* (New York: Praeger, 1975) pp. 2–46; Jon Woronoff, *Organizing African Unity* (Metuchen, N.J.: Scarecrow Press, 1970).

3. Yashpal Tandon, "The Organization of African Unity: A Forum for African International Relations," *The Round Table*, no. 246 (April 1972), pp. 221–30; Tunde Adeniran, "Pacific Settlement among African States: The Role of the Organization of African Unity," *Conflict Quarterly* 2, no. 2 (Fall 1981); A. Bolaji Akinyemi, "Africa—Challenges and Responses: A Foreign Policy Perspective," *Daedalus* 3, no. 2 (Spring 1982), pp. 247–53.

4. Preamble, Charter of the Organization of African Unity.

5. Louis B. Sohn, "The Human Rights Law of the Charter," *Texas International Law Journal* 12, no. 2, 3 (Spring, Summer 1977), pp. 129–40.

6. Es'kia Mphahlele, "Africa in Exile," *Daedalus* 3, no. 2 (Spring 1982), pp. 29–48.

7. The Commission of Mediation, Conciliation and Arbitration was set up, but it never handled any of the many disputes with which the OAU has dealt. Instead, the organization has always had recourse to ad hoc commissions and

committees, usually composed of heads of state or government. The 1977 Summit Conference which assembled in Libreville, Gabon, decided to replace the Commission by a Standing Committee with a membership of seven states.

8. Osita C. Eze, "Background Paper," United Nations "Seminar on the Establishment of Regional Commissions on Human Rights with Special Reference to Africa, Monrovia, Liberia, 10-21 September 1979," UN Doc. HR/Liberia/1979BP/3; Woronoff, *Organizing African Unity.*

9. O. Okongwu, "The OAU Charter and the Principle of Domestic Jurisdiction in Intra-African Affairs," *Indian Journal of International Law* 13, no. 4 (1973), pp. 589-93; A.B. Akinyemi, "The Organization of African Unity and the Concept of Non-Interference in Internal Affairs of Member States," *British Yearbook of International Law, 1972/1973*; S. Azadan Tiewal, "Relations between the United Nations Organization and the Organization of African Unity in the Settlement of Secessionist Conflicts," *Harvard International Law Journal* 16, no. 2 (Spring 1975), pp. 259-302.

10. Zdenek Cervenka, *The Unfinished Quest for Unity, Africa and the OAU* (London: Friedmann and the Scandinavian Institute of African Studies, 1977), pp. 84-109, 140-48. The Angolan Civil War is not entirely over. Guerrilla resistance to the MPLA regime continues, particularly in the central and southern parts of the country.

11. UN Doc. A/PV.2054.

12. UN Doc. A/PV.2055.

13. Coming from a man who was then working for his return to power, Obote's appeal could have been challenged as being in part self-serving. In December 1980 he recaptured political power in Uganda.

14. UN Doc. A/PV.2301. Former Emperor Haile Selassie died in 1975 from what the Ethiopian authorities described as natural causes.

15. Colin Legum, ed., *Africa Contemporary Record, 1975-1976* (New York: Holmes and Meier, 1976), pp. C22-C24.

16. The 1975 Summit Conference provided Mozambique the first opportunity to participate as a new member of the OAU.

17. The new Foreign Minister of Uganda had threatened that Uganda would withdraw from the organization if his delegation was not seated.

18. Legum, *Africa Contemporary Record, 1978-1979* (New York: Africana Publishing, 1979), p. A31.

19. *Africa Research Bulletin (Political, Social and Cultural Series) 1980*, p. 5649A.

20. The development of the movement for international protection of human rights has been traced to humanitarian political intervention in the nineteenth century. See Evan Luard, "The Origins of International Concern over Human Rights," in Evan Luard, ed., *The International Protection of Human Rights* (New York: Praeger, 1967), pp. 7-21.

21. Cervenka, *The Unfinished Quest*, p. 74.

22. Ssalongo Ngoma, "Independent Africa Produces More Refugees," *African Christian* (Nairobi), October 26, 1981.

23. Commission to Study the Organization of Peace, *Regional Promotion and Protection of Human Rights* (New York: The Commission, 1980), pp. 31-45.

24. United Nations, "Seminar on the Establishment of Regional Commis-

sions on Human Rights with Special Refernce to Africa, Cairo, UAR, 2–15 September 1969,'' UN Doc. ST/TAO/HR/38.

25. The International Commission of Jurists organized several seminars in Africa at which the desirability of creating an African regional human rights commission was usually affirmed.

26. United Nations, ''Seminar on the Establishment of Regional Commissions on Human Rights with Special Reference to Africa, Monrovia, Liberia 10–21 September 1979'', UN Doc. ST/HR/SER.A/4.

27. See text of ''Conference on Security and Cooperation in Europe: Final Act, Helsinki, 1975.''

28. Vojin Dimitrijevic, ''The Place of Helsinki in the Long Road to Human Rights,'' *Vanderbilt Journal of Transnational Law* 13, nos. 2–3 (Spring-Summer 1980).

29. Dante B. Fascell, ''The CSCE Follow-up Mechanism from Belgrade to Madrid,'' *Vanderbilt Journal of Transnational Law* 13, nos. 2–3 (Spring-Summer 1980).

30. The position of Chairman is not provided for in the OAU Charter. However, over the years, it has become traditional for the head of state or government of the country where the annual Summit Conference takes place to chair the meeting and thereafter act as chief political spokeman of the organization until the next Summit Conference. It is now also customary for the Chairman of the OAU to address the annual regular session of the United Nations General Assembly.

31. International Commission of Jurists, *Uganda and Human Rights* (Geneva: ICJ, 1977).

32. *Facts on File, 1975,* pp. 739D1–D3.

33. Legum, *Africa Contemporary Record, 1977–1978,* (New York: Africana Publishing, 1978) p. C48.

34. Amy Young–Anawaty, ''Human Rights and the ACP-EEC Lomé II Convention,'' *New York University Journal of International Law and Politics* 13, no. 1 (Spring 1980), pp. 63–98.

35. Legum, *Africa Contemporary Record, 1972–1973* (New York: Africana Publishing, 1973), p. B511.

36. *Africa Research Bulletin (Political, Social and Cultural Series) 1979,* p. 5373C.

37. Susan Cronjé, *Equatorial Guinea, the Forgotten Dictatorship* (London: Anti-Slavery Society, 1976).

38. Ibrahim J. Wani, ''Humanitarian Intervention and the Tanzania-Uganda War,'' *Horn of Africa* 3, 2 (n.d.).

39. *Africa Research Bulletin, (Political, Social and Cultural Series), 1979,* p. 5329B.

40. Text of Resolution in United Nations, ''Cooperation between the United Nations and the Organization of African Unity,'' UN Doc. A/34/552; Joseph Margolis, ''Dissension and Resolution,'' *Africa Report* 24, 5 (September-October 1979); pp. 52–55; *West Africa,* 30 July 1979, pp. 1355–57; *Africa Research Bulletin, (Political, Social and Cultural Series), 1979,* pp. 5328A-30B.

41. Warren Weinstein, "Africa's Approach to Human Rights at the United Nations," *Issue* 6, no. 4 (Winter 1976), pp. 14–21; and "Human Rights in Africa: A Long-Awaited Voice," *Current History* 78, no. 455 (March 1980), pp. 97–101, 130–32.

CHAPTER SEVEN

The Banjul Charter on Human and Peoples' Rights: A Legal Analysis

RICHARD GITTLEMAN

The Eighteenth Assembly of Heads of State and Government of the Organization of African Unity (OAU) meeting in Nairobi, Kenya, June 24–28, 1981, took a historic step toward the protection of human rights in Africa when it adopted the Banjul Charter on Human and Peoples' Rights.[1] The Charter represents the culmination of a two-year drafting process.[2]

The stated objective of the drafters was to prepare an African Charter on human rights that was based upon African legal philosophy and responsive to African needs.[3] To the legal experts assembled in 1979 at Dakar, Senegal, to prepare the first draft of the proposed African Charter, problems unique to Africa justified their departure from the models created by the European Convention for the Protection of Human Rights and Fundamental Freedoms (European Convention)[4] and the American Convention on Human Rights (American Convention).[5] In addition, the experts rejected the charter format proposed at the United Nations–sponsored Monrovia Seminar on the Establishment of Regional Commissions on Human Rights with Specific Reference to Africa, held earlier in the same year. The proposals of that Seminar simply set out applicable standards as embodied in other international covenants and declarations, whereas the Banjul Charter, as it finally emerged, catalogued specific rights to be protected.[6]

The purpose of this chapter is to analyze some of the more salient legal issues presented by the Banjul Charter, with particular attention to the binding nature of the document, "clawback" clauses, questions surrounding permissible state derogation from the Charter, and the proposed African Commission on Human and Peoples' Rights.

ANALYSIS OF THE CHARTER

The African Charter is divided into three parts. Part I sets out rights and duties in two chapters. Chapter I sets out the rights to be protected under the Charter, while Chapter II sets out the individual's duties toward "his family and society, the State, and other legally recognized communities and the international community."[7] Part II of the Charter, composed of four Chapters, elaborates on the measures to safeguard the rights articulated in Part I. Chapter I calls for the establishment of the African Commission on Human and Peoples' Rights and lays out the structure of the Commission in detail. Chapter I concerns the functions of the Commission while Chapter III deals with the procedure of the Commission. The final chapter of Part II indicates the applicable principles by which the Commission will secure the protection of human rights in Africa. Finally, Part III establishes general provisions concerning the commencement of the African Commission on Human and Peoples' Rights.

Comparison of African Charter with Other International Instruments

The Preamble to the African Charter on Human and Peoples' Rights differs dramatically from the preambles to other regional conventions for the protection of human rights, and it merits close examination because it reflects the significant themes of the Charter. The intent of the framers was to create a charter inspired by African legal philosophy and responsive to African needs. The Preamble indicates that the Charter draws its inspiration from the Charter of the OAU, which stipulates that "freedom, equality, justice, and dignity are essential objectives for the achievement of the legitimate aspirations of the African peoples."[8] The Preamble reaffirms

> the pledge . . . made in Article 2 of the [OAU] Charter to eradicate all forms of colonialism from Africa, to coordinate and intensify . . . cooperation and efforts to achieve a better life for the peoples of Africa, and to promote international cooperation having due regard to the Charter of the United Nations and the Universal Declaration of Human Rights.[9]

In keeping with its peculiarly African inspiration, the Charter relies upon "historical tradition and the values of African civilization,"[10] and reminds member States of their duty to "eliminate colonialism, neocolonialism, apartheid, zionism, and to dismantle aggressive foreign military bases."[11]

Thus, one respect in which the Charter differs from the American and European Conventions is its reliance on principles primarily African in nature. Yet the distinct African nature of the principles recited in the Preamble do not alone indicate the extent to which the Banjul Charter stands apart from the European and American Conventions. The sixth clause of the Preamble illustrates that the Charter embodies a concept of duty different from that contained in the European and American Conventions. It provides that "the enjoyment of rights and freedoms also implies the performance of duties on the part of everyone."[12] In other regional human rights instruments, the concept of "duties" refers only to the obligation of a State toward its citizens or toward citizens of another State coming within its jurisdiction.[13] Occasionally, obscure references are made concerning the individual's responsibility to the community.[14] The African reference, as the Charter makes clear, imposes an obligation upon the individual not only toward other individuals but also toward the State of which he is a citizen.[15] The notion of individual responsibility to the community is firmly ingrained in African tradition and is therefore consistent with the historical traditions and values of African civilization upon which the Charter relied. The inclusion of this far-reaching clause has roots, however, in factors other than mere tradition and, to a large extent, explains the various tensions throughout the Charter.

The socialist States such as Mozambique and Ethiopia had a difficult time reconciling traditional human rights conventions with socialist philosophy. The notion of "individual" in a socialist State differs markedly from the notion in a capitalist State. As a result, to ensure the eventual adoption of the Charter by all States, the drafters in Dakar stated that if the individual is to have rights "recognized" by the State, he also must have obligations flowing back to the State. The drafters believed that references in extant international instruments to an individual's obligations were so vague as to be meaningless. For this reason, the African Charter attempts to rectify this concern by enumerating those obligations imposed upon the individual. In addition, the Preamble stresses the importance of economic, social and cultural rights:

> It is henceforth essential to pay a particular attention to the right to development and that civil and political rights cannot be dissociated from economic, social, and cultural rights in their conception as well as universality, and that the satisfaction of economic, social, and cultural rights is a guarantee for the enjoyment of civil and political rights.[16]

The African Commission is charged with the responsibility of interpreting this clause;[17] however, its language indicates the possibility that preference will be given to economic and social programs where they collide with civil and political rights. The extent to which this reading of the provision is correct will have to await practical application of the Commission.

In summation, the African Charter's preamble serves as a guide for the significant themes that run throughout the entire Charter. First, the African Charter relies heavily upon African documents and traditions rather than upon United Nations declarations and covenants. Second, while individuals enjoy certain rights under the Charter, they also are obligated to fulfill certain duties toward other individuals as well as toward the State of their citizenship. Finally, economic, social, and cultural development is a top priority. The extent to which the right to development supersedes civil and political rights is not clear, however, and must await future clarification. The following subsections will examine substantive provisions of the Charter that evidence these major principles embodied in the Preamble.

Legal Effect of the African Charter: Binding versus Non-Binding

An important aspect of a human rights document is its legal effect. While the Banjul Charter could be interpreted as a non-binding instrument, an argument could be made that it was nevertheless designed to be of a binding nature.

Member states of the OAU who are parties to the Banjul Charter have an obligation to "recognize the rights, duties and freedoms enshrined" in the African Charter and to "undertake to adopt legislative or other measures to give effect to them."[18] This language varies substantially from the American Convention and also from prior drafts of the present African Charter. According to Thomas Buergenthal, under Article 1 of the American Convention a state has the negative obligation "not to violate an individual's rights" and may also have the obligation to adopt "affirmative measures necessary and reasonable under the circumstances 'to ensure' the full enjoyment of the rights the American Convention guarantees."[19] It is not clear that the African Charter requires an equally strong obligation from member states. The earlier Dakar Draft required that states "shall recognize and shall *guarantee* the rights and freedoms stated in the present Convention [sic] and shall undertake to adopt, in accordance with the constitutional provisions, legislative and other measures to *ensure* their respect."[20] The elimination of the vital words "guarantee" and "ensure" from the final draft deprives the Charter of much of its force. This language was eliminated apparently to make the Charter more acceptable to those governments concerned about the effect of a human rights covenant upon national sovereignty.

The recognition of rights without a guarantee of their implementation could allow one to interpret the Charter as merely a set of rights to be promoted rather than protected.[21] This argument is contradicted, however, by the Article 1 clause that obligates member states to "undertake to adopt legislation or other measures to give effect to [the Charter]."[22] Unfortunately, the deletion of the express guarantee and obligation to ensure protection of rights may serve as evidence to support the proposition that the Charter is of a non-binding, i.e., non-protective nature.

Not all human rights systems, however, began with a legally binding charter or convention. The Inter-American human rights system, for example, began with the American Declaration of the Rights and Duties of Man adopted in 1948.[23] As a declaration, the document imposed no binding obligation upon states but merely constituted a "'promotional' . . . statement of goals for States to achieve progressively."[24]

Like the American Declaration in the Americas, the African Charter lays the foundation for a human rights system in Africa, and in this respect appears to be designed as a binding instrument. Not only does the Charter establish a duty on states to enact legislation to give effect to the Charter's provisions, but it also establishes a commission to oversee the protection of enumerated rights, implying that states are bound to respect these rights. To declare otherwise would ignore the function of the Commission to "ensure the *protection* of human and peoples' rights under conditions laid down by the present Charter."[25] This interpretation of the Charter as a binding document would have been even more persuasive had the original language of the Daker Draft been retained—language guaranteeing rights and ensuring their implementation at the state level.[26]

The Charter's Limitations of Granted Rights

Relevant International Instruments Protecting Individuals Against State Abuse   The existence of an international human rights regime protecting the individual against state abuse is no longer an aspiration but rather a "political fact." The cornerstone of this developing system is the Universal Declaration of Human Rights passed as a nonbinding UN General Assembly resolution in 1948. Since that time states have assented to a global venture to regulate state behavior with regard to individuals within a state's own territory. Their participation is manifested in the International Covenant on Civil and Political Rights and in the Optional Protocol[28] as well as in the European Convention, the American Convention, and the African Charter. Professor Louis Henkin points out that the foregoing instruments do not create rights but merely recognize rights already in existence "in some other moral or legal order."[29] By ratifying a human rights instrument, a state is recognizing the existence of these rights and, more important, is agreeing to incorporate this standard into its own domestic legal system.[30] After ratifying such an international instrument, a state is stopped from refusing to permit the international community to discuss alleged breaches of the instrument on the ground that such discussion violates the breaching State's sovereignty. Under the basic principle of *pacta sunt servanda*, a state is bound by its treaty obligations.[31] Where a treaty, as in the present case, imposes external constraints upon a state's actions toward persons within that government's territorial jurisdiction, a state may not avoid the treaty obligation, since it entered into a consensual agreement to permit such interference; therefore, any alleged violation of the treaty becomes an issue of international concern. This concept is fundamental to human rights in general and to the derogation question in particular.[32]

Derogation Clauses, Clawback Clauses, and the African Charter The African Charter contains no specific provision entitling a state to derogate from its obligations, i.e., to temporarily suspend a right guaranteed under the Charter. Many of the provisions, however, contain "clawback" clauses[33] that entitle a state to restrict the granted rights to the extent permitted by domestic law.[34] As the following discussion will demonstrate, such protection is substantively questionable.

Clawback clauses are not the same as derogation clauses[35]—and do not provide the individual the same degree of protection provided by derogation clauses contained in other covenants and conventions.[36] Derogation clauses restrict a state's conduct in two important ways. First, they limit the circumstances in which derogation may occur. For example, under the European Convention, derogation can occur only "in time of war or other public emergency threatening the life of the nation."[37] Second, derogation clauses define rights that are nonderogable and must be respected, even when derogation is permitted. The effect of derogation clauses, therefore, is to carefully define the limits of state behavior toward its nationals during times of national emergency—a time when states are most apt to violate human rights.[38]

While derogation clauses permit the suspension of previously granted rights, clawback clauses restrict rights *ab initio*. As a result, clawback clauses tend to be less precise than derogation clauses because the restrictions they permit are almost totally discretionary. The granted right may be restricted by local law or the existence of a national emergency—two very vague and limitlessly broad standards. By virtue of these vague standards, clawback clauses do not provide the external control over state behavior that derogation provisions provide. Evidence comes from examining the protection given the right to liberty.

Under Article 6 of the Charter, "every individual shall have the right to liberty and to the security of his person."[39] Furthermore, "no one may be arbitrarily arrested or detained." Yet the Charter qualifies these guarantees with a clawback clause: "No one may be deprived of his freedom except for reasons and conditions previously laid down by law."[40] The Charter contains, however, no definition of these reasons and conditions.

A comparison with the European and American Conventions demonstrates the deficiency of the African Charter provision. The American Convention closely parallels the African Charter;[41] however, the American Convention lays out additional minimum procedural safeguards to ensure that the right to liberty is not a mere "paper" right. The American Convention provides that the detained be brought promptly before a judge, that he be entitled to a trial within a reasonable time or be released, and that such release may be conditioned upon certain guarantees to ensure his appearance for trial.[42] In addition, anyone deprived of his liberty is guaranteed recourse to a competent court to determine the lawfulness of his detainment. Furthermore, in those countries that permit one threatened with arrest to petition the court for a ruling on the lawfulness of such a threat, that right is one from which derogation is not permitted.[43]

The European Convention addresses the right to liberty from a different perspective, but the result is similar. It provides for comprehensive protection of individual rights as well, yet the European Convention proclaims that no one shall be deprived of his liberty except in certain situations.[44] The European Convention also sets out procedural safeguards by requiring the accused to be promptly informed of the reason for his arrest in a language he understands.[45] Finally, the European Convention allows the victims of any violations of these provisions the right to compensation.[46]

By providing comprehensive procedural safeguards regarding the right to liberty, both the European Convention and the American Convention seek to provide external restraints upon governmental behavior. These external restraints serve two separate purposes. First, they ensure that a state's laws conform to the minimum safeguards provided for by the convention or charter. Second, they ensure that governmental activity, if it violates both national law and the convention, is reviewed in a forum more sympathetic to the victim than the courts of the breaching state party.

In light of these safeguards, the African Charter is woefully deficient with regard to the right to liberty. As that right is subject to national law, the Charter is incapable of supplying even a scintilla of external restraint upon a government's power to create laws contrary to the spirit of the rights granted. Even the African Commission's ability to provide some external restraint in situations where governmental activity contravenes a national law is highly questionable. Without precise legal guidelines, the Commission will be severely handicapped in dealing with such situations.

Thus the absence of such protection seriously undermines the effectiveness of Article 6, and an individual is given no greater protection than she or he would have under domestic law. Even if such protection is adequate in most situations, the Charter does not exist to cover most situations; its purpose is to deter the occasional abuses a government imposes upon its citizens. This problem could be averted if the Charter—modeling itself on the European Convention—expounded on and clarified the situations in which deprivations of liberty are permissible, by enumerating a specific list of exceptions to the right to liberty and by setting forth appropriate procedures to be followed.

The Effect of Domestic Law and International Instruments upon the African Charter's Limitations on Granted Rights The preceding discussion of clawback clauses in the African Charter has demonstrated the need to search outside the Charter itself for interpretation of such phrases as ''in accordance with the law'' and ''by the law.''[47] In light of the Charter's inclusion of clawback clauses and omission of a derogation provision, an examination of other international instruments and relevant domestic law suggest alternative safeguards to protect Charter-given rights from governmental abuse. Separate analyses of these intentional inclusions and omissions in the African Charter reveal the distinct effects of each.

Clawback Clause Interpretation

Under a narrow interpretation of a phrase such as "in accordance with the law," the African Commission, when established, could confine itself to considering only domestic law, thereby granting a right to the extent that the right conforms to local law. Yet an examination of the derogation provision of the Constitution of the Republic of Zaire illustrates the inadequacy of such a domestic law interpretation. The Zaire Constitution states:

> If serious circumstances imminently threaten the Nation's independence or integrity or cause an interruption in the regular functioning of the organs of the Popular Movement of the Revolution or jeopardize vital State interests, the President of the Popular Movement of the Revolution, the President of the Republic, may proclaim a state of emergency, with the consent of the Political Bureau.
>   He shall so inform the Nation by message.[48]

The Zaire Constitution nowhere defines the phrase "serious circumstances imminently threaten[ing] the Nation's independence or integrity." The event triggering a state emergency may be any occurrence that merely "jeopardize[s] vital State interests." The lack of a definition of the type of action deemed to jeopardize a vital State interest renders this phrase dangerously vague. Furthermore, the Zaire Constitution permits the suspension of guarantees during a state of emergency. It empowers the President "to take all measures required by the circumstances," specifically permitting him to "restrict the exercise of individual liberties and certain fundamental rights."[49]

Although the consent of the Political Bureau is required before the President can declare such a state of emergency and suspend guarantees, it is not clear that the requirement of consent will serve as an effective check on the President. As the President has the power to appoint and dismiss Political Bureau members,[50] the Bureau could consist of parties dependent on the President and consequently in line with his views. Hence as the Zaire Constitution provides insufficient guidelines for interpretation of its provisions permitting derogation from guaranteed rights, domestic law can be viewed as an inadequate tool for construing the provisions of the African Charter.[51]

Under a second and broader interpretation of the Charter, the Commission, when established, will not need to restrict itself to domestic law but may interpret the clawback clauses in light of international law. The Commission is empowered to use as applicable principles, provisions of the Charter of the United Nations and other instruments adopted by African countries in the field of human and peoples' rights, as well as provisions of various instruments adopted within the specialized agencies of the United Nations of which the parties to the African Charter are members. Conceivably, therefore, when faced with the task of determining whether an act is "within the law" or "in accordance with the law," the Commission can refer to instruments and principles outside the African Charter that restrict government behavior to a greater degree than the Charter itself. In this way the Commission would be able to draw upon more definite provisions contained in other international instruments in order to provide an interpretive base for the Charter's broad provisions.

Article 6 of the Charter, the right to liberty, provides a suitable example. Article 6 provides that "no one may be arbitrarily arrested," yet an individual "may be deprived of his freedom . . . for reasons and conditions previously laid down by law."[52] Article 9 of the International Covenant on Civil and Political Rights contains a similar provision.[53] However, the Covenant continues where the Charter leaves off and carefully describes the limits within which domestic law must remain:

> Anyone who is arrested shall be informed, at the time of his arrest, of the reasons for his arrest and shall be promptly informed of any charges against him.
> Anyone arrested or detained on a criminal charge shall be brought promptly before a judge or other officer authorized by law to exercise judicial power, and shall be entitled to trial within a reasonable time or to release. It shall not be the general rule that persons awaiting trial shall be detained in custody, but release may be subject to guarantees to appear for trial, at any other stage of the judicial proceedings, and, should occasion arise, for execution of the judgement.
> Anyone who is deprived of his liberty by arrest or detention shall be entitled to take proceedings before a court, in order that that court may decide without delay on the lawfulness of his detention and order his release if the detention is not lawful.
> Anyone who has been the victim of unlawful arrest or detention shall have an enforceable right to compensation.[54]

Article 6 of the African Charter contains none of the specificity of Article 9 of the International Covenant on Civil and Political Rights. Since the Commission is charged with the interpretation of the Charter,[55] it could thus adopt Article 9 as an interpretation of Article

6. The attractiveness of this procedure lies in the flexibility given the Commission. Where political reality collides with an unpopular judicial determination, a mutually acceptable compromise can be worked out through the Commission's broad interpretive powers—a solution that would greatly facilitate the acceptance of Commission decisions by the Assembly of Heads of State and Government. Ideally, judicial decisions could increasingly become less dependent upon political considerations.

In many cases, the Commission will not need to "interpret" Charter provisions in light of Covenant provisions but may directly apply the appropriate article of the Covenant or other international instruments as controlling law. For example, Article 6 of the Charter allows arbitrary arrest for reasons and conditions. When party to the Covenant, a country has a contractual obligation, under *pacta sunt servanda*, to abide by the Covenant; hence its provisions conceivably constitute "condition[s] previously laid down by law" as required in Article 6 of the Charter. Article 9, therefore, may be directly applied by the Commission as an interpretation of the Charter's Article 6.

If the Commission is willing and able to adopt the above interpretive procedure. Article 6 (the right to liberty), Article 9 (the right to information), Article 10 (the right to free association), Article 11 (the right to assembly), Article 12 (the right to freedom of movement), Article 13 (the right to participate in government), and Article 14 (the right to property) will provide a greater amount of substantive protection for the individual than each of the provisions standing alone. The Commission's autonomy in its interpretive powers is therefore imperative and Commission members must be chosen to serve in personal rather than official, governmental capacities.[56] A Commission that is able to maintain autonomy from political forces will be able to put forward solutions that not only follow the rule of law but also are politically acceptable.

Interpretation of the Omission of a Derogation Clause

Just as the African Commission could interpret the clawback clauses through recourse to other international instruments as a means of providing greater protection for the individual, the Commission also could look to the derogation provision of the International Covenant on Civil and Political Rights to prevent governmental abuses during a state of emergency.

The scope and limitations of permissible state derogation are set out in Article 4 of the Covenant:

1. In time of public emergency which threatens the life of the nation and the existence of which is officially proclaimed, the States Parties to the present Covenant may take measures derogating from their obligations under the present Covenant to the extent strictly required by the exigencies of the situation, provided that such measures are not inconsistent with their other obligations under international law and do not involve discrimination solely on the ground of race, colour, sex, language, religion, or social origin.

2. No derogation from Articles 6, 7, 8 (paragraphs 1 and 2), 11, 15, 16, and 18 may be made under this provision.

3. Any State Party to the present Covenant availing itself of the right of derogation shall immediately inform the other States Parties to the present Covenant, through the intermediary of the Secretary-General of the United Nations, of the provisions from which it has derogated and of the reasons by which it was actuated. A further communication shall be made, through the same intermediary, on the date on which it terminates such derogation.[57]

The second clause of Article 4 (1) indicates that any public emergency will permit derogation as long as it threatens the life of the nation. Currently no case law exists interpreting Article 4 of the Covenant; however, the substantially similar Article 15 of the European Convention has received some attention.[58] For example, in the *Greek Case*,[59] the European Commission on Human Rights articulated four elements that constituted a "public emergency threatening the life of the nation" under the European Convention. These elements were:

1. An actual or imminent emergency;
2. involving the whole nation;
3. threatening the continuance of the organized life of the community;
4. for which the normal measures or restrictions permitted by the Convention for the maintenance of public safety, health, and order are plainly inadequate.[60]

The second element should properly be read to include insurrections that threaten only a portion of the country.[61] It should be added, however, that proportionality or "the extent strictly required by the exigencies of the situation"[62] mandates that where a government decides to derogate, it may do so only in those areas affected by the emergency. It would therefore be improper for a state to suspend the right of freedom from arbitrary detention in areas where there was absolutely no emergency or threat of emergency.[63] Finally, other situations threatening disasters constitute emergencies and would trigger the right to derogate.[64]

Who is to determine whether a situation constitutes a public emergency threatening the life of the nation and whether the particular government response was "strictly required by the exigencies of the situation"? In interpreting the derogation provision of the European Convention, the European Court in *Ireland versus United Kingdom* stated:

> It falls in the first place to each Contracting State, with its responsibility for "the life of [its] nation," to determine whether that life is threatened by a "public emergency" and, if so, how far it is necessary to go in attempting to overcome the emergency . . . . In this matter Article 15 §I leaves those authorities a wide *margin of appreciation*.
>
> Nevertheless, the States do not enjoy an unlimited power in this respect . . . . The domestic margin of appreciation is thus accompanied by a European supervision.[65]

This language indicates that international bodies maintain reviewability over a state's determination of not only what actions are required by the exigencies of the situation but also what constitutes a public emergency.[66] The African Commission, therefore, should have no difficulty in reviewing state discretion (the margin of appreciation) where the state concerned is a party to the International Covenant and is thereby bound by its restrictions. Yet the extent of reviewability is not clear where the state concerned is not a party to the Covenant. In the interest of consistent judicial determination, the Commission should apply, as in the case of the clawback clauses, the same reviewability standards to those countries not party to the Covenant. This solution is possible particularly where the state concerned has a derogation provision in its constitution similar to the Covenant.[67]

Derogation clauses do not authorize the suspension of all rights granted under the instrument. Under Article 4(2) of the Covenant, the following articles may not be derogated from, notwithstanding the existence of a public emergency: Article 6 (right to life), Article 7 (freedom from torture and cruel, inhuman, or degrading treatment or punishment), Article 8 (1) and (2) (freedom from slavery and servitude), Article 11 (freedom from imprisonment for failure to fulfill a contractual obligation), Article 15 (freedom from *ex post facto* laws), Article 16 (right to recognition as a person before the law) and Article

18 (freedom of thought, conscience, and religion).[68] While the Covenant explicitly forbids a state to derogate from the above rights, some vital rights are derogable under certain Covenent provisions: Article 9 (freedom from arbitrary arrest or detention), Article 14 (right to a fair trial), and Article 17 (freedom from arbitrary or unlawful interference with privacy, family, house, or correspondence).

Does this mean, then, that derogable rights (as opposed to non-derogable ones) are automatically suspended when a state declares an emergency? The answer is an emphatic no. As described earlier, a state of emergency in only one sector of the country will not authorize a nationwide state of emergency unless the "exigencies of the situation" warrant such a move. A right may be derogated from only when it is necessary in order to deal with the emergency and then only to the extent that it is proportional to the emergency, in other words, to the extent strictly required by the exigencies of the situation.[69]

In conclusion, the importance of looking to both domestic law and other international agreements to interpret the African Charter is crucial as a means to safeguard individual rights during a state of emergency. The Commission's use of other legal instruments, particularly the International Covenant on Civil and Political Rights, would enable it to implement the Charter-given rights seemingly undermined by the clawback clauses and broad derogation provision. In addition, an understanding of the structure and procedures of the Commssion aids in predicting its effectiveness in implementing the Charter.

ESTABLISHMENT AND ORGANIZATION OF THE AFRICAN COMMISSION ON HUMAN AND PEOPLES' RIGHTS

This final section will briefly describe the provisions of the Charter relating to the African Commission. As the entity charged with interpreting the Charter, an examination of its structure and procedures is necessary.[70]

Election of Members

By the terms of the Charter, the African Commission on Human and Peoples' Rights shall consist of eleven members serving in their personal capacity. Four months prior to elections, the Secretary-General of the Organization of African Unity will invite states party to the present Charter to nominate up to two candidates. A state may nominate a candidate from its own state, but if a state nominates two candidates, one may not be a national of that state. In any case, a candidate may not be nominated if he is not a national of a state party to the present Charter.

As soon as the Secretary-General has compiled the names of the candidates, he is required to make an alphabetical list and submit it to the Heads of State and Government at least one month prior to elections. The members of the Commission are then elected by secret ballot by the Assembly of Heads of State and Government at its annual summit meeting. Each member of the Commission serves a six-year term and is eligible for reelection. The Commission, once elected by the Heads of State and Government, elects its own officers and establishes its own rules of procedures. The Commission will meet ''whenever necessary'' but will be convened by its Chairman at least once a year.

Communications to the Commission

The Charter creates two types of communications, each of which is considered by means of a different procedure. The first classification concerns communications from states.

A state party to the Charter that has good reason to believe that another state party has violated the provisions of the Charter may by written communication bring the matter before that state or before the Commisison. In either case, the communication shall be addressed to the Secretary-General of the OAU, the chairman of the Commission, and the accused state. This provision indicates that by becoming a state party to the African Charter, a State automatically recognizes the competence of the Commission to hear complaints against that state. As a result, this provision greatly facilitates the authority and usefulness of the Commission.[71]

The state party to whom the communication is addressed has three months to respond to the enquiring state. Such explanation ''should include as much as possible relevant information relating to the laws and rules of procedure applied and applicable and the redress already given or course of action available.''[72] The objective of the Commission in such state-to-state dealings is to encourage the parties to reach an amicable settlement between themselves. If, however, the states cannot reach a mutually satisfactory agreement, either party may submit the matter to the Commission and notify the other state of such action. The Commission will only consider the matter after all domestic remedies have been exhausted.

Once the matter is before the Commission, that body is given broad investigatory powers under Article 46, which states in part: ''The Commission may resort to any appropriate method of investigation.'' While the Charter expressly states that the Commission may request all relevant information from the states concerned in either written or oral form, there is no express indication as to whether the Commission can undertake fact-finding missions. Article 46, which applies to the procedure concerning communications from states as well as from those not parties to the Charter, could be interpreted as allowing such investigations.

When the Commission has gathered sufficient information about a state-communicated matter, and has determined that an amicable solution is impossible, it writes a report stating the facts and its findings. The report is then submitted to the Assembly of Heads of State and Government. Article 53 provides that "While transmitting its report, the Commission may make to the Assembly of Heads of State and Government such recommendations as it deems useful." Although vague, this language indicates that the recommendations of the Commission are to be made to the Assembly of Heads of State and Government and are not to be incorporated into the report. The importance of this provision rests in Article 59, which states that the report of the Commission (regardless of whether it concerns a communication brought by a state, an individual, or a non-governmental organization) will be published only when the Assembly decides it should be. Under no circumstances will the recommendations of the Commission be made public without the prior approval of the Assembly of Heads of State and Government.

Under Article 55 there is no limit as to who may file a communication before the Commission as long as Article 56 is followed. Article 56 states that communications, other than those of state parties, will be considered if they: (1) are compatible with the Charter of the OAU and the Banjul Charter; (2) are not written in disparaging or insulting language; (3) are not based exclusively on reports disseminated through the news media; (4) are sent within a reasonable time after exhausting local remedies; and (5) do not deal with cases already settled by those states in accordance with various international instruments. While an individual may bring a petition before the Commission, it is unclear whether individual petitions will be considered independently or will be considered only "after deliberations of the Commission [in which] one or more communications apparently relate to special cases which reveal the existence of a series of serious or massive violations of human and peoples' rights."[73] Where such a situation exists, the Assembly of Heads of State and Government may, at its discretion, then request the Commission to undertake an in-depth investigation.

The fact that the Assembly must authorize the Commission to issue a report on non-state-reported communications suggests that the Commission merely functions as a subcommittee of the Assembly, with no independent authority of its own. It can be hoped that this question will be resolved when the Commission writes its own rules of procedure, which it is empowered to do under Article 42(2).

CONCLUSION

Like all human rights instruments, the African Charter is as much a political document as it is a legal one. Several of the delegates in Nairobi expressed the view that although the standards of the Charter were vague, the Commission was given sufficient flexibility to interpret the Charter in a manner consistent with other international instruments, and that despite the unique concept of peoples' rights and the firm obligation imposed upon individuals by their states, the Commission's decisions would closely parallel those of similar international organizations charged with the protection of human rights. This view seems reasonable and if realized will provide not just Africa but the entire world with a valuable mechanism for futhering the cause of individual rights.

However, the steps from espoused aspirations to practical reality are difficult. The OAU might do well to consider the possibility of creating a temporary African Commission charged solely with the task of promoting the principles embodied in the Charter prior to the actual commencement of the Commission provided for in Article 30. In addition to providing an immediate promotional institution, the Temporary Commission could lay the groundwork for resolving some of the major problems that will confront the permanent Commisison.

The two most pressing issues deal with restriction on rights granted by the Charter. The lack of a derogation provision places on the Commission the unenviable task of determining when a government has acted improperly during a declared state of emergency. The presence of clawback clauses requires the Commission to determine what applicable standards should be used in defining the phrase "in accordance with the law."

The satisfactory resolution of these issues necessitates a broad interpretation of the Charter so as to apply external norms to the vague Charter provisions. This result will be possible only if the Commission is permitted to carry out—with a minimum of interference from the Assembly of Heads of State and Government—its Charter-given mandate to interpret all Charter provisions. An autonomous Commission with members represented in their personal capacity is a fundamental requirement for the successful operation of the Commission and the subsequent implementation of the substantive protective safeguards of the African Charter on Human and Peoples' Rights.

NOTES

1. *African Charter on Human and Peoples' Rights*, adopted June 27, 1981, OAU Doc. CAB/LEG/67/3/Rev. 5, reprinted in "Report of the Secretary-General on the Draft African Charter on Human and Peoples' Rights," OAU Doc. CM/1149 (XXXVII) (Annex II) 1981. The full text of the Charter is reprinted in Appendix 2 of this book.

2. At the Sixteenth Ordinary Session of the Assembly of Heads of State and Government in Monrovia, Liberia, in 1979, decision 115 (XVI) called for the preparation of a preliminary draft of an African Charter, "to make provision for the establishment of organs and for the promotion and protection of human and peoples' rights." OAU Doc. AHG/115 (XVI). The first draft of the proposed African Charter was prepared in Dakar, Senegal, during November and December of 1979. OAU Doc. CAB/LEG/67/3/Rev. 1 (1979). This document will be referred to here as the Dakar Draft.

3. *Réunion des experts pour l'élaboration d'un avant-projet de Charte Afrique des droits de l'homme et des peuples*, 1–2, Dakar, Senegal (1979) (on file with the International Human Rights Law Group, Washington, D.C.) (mimeographed).

4. *European Convention for the Protection of Human Rights and Fundamental Freedoms*, signed Nov. 4, 1950, entered into force Sept. 3, 1953, *United Nations Treaty Series* 213, p. 222.

5. *American Convention on Human Rights*, signed Nov. 22, 1969, entered into force July 10, 1978, *Organization of American States Treaty Series*, no. 36, p. 1.

6. The United Nations Seminar in Monrovia set out its proposed standards in two articles:

> Article 2: The Commission shall be guided by the international law of human rights, including the provisions of specific African instruments on human rights which may be concluded, such as a declaration, a charter or a convention, the provisions of the United Nations Charter, the Charter of the OAU, and the Universal Declaration of Human Rights, and the provisions of other United Nations and African instruments in the field of human rights, especially the International Covenant on Economic, Social and Cultural Rights, the International Covenant on Civil and Political Rights and the optional protocol thereto, the International Convention on the Elimination of All Forms of Racial Discrimination, the International Convention on the Suppression and Punishment of the Crime of *Apartheid*, the United Nations Convention and Protocol Relating to the Status of Refugees, the OAU Convention Governing the Specific Aspects of Refugee Problems in Africa, and the OAU Convention on the Elimination of Mercenarism in Africa, as well as the provisions of instruments adopted within specialized agencies of the United Nations, such as ILO, UNESCO, FAO, and WHO.
>
> Article 3: The Commission shall also have regard to other international conventions, whether general or particular, establishing rules expressly recognized by the States members of the OAU; to African practices consistent with international human rights standards evidencing customs generally accepted as law; and to the general principles of law recognized by African nations, judicial decisions, and the teachings of authoritative authors as subsidiary means for the determination for the rules of law.

United Nations, "Seminar on the Establishment of Regional Commissions on Human Rights with Special Reference to Africa, Monrovia, Liberia, 10–21

September 1979,'' UN Doc. ST/HR/SER. A/4 (1979). An interesting, although out of date, study conducted by the Commission to Study the Organization of Peace prior to the adoption of the Banjul Charter, recommended adoption of principles contained in the Monrovia proposal rather than those contained in the Dakar Draft. The basis of this commission's argument is that the Monrovia proposal is a "means"-oriented document, that is, it focuses on form rather than substance; the Dakar Draft, as an "ends"-oriented document, focuses on substance rather than form. *Regional Protection and Promotion of Human Rights in Africa* (New York: The Commission, 1980), p. 7. Since much of the substance of the Charter is highly controversial, it may take considerable time for the necessary parties to agree upon acceptable arrangements.

7. See *African Charter*, Articles 27–29.

8. *Charter of the Organization of African Unity*, Preamble, clause 3.

9. *African Charter*, Preamble, clause 3. The eminent Nigerian jurist T.O. Elias has argued that the language of the OAU Charter "having due regard to the Charter of the United Nations and the Universal Declaration of Human Rights" demonstrated "not only the adherence of the Member States to the Principles of the [UN] Charter, but also their awareness of the need to realise the goal of international co-operation in practical terms." Quoted in Zdenek Cervenka, *The Organization of African Unity and Its Charter* (New York: Praeger, 1969), p. 109. Dr. Cervenka has disputed this view. He grants credibility to Elias' view, however, by stating that "there is no legal provision in the OAU Charter which indicates the kind of relationship that is to exist between the OAU and the UN" (p. 110). The African Charter on Human and Peoples' Rights offers little assistance on the subject. Its applicable standards incorporate both African and UN documents, while indicating no preference. The resolution of this issue will depend on how the Commission chooses to interpret the conflicting provisions.

10. *African Charter*, Preamble, clause 4. The scope of this paper does not permit a detailed discussion concerning the effects of traditional African values upon human rights. The abundant literature indicates that traditional African values encompass most human rights; however, some traditional values are obstacles for a few contemporary rights. For a discussion of the influence of traditional African societies on modern human rights concepts, see Hurst Hannum, ''The Butare Colloquium on Human Rights and Economic Development in Francophone Africa,'' *Universal Human Rights* 1, no. 2 (1979), pp. 64–69, and Chapters 2, 3, and 4 of the book in hand.

The inclusion of the term "zionism" in the Charter has created considerable controversy. The author was told by a high OAU official that the Libyans introduced the term during the first drafting session in Banjul and it was immediately placed in brackets in the text. As soon as it was introduced, however, Foreign Minister Mogwe of Botswana protested that Zionism was not an African problem. He further argued that it would be a dangerous precedent to import non-African problems into an African organization. No one responded to Mr. Mogwe, and it was assumed that the phrase would be omitted from the Charter unless the Assembly of Heads of State and Government voted to retain the term in Nairobi. OAU records do not reveal such a vote was ever taken, however, and the term "zionism" has inexplicably been included in the final draft.

11. *African Charter*, Preamble, clause 8. The text of the Dakar Draft used the following language: "Conscious of the duty to achieve the total liberation of the African territories that are not yet independent." Dakar Draft, (see note 3 above), Preamble, clause 9. The added reference in the African Charter to "neocolonialism, apartheid, zionism, and the dismantling of aggressive foreign military bases" demonstrates the drafters' breadth of concern about foreign intervention.

12. *African Charter*, Preamble, clause 6.

13. For a more comprehensive view of the limitations of an individual's duties to the community, see E. Daes, "Study of the Individual's Duties to the Community and the Limitations on Human Rights and Freedoms under Article 29 of the Universal Declaration of Human Rights," UN Document E/CN.4/Sub.2/432 Rev. 1, Add. 1-6 (1979).

14. The American Convention does mention the individual's obligation to his family, community, and mankind. See *American Convention*, Article 32. The Universal Declaration of Human Rights also provides that "everyone has duties to the community in which alone the free and full development of his personality is possible." *Universal Declaration*, Article 29 (1). It is an open question, however, as to whether "community" equals "state."

15. Neither the European Convention nor the American Convention mentions such an obligation by the individual to the state. The American Convention starts with a completely different premise: "Recognizing that the essential rights of man are not derived from one's being a national of a certain state, but are based upon attributes of the human personality . . . ." *American Convention*, Preamble, clause 2. See also *International Covenant on Civil and Political Rights*, Preamble, clause 2: "Recognizing that these rights derive from the inherent dignity of the human person. . . ."

16. *African Charter*, Preamble, clause 7.

17. Ibid., Article 45 (3).

18. Ibid., Article 1.

19. Thomas Buergenthal, "The Inter-American System for the Protection of Human Rights," in T. Meron, ed., *Teaching International Protection of Human Rights* (forthcoming).

20. Dakar Draft, Article 1 (See Note 3, above) (emphasis added).

21. See *African Charter*, Article 25. As the language of the Charter reveals, there is no express guarantee of rights:

> States Parties to the present Charter shall have the duty to promote and ensure through teaching, education, and publication, the respect of the rights and freedoms contained in the present Charter and to see to it that these freedoms and rights as well as corresponding obligations and duties are understood.

22. Ibid., Article 1.

23. *American Declaration of the Rights and Duties of Man*, May 2, 1948.

24. Commission to Study the Organization of Peace, "Regional Protection and Promotion of Human Rights in Africa," p. 9.

25. *African Charter*, Article 45 (2) (emphasis added).

26. Compare *Dakar Draft*, Article 1 ("guarantee" and "undertake . . . to

ensure") with the *African Charter*, Article 1 ("recognize" and "undertake to adopt"). Several of the drafters expressed to the author the view that the African Charter is a well-balanced compromise between recognized legal norms and political reality.

27. Louis Henkin, ed., *The International Bill of Rights* (New York: Columbia University Press, 1981), p. 6.

28. *Optional Protocol to the International Covenant on Civil and Political Rights*, 16 December 1966, G.A. Res. 2200 (XXI) (1966), entered into force March 23, 1976.

29. Henkin, *The International Bill of Rights*, p. 15.

30. International human rights conventions or covenants that are binding upon member states contain provisions similar to Article 1 of the African Charter, which provides: "The Member States of the Organization of African Unity parties to the present Charter shall recognize the rights, duties, and freedoms enshrined in this Charter and shall undertake to adopt legislative or other measures to give effect to them." *African Charter*, Article 1. See *American Convention*, Article 2; *European Convention*, Article 1; *International Covenant on Civil and Political Rights*, Article 2.

31. The principle of *pacta sunt servanda* has long been a recognized rule of customary international law, and was codified in the *Vienna Convention on the Law of Treaties*, opened for signature May 23, 1969, Article 26, UN Document A/Conf. 39/27, p. 289, entered into force Jan. 27, 1980.

32. In effect, a state is agreeing to permit the international community to protect the State's citizens and anyone else coming within the state's territory from abusive action and derogation from basic fundamental guarantees.

33. Rosalyn Higgins defines the term "clawback" as a clause "that permits, in normal circumstances, breach of an obligation for a specified number of public reasons." "Derogations under Human Rights Treaties," *British Yearbook of International Law* 48 (1978), p. 281. She distinguishes the clawback clause from derogations in a strict sense, which "allow suspension or breach of certain obligations in circumstances of war or public emergency." See Robert Norris and Paula Reiton, "The Suspension of Guarantees," *American University Law Review* 30 (1981), pp. 189–93.

34. *African Charter*, Articles 8–14.

35. Compare Joan Hartman, "Derogation from Human Rights Treaties in Public Emergencies," *Harvard International Law Journal* 22 (1981), p. 6 (interpreting derogation clauses as being a restrictive type of clawback clause), with Higgins, *Derogation Under Human Rights Treaties* (distinguishing clawback from derogation clauses).

36. See American Convention, Article 27; *European Convention*, Article 15; *International Covenant on Civil and Political Rights*, Article 4.

37. European Convention, Article 15 (1).

38. The American Convention contains the most extensive list of non-derogable rights. See *American Convention*, Article 27 (2). Article 27 (1) reads as follows:

> In time of war, public danger, or other emergency that threatens the independence or security of a State Party, it may take measures derogating from its obligations under the present Convention to the extent and for the period of

time strictly required by the exigencies of the situation, provided that such measures are not inconsistent with its other obligations under international law and do not involve discrimination on the grounds of race, color, sex, language, religion, or social origin.

39. *African Charter*, Article 6.

40. Ibid., Article 6.

41. Provisions similar to those in the African Charter read:
   1. Every person has the right to personal liberty and security.
   2. No one shall be deprived of his physical liberty except for the reasons and under the conditions established beforehand by the constitution of the State Party concerned or by a law established pursuant thereto.
   3. No one shall be subject to arbitrary arrest or imprisonment.

American Convention, Article 7.

42. Ibid., Article 7 (5).

43. Ibid., Article 7 (6).

44. (1) Everyone has the right to liberty and security of person. No one shall be deprived of his liberty save in the following cases and in accordance with a procedure prescribed by law:

(a) the lawful detention of a person after conviction by a competent court;
(b) the lawful arrest or detention of a person for non-compliance with the lawful order of a court or in order to secure the fulfillment of any obligation prescribed by law;
(c) the lawful arrest or detention of a person effected for the purpose of bringing him before the competent legal authority on reasonable suspicion of having committed an offense or . . . to prevent his commiting an offense or fleeing after having done so;
. . . .
(f) the lawful arrest or detention of a person to prevent his effecting an unauthorized entry into the country or of a person against whom action is being taken with a view to deportation or extradition.

European Convention, Article 5(1).

45. Ibid., Article 5(2).

46. Ibid., Article 5(5).

47. See *African Charter*, Articles 6, 9 (2), 10 (2), 11, 12 (4), 13 (1), 14.

48. 48. Zaire Constitution, Article 48 (1974, amended 1978).

49. When military law or a state of emergency has been proclaimed, the President of the Popular Movement of the Revolution, the President of the Republic, shall be empowered to take all measures required by the circumstances.
   In particular, he may restrict the exercise of individual liberties and certain fundamental rights under conditions determined by this Constitution and by law.
   In addition, he may suspend in all or in part of the national territory, and for the duration and infractions which he may determine, the repressive action of ordinary jurisdictions and substitute that of military jurisdictions. However, he may not infringe upon rights to defense and to appeal.

Zaire Constitution, Article 49.

50. Ibid., Article 40.

51. This sytem constrasts with that provided for in the International Covenant. See text below accompanying Note 57.

52. See *African Charter*, Article 6.

53. Everyone has the right to liberty and security of person. No one shall be subjected to arbitrary arrest or detention. No one shall be deprived of his liberty except on such grounds and in accordance with such procedure as are established by law. *International Covenant on Civil and Political Rights*, Article 9(1).

54. Ibid., Article 9 (2)–(5).

55. See *African Charter*, Article 45 (3).

56. The Dakar Draft contained an article that stated: "The office of a member of the Commission shall be incompatible with that of a Government member or of a member of the diplomatic corps." *Dakar Draft*, Article 32. This provision was the subject of a two-day debate and was not adopted because of a lack of consensus. In one of the only votes taken concerning the provision, its inclusion in the Charter was defeated fifteen votes to twenty. While the members of the Commission are to serve in their individual capacities, the defeat of this provision indicates that the contrary may prove to be true.

The make-up of the Commission is of obvious importance. It was conceded by one of the Charter drafters that a Commission interpreting the Charter narrowly could construe such phrases as "in accordance with the law" or "within the law" to preclude any action by the Commission where the local law contrary to the Charter was sanctioned by national security—regardless of how tenuous the claim.

57. *International Covenant on Civil and Political Rights*, Article 4. The term "public emergency" corresponds to "war, public danger, or other emergency" in the American Convention, Article 27. The corresponding language of the European Convention reads "war or other public emergency." *European Convention*, Article 15(1).

Yet as Buergenthal points out, the omission of the word "war" in the Covenant was no accident. Article 2(4) of the United Nations Charter prohibits any member state from resorting to the use of force against the territorial integrity of any other state. Thus the inclusion of the word "war" in Article 4 of the Covenant would symbolically weaken the UN concept of the illegality of war, even though war is most definitely a public emergency within the meaning of Article 4, in that all wars threaten the life of nations. "While it was recognized that one of the most important public emergencies was the outbreak of war, it was felt that the Covenant should not envisage, even by implication, the possibility of war, as the United Nations was established with the object of preventing war." Thomas Buergenthal, "To Respect and to Ensure: State Obligations and Permissible Derogations," in Henkin, *The International Bill of Rights*, pp. 72–79.

58. (1) In time of war or other public emergency threatening the life of the nation any High Contracting Party may take measures derogating from its obligations under this Convention to the extent strictly required by the exigencies of the situation, provided that such measures are not inconsistent with its other obligations under interantional law.

(2) No derogation from Article 2, except in respect of deaths resulting from lawful acts of war, or from Articles 3, 4 (paragraph 1), and 7 shall be made under this provision.

(3) Any High Contracting Party availing itself of this right of derogation shall keep the Secretary-General of the Council of Europe fully informed on the measures which it has taken and the reasons therefor. It shall also inform the Secretary-General of the Council of Europe when such measures have ceased to operate and the provisions of the Convention are again being fully executed.

European Convention, Article 15.

59. *The Greek Case*, *Yearbook of the European Convention on Human Rights* 12, (1969), pp. 11–697.

60. Ibid., p. 72.

61. Compare Buergenthal, "To Respect and to Ensure," p. 80 (public emergency need not threaten entire nation), with Hartman, "Derogation from Human Rights Treaties," p. 16 (entire state must be threatened).

62. *European Convention*, Article 15 (1).

63. See Norris and Reiton, "The Suspension of Guarantees," p. 201: "Inasmuch as the legitimacy of a state of exception is derived from its necessity, there is an implied restriction to the geographical area affected by the special circumstances."

64. Buergenthal, "To Respect and to Ensure," p. 79.

65. *Ireland v. United Kingdom* 25, European Court on Human Rights, Judgment of 18 January 1978, Ser. A, no. 25, pp. 78–79 (emphasis added).

66. See Buergenthal, "To Respect and to Ensure," pp. 81–82.

67. For example, the derogation provision in the Nigerian Constitution provides:

> (2) An Act of the National Assembly shall not be invalidated by reason only that it provides for the taking, during periods of emergency, of measures that derogate from the provisions of section 30 [right to life] or 32 [right to personal liberty] of the Constitution; but no such measures shall be taken in pursuance of any such Act during any period of emergency save to the extent that those measures are reasonably justifiable for the purpose of dealing with the situation that exists during that period of emergency:
> Provided that nothing in this section shall authorize any derogation from the provisions of section 30 of this Constitution, except in respect of death resulting from acts of war or authorize any derogation from the provisions of section 33 (8) [freedom from *ex post facto* laws] of this Constitution.
> (3) In this section, a "period of emergency" means any period during which there is in force a Proclamation of a state of emergency declared by the President. . . .

Nigerian Constitution, Article 4 (2)–(3). See text at Note 49, above, for the derogation provision in the Zaire Constitution.

68. *International Covenant on Civil and Political Rights*, Article 4(2). The European Convention contains only four non-derogable rights: the right to life, freedom from slavery, freedom from torture, and freedom from *ex post facto* laws. *European Convention*, Article 15. The American Convention possesses the most extensive list of non-derogable rights. It includes the seven in the International Covenant, with the exception of freedom of conscience, and in addition includes the rights of the family, the right to a name, the rights of a child, the right to nationality, and the right to participate in government. *American Convention*, Article 27 (2). The American Convention also provides that the judicial guarantees essential for the protection of such rights are themselves non-derogable.

69. The individual safeguards within a single provision should also be retained to the limitations of necessity and proportionality. For example, Article 14 of the Charter, dealing with the right to a fair trial, contains specific procedural safeguards, such as the presumption of innocence, the right to be informed promptly of the charged offense, the right to be present at trial, and the double jeopardy provision. These enumerated rights should not be derogated from even in an emergency situation, as they provide vital protection to the individual and impose only minor burdens on a state—if any at all.

Even the inability to impose procedural safeguards on a government intent upon depriving its citizens of all civil and criminal guarantees does not in itself invalidate this principle.

70. Part II (Articles 30–63) of the Charter deals with the Commission's establishment and organization (Chapter I), mandate (Chapter II), procedures (Chapter III), and applicable principles (Chapter IV). Part III (Articles 64–68) concerns general enactment provisions. See *African Charter*, Articles 30–68.

71. The American Convention provides that a state party to the Convention may file an additional communication against another state party only if both states have deposited declarations recognizing the competence of the Commission to examine such communications. *American Convention*, Article 45(2). The European Convention also requires mutual recognition of the competence of the Commission. *European Convention*, Article 25 (1).

72. *African Charter*, Article 47.

73. Ibid., Article 58(1).

CHAPTER EIGHT

Human Rights Non-Governmental Organizations in Black Africa: Their Problems and Prospects in the Wake of the Banjul Charter

HARRY M. SCOBLE

Human rights and development are intertwined. There cannot be lasting progress in one without progress in the other. Yet "rights," as enforceable claims, are not given. They are taken, through successful struggle by the relatively less powerful against the political elite. A society and polity does not necessarily require explicit human rights non-governmental organizations so long as "freedom of association" (in the lawyer's formulation) or "political pluralism" (in the political scientist's) prevails. In the absence of such conditions, as I shall demonstrate for Africa as a whole, the role of non-governmental human rights organizations becomes all the more central. Every political elite on that continent has the right to declare states of exception—of emergency, siege, or martial law—and thereby close down the legitimate struggle for rights by suspending freedom of association. The lack or severe weakness of domestic means to protect human rights places all the greater burden on those few organizations and institutions that exist.

Human rights non-governmental organizations (NGOs) carry out six key functions:

1. information gathering, evaluation, and dissemination;
2. advocacy;
3. humanitarian relief and/or legal aid to victims and families;
4. building solidarity among the oppressed, and internationalizing and legitimating "local" concerns;
5. moral condemnation and praise; and
6. lobbying national and intergovernmental authorities.

Information gathering, evaluation, and dissemination, or "information processing" (the shorthand term I shall employ), is the prime function of human rights NGOs. Without information on the status of human rights observance, and the particular nature and context of human rights violations, there is little hope for the protection of human rights. Information processing constitutes a set of discrete but interrelated activities involving the social-scientific conceptualization of one or more human rights, following by the gathering of information relevant to the main dimensions of the concept(s). During and after this activity, evaluation occurs, a process of simultaneously judging both the source of the data and the quantity and quality of the data from that source. After the quality of the information has been judged, the human rights NGO then makes decisions concerning the classification of its information—some of which will be intraorganizationally "classified" (essentially, censored, in order to protect the sources), the remainder of which can be publicized. Finally, and in all cases, the human rights NGO seeks to disseminate some part of the information.

Human rights NGOs *must* undertake this information-processing function for two basic reasons. First, no other agency has done, or is adequately doing, this primary function; and, secondly, anything else that the NGOs attempt to do—whether individually or collectively; whether on "public education," law drafting, or implementation of existing international standards; whether ameliorative, eradicative, or preventive—ultimately is conditioned upon how well the organization is perceived by relevant others as performing this prime function. Without accurate and timely information, there can be no rational and effective NGO policies on human rights. And without such NGO policies, human rights will constitute only a weapon for continuing the Cold War by additional ideological means or for fighting North-South battles at the rhetorical level.

Advocacy, essentially a legal term, means pleading the cause of another. It is clearly dependent upon information processing, yet goes beyond that, for it entails actively utilizing the information in order to take up the case of those whose rights are violated. If rights are being systematically violated, it means that the victims are unable to defend themselves within their own political system—either because they are unaware of their rights and of the injustices done to them, which is rare, or because that system denies them the resources to assert themselves and heavily sanctions them for trying. Advocacy thus means speaking for those who cannot speak, and embraces a broad range of communications activities: public education, consciousness raising, the enlisting of co–interest groups that ought logically to be concerned, and constituency building. It may entail attempting to place the information in the electronic and other mass media; it certainly involves getting that information into the quality media to reach various elites and their attentive publics.

At times, advocacy has involved breaking altogether new ground, focusing attention on an issue that had been totally ignored and completely outside the public consciousness. This was the case when Michael Scott, an Anglican clergyman, became the first Western spokesman on behalf of the Herero people of South West Africa (Namibia) in the early 1950s, and of the organizations which at that time became advocates of racial justice in Southern Africa: the London-based Africa Bureau, the American Committee on Africa, and the Fellowship of Reconciliation.[1] Today, Transafrica, a new Washington-based organization, seeks to establish the condition and concerns of the black peoples of Africa and the Caribbean as relevant to American publics and institutions.

Since World War II, there has been a veritable explosion in the number of non-governmental organizations concerned with the defense of human rights and fundamental freedoms. Nonetheless, one must immediately recognize two additional facts of political relevance. First, it must be conceded that the resources of these now numerous organizations remain very limited. The governments of the world in the aggregate spend more on armaments and "defense" in a few minutes than the combined *annual* budgets of all existing human rights NGOs. And because resources are so minimal, there are few NGOs that are truly universalistic in their geographic scope or comprehensive in their concern for all human rights; in fact no NGOs satisfy both of these criteria. Rather, as a matter of practical necessity, there is specialization and concentration by each agency on one issue, one population segment, or one geographical area. Thus the name of the International Defence and Aid Fund for Southern Africa indicates its geographic self-limitation, while Survival International stretches its meager resources in defense of indigenous peoples everywhere. Therefore, in examining the growth of human rights organizations since World War II, it should be clear that not all "good causes" have advocacy groups to advance them. This is especially evident in the case of human rights NGOs and the black African nations.

Despite their growth in numbers, the overwhelming majority of existing human rights NGOs remain located in the Western industrialized nations. The political significance of this fact—in terms of a conscious or unconscious bias in favor both of civil and political rights and of governmental and political structures modeled on those of the West—was probably much greater in the 1960s than it is at present. Since 1970, most Western-based human rights NGOs have broadened their concerns in a more balanced fashion that accommodates economic, social, and cultural rights as well as the civil and political ones. The older, established organizations—perhaps the case of the International Commission of Jurists is the most dramatic, since it was created in 1952 as an instrument in the Cold War—changed in response to the concrete world situation. This was largely a result of critical reflection and self-evaluation, but also a response to a changing constituency. Furthermore, new groups were formed in the context of this changed environment. Perhaps most important, the formation, survival, and operation of human rights NGOs within the Third World has meant that the Western-based groups have now to take account of them and their definitions of reality. To do otherwise would be to forfeit credibility and relevance.

Advocacy involves taking information about events and converting it into an issue on the public agenda. This is also a process whose outcome is uncertain; there exists little systematic, action-relevant knowledge on why some attempts succeed while others, equally compelling on their face, fail. Nonetheless, one can say that, where advocacy has been successful, it results—as intended—in an expansion of public attention to an issue. In addition, successful advocacy raises the issue from the national (or subnational) arena in which the victimization takes place to a higher transnational if not intergovernmental level in which the oppressors may have to face some consequences for their repressive actions. It creates this possibility (not probability) of risk by increasing the number of potential participants in the underlying conflict represented by the issue, bringing in non-nationals with their own political resources on the side of the victims.

The provision of *humanitarian relief and legal assistance* is also a function of human rights NGOs. To advocate the cause of human rights victims and their families without at the same time addressing their immediate material needs would undermine the sincerity and credibility of human rights organizations, especially of Western-based ones with obvious control over or access to superior resources.

There is some evidence of an evolution, in both religious and secular humanitarianism, from a crisis-oriented reactive response of direct dole to a longer-term strategy of protracted struggle, including an effort to help immunize potential political targets from the worst forms of economic deprivation that repressive regimes seek to impose. This is how we can interest the "theology of liberation" and especially the effort, begun in the 1960s by the Roman Catholic Church in Latin America, to implement the new theology in the pastoral program of establishing *comunidades de base* (self-sustaining small "base communities"). A further example is furnished by the relief program fund of Amnesty International (AI), the expenditures from which, during the past five years, have equaled anywhere from 7 to 21 percent of its annual operating budget. Some of these disbursements are part of a revolving capital-loan fund to enable former prisoners of conscience, families of "disappeareds," and similar political victims to purchase fishing boats, equipment to establish a small bakery, supplies for cottage industry, and other self-help projects in targeted Third World countries, including well-established relief projects in Southern Africa. AI's relief program now also includes a contingency fund, from which financial assistance has been provided "to South African, Ugandan, and Ethiopian refugees, including former prisoners of conscience, [and] people who might have become prisoners of conscience had they stayed in those countries . . . ."[2]

Legal assistance includes a large number of law-related activities. For example, direct legal assistance to "criminal" defendants is, of course, critical in the struggle for human rights. If citizens can be detained indefinitely without charges or trial, or tortured to coerce false confessions upon which they are subjected to long-term imprisonment or official murder, then it is clear that no other rights will be respected. This was the primary impetus behind the establishing of the British-based Aid and Defence Fund for Southern Africa.

Building solidarity among the oppressed is a function which incorporates all the activities associated with the three functions already elaborated, yet it goes beyond information processing, advocacy, and humanitarian relief legal assistance. In the first instance, it entails maintaining personal contact with the oppressed to demonstrate that they are not alone, that they have not been forgotten in their struggle. Recently, professional organizations have demonstrated a willingness to express collegial solidarity, as well.

In the case of Africa generally, the special human rights committee of the Inter-Parliamentary Union, PEN International, the London-based "Index on Censorship," the Freedom to Publish Committee of the American Association of Publishers, and the Human Rights Sub-Committee of the Overseas Press Club, among others, have all taken public stands in defense of black African colleagues whose rights were being violated. But it is perhaps in the context of the Southern African struggles that the process of building personal and political solidarity is revealed in its fullest dimensions. Here, George Shepherd has substituted the term "liberation aid," of which "the central theme is transnational political support from one group to another across national boundaries to achieve a common objective, the realization of human rights by those who are oppressed."[3]

In the case of British and American participants in the anti-apartheid struggle, the building of solidarity has entailed a wide variety of activities: campaigning against the sale of South African Krugerrands and for ending sports contacts with the Republic of South Africa; exposing the complicity of the British and American governments in permitting domestic corporations to evade the UN-voted arms embargo against South Africa and the trade embargo against Rhodesia; pressuring commercial banks to cease loans to the South African government and persuading other institutions (e.g., churches, universities) to divest themselves of the stocks of corporations with major holdings in South Africa; and many other actions.

Furthermore, at least in the case of the anti-apartheid movement, the building of solidarity has also encompassed direct material assistance to the indigenous liberation movements. For instance, the World Council of Churches (WCC) voted at its 1968 Uppsala Assembly to initiate a Programme to Combat Racism. Beginning in 1970, the WCC has made financial grants to liberation movements ''for the purpose of helping with the costs of administration, education, and medical programs.''[4] While the WCC Programme is in fact worldwide, it is also true that approximately one-half of its total disbursements over the past dozen years has been focused upon Southern African liberation movements (e.g., the Patriotic Front in Zimbabwe, SWAPO in Namibia). In such a setting of armed struggle, these WCC actions have been highly controversial, both within the anti-apartheid movement as a whole and within the mainline Protestant churches. In 1978 the Salvation Army suspended its membership in the Council over precisely this issue, the more conservative Protestant denominations in Western Europe and North America have refused to make contributions to the Programme fund, and the latter denominations' political allies have been eager publicly to misunderstand or deliberately distort the purposes of the WCC. Indeed, this example probably illustrates the severest test for Western-based organizations in expressing solidarity with the oppressed of the Third World: that the action is taken in the face of real and non-trivial costs.

Moral condemnation and praise constitute a fifth, separate function of the human rights NGO, one which flows logically from and particularly depends upon the credibility of the organization (or of its trusted allies) as an information-processor. By comparison with other major international actors, notably nation-states and multinational corporations, human rights NGOs are weak in traditional political resources: They have no guns, little money, and frequently small membership. They do, however, have moral authority, particularly where they have developed a reputation for non-partisan commitment to the protection of human rights as well as credibility as processors of information on violations. The capacity to produce a factually based moral condemnation of a repressive regime is the major ''power'' that the NGOs possess. Denunciations by the human rights NGOs employing the ''power of pitiless publicity'' can operate as a major disincentive to repressive governments, because repressive elites normally seek to convert their influence and especially their power into authority, whereas moral condemnation denies them precisely that desired legitimacy.

Lobbying is the final function undertaken by non-governmental organizations devoted to human rights. Several qualifications must be noted. First, lobbying can only occur in those First and Third World systems that recognize the legitimacy of private associations and permit them to take public stands on pending policies—including opposing the policies of the government of the day. Second, human rights organizations are weak in conventional political resources for lobbying. Nevertheless, no government—particularly a Western one—is wholly monolithic. The moral and legal commitment of human rights NGOs, together with their capacity to generate information on violations which may be denied but cannot be disproven, has provided them access to similarly committed legislators and civil servants. Together, in a kind of reciprocal, indeed symbiotic, interaction they have engaged in cooperative coalition building, one result of which, this past decade, has been the institutionalization of concern for human rights within Western governmental structures.

With this discussion of NGOs' functions as background, we turn now to consideration of statistical and case-study material on human rights NGOs in or focused on Africa.

The Nature, Scope, and Character of African Human Rights Non-Governmental Organizations

Table 8.1 below presents data on two elementary measures: the percentage of countries in a given subregion which had one or more human rights NGOs and the mean ("average") number of such groups per country where they in fact exist. When employed together, these provide a useful comparative indicator of the extent to which these crucial private associations have developed in Third World societies.

Of the twenty-nine groups listed in Table 8.1, two (the OAU and Ghana National Committees against Apartheid) are sponsored by governments. Closer examination of the remaining twenty-seven shows the generic weakness of the human rights movement in black Africa. Five are women's organizations; eight are church- or religious-oriented; four concern writers and/or journalists; six are lawyer's organizations; and the final four are sections of Amnesty International. The various women's organizations focus primarily on women in development, rather than on the broad spectrum of human rights issues. At least five of the religious groups are weak, sectarian, and only tangentially involved in human rights issues; the others are

Table 8.1: Regional and Country Focus of Human Rights Non-Governmental
Organizations Concerned with the Third World Based in the
United States (1980) and in Western Europe (1982)

Focus within the Third World	United States		West Europe	
	Number	Percent	Number	Percent
AFRICA*	29	27	44	27
General region	6		4	
Specific country	23		40	
(South/Southern Africa)	(23)		(25)	
ASIA*-PACIFIC	35	32	30	18
General region	8		0	
Specific country	27		30	
LATIN AMERICA/CARIBBEAN	45	41	91	55
General region	18		23	
Specific country	27		68	
TOTALS	109	100%	165	100%

*excludes all Middle East

SOURCES: *North American Human Rights Directory* (1980) and *Human Rights Directory: Western Europe* (1982), Washington: Human Rights Internet.

limited in resources or only active episodically. The three African national "PEN Centres" are small and weak, seeking primarily to defend the occupational interest of writers. With respect to lawyers' organizations, two are national support sections of the International Commission of Jurists. The Human Rights Committee of the Nigerian Bar Association must, because of its inactivity since its publicized formation, be judged symbolic, perhaps honorific for the officers designated. The African Bar Association, English-speaking and based in Kenya, has encouraged the drafting of a human rights charter for Africa, and now encourages ratification of the Banjul Charter, but at no point sought corporate participation in the drafting of that convention. The Institute for Human Rights Education was formed in Dakar, Senegal, in 1979, with the endorsement and limited financial support of UNESCO; it is still struggling to develop structure, resources, and programs, now under the aegis of the Inter-African Union of Lawyers (IAUL). The IAUL has created its own non-governmental Commission on Human Rights and the Rights of Peoples. Finally, the four national sections of Amnesty International follow overall AI procedures, meaning that, apart from campaigning within their own countries for the elimination of torture and abolition of capital punishment, they are otherwise forbidden as Amnesty members from concerning themselves with domestic violations of the security and integrity of the person.

Finally, one should note the current absence from black Africa of three types of organizations: ecumenical organizations, associations of families and relatives of political prisoners to collect and verify information on such detainees, to campaign publicly for their release, and to reach out to international organizations; and private groups of lawyers and others created to litigate and lobby on domestic civil liberties issues. Their non-existence in Africa underscores the weaknesses of African human rights NGOs.

One explanation for the relative weakness of the human rights movement in black Africa, to be examined in greater detail below, is the regional and country-specific focus of human rights organizations based in the West. Table 8.1 shows that the largest proportion of all non-universal NGOs based in both the United States and Western Europe focuses on the Latin American/Caribbean region. Only slightly more than a quarter of these human rights NGOs are concerned with the region or specific countries of sub-Saharan Africa. Further, apartheid dominates their interest. For Westerners and black Africans alike, the persistence of gross racial injustices in South Africa apparently inhibits the development of human rights NGOs concerned with other African states.

THE FEW, WEAK HUMAN RIGHTS ORGANIZATIONS IN AFRICA: DOES POVERTY EXPLAIN ALL?

Having documented the relative weakness of the human rights movement in black Africa, we must identify and evaluate potential explanatory factors. In the pages that follow, we briefly examine four broad factors as possible explanations for this weakness.

One explanation might be that the magnitude of human rights crises is much less in Africa than elsewhere in the Third World. According to this line of reasoning, human rights organizations are created in response to perceived needs; therefore, the lack of such private associations reflects the generally favorable human rights climate in Africa.

While it would be impossible to disprove this claim with quantitative data on the frequency and severity of violations that would permit unambiguous intra-Third World comparisions, nonetheless sufficient "anecdotal" evidence of severe and frequent African violations exists to require that we reject the claim. For instance, Argentine-style "disappearances" following the detention of politicals by government agents have occurred in Ethiopia and Zaire. Guatemala-style kidnappings (and kidnap-murder) of government opponents have been documented in Lesotho. Where several Arab nations have sought to destroy independent bar associations, the

Sudan, Zambia, and Tanzania have interfered with the free practice and provision of legal services. Most Asian and Latin American regimes have responded with repression to any move toward economic or political independence on the part of national trade unions; so also have the governments of Ghana, the Ivory Coast, Sierra Leone, Togo, Upper Volta, and Zambia. Judicially-ordered floggings and public amputations (at least three) have taken place in Mauritania—where slavery persists. College students held in detention have been killed in Zaire. Throughout Africa generally, "treason" and especially "sedition" trials appear with frequency, and the ease with which real and imagined political opponents can be locked up indefinitely at the pleasure of the executive power and with no judicial process is no less than that of the most repressive governments elsewhere in the Third World. Moreover, this broad survey of recent violations—drawn from the two most recent annual reports of Amnesty International—takes no account of the long periods of brutal misrule by Idi Amin in Uganda, President Macias of Equatorial Guinea, and the self-proclaimed Emperor Bokassa of the Central African Republic.

If the apparent need exists, why hasn't it called forth the appropriate organizational response? Some might point to the contemporary and continuing refugee crisis in Africa as an explanatory factor. Half the world's refugee population recognized by the UN High Commissioner for Refugees is located in Africa: 6.3 million non-resettled refugees within Africa, of which 43 percent are internally displaced, out of a world total of 12.6 million in 1981.[5] But does it seem reasonable to suppose that the refugee problem totally swamps African capabilities, in the sense of absorbing all their potential voluntary organizational resources? Clearly, the massive numbers of refugees places a severe strain on those organizations traditionally concerned with humanitarian relief, such as the African Christian churches, which are, in the first instance, weak institutions—especially when compared with those in Latin America. However, on-site humanitarian assistance by indigenous churches is augmented by a very large number of intergovernmental and governmental programs and especially by non-African international and national voluntary relief agencies. For these reasons, the large refugee problem does not seem adequately to explain the lack of secular human rights organizations in Black Africa.

We come to the "obvious" explanatory factor, poverty: Employing World Bank worldwide data on average per capita Gross National Product for 1970–1975, there are 42 nations in the world with an annual per capita income of less than $300 (US). Of these, 27 are African, 10 Asian, 4 Middle Eastern, and only 1 (Haiti) in the Latin

American-Caribbean region. Certainly, poverty is part of the weak basis for alternative institutions (such as churches, private universities, an independent bar, privately controlled newspapers, etc.) which elsewhere generate interests—and the possibility of human rights organizing around them—different from and potentially opposed to those of government. In Africa, new governmental institutions, although "thin" and fragile, stand relatively alone and unchallenged. Furthermore, of these 27 poorest African nations, precisely two-thirds exhibited rates of adult literacy (for those 15 or more years old) of 20 percent or less for this same time period. If we analogize from the sociological studies of Western societies, where the objective indicators of socioeconomic status (and particularly that of years of formal education) are directly correlated with membership in voluntary associations, then one must conclude that the pool of potential recruits for human rights or any other private organizations is extremely constricted in Africa. However, the economic base of society is not wholly determinative. (If it were, there would be no deviant cases to explain—such as wealthy countries like Saudi Arabia that lack private associations of all types, or Sri Lanka, one of the poorest, with a robust associational life, including human rights associations.) Therefore, there remains a fourth factor for consideration.

This factor is the nature of the ethnic community, and its structure, subdivisions, and processes in traditional African society, as these have interacted with the desires of the political elite. In general, the ethnic community is land-based and territorially segregated, coterminous with neither the full territory nor the total population of the new nation. Membership is exclusive, acquired by the accident of birth and not voluntarily relinquished; it is also inclusive in the sense that collectively defined criteria (of lineage, sex, age, and so forth) determine the status of the individual, providing him or her access to all the intraethnic subgroupings relevant to life. A complex internal political process of patronage and clientage prevails. Individual achievement is irrelevant because social identity, in the words of M.G. Smith, "is ascriptive and corporate in base and significance."[6] Moreover, citizenship, and the specification of all rights and duties attaching thereto, is defined wholly in terms of membership in the ethnic community—not yet the nation-state.

Meanwhile, however, the struggle for national self-determination has necessitated the superimposition of modern organizational forms—political parties, government bureaucracies, economic corporations—on this traditional base. In this process, the ethnic community, as the repository of all relevant demands, expectations, and identifications, became the sole meaningful basis for organizing political parties. But, where independence was begun with a multi-party system, it has now in almost all instances given way to a one-party system maintained by the legal authority and coercive power of the state. And the state, whether officially capitalist or socialist, is the main (if not sole) engine for development of the economy. Thus, in a multi-ethnic population, to the extent that the single dominant party is based on just one ethnic community (whether minority, largest plurality, or even absolute majority), members of this dominant ethnic group—especially those with higher education—have positive incentives to maintain the existing system. More highly educated individuals of subordinate ethnicity may seek a depoliticized accommodation within the system, uneasily serving as technocratic assistants in the process of governance and avoiding any other organizational activity. For all other out-group members, residual interethnic enmities may keep them divided and ruled, but in any event the attempt to form a human rights organization in such cases would be viewed with alarm by the political elite, being interpreted as the formation of a covert political party. In short, a complex of modern institutional factors based on the pervasive high salience of ethnic identity operates both positively and negatively to inhibit formation of secondary associations, especially overt human rights organizations.

INDIGENOUS HUMAN RIGHTS NON-GOVERNMENTAL ORGANIZATION STRATEGIES FOR THE FUTURE

Clearly, discussion about the presence and impact of human rights NGOs in Africa demands further research. However, their relative weaknesses calls for a pessimistic outlook on both the magnitude and nature of violations of human rights in black Africa.

As indicated, the cultural and sociological bases for autonomous human rights organizations are very limited; nor are these subject to large and sudden change. Furthermore, there is little evidence that African human rights NGOs as such have played other than a very general role of taking a favorable public stance toward informing Africans about their rights, along with the idea that there ought to be an African regional treaty for the promotion and protection of human rights. Certainly there is no evidence that existing indigenous groups have played a role in the systematic monitoring and public condemnation of African regimes guilty of significant violations. Neither is there reason to predict that such African NGOs can play other than a subsidiary, supportive, and generally promotional role in the foreseeable future.

Since the African Charter of Human and Peoples' Rights is now an accomplished fact, African human rights NGOs would hardly want to oppose it; it would be the height of political unrealism, in terms of their potential impact, to argue that acceptance of the new Banjul Charter be made conditional upon immediate substantive amendments. (The present African political situation is totally unlike the experience of the early United States in which the anti-Federalists had the negative capacity to exact the first ten amendments — the Bill of Rights—as the price for ratification of the Constitution of 1787.) Nor can African NGOs now remain silent during the current campaign for the ratification of the new convention, for that would expose them to the charge of inauthenticity. All they can do is publicly urge African states to ratify or accede to the Charter. Once the twenty-sixth state has done so, or as this threshold is approached, presumably the African NGOs can then also discreetly lobby for significant action to strengthen the Charter. This activity would be aimed at getting genuine human rights proponents nominated and elected to the new African Commission on Human and Peoples' Rights (under Articles 31–34), in the hope that a majority of this first Commission will be predisposed to the development of rules of procedure (under Article 42, section 2) which permit the intergovernmental agency the most active role possible and which also allow an active role by both indigenous and external human rights organizations.

Initially, the prospects for such outcomes favorable toward both an activist Commission and the emergence of active and effective African NGOs seem exceedingly dim. This is so for three interrelated reasons: the probable politics of the selection of members for the new, eleven-man African Commission; the silence of the Banjul Charter with regard to non-governmental organizations; and substantive changes made in the body of the charter, between the first and the final drafts, which strongly suggest a growing awareness on the part of incumbent African political elites of the "need" to prevent just such outcomes.

First, section 2 of Article 31 of the International Covenant on Civil and Political Rights specifies that, in the election of the eighteen-member Human Rights Committee, "consideration shall be given to equitable geographical distribution of membership and to the representation of the different forms of civilization and of the principal legal systems." By contrast, the Banjul Charter is silent, its relevant language Article 32 prescribing only that no more than one member of the new African Commission may be elected from any one signatory state. Yet it seems highly probable that interstate and interbloc political bargaining will produce an informal understanding establishing very similar rules of the game for allocating seats on the African Commission. This selection process is likely to bring onto the Commission individuals whose culture, religion, and/or ideology is opposed to the idea that individual civil and political rights have any proper place in a scheme of human and peoples' rights, especially given the conditions of Western-originated apartheid racism. Nor is this all. The probable process of selection will bring onto the commission individuals who are convinced that only duly constituted—meaning, at base, de facto—governments have the moral and legal right to judge whether whichever rights are recognized are being violated, and to identify the causes of violations. In short, it is not likely that Commission members would be responsive even to *strong* African human rights NGOs devoting significant attention to civil and political rights. But African NGOs in fact are not strong, and the paucity and weakness of indigenous human rights organizations create a vacuum that international human rights NGOs cannot hope to fill, since they are Western, meaning both white and wealthy.

A second factor overlaps the first. The new African Charter, by explicit contrast with the UN, the European, and the Inter-American human rights systems, is utterly silent as already indicated concerning non-governmental organizations. The silence is deliberate, reflecting not mere indifference or inadvertence but rather the active hostility of most African elites, and in particular the governing elites of most African countries, toward any social formation disrupting their conception of the natural identity of interests of the individual and his society.

The introductory statement to the first revised draft of the Banjul Charter includes two assertions making this philosophical position quite clear. The first states: "In traditional African societies, there is no opposition between rights and duties or between the individual and the community. They blend harmoniously." And the second: "The conception of an individual who is utterly free and utterly irresponsible and opposed to society is not consonant with African philosophy."[7] So long as this philosophy remains operative, the African Commission will be compelled to deny standing or any other legitimacy and access to any African organization—however indigenous—that appears to monitor governmental violations of civil and political rights.

Third and perhaps most important, substantive changes were made between the first and final versions of the African Charter which have the effect (and thus seem to reflect the intention) of severely limiting—if not totally precluding—the possibility that indigenous human rights organizations could develop an active and cooperative relationship with the African Commission on Human and Peoples' Rights. These changes had the combined effect of: (1) enlarging the realm of permissible state compulsion by a signatory nation; (2) reducing the autonomy and juridical role of the intergovernmental African Commission; and (3) rendering the right to freedom of association extremely problematic.

First, the increased power of potentially repressive regimes can be inferred from changes in the wording of the very first article of the convention. Originally this read as follows. "The States Parties shall recognize and shall guarantee the rights and freedoms stated in the present Convention and shall undertake to adopt, in accordance with their constitutional provisions, legislative and other measures to give effect to rights and freedom [sic] enshrined in this Convention." Clearly, the verb form is in the imperative mood, the language employed is that of command; it relates solely to whatever human and peoples' rights and freedoms are being specified in the document; and it further indicates an intent to require of the signatory a good-faith effort, consistent with its constitution, to provide a domestic legislative basis for such rights (e.g., national laws that establish judicial remedies, civil and/or criminal, for the improper executive denial of the rights).

In its final version, however, the same article now reads: "The Member States of the Organization of African Unity, parties to the present Charter, shall recognize the rights, *duties*, and freedoms enshrined in this Charter and shall undertake to adopt legislative *or other measures* to give effect to them." Emphases have been added to highlight one critical addition to the language and an equally important "either/or" weakening of the permissible means by which signatory states may seek to satisfy the mandate that their laws conform to the convention: "Duties" have been interposed between "rights" and "freedoms"; all three relationships between the self and relevant others are granted equal juridical status; and the obligation of the nation-state to recognize any one of these relationships may be met non-legislatively, by "other measures." This new wording grants the same status to two "entities," namely, "rights" and "duties," which are dissimilar. For example, to have a right does not mean that one has a legal (as against a moral, because socially and politically desirable) duty to exercise it. Specifically to have a right to free speech (provided in very qualified form in Article 9 of the Banjul Charter) cannot clothe the state with the legal authority to legislate criminal penalties for one's conscious decision not to make use of that right. Yet a duty may be treated in either a positive or a negative fashion. It may be specified in language such that one *must act* in a certain way, or negatively that one *must refrain from acting* in a certain way. In either case, the willful failure to perform the designated duty provides the occasion for the government to impose severe sanctions (including the withholding of valued indulgences which would otherwise be offered). Meanwhile, we know of no systematic theory of legislation in which executive decrees do not have less weight and value than formally enacted legislation.

The second category of changes deals with the autonomy and juridical role of the African Commission to be set up under the Charter. In the first draft, clause 2 of Article 45 on the mandate of the African Commission on Human and Peoples' Rights originally stated that the new commission "shall: . . . (2) Formulate and lay down principles and rules aimed at the solution of legal problems relating to human rights and fundamental freedoms upon which African governments *shall* base legislation." The emphasis underlines the language of command being employed. Clause 2 in its original form also provided an authoritative hierarchy of institutions, assigning to the new Commission the role of devising the general legal principles to be utilized in resolving such problems; the member states are obligated to employ these "principles and rules" in enacting national legislation conforming to the purposes of the convention. The underlying intention, we infer, was to further the Pan-African political—and, indeed, general legal—goals of consistency, uniformity, and predictability in the behavior of some fifty states as the units of action. In the adopted version, however, the clause has been weakened to the permissive form: "upon which African Governments *may* base their legislations." The potential juridical role of the African Commission was substantially reduced; the probability that purely political and other non-legal factors will produce a degree of legal anarchy was greatly enhanced.

Similarly, the autonomy of the African Commission was reduced between the first and final drafts with regard to its own rules of procedure. The original Article 46 initially began: "The Commission may resort to all methods of investigation . . . ." Assuming a consensus among the first members of the new commission, this language was certainly broad enough for them to have vested themselves with whatever methods other human rights commissions have utilized in the past, including on-site inquiry into allegations of recent or ongoing violations, and with any other methods necessary to inform themselves in a complete, accurate, and timely manner. It would have permitted a new Commission, itself weak in resources and lacking even a library, to accord privileged access to international (meaning external) human rights NGOs widely respected for their information-processing function; equally, it would have permitted the Commission or a designated subcommittee to travel outside the continent if the only relevant information concerning an African issue were elsewhere.[8] By contrast, the language of Article 46 as finally adopted substitutes "any appropriate method" for "all methods."

The third category of change of immediate importance for indigenous human rights NGOs is to be found in Article 10. The article initially read as follows: "1. Every person shall have the right to freely form associations with others, provided that he abides by the law. 2. No one may be compelled to join an association." While less than identical, this original formulation was close to both Article 20 of the Universal Declaration of Human Rights and Article 22 of the International Covenant on Civil and Political Rights on the same subject. In its final form, however, the same article now reads: "1. Every individual shall have the right to free association provided that he abides by the law. 2. Subject to the obligation of solidarity provided for in Article 29, no one may be compelled to join an association." This wording differs even further from that commonly appearing elsewhere in human rights treaties. The right appears to be diluted, at the same time that the addition of the qualification to section 2 raises the possibility that the domain of legitimate state compulsion has been enlarged.[9]

Beyond these very specific considerations, overall how should one appraise the Banjul Charter? From the perspective of human rights NGOs, indispensable for effective human rights, the new African Charter of Human and Peoples' Rights must be judged a very weak instrument, a minimalist approach when compared to the International Covenant on Economic, Social and Cultural Rights (ICESCR) and the International Covenant on Civil and Political Rights (ICCPR). The weakness is evident in three broad areas. The Charter is weak, first, because the human rights granted are limited in number and defined in a most equivocal manner. As Richard Gittleman points out above, the new Charter contains no specific derogation proviso on how and which rights might permissibly be suspended under wartime or other abnormal conditions. (By contrast, see Article 4 of the ICCPR.) Further, the specification in Articles 27–29 of the individual's duties and obligations to the state generate the high probability of conflict with the enumerated rights guaranteed him or her (as examined in more detail below). In addition, the "people" to whom rights collectively attach is nowhere defined—deliberately so[10]—and this creates an additional probability that future usage will juridically exempt instances in which repressive national elites decide that it is necessary to sacrifice individual claims to the imperatives of an alleged collectivity. Yet perhaps the most important feature—and failure—of the Charter, as Gittleman stresses, is the excessively conditional language by which rights are recognized even under the most normal of circumstances (i.e., the prevalence of the so-called "clawback clauses" in the statement of those human rights which fall into the civil-political category).

This broad criticism requires amplification. Specifically, for instance, Articles 6 and 7 deal with civil liberty and criminal justice. According to the rapporteur at the 1981 Nairobi Ministerial Meeting, which acted on the final draft of the Banjul Charter, Keba M'Baye, the Chairman of the Group of Experts which prepared the preliminary draft, thought these one of the significant features of the new human rights convention. M'Baye is summarily quoted as having singled out "the deliberate briefness of the articles . . . with respect to the provisions relating to justice whose conception may differ according to the political choice of the State."[11] To be sure, the political accommodation of common law, Napoleonic Code, Koranic-Shari'a, and Marxist-Leninist legal systems would be no mean feat. Yet in a charter purporting to guarantee individual rights one might reasonably expect to find stated a minimum guaranty that, under ordinary circumstances, all trials would be conducted by a *civilian* judiciary in open courts. But no such qualifying language is to be found in the charter; yet the "right to defence" (including right to counsel of one's choice), which *is* incorporated in the language of Article 7, will most likely prove meaningless in cases tinged with political considerations if it can only be exercised within the closed confines of a military court or similar "special" tribunal.

Articles 14–18 of the Banjul Charter incorporate economic, social, and cultural rights. Concerning this, the rapporteur has quoted M'Baye to the effect that "the concise and general formulation adopted . . . is in line with the concern to spare our young states too many but important obligations. In effect, these rights of the second generation are rights which entail benefits from the State."[12] Again, the statement is in accord with contemporary thinking of human rights advocates. Economic "rights" are conditional, future benefits progressively to be achieved. Nonetheless, the complete silence of the new convention with regard to "trade unions" is in marked contrast to the specificity of Article 8 of the ICESCR on this subject. And if trade unions are silently subsumed under freedom of association, then the revised section of Article 10 only promises ambiguously that "every individual shall have the right to free association provided he abides by the law." Indeed, the revised second section of the same article leaves it unclear whether the individual might not be legally compelled to join a government-controlled trade-union organization of the Communist style in Poland.

The second broad weakness in the Banjul Charter is to be found in its apparent major reliance (in Articles 47–53) on state action, especially state-to-state complaint procedures, to initiate implementation. Enough time has passed with regard to the initial high hopes held for such a "horizontal" procedure under the UN human rights regime to suggest that such expectations were politically naive. In fact, the state-to-state complaint process has only worked well under the regionally much more homogenous European Human Rights Convention. Given the general history of inaction under the procedure, and the further fact that all of those involved in the drafting of the Banjul Charter consciously resisted compensating for probable state inaction by providing for an active and action-initiating role on the part of human rights NGO's, then one must tentatively conclude that they have contrived a largely cosmetic instrument calculated to be minimally intrusive where the fundamental human rights issue of how a government treats its own citizens is at stake.

This regrettable conclusion gains further credence when one examines the third broad weakness of the charter, the restricted definitions of the functions and authority of the African Commission on Human and Peoples' Rights. For example, Gittleman notes that it can be argued that even the revised language of Article 46 is broad enough to pemit onsite investigation by the Commission. But the life of the law is through experience, including politics, and not through logic. If one considers on-site investigation a mere "procedure," then technically a simple majority of the Commission could establish this with the authority granted it under section 2 of Article 42 ("The Commission shall lay down its rules of procedure"); yet if it is a "function," this fact is nowhere specified in the critical Article 45. And since on-site inquiry is a most sensitive political activity (because it constitutes a supranational calling into question of the veracity and indeed legitimacy of a sovereign), the first time that the issue arises it would seem destined for submission to the Assembly of Heads of State and Government—for whom inaction, a decision not to decide, would seem more prudent than the establishment of a "bad" precedent.

In addition to problems concerning the potential role of the Commission, the new charter requires that, in state-to-state or single-state proceedings, where mediation and conciliation by the Commission are impossible, the African Commission will then separately submit both a report and its recommendations to the OAU Assembly. The recommendations are not to be made public. The Commission's report ("stating the facts and its findings") *may* be made public, but only upon the decision of the Assembly. Such restrictions further reflect the intention to maintain a cautious, tight political rein on the African Commission on Human and Peoples' Rights.

Meanwhile, "other communications"—including those from indigenous or external NGOs—must be screened by the African Commission to meet criteria of admissibility. These (specified in Article 56) are no more difficult to satisfy than those currently required in other (e.g., the UN or Inter-American) systems. Section 1 of Article 58 requires the Commission to deliberate upon admissible communications to determine if they "apparently relate to special cases which reveal the existence of a series of serious or massive violations . . . ." Whether this threshold test presents greater difficulties than, or merely the same ones as, the UN's formulation remains for the future to reveal. In any event, if the Commission's deliberations on complaint petitions lead it to the conclusion that they do reveal "a series of serious or massive violations," it must first notify the Assembly of this fact. Following this, according to section 2 of the same article, the Assembly "may then request the Commission to undertake an in-depth study of these cases . . . ." Certainly, it can—and undoubtedly will—be argued that this means that the African Commission can independently receive petitions from NGOs or individuals; yet it cannot independently investigate them unless it first obtains a specific mandate from the higher political organ, the Assembly. In short, although the language of Article 46 is seemingly broad, it in fact is restricted to *how* the Commission may proceed with an in-depth study; *when* it may investigate, however, is a decision which—like on-site inquiry—is reserved to the Assembly. If these restrictions prevail, and the continental balance of political forces is overwhelmingly in their favor at present, they not only reduce the functional status of the new Commission to acting as a subject-matter subcommittee of the Assembly (as Gittleman notes), they cripple the necessary and vital role that could be played by human rights NGOs in the process.

Furthermore, Article 59 raises additional inhibitions on the potential role to be served by NGOs. It requires that all proceedings of the African Commission, regardless of the source of the communications being considered, "shall remain confidential until such a time as the Assembly . . . shall otherwise decide." Yet the persistence of official secrecy—the refusal of intergovernmental human rights agencies to publicize the fact that they have taken official cognizance of well-documented violations—is one of the governmental face-saving procedures that most human rights NGOs have sought to banish, on the grounds that secrecy encourages the violators, delaying the ending of violations or even more substantial internal political change. Furthermore, the potential impact of the NGOs has been described as "the mobilization of shame," and this cannot be accomplished without the widest publicity on violations and violators alike. At the minimum, therefore, the politics of the African situation require that those who submit allegations of violations to the Commission be in no way associated with other individuals and groups that publicize the identical facts in their campaigning efforts to build public awareness and condemnation. While it is currently true that petitioners to the African Commission will have no consultative status that can be suspended or revoked, it is not beyond the realm of possibility that an angry Assembly majority of affronted nation-states would instruct the new Commission to refuse to accept or otherwise consider any communications from a person or organization deemed by the Assembly to have violated its rule of confidentiality.

So much for the fundamental weaknesses of the Banjul Charter, with regard both to the specification of the human rights to be promoted and protected and to the creation of the institutional mechanism and procedures by which these rights are to be propagated and implemented. Lastly, it is necessary to consider the legal and political implications of the fact that this African Charter of Human and Peoples' Rights is an attempt not only to include "first-," "second-," and "third-generation" rights, but also to incorporate countervailing duties and obligations within the same unitary structure.

While Articles 27 and 28 assign the individual various duties with regard to "family," "fellow beings," and "others," it is Article 29 that is of greatest concern. It is this article that makes concrete "the obligation to solidarity" only vaguely referred to in the revised second section of Article 10 ("Subject to the obligation of solidarity . . . , no one may be compelled to join an association"). In point of fact, Article 29 is most comprehensive and specific in its imposition on the individual of obligations to a variety of solidarities; it reads, in part:

> The individual shall also have the duty: . . . ; (2) To serve his national community . . . ; (4) To preserve and strengthen social and national solidarity . . . ; (5) To preserve and strengthen the national independence and the territorial integrity of his country . . . ; (7) To preserve and strengthen positive African cultural values . . . ; (8) To contribute . . . to the promotion and achievement of African unity.

It will not do to dismiss these stated solidarities as non-operational objectives or the kind of high-blown rhetoric normally relegated to flowery preambles. Article 29, in combination with the ambiguities of Article 10 and/or the broad grant of power to accomplish the mandated state duty of Article 1, is entirely open-ended enough to legitimize one or another of several conceivable *anti*-human rights regimes.

One broad possibility is that African governments will choose to place a positive stress on the duties embraced in Article 29. That is, Articles 29 and 10 together can be read as permitting compulsory membership in a formal organization manifestly devoted to one or more of these corporate solidarities. As a specific example, if one examines the basic documents of African political parties (their founding charters, constitutions, statutes, platforms, etc.), it is evident that most of these—and certainly those of the dominant parties—claim total dedication to these worthy ends. Given this fact, it would be but a short step, and one which is permitted if not encouraged by the Banjul Charter itself, to making membership in the ruling party both mandatory and exclusive. Where these twin conditions obtain, discipline can then be forcibly exacted. Such compulsion, in all probability, need not directly affect all ordinary citizen-subjects, for there is no necessary virtue in forcing all adults, including illiterate peasants, into a mass party. On the other hand, the net of compulsion could, and most likely would, be cast broadly enough to enmesh all those in the urbanized, modernized sectors—all those, in short, with the resources for potential political dissent and who might be motivated to lead, represent, and speak on behalf of excluded groups. This joint reading of Articles 10 and 29, moreover, would merely confirm existing trends toward single-party systems in the newly independent nations; it would thereby legitimize barriers against the emergence of the concept of a loyal oppositon.

Somewhat less compulsory, yet equally harmful to the status of domestic human rights, would be the ruling party's utilizing its control of governmental institutions to establish a national-level commission on human rights, say, a Commission in Defence of the Banjul Charter, which could permit the political elite to preempt the social field and thereby monopolize all internal discourse on human rights issues. Such a national human rights commission would serve primarily as an instrument of foreign policy for its government.

These possibilities, of which several variants undoubtedly exist that need not be spelled out here, have been derived from the logical incompatibilities of Articles 10 and 29 in relation to each other. It would probably be more politically realistic to anticipate that African governments will be tempted, once again permitted or encouraged by the inconsistencies embedded in the Banjul Charter, to employ Articles 10 and 29 in combination and take a strongly negative approach to human rights in order to uphold the solidarity duties of the individual.

In simplified schematic form, the sources of human rights violations in Africa (as in the Third World generally) are two-fold: external, arising in the environment of international relations in all their forms, and internal, arising from the nature of the domestic political system.

The denials of peoples' rights in the Third World, including simply the failure to achieve them in any greater degree, have external causes. While visible domestically in the tragic dilemma of an excess of popular expectations, demands, and needs over resources available to satisfy them, yet the dilemma is external in origin. It derives from colonial history, specifically from the fact that formal political independence was gained only after these colonized territories and populations had been integrated into global structures of economic, political, and social power disadvantageous to their needs.

Even so, imagine the miraculous; let us suppose that a just New International Economic Order were to be achieved by tomorrow morning. Would there then be any warrant for assuming that denials and active violations of peoples' and human rights would disappear overnight as well? I think not. There are domestic causes as well, of which official corruption, nepotism, and governmental incompetence are probably only the most visible symptoms. That is, the underlying cause being reflected in these epiphenomena is what Robert Dahl has termed the "cumulative inequalities" upon which the political system is based and which, in turn, are the outcomes processed by these systems.[13] In many African systems, including those which entered the postindependence period with the most favorable economic conditions, a numerically tiny social group controls all political power; it is drawn entirely or disproportionately from a single ethnic community; the monopoly of political power also yields monopolized access to income and wealth within the system. Whether the development scheme is formally state capitalism or socialism, the socialized investment function is controlled by a governmental apparatus that in turn is controlled by the single party (or the "apolitical" military). Top-down planning is the rule. The individual has a right only to be "developed" at a pace and in a manner determined by the political elite; the individual has no right to participate in or to influence this development process—only a distant future right to contingent benefits. Politics thus become the process of suppressing the natural domestic conflicts that would otherwise emerge from these reinforcing ethnic, class, and power inequalities. Bureaucratic authoritarianism, most fully developed in Latin America but emerging elsewhere in the Third World, is both the means and the end result of such suppression.

Finally, in the absence of rule by murderous rampage, normal politics under conditions of cumulative inequalities is a process of making peaceful changes *legally* impossible. For example, the white rulers of the South African Republic have been punctiliously legalistic in carrying out a most vicious racism. Repressive rule *by* law is altogether common among the nations of this era.

The relevance of the above points becomes starkly evident when one recalls, from the final language of Article 1 of the Banjul Charter, that the member states of the Organization of African Unity have collectively granted themselves the mandate to give effect to the Charter's duties, as well as to its rights and freedoms, by adopting legislative or other measures. If, as established in Article 29, the individual has a duty to strengthen national solidarity, to preserve the territorial integrity of his country, to promote African unity, then the adequacy of his performance of such duties will be judged by the relevant national elite. Whether African elites are more insecure than other Third World elites may be unanswerable empirically; in any event, most African elites derive significant benefits from existing cumulative inequalities and, like all elites elsewhere, they have both motivation and means to preserve their power and privilege within the system, in the name of preserving the system itself. For such self-gratifying purpose, Article 1 may be read as empowering insecure elites to issue executive decrees by which to criminalize what they perceive as the negative consequences to such various specified solidarities arising from the individual's exercise of his (conditionally granted) freedoms to assemble (under Article 11), to express and disseminate his opinions (under Article 9), to associate with others (under Article 10). For instance, since ethnicity and geography are intimately related in most parts of Africa, any political brief by or for a powerless ethnic community can readily be interpreted as a threat to the territorial integrity of the nation-state. Therefore, under the guise of reasons of state and similar obligations of solidarity, ordinary political speech can and will *legally* be labelled as the crime of treason or sedition because one can find no basis, within the terms and logic of the Banjul Charter, upon which to call the sophisticated, post-Amin legalistic tyrant to task. Given its unresolved ambiguities and contradictions, the new African Charter is capable of legitimizing a cruelly perverted jurisprudence of human rights under which the individual is permitted no more than the right to engage in public praise of the omnicompetent ruling party, or its leader.

In raising these problems, I am not asserting that all African signatories to the Banjul Charter will take one of these repressive routes. Nor would I predict that no signatory or group of signatories will seek to employ the treaty's procedures and the African Commission to challenge a perverted course so destructive of human rights. To the contrary, I am asserting two brief, pessimistic points: that one or more nations can and will manipulate the contradictions embraced in the Charter to establish an *anti*–human rights regime; and also that no nations, however indignant, will be able to employ the Charter successfully to call the violators to account. At the same time, there is nothing in the Banjul Charter that would prevent a member state from doing far more in the way of promoting and effectively protecting individual rights than that which is so conditionally prescribed in the document. As a regional mechanism for the collective protection of individual or group rights of a political nature, the Banjul Charter comes desperately close to being a snare and a delusion. This is so because, in searching the document for an irreducible minimum of such rights that could be protected, and for an associational basis for self-protection, one finds that there is neither.

NOTES

1. See, in particular, George W. Shepherd, Jr., *Anti-Apartheid: Transnational Conflict and Western Policy in the Liberation of South Africa* (Westport, Conn.: Greenwood Press, 1977), pp. 33–36, and Roger S. Clark, "The International League for Human Rights and South West Africa, 1947-1957: The Human Rights NGO as Catalyst in the International Legal Process," *Human Rights Quarterly* 3, no. 4 (Fall, 1981), pp. 101–36.

2. See the annual reports of Amnesty International for 1977–1981. For AI's contigency fund, see *Amnesty International Report 1978* (London: Amnesty International, 1979), pp. 25 and 288–93 for the supporting statistical data.

3. Shepherd, *Anti-Apartheid*, p. 120.

4. Ibid., pp. 125–26.

5. The data are from "1981 World Refugee Survey" published by the U.S. Committee for Refugees (USCR) (New York: 1982), pp. 32–33. These statistics, for the first time, constitute an attempt by the USCR to define as "refugees" only those persons still in need of permanent homes (i.e., non-resettled) in contrast to the higher refugee statistics reported by the UN High Commissioner for Refugees (UNHCR) (whose office retains in its totals those persons permanently resettled in third countries until such time as they legally acquire their new nationality). The latter precaution by the UNHCR is maintained in case those permanently resettled may again need the legal protection of the UN Office; but in practice, according to the U.S. Committee for Refugees, very few permanently resettled refugees ever need to call upon the

UNHCR again for assistance. Therefore, the lower statistic is a more realistic definition of the problem.

6. See M.G. Smith, "Institutional and Political Conditions of Pluralism," in Leo Kuper and M.G. Smith, eds., *Pluralism in Africa* (Berkeley and Los Angeles: University of California Press, 1969), ch. 2, pp. 27–65, at p. 58.

7. "African Charter of Human and Peoples' Rights, Meeting of Experts for the Preparation of the Draft African Charter of Human and Peoples' Rights, Dakar, Senegal, 28 November to 8 December 1979." OAU Doc. CAB/LEG/67/3/Rev. 1 (quotations at pp. 3 and 2, respectively).

8. The case of the 1979 downfall of "Emperor" Bokassa of the Central African Republic is relevant to this point. Amnesty International first publicized the killings of school children (mostly ages 12 to 16 but some as young as 8) on May 14, 1979. Ten days later, after government denials that any pupils under the age of 16 had been arrested and that any of those detained had been killed, at a francophonic conference of African heads of state, Bokassa admitted to newsmen that some young people had been killed the month earlier. (Practically simultaneously, his ambassador in Paris held a news conference confirming the accuracy of the AI report of fifty to one hundred deaths.) Thereupon, five governments at the conference—the Ivory Coast, Liberia, Rwanda, Senegal, and Togo—established an ad hoc commission of inquiry, sending it immediately to Bokassa's capital, Bangui. We note that "members of the commission also visited London and held formal discussions with Amnesty International." (*Amnesty International Report 1980*, London: Amnesty International, 1981, p. 36.) The report of the five-nation commission, publicized in August, found that government security forces had killed as many as one hundred fifty school children. (They had been demonstrating against an Imperial decree ordering them to purchase and wear special school uniforms; some reports indicate that a boutique owned by the Emperor's wife was the sole source of supply.)

9. Of added relevance to the future status of African human rights NGOs, certain stylistic changes were made in the Charter which have substantive effect. The first draft of the Banjul Charter, in speaking of *human* rights, uniformly throughout employs the noun "person" but, in the final version, in every instance this has been changed to "individual" as the referent of the right. I infer that the consistent change was deliberately made to avoid the possibility that subsequent African jurisprudence might treat the business corporation as an artificial person with public law rights attaching to it.

After all, American constitutional law and politico-legal history are quite well known to Third World jurists and lawyers. African jurists in particular are well aware of the perverted logic by which the U.S. Supreme Court, beginning in 1886, interpreted the language of the Fourteenth Amendment—which was clearly intended to protect the freed slaves—so as to protect business corporations from governmental regulation. Also, the attitudes of Third World elites toward multinational corporations include both fear and anger, as is well documented. However, in avoiding the possibility of legal protection for such business corporations, the African draftsmen have also excluded the possibility that their emerging human rights jurisprudence might afford protected status to not-for-profit incorporated entities such as churches or non-governmental organizations manifestly dedicated to human rights.

10. Unfortunately, in discourse in international law and politics, "people" is used in at least three different ways: in the struggle for the self-determination of a people (the right to political independence); in reference to the economic, social, and cultural rights collectively of a people (as citizens within a nation-state); and, finally, in reference to the right of a people in a society organized as government and state against claims of other peoples so organized (as an attribute of sovereignty). Operationally, one suspects, "peoples" will be given concrete referents primarily in the case of the anti-apartheid struggle and, in the name of all Africans as represented by member states of the OAU, on issues of imperialism and all forms of neocolonialism. If so, one of the major political purposes of the new Charter is to buttress the claims of the Movement of Non-Aligned Countries/Group of 77 for a New International Economic Order, a New International Information Order, and so forth. One of the consequences, unintended or otherwise, may be to diminish the claims of individuals-within-the-people in the second, collective usage above.

11. OAU Document CM/1149 (XXXVII), Annex I, p. 4.

12. Ibid.

13. Robert A. Dahl, *Who Governs? Democracy and Power in An American City* (New Haven: Yale University Press, 1961), p. 85.

III

Problems of Development and Human Rights from an International Perspective

---

INTRODUCTION

Since World War II, increasing international attention has been devoted to defining and realizing basic goals in human rights and development. However, despite the prominence of these matters as global agenda items, and their extensive normative and institutional history within the UN system, problems of human rights violations and underdevelopment still persist throughout much of the Third World. Current attempts to devise more effective policies to deal with these problems frequently have become stalemated in North-South deliberations, reflecting continuing political differences as to how human rights and development questions should be approached and resolved within the international community. For example, many developing countries argue that only a major restructuring of the international economic system—the New International Economic Order (NIEO)—can permit development and the protection of human rights within these societies. Western governments, on the other hand, have tended to emphasize civil and political matters in their human rights policies, and they question claims that greater international economic redistribution will alleviate conditions of underdevelopment in Third World societies.

Despite these disagreements, there is growing recognition that human rights and development are related aspects of each other's accomplishment and as such remain mutually conditioning factors. This section examines the relationships between development and human rights, as well as the impact of global trends in these areas upon African countries.

In his chapter, Ronald Meltzer explores the changing content and character of international human rights and development, particularly within the context of North-South relations. He indicates different areas of convergence between human rights and development—

conceptually, politically and institutionally. He suggests that an adoption of a more integrated approach to these matters can help overcome many of the problems found within each realm. Meltzer then examines how these linkages were handled within a key set of North-South negotiations for African states: the formulation of the Lomé II Convention between the European Community and the African-Caribbean-Pacific states. The renegotiation of the Lomé agreement in 1979 illustrated continuing problems that confront human rights and development matters within North-South relations. For the most part, human rights and development questions were treated as conceptually distinct and narrowly defined phenomena, and their discussion within the Lomé II negotiations eventually turned into an antagonistic political sideshow. The experience of the Lomé II renegotiation process also revealed the limits of state action in the formulation and implementation of human rights and development activities.

Timothy Shaw looks at the connections between human rights and development by examining the position of African states within the world system. In his chapter, he argues that the status of human rights and development within societies is not simply the function of the African regimes themselves, but the result of their historical and structural dependency in international economic and political relations. Using a world systems approach, Shaw assesses the prospects for self-determination within Africa, as well as the different international programs—the OAU Lagos Plan and the World Bank's Agenda for Action—formulated to advance economic and social development. Shaw concludes that African steps towards human rights and development remain severely limited by continuing historical patterns of dependency characterizing Africa's position within the world system.

The issue of self-determination stands at the center of human rights and development questions concerning Africa. The postwar era has witnessed an extensive process of political decolonization within the continent, leading to the creation of independent sovereign states which have sought increased self-determination as a fundamental priority of government. Clearly, this process has not been completed, given Africa's continuing economic dependence upon the West and the residues of its colonial past.

Perhaps the most blatant and obvious limit to the achievement of self-determination within Africa has been the case of Namibia, which remains under South Africa's control despite UN revocation of its mandate. Namibia has been the focus of recent multilateral efforts to rectify this basic—and anachronistic—denial of human rights. George Shepherd's chapter examines the factors which have prevented

Namibian independence. In particular, he shows how human rights considerations in this context have been shaped by broader international economic and strategic constraints. Shepherd also analyzes the motivations and interactions of the Western "contact group" which has sought a negotiated settlement for Namibian independence. In his chapter, he suggests basic principles for a viable approach to this human rights dilemma.

The chapter by Jack Donnelly focuses on an important manifestation of the connections between human rights and development—the espousal of a "right to development" by the Third World. Donnelly evaluates the origins of the claim that development itself is a basic human right, and he examines its moral and legal foundations. Despite its growing importance as a political statement, Donnelly argues that the right to development—a "third generation" of human rights—contains numerous fallacies of law and logic. He concludes by suggesting several principles for thinking about human rights and development questions. From his perspective, focusing on the right to development is an inappropriate way to deal with these matters and a wrong-headed approach to making the necessary connections between human rights and development.

CHAPTER NINE

International Human Rights and Development: Evolving Conceptions and Their Application to Relations between the European Community and the African-Caribbean-Pacific States

RONALD I. MELTZER

Despite their normative importance, attempts to advance international human rights and development in Africa confront major obstacles at all levels of political activity—domestic, regional, and international. As indicated in several preceding chapters, even the most cursory examination of many African societies reveals the persistence of widespread poverty and government repression. In addition, there has been a remarkable consensus of pessimism emanating from the United Nations, the World Bank, the International Monetary Fund, and elsewhere, indicating that large portions of the population in this area of the world will face even bleaker prospects during the 1980s.[1]

Over the past two decades, connections between underdevelopment and human rights violations have frequently become apparent. In many African countries, basic freedoms and individual liberties have been suspended or transgressed in the name of some other sanctioned value—unity, decolonization, economic progress, or national security. State leaders often claim that within societies already burdened with pressing needs and instabilities, the vast demands of development require what Robert Heilbroner called "iron governments." In effect, this perceived necessity would set lower standards and priorities for the protection of human rights and individual needs.[2] Moreover, in Africa and other areas of the developing world there has been a growing appeal to what Foaud Ajami has called "the latest narcotic" peddled within these societies—the promise of a return to authenticity and original tradition to improve living conditions. In Zaire, Uganda, and elsewhere, this emphasis upon traditional practices has acted in many instances to cover up the decay, dress up the tyranny, and run away from the dependency that these countries—and their people—experience.[3]

This chapter explores the changing content and character of international human rights and development. It focuses upon recent formulations in these areas and their conceptual, political, and institutional connections, especially in the context of North-South relations. This chapter also will examine the formulation of the Lomé II Convention between the European Community (EC) and the African-Caribbean-Pacific (ACP) states during the 1977–79 period to illustrate how linkages between human rights and development have been approached in North-South negotiations affecting Africa. As will be seen, the renegotiation of this EC-ACP association agreement provides telling insight into the difficulties of pursuing international human rights and development objectives, as well as attempts to forge meaningful connections between these two policy areas.

THE CHANGING CONTENT AND CHARACTER OF INTERNATIONAL HUMAN RIGHTS AND DEVELOPMENT

Over the past few decades, the definition and scope of international human rights have been broadened considerably, a development that has mirrored the changing configuration and viewpoints of United Nations membership.[4] Within the United Nations, the earliest and most recognized focus of human rights dealt primarily with "fundamental freedoms" of individuals. Beginning in the 1960s, however, normative development in the area of international human rights was extended to collectivities, especially concerning economic, social, and cultural rights. This emphasis could be seen, for example, in the 1966 UN covenants on human rights. As indicated in the preceding chapters, the Banjul Charter went even further in recognizing African peoples' rights to economic, social, and cultural development, a satisfactory environment, and peace and security. Thus, current international human rights formulations embrace an impressive array of subjects and norms, involving individual and collective rights that extend across civil, political, economic, social, and cultural terrains.[5]

Definitions about international human rights derive from many different traditions and bodies of thought.[6] As illustrated in earlier chapters, Western perspectives on human rights have focused largely upon the state as the primary threat to individual rights and liberties. Emphasis has been placed upon limiting the power and arbitrariness of the state and providing the individual with recourse to and standing before the state on such matters. Developing nations and socialist states, however, do not necessarily share this perspective. Indeed, Western notions frequently have been criticized in these quarters as a partial and even misguided formulation of human rights—an ideology of abundance. Third World and socialist criticisms generally have stressed that the protection of human rights is not tied exclusively to violations by the state. It must also cover societal conditions, that is, the provision of economic and social well-being.

These contending views can be seen in each side's basic emphasis in approaching the protection of human rights. As Kenneth Boulding has noted, Western conceptions of human rights have traditionally focused upon "form"—procedures to insure the protection of the individual and to offer remedies in times of possible violation. Third World and socialist formulations, however, have emphasized "substance"—an enumeration of rights and obligations specifying social and economic objectives. But each perspective has evidenced its own weaknesses. Just as the Western liberal view has been vulnerable to criticisms concerning economic and social injustice, so the Third World and socialist formulations are open to charges of state tyranny.[7]

These contentions concerning human rights have become increasingly important in North-South relations, particularly in connection with international development issues. For example, Western economic perspectives on North-South relations have focused primarily on the private marketplace as the basis for generating economic development, as well as distributing economic justice and well-being. But as Sylvia Ann Hewlett has noted, there has been no natural affinity that has been proven between the Western prescriptions for economic growth, political freedom, and social justice in the contemporary development process. More often than not, the Western growth strategies pursued by developing states have been indifferent to equity considerations, and governments frequently have relied upon repressive internal policies for their institution and maintenance.[8] Thus, for many developing countries, the Western economic model has failed systematically to resolve domestic inequities of distribution, wealth, and power. In addition, Western nations have opposed most proposals for international economic restructuring regarded by the developing world as necessary to correct prevailing market failures. The maintenance of these positions on North-South matters has had a significant effect upon how human rights issues have been approached by developing countries. It has led to a discrediting of Western formulations about international human rights in the Third World, and has permitted a backing off from their implementation.[9]

Some time ago, Rupert Emerson suggested that any viable formulation of international human rights would need to make greater connections between such human rights and the advancement of global development and world peace.[10] These types of relationships have been increasingly emphasized in various UN forums. One such effort involves what has become known as the right to development.[11] But as the Donnelly chapter indicates, despite affirmation by the UN Commission on Human Rights, its content and effects still remain at rather primitive stages of development.[12] Furthermore, the necessary steps to get binding convenants to respect such rights and machinery to implement these covenants are not likely to occur soon, if at all, since the right to development touches upon major points of controversy in North-South relations.[13]

Nevertheless, the idea of the right to development and its far-reaching connections point up significant changes that have occurred in development thinking over recent decades. These modifications reflect not only changing values about what development entails, but also represent a response to the meager results gained from successive attempts to devise and implement international development strategies. Indeed, despite more than a decade of international conferences and proclamations, North-South deliberations on these matters have been reduced largely to ritualism and stalemate.

Such failures of past North-South efforts indicate that prevailing approaches to international development need to be recast. First, the notion of internal reform within developing societies must be given more serious consideration as an important complement to international economic reform. As Mahbub al Haq has argued, all too often, the proposal of a New International Economic Order (NIEO) has become the "soft option" for leaders within the developing world who remain unable or unwilling to confront their own domestic situations. Second, it is important to discard the view that NIEO is a condition or outcome that is to be granted by the North. Instead, such change should derive from the actions of developing countries themselves, with or without the collaboration of the North. Third, the North must understand its own interests in restructuring the international economic order. These interests are reflected in the growing reliance of Western nations upon the South for trade and resources, as well as in efforts to insure that continuing Third World economic problems do not engulf an already deteriorated international economic order. Thus, the North should no longer view development problems as issues that can be put off or considered unrelated to its own economic difficulties. Finally, it is necessary to rectify what has been a major shortcoming of past development strategies: the tendency to ignore the social and human aspects of development, or what one observer called the *requirements* side of the development question.[14]

The past three decades have witnessed several major changes in prevailing international strategies for development. The first UN

Development Decade, of the 1960s, was concerned primarily with rates of economic growth achieved by developing countries. It included only superficial reference to the promotion of social progress and human rights. In the 1970s, this limited approach was revised to grant greater attention to social justice and human needs. But international development programs still treated social and human aspects of development in a vague and extraneous manner, particularly in comparison with specific targets outlined for economic growth and resource transfers. This distinction between the different aspects of international development has been continued and reinforced in the major UN resolutions and declarations relating the establishment of NIEO.[15]

As the Shaw chapter below indicates, the more recent formulations, such as the OAU Lagos Plan of Action, reflect new directions in development thinking. First, the fulfillment of *basic human needs* is central to realizing effective development. Such needs contain two key dimensions—material and non-material. The provision of individual and family needs, such as food, shelter, and clothing, as well as essential public services, such as water, sanitation, health, and education, constitute basic material needs. Non-material aspects include respect for individual choice and self-determination. Second, effective development is predicated upon *endogenous* rather than exogenous patterns of economic relations. At its base, endogenous development entails more autonomous domestic economic planning that focuses upon the satisfaction of internal needs and societal potential. Such an emphasis would result in a restructuring of the national economy's relationship to the world economic system. A third component would be the maximazation of *self-reliance*. Related to the idea of endogenous development, self-reliance not only calls for the selective adoption of links to external economic relations, but, perhaps more important, involves efforts to cultivate reliance upon local resources and capacities. Finally, a more viable approach to development requires significant public *participation*—the continuous, widespread, and conscious effort to make all segments of society engage in the development process, and to ensure that development choices more accurately reflect popular desires.[16]

As an integrated process and outcome, then, several propositions can be made about development.[17] First, collective and individual development promote one another; the achievement of one dimension at the expense of the other can be only self-defeating. Second, development cannot be seen simply as economic growth and industrialization, nor can it result from an exclusive emphasis upon these factors. Its essential elements also include improved living conditions, social change, and close attention to the qualitative impacts of economic activity.[18] Thus, as the 1980 Brandt Commission Report noted, development has come to mean "more than a passage from poor to rich, from traditional rural economy to sophisticated urban"; instead, development "involves a profound transformation of the entire economic and social structure," carrying with it "not only the idea of economic betterment but also of greater human dignity, security, justice, and equity."[19]

HUMAN RIGHTS AND DEVELOPMENT: CONCEPTUAL, POLITICAL, AND INSTITUTIONAL CONNECTIONS

Recent formulations about international human rights and development reveal several connections that can be made between these two areas—conceptually, politically, and institutionally. In many respects, establishing such linkages would help overcome problems that have been experienced in each realm. At the conceptual level, the notion of development has explicit links to human rights. Even beyond debates about its existence as a right, development can be viewed as a basis for the enjoyment of human rights, providing access to the means necessary to realize the types of human rights specified in the Universal Declaration and the International Covenants.[20] A more integrated approach to development and human rights also can remedy previous blindspots and distortions associated with past conceptions. For example, linking human rights and development would mean that a major dimension of development—the human and social aspects—would be considered an integral component of both the human needs, an important shortcoming in previous development strategies. In this manner, the concept of development is expanded to avoid the prior constraints and pitfalls of emphasizing economic growth, and key aspects of development can be treated as human rights—the right to food, shelter, education, and meaningful survival.[21]

The conceptual links between human rights and development are highlighted perhaps most clearly when the notion of public participation is introduced. In effect, such participation can be seen as a linchpin of the development process, helping to ensure that needs are met, energies are mobilized, and outcomes are more responsive to collective and individual wills. Thus, public participation acts as a vital basis upon which concepts of development and human rights can interrelate and become mutually supporting.

A more integrated approach to development and human rights also has important implications politically. Many of the political trade-offs and straw men troubling North-South relations could be avoided or addressed more effectively by relating human rights and development factors. For example, past international deliberations dealing with NIEO and other development matters frequently floundered or became further politicized when human rights issues were raised. In this context, the protection of international human rights became a rather tattered Western banner waved before the developing world as a response to calls for NIEO. The result was the creation of a false trade-off, in effect sidetracking or discrediting activities in support of both sets of objectives.

A similar interaction occurred with respect to the notion of basic needs. The Western emphasis upon basic needs was viewed with strong suspicion within the Third World. It was seen as an attempt to establish a global bottom-line without addressing fundamental questions of hierarchy, decision making, and distribution within international economic relations. As a consequence, discussions about meeting basic human needs within underdeveloped societies became stalemated and rancorous. Similarly, North-South relations often became bogged down over issues of priority among development objectives, principally concerning the reduction of international inequalities versus the pursuit of internal reforms. Again, discussions spiraled into false trade-offs and recriminations. For example, in the Third World, standards of equity and fairness were applied between rich and poor globally, but not at home. Among Western governments, the need for domestic political and civil liberties within developing nations took priority over problems of international economic justice and opportunity.

Clearly, a more integrated approach to human rights and development would help avoid these types of distinctions and the posturing that have long exacerbated North-South relations. No doubt substantial policy differences persist between developed and developing countries, creating major obstacles to resolving global development and human rights issues. But serious consideration of more recent formulations in these areas could reduce the basis for continued politicization—or least provide less cover for each side's actual motivations and dynamics.

An integrated approach to development—one with clear links with human rights—also has important implications institutionally. The UN system has long addressed linkages between international human rights and development. For example, the Charter makes reference to these types of connections, and as early as 1957, the General Assembly called for programs to combine human and social progress as a basis for achieving development.[22]

However, the United Nations remains unprepared institutionally to approach development on a multidisciplinary or intersectoral basis. Recent UN restructuring activities in the economic and social sectors have sought to integrate different aspects of development programming, as well as coordinate different levels of activity (intergovernmental, interagency, and inter-Secretariat). However, very little progress has been achieved on UN institutional reform in this respect. The obstacles have included: political differences among member states as to the goals and authority of UN organs dealing with development; bureaucratic conflicts among UN bodies concerning jurisdictional issues; and major organizational design problems in creating new intersectoral capacities within a system that has long been highly compartmentalized and pluralistic.[23]

Recent UN development strategies have emphasized program decentralization and collective self-reliance within developing countries. As a result, regional and local institutional capabilities have become more important in realizing development objectives. Indeed, the most fruitful institutional focus in the development process, along with establishing links to human rights, may be at the local or grassroots level. In terms of resource planning and utilization, this level of activity could be the most efficient and dynamic institutionally, and it could also help ensure maximum public responsiveness in the development process. At the local level, non-governmental organizations (NGOs) can play particularly useful roles in this regard. As the chapter by Harry Scoble, above, points out, NGOs can offer alternative and supplementary services in defining and meeting human rights and development objectives.[24] However, further institutionalization of the development process in this manner still confronts a basic problem of implementation, that is, the design of criteria and measures for monitoring organizational compliance with prevailing standards.[25]

LINKAGES BETWEEN HUMAN RIGHTS AND DEVELOPMENT: THE FORMULATION OF THE LOMÉ II CONVENTION

The development policies and prospects of most African states have been linked historically to economic relations with members of the European Community. These economic ties date back to the formation of the European Community in 1958 and have been institutionalized through various association agreements. From the Yaoundé I Convention in 1963, which involved some eighteen Associated African States and Madagascar (ASSM), to the Lomé II Convention of 1979, which applied to fifty-eight African-Caribbean-Pacific states (ACP), this system of association expanded into full-scale trade and development assistance agreements which have been described as a "model for relations between developed and developing countries."[26]

The evolution of these EC-ACP association agreements has reflected changing African development policies, as well as the outcome of bargaining between the two major groupings. The first Lomé Convention, concluded in 1975, sought to improve upon the limited trade and development assistance provisions of Yaoundé. It dealt with five major areas: trade cooperation: export earnings from commodities; industrial cooperation; financial and technical cooperation; and joint EC-ACP institutions. The Lomé Convention included major revisions of Yaoundé's terms and arrangements. Of particular importance were new provisions for the stabilization of export earnings (STABEX) and industrial cooperation. One vital aspect of Lomé, which has distinguished this agreement from others in North-South relations, has been its intended comprehensiveness as a development instrument. Towards this end, the framework of Lomé I and II has rested upon "four cornerstones" that seek to solidify EC-ACP relationships in a systematic fashion. These include:

> legal certainty in the relations between economically unequal partners on the basis of a freely negotiated agreement;
>
> a single agreement governing relations between all countries, which rules out any influence upon, or discrimination against, the economic systems, forms of government, or development models of individual partners; thus cooperation is marked unequivocally by non-alignment and mutual respect for national and cultural independence;
>
> general arrangements for every conceivable form of cooperation; with the variety of precisely defined instruments available, it is possible to provide each ACP country those measures best adapted to its particular economic structure, its degree of development, its requirements, and its own priorities;
>
> a permanent dialogue between the developed and developing members, guaranteed by an institutional structure taken over from the first Lomé Convention and further strengthened by new consultation procedures.[27]

The Lomé I Convention remained in force for five years, expiring on February 29, 1980. Since Lomé II was seen as a continuation and elaboration of EC-ACP relations, negotiations for a new Convention were planned as part of this ongoing association. The renegotiation process began on July 24, 1978, involving all the major bodies dealing with EC-ACP relations: the EC Council and Commission, the European Parliament, the ACP-EEC Council of Ministers, and the ACP-

EEC Consultative Assembly and its Joint Committee. Predictably, each side of the EC-ACP groupings took opposing views of the content of the new Convention. In general, the ACP states called for a radical restructuring of Lomé I to provide greater economic benefits and authority to recipients. The EC members adopted a much more limited perspective in revising the past Convention.[28] Well before the official renegotiations were scheduled to convene, however, another key issue was raised—the introduction of a reference to human rights within the framework of the Convention. This matter subsequently became a major point of contention within EC-ACP negotiations.

The possibility of including a human rights provision within a new Lomé Convention surfaced initially at the 1977 ACP-EEC Council meeting. Several European members were very concerned about the extent to which Community economic assistance programs supported regimes, such as those of Amin, Bokassa, and Macias Nguema, that clearly violated human rights. They sought to gain a basis for condemning such action, if not ensuring a stronger commitment to respect such rights. This type of sentiment similarly led to the so-called Uganda guidelines which the EC adopted in June 1977. In the face of highly publicized abuses of basic human rights in Uganda, the European Nine agreed that their economic assistance programs should not support the Amin government and should remain restricted solely to improving living conditions for the Ugandan people. However, these guidelines were very difficult to implement, since major Community assistance provisions, such as STABEX, could not be controlled in such a manner.[29] Indeed, these difficulties led some European states to seek more definitive instruments for dealing with human rights violations within the Lomé framework.

Prior to the renegotiation process, ACP states expressed reservations about dealing with the issue of human rights and generally sought to put off its consideration. They expressed concern that any reference to human rights within the Convention could be used as a pretext for intervening in their countries' internal affairs, arguing in addition that such treatment of human rights matters more appropriately belonged in other international forums. African members also thought that human rights represented a highly complex and subjective concept, posing too many political problems for inclusion in what was seen as an essentially economic agreement. Moreover, ACP spokesmen drew sharp distinctions between human rights violations in South Africa and those found elsewhere on the continent; they were unwilling to deal with human rights matters in any consolidated fashion.[30]

Despite some early indication of a possible EC-ACP compromise on human rights within Lomé II, the positions of each side grew farther apart over time. For example, the ACP Council of Ministers met in Lusaka in December 1977 and adopted a resolution stating that the Lomé convention dealt essentially with trade and development assistance, and therefore was unsuited for any consideration of human rights.

Within the European Community, the Commissioner for Development, Claude Cheysson, stated in February 1978 that human rights should appear in a renegotiated economic assistance agreement with the ACP. He noted that a major shortcoming of Lomé I was its failure to specify the "ultimate objective" of social and economic development. While emphasizing that the EC should not use development assistance measures to interfere with the domestic affairs of other sovereign states, the European Commission eventually suggested two guidelines for dealing with human rights within Lomé II. First, there should be a preambular clause stating unequivocally the signatories' obligation to observe fundamental human rights. Second, the EC should undertake an internal commitment to condemn publicly any infraction of human rights by any of the signatories. Such a condemnation would not necessarily lead to a termination of commercial relations, but it could affect aid transfers to violators.[31]

The European Parliament similarly focused upon a reference to human rights within the Lomé framework. On November 23, 1978, it adopted a resolution calling for "great care and a high degree of responsibility" in approaching human rights. Such caution reflected underlying disagreements within the Community. For example, in the Parliament, Socialist and Conservative groups favored specific references to human rights, especially Articles 3–14 of the Universal Declaration. But Christian Democrats argued that Lomé had been intended primarily for trade and economic development, noting that different contexts for human rights exist among the EC and ACP states.

These divergent EC perspectives also were evident in intergovernmental deliberations. In various EC forums, British and Dutch representatives called for the inclusion of an operational clause within Lomé II that could free EC members from obligations to ACP states committing gross violations of human rights. Both governments emphasized the importance of public support to continued development assistance programs and questioned their long-term political viability in the face of recipients' human rights abuses. But other member states, such as France, Belgium, and Germany, sought to limit consideration of the issue and to avoid any interference with what was viewed as the primary task of Lomé II: the renegotiation of a trade and economic assistance agreement between the Community and its associated ACP states. By the time renegotiation officially began in July 1978, however, the Nine had reached a compromise on the matter. They would attempt to incorporate a reference to human rights within the preamble of the new Convention, although it was clear that the practical effects of such action were questionable.[32]

When the EC-ACP Council of Ministers met formally to open the Lomé renegotiations, each side held opposing positions on the issue of human rights. Indeed, these differences deepened throughout the renegotiation period. The ACP states remained steadfastly opposed to a human rights initiative within Lomé, viewing its inclusion as a "dangerous and uncalled-for precedent" within ACP-EC economic relations. Moreover, they criticized the narrowness of EC conceptions of human rights, which emphasized civil and political rights within ACP members while showing little interest in the rights of ACP migrant workers within Europe. The EC representatives did acknowledge that any human rights provisions required reciprocal application, but they were clearly reluctant to assume specific obligations vis-à-vis foreign workers. Indeed, the Nine eventually rejected an ACP declaration on non-discriminatory treatment for ACP migrant workers, effectively precluding what might have been their only positive leverage to gain ACP approval for a human rights component within Lomé II.

Throughout these negotiations, compromise proposals regarding a human rights provision within Lomé were entertained. For example, one such compromise suggested a reference to the "promotion of human dignity" in the Convention. But by the close of the fourth annual meeting of the ACP-EEC Consultative Assembly, in early October 1979, a final resolution on the renegotiation of Lomé II was adopted without agreement on human rights. Thus, when the Convention was signed on October 31, 1979, it contained no direct mention of human rights in any form.[33]

At the signing of the Lomé II Convention, EC and ACP representatives commented on the importance of human rights, seeking to reduce the issue's prominence and controversy within the specific framework of this new agreement. Each side noted the independent action it had taken on the matter in other institutional arenas. For example, in July 1979 the OAU had resolved in Monrovia to draft an African charter on human rights and establish regional mechanisms for their protection. In part, this OAU action represented an attempt to respond to foreign criticisms concerning the ACP position during the renegotiation period and, more important, to insulate future economic agreements from similar EC human rights initiatives. When Lomé II was signed, the President of the ACP Council of Ministers, H. Bernard St. John, asserted that the Monrovia resolution made clear that "our concern for human rights is no less than yours."[34] In addition, as described earlier in chapters by Claude Welch and Edward Kannyo, the deposition of Amin, Bokassa, and Macias Nguema suggested that human rights abuses in Africa could be rectified through internal action.

Within the European Community, the Nine eventually adopted an internal statement declaring their intention to take "appropriate action" to insure that aid benefits would be limited only to the neediest in cases of flagrant human rights violations. In effect, this declaration amounted to a reiteration of the Uganda guidelines. Thus, the renegotiation process did not succeed in giving expression to earlier EC intentions to link human rights and development within the context of Lomé.[35]

CONCLUSION

The experience of the Lomé II renegotiation process offers important insights into how human rights, development, and their possible linkages are treated within contemporary North-South relations. Conceptually, politically, and institutionally, EC-ACP interactions concerning Lomé II offer graphic evidence of the types of pitfalls noted earlier in this chapter. Conceptually, human rights and development were considered as distinct phenomena, and their individual treatment similarly reflected narrow notions of what each objective constituted. For example, the thrust of what the EC sought to include as a human rights initiative in Lomé II was largely a series of fundamental freedoms associated with Articles 3–12 of the Universal Declaration. As noted, this emphasis on basically civil and political rights, particularly to the exclusion of other human rights in economic and social realms, tended to fragment discussion of human rights and development, making their linkage within Lomé II virtually impossible.

Interestingly, ACP treatment of human rights matters within the renegotiation similarly reflected narrow conceptions. Aside from references to the economic and social rights of ACP migrant workers in Europe, ACP statements concerning human rights remained largely confined to civil and political matters, and they were addressed in isolation from the major development provisions of Lomé II. Perhaps this ACP perspective on human rights was aimed as a response to EC initiatives. As seen in earlier chapters, subsequent treatment of human rights within the Banjul Charter eventually took on much broader conceptual dimensions concerning individual and peoples' rights.

Lomé II's treatment of development also was limited conceptually, particularly with respect to its social and human aspects. The Convention, as it was formulated, contained six major areas of emphasis:

promotion and development of trade between the ACP and the European Community;
industrialization of the ACP states, the main prerequisite for their economic development and for increased trade to the benefit of these countries;
stabilization of export earnings from commodities;
improvements in the agricultural sector, with the particular aim of guaranteeing the ACP's food supply;
intensification of regional cooperation among the ACP countries;
special measures for the least-developed ACP countries.[36]

Although Lomé II did contain specific provisions bearing upon social and human aspects of development, most particularly the agricultural cooperation activities and integrated rural development projects, the new EC-ACP arrangements constituted primarily a conventional trade and aid agreement. As in the case with many such pacts, much more specificity and emphasis were given to economic growth, trade, and financial transfer targets than to such matters as human needs, the level of participation, and social conditions. Thus Lomé II did not go very far either in advancing a more integrated approach to development or in making direct links between development and human rights within its framework.[37]

Politically, attempts to introduce a human rights provision into Lomé II fell victim to many of the false trade-offs and politicized dynamics that have characterized other North-South proceedings in the past. The ACP states viewed the EC efforts with a great deal of suspicion, particularly given the divergént perspectives each side took concerning the types of changes Lomé II should incorporate vis-à-vis earlier economic assistance agreements. At best, the ACP members perceived the issue of human rights as a distraction from their principal mission. At worst, these states were concerned about the use of human rights as a basis for legitimizing foreign intervention and escaping economic assistance obligations. As a foreign minister from one ACP nation stated, the EC human rights initiative was seen as a neocolonial holdover, maintaining the ''right to sit in judgment of our internal policies.''[38]

Within the European Community, political commitment to integrating human rights into a comprehensive development program also was not deeply rooted. Some governments saw the inclusion of such a provision within the Lomé II Convention as a needed leverage or escape valve to deal with human rights violations in ACP recipients. The continuing embarrassment and public recrimination associated with the Uganda experience, as well as a desire to avoid future predicaments of this kind, were important motivations behind EC efforts. Moreover, the Community's unwillingness to entertain human rights provisions applying to ACP migrant workers in Europe also revealed a lack of EC political will to gain an effective integration of human rights and development within the Lomé II Convention. Thus, the issue of human rights and its place within the Lomé framework became a political side show, resulting in mutual antagonism and a reinforcement of the separation of human rights and development in EC-ACP relations. As noted, to forestall a repetition of this episode in future negotiations, the African states chose to pursue whatever human rights course they would follow within an arena—the OAU—that would not be subject to such EC pressure and intrusion.

The treatment of human rights within the renegotiation of Lomé II was also problematic institutionally. Indeed, very little consideration was given to institutionalizing the protection of human rights, that is, how they would be structured, implemented, and monitored for compliance. Perhaps the most detailed proposal along these lines came in a 1978 European Parliament report. This so-called Broeksz Report suggested the establishment of an independent ACP-EC institution that would review and pass judgment on human rights violations. This body would apply its provisions to both EC and ACP countries and operate by majority decisions. Moreover, it would recommend actions in response to such violations, ranging from an expression of indignation to actual economic sanctions. But no real plans were presented for the functioning and organization of such a body, nor for criteria to determine compliance with human rights standards.[39] In large part, this lack of institutionalization derived from the early and clear-cut obstacles that the inclusion of a human rights provision faced in the renegotiation process. In effect, the EC-ACP deliberations never got past the first step of considering its appropriateness and acceptance within the Lomé framework.

Major institutional inadequacies were also apparent in the possible linking of human rights considerations with Lomé II trade and development assistance. As noted, the Convention contained many more specific targets and bases for institutional actions in the strictly economic areas of the development programs than it did in the social and human realms. For example, sections dealing with STABEX and the European Development Fund (EDF) had clear quantitative criteria for performance. But provisions for individual and group participation in various local development projects remained vague and ineffective.[40] Moreover, Lomé II did not promote opportunities for institutionalizing the development process beyond traditional governmental boundaries. In most instances, the Convention left the formulation and implementation of development programs up to the individual ACP states. Given the importance of NGOs and community-based groups in fostering a more integrated approach to development, including broader linkages to human rights, Lomé II did not advance institutionally these policy areas and their interrelationships.

The experience of the Lomé II renegotiation process points up the limits of state action in the formulation and implementation of human rights and development activities. In many respects, the establishment of a more integrated approach to human rights and development has been hindered directly by states' policies and interactions. Their involvement in these matters also has undercut the capacities of intergovernmental organizations to link human rights and development. Not surprisingly, many of the concepts, roles, and functions elaborated within recent formulations of human rights and development focus more and more upon non-state actors and decentralized activities—not only to supplement state and interstate actions on these matters, but also to compensate for prevailing state practices.

NGOs and community-based activities have become increasingly important components for gaining improved human rights and development records within developing countries. Yet there is a distinct lack of these types of organizations and resources within Africa, even in comparison to other regions within the developing world. Although the adoption of the Banjul Charter of Human and Peoples' Rights may provide a new stimulus for dealing more effectively with these matters, significant conceptual, political and institutional obstacles exist and the prospects for realizing human rights and development objectives remain clouded in Africa.

NOTES

1. For discussion of recent forecasts about global development prospects, see S. J. Burki, "The Prospects for the Developing World: A Review of Recent Forecasts," *Finance and Development* 18 (March 1981), pp. 21–24.

2. See Robert Heilbroner, *An Inquiry into the Human Prospect* (New York: Norton, 1974).

3. Fouad Ajami, "The Fate of Nonalignment," *Foreign Affairs* 59 (Winter 1980/1981), p. 379.

4. See Stephen Marks, "Development and Human Rights: Some Reflections on the Study of Human Rights, Development and Peace," *Bulletin of Peace Proposals* 8, no. 3 (1977), pp. 237–38.

5. Philip Alston and Asbjorn Eide, "Discussion Paper," prepared for the African Seminar on Human Rights and Development, University College, Gaborone, 24–29 May 1982 (mimeographed) pp. 2–4.

6. See Malcolm Richardson, *Human Rights, Human Needs, and Developing Nations: A Bellagio Conference, June 26–30, 1980* (New York: The Rockefeller Foundation, 1980) for discussion of different perspectives on human rights within various regional contexts. See also J. F. McCamant, "Social Science and Human Rights," *International Organization* 35 (Summer 1981), pp. 531–552, for reference to different approaches to international human rights.

7. See Fouad Ajami, *Human Rights and World Order Politics*, Working Paper no. 4, Institute for World Order. (New York 1978), pp. 5–8.

8. Sylvia Ann Hewlett, "Human Rights and Economic Realities: Trade-offs in Historical Perspective," *Political Science Quarterly* 94, no. 3 (Fall 1979), pp. 453, 463.

9. See Richardson, *Human Rights, Human Needs, and Developing Nations*, pp. 8–10, and Ajami, *Human Rights and World Order Politics*, pp. 5–8.

10. See Rupert Emerson, "The Fate of Human Rights in the Third World," *World Politics* 27, no. 2 (January 1975) pp. 201–226. See also Ajami, *Human Rights and World Order Politics*, pp 14–15.

11. See "Report of the Secretary-General to the UN Commission on Human Rights," UN Doc. E/CN.4/1334, 2 January 1979; and Hector Gros Espiell, "The Right to Development as a Human Right," *Texas International Law Journal* 16 (Spring 1981), pp. 189–205, for further discussion of this point.

12. See UN Doc. E/CN.4/AC.34/WP.23, 12 January 1982, pp. 2–3 and Alston and Eide, "Discussion Paper," pp. 41–44.

13. See Laura Garnick and Carol Cosgrove Twitchett, "Human Rights and a Successor to the Lomé Convention," *International Relations* 6, no. 3 (May 1979), pp. 541–42.

14. See Mahbub al Haq, "Negotiating the Future," *Foreign Affairs* 59 (Winter 1980/1981), pp. 398, 400–404, and "The Historical Context of the North-South Relationship and the Role of the United Nations System in the Evolution of This Relationship," North-South Roundtable, Society for International Development, Rome, 18–20 May 1978, Background Document NSRT/INF.1, p. 3.

15. See "The Historical Context", pp. 8–28, for further discussion.

16. See Hurst Hannum, "The Butare Colloquium on Human Rights and Economic Development in Francophone Africa: A Summary and Analysis," *Universal Human Rights* 1, no. 2 (April-June 1979), p. 73, for reference to the importance of participation as a component of development strategies.

17. See *Bulletin of Human Rights*, no. 29 (July–September 1980) (Division of Human Rights, United Nations), p. 4, for a report on the importance of integration in development, as noted at a United Nations Seminar on the international economic order and human rights, Geneva, July 1980.

18. See Gros Espiell, "The Right to Development as a Human Right," pp. 200–204.

19. See "Report of the Seminar on the Relations That Exist between Human Rights, Peace, and Development," New York, 3–14 August 1981. UN Doc. ST/HR/SER.A.10, p. 16.

20. See "Seminar on the Relations That Exist", p. 19.

21. Despite conceptual links of this sort, many practical problems of implementation remain. See Alston and Eide, "Discussion Paper," p. 289, and "Seminar on the Relations That Exist", p. 49, for references to disappointment with the International Development Strategy on this matter.

22. See *United Nations Action in the Field of Human Rights, 1980* (New York: United Nations Publication, 1981), pp. 251-55.

23. See Ronald I. Meltzer, "Un Structural Reform: Institutional Development in International Economic and Social Affairs," in Toby Trister Gati, ed., *The US, the UN, and the Management of Global Change* (New York: New York University Press, 1983), for further discussion of UN institutional change with respect to evolving global development challenges.

24. For a good example of one such NGO operating in this manner, see "Participation of the Rural Poor in Development," *Development: Seeds of Change* 1 (1981), pp. 62-64, on the operations of a project sponsored by the International Center for Law in Development.

25. See Marks, "Development and Human Rights," p. 242.

26. See European Community Doc. 1-559/80, 17 November 1980, p. 24, which refers to this characterization in the Preamble of the Lomé II Convention.

27. Ibid., p. 28.

28. See Garnick and Twitchett, "Human Rights and a Successor," p. 541.

29. See Ibid., p. 543.

30. See Amy Young-Anawaty, "Human Rights and the ACP-EEC Lomé II Convention: Business as Usual at the EEC," *New York University Journal of International Law and Politics* 13, no. 1 (Spring 1980), p. 80.

31. See Ibid., pp. 81-84, and Garnick and Twitchett "Human Rights and a Successor," p. 547, for more on these discussions.

32. See Young-Anawaty "Human Rights and the ACP-EEC," pp. 85-86, and Garnick and Twitchett, "Human Rights and a Successor," pp. 547-51.

33. See Young-Anawaty, "Human Rights and the ACP-EEC," pp. 88-90.

34. Ibid., p. 93.

35. Ibid., p. 94.

36. EC Doc. 1-559/80, p. 31.

37. See Nantang Jua, "ACP-EEC Lomé Regime: Implementing the Comprehensive Development Strategy" (Ph.D. dissertation, State University of New York at Buffalo, 1982), for additional discussion along these lines.

38. "Changes Needed for Lomé Two," *Africa* 81 (May 1978), p. 62.

39. See Garnick and Twitchett, "Human Rights and a Successor," pp. 545-46.

40. See Jua, "ACP-EEC Lomé Regime."

CHAPTER TEN

The Political Economy of Self-Determination: A World Systems Approach to Human Rights in Africa

TIMOTHY M. SHAW

In terms of the denial of human rights and fundamental freedoms in independent African states, the OAU's record has been dismal . . . . Besides the dictatorial nature of most of the governments in Africa, there are other important barriers to its effectiveness. These include the dominant position of African governments in the countries' socio-economic life, the ideological orientation of some of the OAU member states, the traditional and cultural values, and religion.

—Olajide Aluko

Human rights in Africa, like human rights in the Western world, are continually threatened by the interests of the ruling class.

—Rhoda Howard

Until very recently the OAU did not have any idea of human rights other than those borrowed from the Western liberal tradition . . . products of the Western ascendancy in world affairs.

—Olajide Aluko

The analysis presented in this chapter of the elusive goal of African self-determination is based on the premise that human rights and needs in Africa, as elsewhere, are inseparable from the continent's historical inclusion and contemporary position in the world system. The definition and realization of human rights cannot be considered out of historical or structural context. The world systems perspective, while not conceived with human rights per se as either factor or focus, constitutes an appropriate framework through which to better explain and evaluate such rights and needs. Quite clearly, fewer prerequisites and less promising prospects for the satisfaction of human rights and needs are hardly to be found in any region of the globe over the remaining two decades of the twentieth century than in Africa.[1]

A world systems approach to human rights, as to other elements of social behavior, is characterized by a concentration on history and structure. Any particular social relation or formation, particularly one at the periphery, is situated within this broader context. So the absence or presence of human rights in Africa is not the function of African regimes alone; rather, it is one result of patterns of dependency over recent decades. Individual presidents and governments have limited influence on the establishment or preservation of rights because of such wider "systemic" factors. Notwithstanding the claims of nationalist movements for freedom from both repression and starvation, most present leaders on the continent lack the means, in terms of political and productive capacities, to begin to provide either facilities or food for their burgeoning populations. Their position at the periphery of the world system constrains both their capacity and their authority.

As the decade of the 1980s opened the tenuousness of rights and needs in Africa was poignantly underlined by two significant and symbolic events. First, the demise of presidential power and popular identity in the very country where the African Charter on Human and Peoples' Rights was first debated and designed. President Jawara and the Gambian people have been incorporated legally and strategically in Senegambia. And, second, the new decade witnessed the preparation and presentation of two alternative development strategies to cope with the continental recession: The OAU *Lagos Plan of Action for the Economic Development of Africa, 1980–2000* and the World Bank's *Accelerated Development in Sub-Saharan Africa: An Agenda for Action.*[2] The latter summarizes succinctly the unenviable condition of Africa today:

> For most African countries, and for a majority of the African population, the record is grim, and it is no exaggeration to talk of crisis . . . Output per person rose more slowly in Sub-Saharan Africa than in any other part of the world, particularly in the 1970s. . . The tragedy of this slow growth in the African setting is that incomes are so low and access to basic services so limited . . . Past trends in African economic performance and continued global recession together explain the pessimistic projections for African development in the 1980s.[3]

The debate about alternative development difficulties and strategies—i.e., between the Lagos Plan of Action and the Agenda for Action—replicates similar contentions about human rights deficiencies. The former, compatible with a world systems perspective, blames external or global factors for Africa's economic and social underdevelopment, whereas the latter, as in a traditional perspective on human rights, is most critical of internal mismanagement. Nevertheless, measures to implement the self-reliant designs of the Lagos

Plan of Action include social transformation—the "equitable distribution of the means of production and the fruits of development and economic growth"—with profound implications for the bases of human rights and needs:

> It requires determined and continuous attention to the provision of opportunities for the total involvement of all segments of the population in the development process and of guarding against undue privileges. It constitutes the heart of a self-renewing society and the generation and sustainment of a self-reliant and self-sustaining economic growth. In this connection, it is recommended that member states should take appropriate measures to ensure that all citizens have equal opportunities to the acquisition of the means of production—education and training including health facilities, physical factors of production, and equitable access to the benefits of development and economic growth—food, water, health services, and money income.[4]

Such a perspective is "radical" in at least three senses. First, it challenges the prerogatives of African regimes to set their own standards. Second, it necessitates change in Africa's place in the world system; otherwise "domestic" development cannot occur. And third, it is "structural," pointing to the bases in political economy of Africa's unsatisfactory record in meeting human rights and needs.

This chapter, like the Lagos Plan of Action, takes it to be axiomatic that the problematic prospects for human rights and needs in Africa are inseparable from the continent's place in the world system. This is especially so when human rights are defined broadly to include basic human needs such as shelter, water, health, and education rather than merely essential legal and political rights. The former basic needs are more clearly related to external exchange and global position, although even the latter essential rights are profoundly affected, directly and indirectly, by external conditions and inputs.

The continent's position at the periphery consists, then, of a structural linkage that involves crucial and cooperative relations among dominant countries, corporations, and classes. These serve to insulate human rights violations in Africa by erecting a wall of "sovereignty" around a set of transnational connections which in fact undermine the bases of the continent's ability to meet right and needs. Together these generate the growing contradictions between Africa's ideologies and practices on human rights: the dialectic between formal adoption of "international" standards and real application of more indigenous criteria. They also constitute the major explanation for the gap between the continent's rich resources and poor condition. Exchange is unequal, so the benefits of production flow out to the metropole, leaving little for either the local bourgeoisie or the proletariat. However, the indigenous ruling class, even in conditions of recession, is able to insert its interests effectively into the transnational nexus, often at the cost of local non-bourgeois—proletarian and peasant—living standards and life styles.

No analysis of the distribution or incidence of human rights can be undertaken, then, wtihout reference to uneven patterns of incorporation and exchange in the world sytem. The reason for the superior potential for satisfaction of human rights and needs at the center is the converse of that at the periphery: the prospects for surplus production, accumulation, and distribution. Differential incorporation is, of course, a function of country, class, and corporation over time; and changes and cycles in the world capitalist system are not completely mechanistic. So in theory the semi-periphery, an intermediate formation between center and periphery, has greater opportunities to meet rights and needs than the real periphery. Yet actual achievements depend on the person of the head of state, the ideology of the regime, and the character of the government. Nevertheless, the descent into anarchy[5] in parts of the periphery is clearly unpropitious for either human rights or needs, as well as being one result of global recession and continent-wide crisis.

Without some type of world system perspective, the consideration of human rights in Africa lacks an appropriate framework for analysis. The satisfaction of human rights and needs is not a function of president, polity, or ideology alone, but rather a function of modes and relations of production. Self-determination at the level of politics is intrinsically related to that at the level of economics. Participation and production cannot be divorced. Hence the world systems perspective adopted in this chapter, with its associated political economy mode of analysis, structural level of analysis, and historical scope of analysis. Any progress towards self-reliance in the future necessitates dealing with analytic, systemic, and inherited factors; hence the pervasive skepticism here about the prospects for any immediate amelioration in the continent's crisis. Even the World Bank in its latest *World Development Report* recognizes the constraints posed by ''external'' conditions on Africa's future:

> Small low-income countries have limited policy options, and global economic conditions are of the utmost importance to them. The development of the poorest, most slowly growing countries in sub-Saharan Africa in the immediate future depends very much on aid and trade trends, but in the longer run, domestic policies are critical.[6]

Given Africa's continuing marginality in the contemporary division of labor, this chapter proceeds from alternative definitions of rights and needs, through current constraints on effective decolonization, and on to the possibilities of self-determination through self-reliance. In addition to being concerned with the definition and distribution of rights and needs, the chapter treats analytic issues throughout, recognizing the superior capability of a world systems approach in terms of the incidence, explanation, and projection of rights on the continent.

My essential theme is that human rights and self-determination cannot be enhanced without a transformation in the nature of the continent's place in the world system. Any African Charter which does not deal with the roots of the issue is unlikely to ameliorate "The African Condition" in a sustained way; hence the need for truly "radical" scholarship and strategies, uncommon characteristics in a rather conservative and cautious continent.

HUMAN RIGHTS IN AFRICA: INDIVIDUAL, INSTITUTIONAL, AND IDEOLOGICAL

One of the least helpful vestiges of colonialism in Africa is the legacy of Western values which inhibits radical rethinking of politics and economics. Liberal assumptions permeate much of the debate about human rights, despite the dramatic differences between the political economies where they were formulated and those in which they are meant to be applied. As Rhoda Howard suggests in her useful *tour d'horizon* of the state of human rights, such assumptions do not fit the African condition:

> In sub-Saharan English-speaking nations a body of Third World countries can be identified which, at least in their ideals, resemble Western democracies, yet which in their practice do not seem able to attain the degree of civil and political liberty to which they ostensibly aspire. This suggests that there may be social, economic, or historical impediments to any implementation of their ideals; in other words, that structures limit the realization of values.[8]

This chapter is concerned with identifying those structures that constrain the achievement of human rights, however formulated. But before turning to these, mention must be made of alternative definitions of such rights. These can be subdivided according to *level* of interaction and *type* of interaction.

First, three major *levels* of interaction can be identified—individual, continental, and global—with the potential for both compatibility and incompatibility between each of them. In the historical and contemporary African context, collective rights have tended to be preferred over individual ones as shown in earlier chapters of this volume. The major recent thrust has been, of course, toward decolonization, both in the postwar period of nationalist movements versus colonial governments, and in the postindependence period of liberation movements versus settler regimes. In general, in both periods such demands have been couched in Western liberal terminology as a means of applying pressure. They have been formulated by African leaders to ensure the success of their claims to succeed metropolitan rulers. This suggests a fourth level of interaction, one to which I return below; namely, the class bases of human rights ideology.

Meanwhile, note needs to be taken of the new efforts of African statesmen to insert a continental definition of rights between the two levels most prevalent in orthodox Western discourse: namely, the individual and the global. The formulation and articulation of an "African Charter on Human and Peoples' Rights" at Banjul in January 1981, subsequently ratified by the Nairobi summit meeting in July 1981, represents (1) a collective assertion of Africa's contemporary distinctiveness, an aspect of continuing decolonization, and (2) a collective recollection of Africa's past distinctiveness, an aspect of a continual quest for legitimization. Adda Bozeman's controversial (because stereotypical) treatise on African notions of war and peace is suggestive of distinctive and alternative concepts of rights:

> Western typologies of violence, then, do not readily accommodate African orientations towards the uses of physical force . . . . all African administrations—both black and white—are authoritarian in the sense that scant attention is paid to democratic principles of rule, majority representations, civil and individualized liberties . . . . The term "human rights" has thus been made to refer exclusively to the "racial rights" of black Africans against African citizens of European provenance . . . . Africans are more at ease with conflict in its multiple manifestations than their contemporaries in Europe and the United States.[9]

And second, three major *types* of interaction can be identified—protection, participation, and satisfaction of needs, i.e., "negative" and "positive" rights. In turn, these are closely related to three different "issue areas"—the legal, political, and economic—which are themselves related to alternative liberal and radical conceptions or definitions of rights.

Asbjorn Eide has provided a useful check list of the first set of types, protection, participation, and satisfaction of needs:

> Only in the context of an organized society with organs of authority does the notion of human rights make sense. As part of political philosophy, "human rights" is a concept expressing the preferred relationship between the individuals and the state. This relationship includes certain freedoms from the stated [sic] (freedom from abuse of authority, from arbitrary arrest, from cruel and inhuman treatment). It also includes the right of the individual to participate in the conduct of public affairs. Further, it includes obligations for the state to secure the satisfaction of needs of all members of society.[10]

In postcolonial Africa, as indicated below, there has been quite a dramatic shift in emphasis away from protection and participation towards satisfaction of needs. In turn, this represents a transition away from the legal and political definition of rights towards the economic. Here, however, note the difference between continental and "global" concerns. In general, the latter, because of the West's continuing ability to lay down norms, concentrates on political and legal rights, whereas the former, because of the elusiveness of development, is increasingly motivated by economic imperatives.

Human rights have begun to be "decolonized" in Africa in two major ways: (1) Orthodox political and legal notions have been "Africanized"; and (2) economic definitions have come to match or eclipse in importance the political and legal. First, as both Howard and Aluko recognize, African statesmen, despite their Western liberal ideology, have begun to redefine rights to take local contexts and concepts into account:

> Civil leaders of most of the independent English-speaking African states do accept, at least publicly, the Western ideals of civil and political freedom, but in so doing they often stress the unique African context of these ideals.[11]

> Most African leaders—like most of their counterparts in Asia and Latin America—believe in the peculiarity of their continent, and the differences in traditions, culture, and values of Africa from those of the Western powers.[12]

Second, African statesmen have begun to give less emphasis to political and legal definitions and greater emphasis to economic definitions. In many ways, this is a response both to the unrelenting process of underdevelopment and to the inability of African regimes to realize legal "protection" and political "participation," given the elusiveness of economic "satisfaction."

FROM DECOLONIZATION TO DEPENDENCE

The nationalist period represented the zenith of concern for political and legal rights of the peoples of Africa. There was widespread consensus in response to unwelcome external control. The inability of African successor regimes to translate political decolonization into economic development has generated two revisions in human rights priorities. First, both because the economic constraints are largely external and because it is convenient to so describe them, African leaders now focus on foreign economic control as they once did on colonial political control. Economic decolonization has succeeded political decolonization as the primary goal. And second, both because of the elusiveness of development and because of the fragility of the state, political and legal rights are no longer just relegated to secondary importance; they are positively and perhaps increasingly transgressed as a means to maintain power. In short, economic demands vis-à-vis external interests, and political and legal abuses with respect to domestic interests, largely characterize contemporary Africa. The latter abuses can, of course, be blamed on the economic constraints—violation of rights is not really Africa's fault but rather a function of its inherited and unfavorable condition—yet Howard rejects such an escape from responsibility:

> In Africa, economic and social conditions are not conducive to human rights. Nevertheless, there is no excuse for some of the abuses of power which occur.[13]

If rights in Africa have become less respected as the date of independence recedes and the prospect of development decreases, then the future prospects of rights in Africa are also likely to diminish. The next twenty years until the year 2000 are unlikely to offer even the minimal growth rates of the first twenty years that followed independence. This trend towards relative and absolute impoverishment has accelerated since the mid-1970s and the advent of global inflation, recession, and protectionism. Given the politics of scarcity, the majority of African regimes are likely to practise what Claude Ake calls "defensive radicalism": the ideology of "African socialism" combined with the reality of African authoritarianism.[14]

This tendency towards repressive regimes is not, of course, confined to Africa. Moreover, indigenous dictatorship was not unknown in the precolonial period. Nevertheless, as Aluko laments, albeit from an essentially liberal perspective:

> In all the OAU member states, the position and powers of the government are all-pervading, and almost all-embracing. Indeed, in the tasks of economic and social development, many African governments perceive individual rights as a luxury which they can ill afford.[18]

Yet if Aluko regrets the centralization of power in Africa because it limits individual rights to expression and accumulation, others might criticize African socialists for being insufficiently radical, for respecting "bourgeois" values too much rather than too little.

In any event, African states, while in general neglecting human rights, can no longer be treated as a homogeneous grouping. Rather, the variety of political economies generates various definitions and treatments of rights; they have realized self-determination to differential degrees. Elsewhere, I have attempted to distinguish among three types of African state: Capitalist, state capitalist, and state socialist.[16] If these distinctions have some general validity, then differences in treatment of human rights issues among them should be quite apparent—the substructure largely determining and certainly constraining the superstructure.

Eide also makes a comparison among states according to whether they are at the center or the periphery and have either a market economy (capitalist) or a planned economy (socialist). Clearly no African state is located at the center; but at the periphery some are more capitalist than others. He includes a rather disparate collection of African countries in his "capitalist" group—Uganda, Kenya, and Zaire; in the "socialist" category he puts Mozambique, Angola, and Guinea-Bissau.[17] Eide suggests that fundamental political and legal freedoms are not well protected in either of the periphery types by contrast to at least the capitalist countries of the center. However, the socialist periphery attempts to satisfy basic economic needs more than the capitalist periphery does. States in the capitalist category

> are, as a rule, very weak both in satisfaction of basic needs for the poorer section of the population and also in fundamental freedoms. In most of these countries there is an extreme maldistribution of income. The more they are integrated in the global market economy, the more severe the maldistribution seems to become. Political participation in many of them has been declining . . . .

By contrast, states in the socialist periphery

> are also weak on fundamental freedoms, but considerably
> stronger than the other group of periphery states with regard
> to economic and social rights. The satisfaction of basic needs
> for the poorer part of the population and the right to work
> have been fairly well safeguarded . . . .[18]

So, at least according to Eide and in opposition to Aluko's assumption, the political economies that are more socialist encourage human rights, especially economic ones, to a greater extent than do the more capitalist political economies. In the latter group, a few individuals may realize the opportunity to accumulate capital and to advance their own rights; but for the majority—the "people"—capitalist regimes in Africa are inferior in terms of their advocacy of rights.

This assertion also runs counter to Howard's assumptions, which, like those of Aluko, are essentially liberal and pluralist. The centerpiece of her policy for enhancing human rights in Africa is "political modernization" or specialization, something more likely to develop under state capitalism than under state socialism. She advocates social pluralism—not revolution—as the means to regulate or moderate state behavior:

> Mediating institutions in Africa such as trade unions or voluntary organizations have neither the membership, the organizational skill, nor the independence to act as "countervailing powers" to the state. Thus the political structure necessary to protect human rights on a day-to-day basis is not yet in existence: until it is, the ruling elites will continue to abuse human rights in their own interests.[19]

So unlike Aluko, whose liberalism is less critical, Howard does begin to situate human rights and self-determination in Africa in the context not only of underdevelopment but also of peripheral social formations.

FROM UNDERDEVELOPMENT TO SELF-RELIANCE

The elusiveness of development and rights has led African leaders to economic as well as political summit meetings. So, in addition to demanding first political and then economic decolonization, they have come to design and declare strategies for effective self-determination. If the first half of the 1960s witnessed a preoccupation with nationalism in black Africa, then the first half of the 1970s was characterized by a preoccupation with liberation in white-ruled Africa; yet both of these movements represented stages in the struggle for *political* emancipation. By contrast, the second half of the 1970s revealed a new preoccupation as the post-Bretton Woods era dawned and projections for a very unpromising future became known: *economic* self-determination.

The 1981 Banjul Charter on Human Rights was preceded by the 1980 Lagos Declaration on economic development. The former called for an African conception of and commission on rights; the latter called for an African common market and common strategy. Before examining the Lagos Plan of Action, two further approaches to identifying and overcoming Africa's underdevelopment should be mentioned, as both relate rights to development, politics to economics.

First, many development experts have come to advocate the satisfaction of what they classify as Basic Human Needs (BHN), rather than the mere maximizing of production. The unhappy experience of African economies since independence, especially since the mid-1970s, has confirmed the imperative of "another way," of alternative strategies. BHN has been espoused as one means to abandon Africa's inheritance of economic extroversion: production and exchange should be internal so that the benefits do not escape into the global economy. Moreover, BHN advocates satisfying the internal need for food, water, shelter, etc., first, before the external demand for primary commodities. Given Africa's characteristic openness and vulnerability, such a transition has an almost revolutionary quality to it. Its basic assumption is that greater autarky would advance development, if development is defined in terms of basic commodities and facilities for the majority of Africa's people. The emphasis in a BHN approach on transforming structures may also make it relevant in the quest for human rights. The reduction of poverty and inequality improves the foundation for rights and dignity, that is, for self-determination.

Second, related to BHN is an innovative method for measuring the realization and distribution of basic benefits throughout the continent. The Physical Quality of Life Index (PQLI) provides one set of indicators for human rights of an economic and educational, rather than political and social, character. But as with other types of data, Africa's present and prospective position is unpromising. As Florizelle Liser, a leading exponent of PQLI, indicates:

In the mid-1970s, on a scale of 0 to 100, Africa had an average PQLI of 32 compared to a Latin Amerian average of 71, a North American average of 95, and a worldwide average of 65. That the PQLI reveals that Africa today is both absolutely and relatively poorer than other developing countries and the industrialized world is no surprise.[20]

And for Africa to achieve a "minimum basic needs target"—a PQLI of 77 (consisting of an average life expectancy of 65 years, 50 or fewer infant deaths per 1,000, and 75% literacy) would require an exceptional disparity reduction rate of better than 5 percent a year until the year 2000:

> Even if a global basic needs strategy were embarked upon in 1980, the disparity between Africa's current performance in regard to critical social indicators and the best expected international performance by the year 2000 is so wide that only a conscious effort to rapidly reduce the gap over the twenty-year period would yield the desired basic needs results.[21]

Nevertheless, Liser paradoxically remains somewhat optimistic that the projected future is so untenable that national and external agencies will combine to develop new BHN strategies to advance PQLI scores. Two contrasting policy options—to enhance the satisfaction of human needs and of human rights—merit more extended discussion.

The OAU Lagos Plan of Action is most compatible with a BHN/PQLI approach to development. By contrast, the World Bank Agenda for Action, despite its association with an international organization that originated and espoused BHN, is skeptical about such new orthodoxies, advocating instead a return to unhindered growth for export. The Lagos Plan seeks to satisfy BHN and human rights directly, whereas the World Bank Agenda suggests growth first and then the meeting of BHN; hence the ambiguity, if not contradiction, between the two documents or declarations. The former is most compatible with a critical world systems perspective, whereas the latter is least so. As a recent Pan-African social science meeting declared:

> The correct orientation and therefore significance of the Lagos Plan of Action is clearly highlighted when it is contrasted with the World Bank Report. The orientation of the two "Plans" are opposite and contradictory, the Lagos Plan of Action advocating a form of development which would benefit the African people whereas the World Bank Report clearly and unambiguously represents the interest of foreign capital. The World Bank Report specifically expresses a very negative and demeaning attitude on the ability of African leadership and institutions. The two documents must therefore be seen as representing sharply opposing points of view concerning African development.[22]

The OAU Lagos Plan of Action is the more authentic and in-digenous approach in terms of origin and orientation. Its "fundamental objective"

> is the establishment of self-sustaining development and economic growth, based on collective self-reliance and aimed at improving the standards of living of the mass of the African people and reducing mass unemployment.[23]

This advocacy of collective self-reliance—a corollary of BHN—is intended "to avoid the terrible specter of increasing mass poverty, unemployment and general instability which all projections of the world economy show will be the lot of the region by the year 2000".[24]

By contrast, the World Bank Agenda for Action is more international in origin and orientation. While claiming compatibility with the Lagos Plan, it does not advocate either national or collective self-reliance. Instead its focus is on "production." Given past trends, especially negative growth in fifteen African countries throughout the 1970s, the Agenda asserts that "a reordering of post-independence priorities is essential if economic growth is to accelerate . . . . Without a faster rate of production increase, other objectives cannot be achieved . . . ."[25] In advocating growth rather than development, and production rather than BHN, the World Bank identifies a set of crucial issues:

> Three major policy actions are central to any growth-oriented program: (i) more suitable trade and exchange-rate policies; (ii) increased efficiency of resource use in the public sector; and (iii) improvement in agricultural policies.[26]

This call for increased production and exports, especially agricultural, is almost the antithesis of the collective self-reliance of the Lagos Plan.

The Lagos Plan had appeared to sound the death knell of outward-looking growth before the Agenda was published:

> Members of the region have tended to be persuaded to believe that the drive-wheel of growth and development is the export of primary products to shrinking and changing world markets for such commodities. It now, however, recognizes that the region's engine of growth and development must consist of a combination of Africa's considerable natural resources, its entrepreneurial, managerial, and technical resources, and its markets (restricted and expanded) to serve the mass of its people, and that in this engine the development of the capital

goods industries is a major component. The region has no alternative today but to map out its own strategies and vigorously pursue their implementation. Its efforts to do so may come to grief if it continues to try to hang on to the very chains that anchor its economies to those of other continents.[27]

It is these "very chains" that the World Bank Agenda seeks to reinforce by advocating agricultural production for export and increased growth rather than development. The Agenda not only disapproves of state socialism in Africa; it also seeks to dismantle existing state structures, claiming, "It is now widely evident that the public sector is overextended, given the present scarcities of financial resources, skilled manpower, and organizational capacity." To reinvigorate industry, it calls for more, not less, foreign and domestic capital, asserting that various "governments have decided on efficiency grounds that the scope of private sector activity should be enlarged."[28]

These two policy prescriptions stand in stark contrast to each other and, if adopted, would lead to markedly different national and continental political economies, with profound implications for human rights. The Lagos Plan seeks to learn from past disappointments and to avoid future difficulties by advocating some disengagement from the world system that the Agenda still sees as the magnet for growth. The adoption of either of these alternative approaches would have a significant impact on human rights as well as on human development, given the connection between political economy and such rights.

THE DIALECTIC OF SELF-DETERMINATION: INCORPORATION VERSUS INDEPENDENCE

Self-determination remains elusive in Africa; human rights and human development have hardly been advanced by either political or economic nationalism. Effective decolonization remains a mirage; both liberal and radical notions of rights are far from realization. This African condition is well described in both its economic and political manifestations by the Lagos Plan:

Twenty years after the majority of African countries have acceded to political independence, the African continent is facing the decade 1980–1990 seriously handicapped by its underdeveloped condition. This underdevelopment is manifested, socially, among other things, by the low level of satisfaction of the basic needs of the population, continued widespread illiteracy, and the persistence of major endemic diseases. This situation is reflected in economic and administrative structures which fail to meet the requirements of development.[29]

The consensual African response to this unacceptable condition is to work towards self-reliance, both national and collective. This strategy is based on the assumption that thereby BHN will more nearly be met. Disengagement from the world system is considered to be a prerequisite for self-determination.

This strategy is, of course, advocated by indigenous leaders who are themselves tied into global networks of diplomatic, strategic, and economic exchange. For them to espouse self-reliance, even at the level of rhetoric, is an indication of the seriousness of the projections for the mid-term future.[30] This is especially so if domestic class consequences of apparently inexorable inequalities are considered. For, as the World Bank Agenda recognizes:

> During the past two decades economic development has been slow in most of the countries of sub-Saharan Africa. When, in the mid-1970's, the world economy experienced inflation and recession, nowhere did the crisis hit with greater impact than in this region.[31]

Even "success stories" like the high-growth, import-substitution, and export-led economies of Kenya and the Ivory Coast—the semi-periphery of Africa—now face difficulties. Although human rights of the negative political and legal kind (protection and participation) are generally respected in these two countries, those of the positive economic variety (satisfaction of needs) are less so. This is particularly worrisome in projecting the future of human rights, for minimal growth even in hitherto expanding economies may retard rights. Again, the World Bank recognizes this prognostication:

> Past trends in African economic performance and continued global recession together explain the pessimistic projections for African development in the 1980's . . . . These prospects and their political, social, and economic implications are not acceptable either to the countries concerned or to the international community.[32]

In response the Bank advocates "privatization" and more concentration on agriculture. But a revival of laissez-faire and external exchange—both, incidentally, rather problematic in a world of recession and protection[33]—may generate authoritarianism rather than humanitarianism. As Ake warns, the absence of growth may retard human rights, so that the choice may no longer be the orthodox one between capitalism and socialism:

> The third historic possibility which lies before Africa is a march to fascism. This could come about in a situation where there was protracted economic stagnation, but not yet revolution.[34]

To avoid both recession and authoritarianism, African leaders have advocated disengagement. an emphasis on BHN and self-reliance. This alternative of relative autarchy involves its own risks, not the least of which is that the African ruling class will be excluded from transnational networks. But this marginalization might occur to most of them in any event as "inter-imperial" rivalries come to dominate North-South relations.

In terms of both development and rights, African states are likely to diverge exponentially over the next twenty years. Only a few political economies will enjoy reasonable rates of growth—e.g., Algeria, the Ivory Coast, Kenya, Nigeria, and Zimbabwe—whereas the majority will suffer both relative and probably absolute impoverishment—e.g., the Sahel, Somalia, Sudan, and Zaire.[35] Given the close relationship among growth and development and human rights, it is in the first, minority category of expanding state capitalist economies that rights are likely to increase.[36] In the second, majority grouping of stagnant or receding state socialist economies, rights are likely to be repressed (*pace* Eide). The former category may be able to take advantage of the World Bank Agenda for expansion through privatization and exportation, whereas the latter grouping, being already less organized, may identify most closely with the OAU Lagos Plan.[37] In such cases, the relative autarky of self-reliance may be associated with authoritarianism because of increased competition for ever-decreasing resources.

The theme of this chapter remains the widespread African assumption that negative rights of protection and participation can only be satisfied when the positive rights of satisfaction of basic human needs are present. The latter tend to be satisfied not only in the more successful states, but also among the more bourgeois classes: Poorer countries and peoples are less able to realize their political, social, and economic rights. Self-determination is an attribute of the rich. Hence the unlikelihood of the Banjul Charter of Human and Peoples' Rights and its proposed regional commission really affecting human rights throughout the continent.

Long after the liberation of Southern Africa, given Africa's continuing dependency, human rights on the continent will remain elusive.

Unless Africa's leaders go well beyond both the World Bank Agenda and the Lagos Plan—i.e., beyond both state capitalism and state socialism towards some form of communalistic and humanistic socialism—they are unlikely to improve the PQLI position or the human rights situation of most of their populations.[38] A world systems approach helps to put such constraints and contradictions into analytic, structural and historical perspective. Only in the semi-periphery—Algeria, the Ivory Coast, Kenya, Nigeria, and Zimbabwe—is growth in personal income and enlargement of human rights at all likely before the end of the century, given continuation of the global recession and the continent's vulnerability. If self-reliance is not advanced in practice at either national or regional levels, then Africa's economic and political prospects may decline even further, especially in the real periphery, with major potential consequences for human rights. As Osita Eze warns:

> Human rights performance in Africa remains precarious . . . .
> Selective emphasis on civil and political rights to the detriment of socio-economic rights and political powers in the hands of a few at the national level have by and large emasculated the enjoyment of civil and political rights by the majority of African peoples.[39]

So, notwithstanding their own treatment under colonial regimes that largely disrespected indigenous political rights and ignored natural economic rights, Africa's leaders are still products of their own political economies, which remain essentially dependent and underdeveloped. Unless they can escape from this external inheritance and unless social revolution brings about dramatic internal changes, the African bourgeoisies are likely at best to encourage reformism and at worst to practice authoritarianism. In either case the prospects for both self-determination and human dignity are slim. Only in a minority of expanding political economies do human rights stand any prospect of improvement in Africa in the mid-term future, this notwithstanding the state capitalist character of such systems. So long as underdevelopment remains ubiquitous, rights will remain elusive.

NOTES

The epigraphs are from Olajide Aluko, "The Organization of African Unity and Human Rights," *Round Table* 283 (July 1981), p. 240; Rhoda Howard, "The Dilemma of Human Rights in Sub-Saharan Africa," *International Journal* 35, no. 4 (Autumn 1980), p. 746; and again, Aluko, "The OAU and Human Rights," p. 234.

1. On Africa's inauspicious inheritance and projections, see Timothy M. Shaw, ed., *Alternative Futures for Africa* (Boulder, Colo.: Westview, 1982), passim.

2. On these two sets of explanations, prescriptions, and projections, see, *inter alia*, Timothy M. Shaw, "Contradictions in the Current Crisis of Capitalism: Competition and Coalition in the OECD and ECA," unpublished paper presented to the Scandinavian Institute of African Studies, Uppsala, September 1982; "Special Issue on the Berg Report and the Lagos Plan of Action," *African Development* 7, nos. 1-2 (January/June 1982), pp. 1-206; and Caroline Allison and Reginald Green, eds., "Accelerated Development in Sub-Saharan Africa: What Agendas for Action?" *IDS Bulletin* 14, no. 1 (January 1983).

3. World Bank, *Accelerated Development in Sub-Saharan Africa: An Agenda for Action* (Washington: International Bank for Reconstruction and Development (World Bank), 1981), pp. 2-4.

4. UN Economic Commission for Africa, "Implementation of the Lagos Plan of Action" (Addis Ababa: ECA, 1982), UN Doc. E/ECA/PSD.2/12/Rev. 1, p. 9.

5. See Timothy M. Shaw, "Beyond Underdevelopment: The Anarchic State in Africa," unpublished paper presented at the Annual Meeting of the African Studies Association, Washington, D.C., November 1982.

6. World Bank, *World Development Report, 1982* (Washington: Oxford University Press, 1982), pp. 35-36.

7. For an introduction to this, see Ali A. Mazrui, *The African Condition* (London: Cambridge University Press, 1980).

8. Howard, "The Dilemma of Human Rights in Sub-Saharan Africa," p. 724.

9. Adda B. Bozeman, *Conflict in Africa: Concepts and Realities* (Princeton, N.J.: Princeton University Press, 1976), pp. 31, 35, and 370.

10. Asbjorn Eide, "The World of Human Rights as Seen from a Small, Industrialized Country," *International Organization* 23, no. 2 (June 1979), pp. 247-48.

11. Howard, "The Dilemma of Human Rights in Sub-Saharan Africa," p. 729.

12. Aluko, "The OAU and Human Rights," pp. 234-35.

13. Howard, "The Dilemma of Human Rights in Sub-Saharan Africa," p. 747.

14. See Claude Ake, *Revolutionary Presures in Africa* (London: Zed, 1978).

15. Aluko, "The OAU and Human Rights," p. 240.

16. See Timothy M. Shaw, "The Political Economy of African International Relations," *Issue* 5, no. 4 (Winter 1975), pp. 671-88, and "Introduction," in Timothy M. Shaw and Olajide Aluko, eds., *The Political Economy of African Foreign Policy: Comparative Analyses* (Aldershot: Gower, 1982).

17. See Eide, "The World of Human Rights," p. 254.

18. Ibid., pp. 253 and 254.

19. Howard, "The Dilemma of Human Rights in Sub-Saharan Africa," p. 746.

20. Florizelle B. Liser, "A Basic Needs Strategy and the Physical Quality of

Life Index (PQLI): Africa's Development Prospects," in Shaw, ed., *Alternative Futures for Africa*, pp. 204 and 208.

21. Ibid., p. 222.

22. "Report of the CODESRIA/ECA Conference of Directors of Social Science Research Institutes and Policy Makers on the Third UN Development Decade, the Monrovia Strategy, and the Lagos Plan of Action, March 1982," *Africa Development 7*, nos. 1–2 (January/June 1982), p. 199.

23. OAU, *Plan of Action for the Implementation of the Monrovia Strategy for the Economic Development of Africa Recommended to First Economic Summit, Lagos, April 1980* (Lagos Plan of Action) (OAU Doc. E.CN.14/781/Add. 1), p. 2.

24. Ibid., p. 3.

25. World Bank, *Accelerated Development in Sub-Saharan Africa*, pp. 4–5.

26. Ibid., p. 5.

27. OAU, *Lagos Plan of Action*, p. 3.

28. World Bank, *Accelerated Development in Sub-Saharan Africa*, p. 5. For a comparison of the Plan and the Agenda, see Timothy M. Shaw, "OAU: The Forgotten Economic Debate," *West Africa*, April 12, 1982, pp. 983–84.

29. OAU, *Lagos Plan of Action*, p. 4.

30. On this contradiction and the fractions within the non-aligned movement, see Timothy M. Shaw, "Non-Alignment and the New International (Economic) Order," in Herb Addo, ed., *Transforming the World Economy? Critical Essays on the New International Economic Order* (forthcoming).

31. World Bank, *Accelerated Development in Sub-Saharan Africa*, p. 2.

32. Ibid., p. 4.

33. See Timothy M. Shaw, *Towards an International Political Economy for the 1980's: From Dependence to (Inter)Dependence* (Halifax: Centre for Foreign Policy Studies, 1980).

34. Ake, *Revolutionary Pressures in Africa*, p. 107.

35. See Shaw, *Alternative Futures for Africa*, passim.

36. On such newly industrializing influential countries (NICs) in Africa, see Timothy M. Shaw, "The Semi-Periphery in Africa and Latin America: Sub-Imperialism and Semi-Industrialism," *Review of Black Political Economy 9*, no. 4 (Summer 1979), pp. 341–58, and, with Donald Crone, "Industrialization and Regionalism in ECOWAS and ASEAN: Nigeria and Indonesia Compared," unpublished paper presented at the Annual Meeting of the Canadian Association of African Studies, Toronto, May 1982.

37. For a critical analysis of country and class positions on these alternative prescriptions, see Timothy M. Shaw, "Which Way Africa? ECA and IBRD Responses to the Continental Crisis," unpublished paper presented to the Scandinavian Institute of African Studies, Uppsala, Sweden, 1982.

38. Dunstan Wai, "Human Rights in Sub-Saharan Africa," in Adamantia Pollis and Peter Schwab, eds., *Human Rights: Cultural and Ideological Perspectives* (New York: Praeger, 1979), pp. 115–44; Emmanuel O. Esiemokhai, "Towards Adequate Defence of Human Rights in Africa," *Quarterly Journal of Administration* 24, no. 4 (July 1980), pp. 451–61.

39. Osita C. Eze, "OAU and Human Rights," *Nigerian Forum* 1, no. 3 (May 1981), p. 93.

CHAPTER ELEVEN

Global Power and Self-Determination: The Case of Namibia

GEORGE W. SHEPHERD, JR.

The claim of colonial peoples to self-determination has been widely recognized in the twentieth century. Yet as the century draws to a close, the limits of this achievement are becoming an increasing problem in international relations. The euphoria of the rapid decolonization of the 1960s has been followed by the sobering realization that the proclamation of the end of Western empire was premature.[1] The status of most of these new states, in political and economic reality, is as surrogates and tributaries of the dominant powers.

The current world system is characterized by the growing cluster of power in the North, principally around the United States and the Soviet Union, and by the increased dependence of the South on the North through economic and military relations with the dominant powers.[2] This relationship of dominance and subordination is the proper context in which to examine the prospects for the achievement of self-determination and basic human rights in Namibia, since the extent to which new states are able to realize these objectives is limited by the power constraints of the international economic and strategic system in which they function.

The right of the people to self-determination in Namibia is well established. This is the basic human right recognized in the twentieth century, incorporated into the UN Charter,[3] and applied to the people of Namibia through a series of decisions of UN committees, World Court decisions, and declarations of policy by all governments concerned, including the Republic of South Africa. In addition to self-determination, these rights include ability to petition for representation and for protection from arbitrary and harmful actions of the South African government. The most decisive implementation of these rights has come through UN action. The series of World Court decisions, culminating in the 1971 Advisory Opinion that upheld the right of the Security Council of the United Nations to terminate the South African Mandate over Namibia, established the fact of violation of rights by South Africa.[4]

Not only has the right to self-determination been endorsed by the United Nations and the World Court, but most states in the world, including all African states, have given de facto recognition to the major Namibian political movement, SWAPO (South West African Peoples' Organization), as the principal, if not exclusive, representative of the Namibian people.[5] Even South Africa has begun to move toward a tribally based form of representative government for Namibia's people.[6] However, the form in which representative government will be achieved, and the rights of people of various other groups besides the majority to be represented and protected are central disputes. But a deeper issue remains. Even if a negotiated settlement is achieved, in many cases of human rights in former colonies, the restructuring of power by the formation of a new government has not enhanced human rights nor provided real independence. In Namibia, a real danger exists that Western interests, working through a new tributary regime, will continue the current pattern of dependence on the West, although reducing South African control. A chief purpose of this chapter is to illustrate the tributary pattern of dependency, for such a pattern directly affects the nature, recognition, and protection of human rights in Namibia.

Colonial territories are one form of the tributary relationship between the powerful states of the core of the international capitalist system and its periphery. South Africa, as the ruling country, is a semi-peripheral middle-range power and a sub-imperial base of the Western core powers.[7] Thus Namibia has been controlled by racial and tribal elites who have served the interests of South Africa and the Western world. The economy has been exploited through white farmers and multinational corporations whose allegiances are to South Africa and the West. As Richard Green saw it, "In its own terms the colonial political economy has been successful. After a slow start, gross domestic product, exports, remittances, settler and corporate incomes have risen precipitately since 1945. For South Africa, the remittances and the captive market (all paid in foreign exchange from globally oriented exports) have been significant."[8] And the strategic significance of the area as a buffer against the increasing pressures of African nationalism from the North and the control of Walvis Bay for Western naval activity around the Cape of Good Hope is well known.

Thus, in terms of strategic political economy, "South West Africa" remains under the rule of South Africa because the dominant forces of the Western world basically support this relationship. The importance of South Africa to the West overrides concerns about growing African hostility and the rising cost of the South African military occupation of Namibia. However, continued South African domination has brought major human rights issues with respect to Namibia to the surface, and the Western powers have sought arrangements that would address flagrant violations of justice and equity in Namibia.

Since the mid-1970s, the West, operating through the Contact Group of Five (the United States, Great Britain, West Germany, France, and Canada) has sought to negotiate a settlement that would move toward political independence for Namibia but at the same time maintain their commitment to the strategic political and economic interests of South Africa. This contradiction has constantly undercut the diplomatic strategies they have utilized.[9] South African leaders have skillfully utilized this Western interest and manipulated the conflict to appear to be accepting reform in favor of rights, while preserving the dependence of Namibia in its tributary role.

This tributary status is a pattern followed in many former colonial territories. It continues the basic dominant-subordinate relationship, despite the granting of "self-determination" and sovereignty in the international system. It is established through the transfer of power to an elite or ruling class whose interests are closely aligned to the former colonial power and the international economic and security system. Such elites may have a popular majority or they may not; but the appearance of majority rule has usually been created through political parties and elections. However, the new ruling group maintains intact the existing economic relationships and security system through financial and trade agreements and, frequently, military agreements that preserve bases and external weapons supply. The new military plays a key role in preserving internal support for the new regime. It also acts as a surrogate for the superpower that has assisted in the birth of a new "independent" nation-state which maintains existing profits, resources, and military relationships and provides the essence of the new tributary system.

Namibia is caught in this tributary system and, if the current trends continue, is apt to become a classic example of the transfer of sovereignty from which the substance of freedom has been extracted by the major powers. The dimensions of this possibility are observable in the structure of Namibia's economy and its political groupings, as well as the political maneuvering over the struggle for Namibia. Attempts of the majority of Namibians to achieve independence through armed struggle and other means do not in themselves assure full independence.

THE SUBORDINATION OF THE ECONOMY

Mining and extraction has become the major industry and primary source of wealth and exports for Namibia, although the majority of whites, like the Africans, are engaged in agriculture. Copper, lead, zinc, and coal are mined on the central plateau. Diamonds, copper, and uranium are the primary exports of companies like de Beers, Amax, Newmont, and Rio Tinto Zinc, and account for 90 percent of all mined wealth. These companies are owned primarily by the U.S. and European multinational corporations with South Africa a secondary partner.[10]

Thus, the major Western powers own and control the most lucrative sections. The expatriation of profits from diamonds and copper has been over 35 percent, a very high proportion for a developing country but typical of Western capitalism in South Africa. In fact, the outflow of dividends was three times the African workers' total annual wages.[11]

The world could function without Namibian exports and, in this regard, only the French would be pressed by the loss of uranium from the Rossing mine. The South African government, however, has earned 60 percent of its South West African revenue from taxes on mining, and, in a time of falling gold prices and a drain on the South African balance of payments, the contribution of Namibia is significant.[12] Thus, South African fears over the loss of the Namibian profits and economic contribution is a factor in its strategic political calculations.

Farming is a secondary industry for the white economy. Only 6,500 white farms occupy the central plateau.[13] Whites, nevertheless, exercise enormous political leverage because they are of German and Afrikaner origin. Thus, the economy is controlled by external interests and the internal distribution favors the tributary class of whites and a few African local and central government personnel. While apartheid has declined in Namibia as a deliberate policy of discrimination, whites run the political economy; as a participant in privilege, there has risen a new tributary class of Africans who support the South African presence and development by the multinational corporations.

The security dimension of this tributary relationship has both South African and Western aspects. NATO powers have made defense of the Cape route a major priority,[14] and with a long, strategically important coastline, Namibia is located on the Western flank of the Cape with the only deep water port in that area at Walvis Bay. Today, Namibia is under military occupation by major South African forces; but even in normal times, the South African Navy uses Walvis Bay, as do occasional NATO task forces. A South African air force base at Rooikop is used as a support strike force and patrol area. The second South African Infantry Battalion Group is stationed at Walvis Bay.[15] Its importance is shown by South African refusal to even consider giving up the port in the current negotiations over Namibian independence. Some Western powers have supported her claims to continued occupation and direct control from Capetown. But the UN has passed Security Council Resolution 432, requesting the reintegration of Walvis Bay into Namibia.

The military occupation of Namibia by South Africa also reveals the scope of their strategic interest. The war with the Peoples Liberation Army of Namibia, an arm of the major African political movement SWAPO (South West African Peoples Organization), has occasionally spilled over into Angola and Zambia. South African army and air force bases have been built along the northern border.[16] The objective of defeating the internal SWAPO insurgency, along with containing the Angolans, Cubans, and Russians to the north of the border, has become a central strategic aim of South Africa. Western powers, while anxious to negotiate the conflict, appear to support South Africa in its objective of preventing the spread of Cuban and Soviet influences into Namibia. South Africa maintains a standing force of 75,000 troops at a cost of nearly a billion Rand a year.[17] The cost of this operation has more than offset the economic gains to South Africa described earlier.[18]

Thus, strategic, political, and economic considerations dominate the issue, while consideration of the right to self-determination is strictly secondary. This conflict of interests can be seen in the policies of the three major actors—the West, South Africa, and SWAPO.

POLICIES OF MAJOR ACTORS

Western powers, as represented by the Contact Group of Five, have disassociated themselves from the military occupation of Namibia and have sought a negotiated settlement in terms of UN resolutions, particularly Security Council Resolution 435, which calls for a cease-fire and a UN-supervised election. The basic policy of the Five, then, has been to mediate among South Africa, the Africans, and the United Nations for a negotiated settlement of the conflict. In reality, however, they accept South African strategic and economic interests as a part of their own broad strategy of dominance in Southern Africa, which would not necessarily be compromised by a popularly based government in Namibia.

The central difficulty has been that any fair election would almost inevitably bring SWAPO to power. The South Africans regard it as a security threat due to its links to Angola, the Cubans, and the Russians. On the other hand, SWAPO has rejected any terms to the settlement which would leave the country under the rule of a tribal-based and tributary elite. There is deep distrust on all sides. The South Africans distrust the UN, SWAPO distrusts the Contact Five, and the Reagan Administration's "constructive engagement" policy with South Africa has aroused latent feelings against U.S. imperialism among the Front Line states.

The Western Five have presented various proposals for settlement since the failure in 1978 of the UN plan for a transitional authority and election.[19] These were based on the concept of a cease-fire and withdrawal of military contingents, followed by a free and fair election of a Constituent Assembly, and the installation of an interim government that would provide for the implementation of a new constitution for an independent Namibia. However, the key underlying issue has been which groups would win the election and control the new government. The latest Western proposals attempted to provide for minority protection within the framework of majority rule through a formula of a two-tier representative system that would give two votes to each citizen, one for party and one for tribal candidates.[20] Because SWAPO rejected this, the proposal has been modified to count a single vote twice. This would enable small minority parties to gain representation. It has made South Africa unhappy, even though it could mean SWAPO would not have a controlling two-thirds of the Constituent Assembly.[21]

However, the formula of tribal representation is regarded by SWAPO and the Front Line African states as a continuation of the earlier Bantustan policies of South Africa by Africans, which is rejected by Namibian nationalists as vehemently as it is by Africans in South Africa. In rejecting the proposal of the Contact Group, Theo Ben Guriab, SWAPO's Permanent Representative to the United Nations, stated, "The Organization of African Unity and SWAPO find this process fundamentally unacceptable since it is intended to keep Namibian people disunited and separate physically . . . ."[22] Thus, they see the Western proposal as connivance with South Africa to prevent the majority party, in this case, SWAPO, from controlling the Constituent Assembly and forming a government.

The Western Five, however, argue that their proposal is no more than the protection and representation of minority interests provided for in many federal constitutions and systems of regional government. However, this attempt to inject a Western formula of democratic representation and protection of minority rights into the conflict, in order to placate South Africa, was ill-advised. It has not been accepted because the formulas have added credence to the SWAPO and Front Line Africans' belief that the West and South Africa are maneuvering to prevent a SWAPO victory and that fundamentally they want to preserve the tributary status of an "independent" Namibia.

South Africa is committed to a continuation of its dominance and control in Namibia under a settlement that will maintain the tributary class in power. Prime Minister Botha considers SWAPO to be "Communist-dominated" and untrustworthy, in terms of South African interests. The right wing of the South African Nationalist Party and the new Conservative Party are convinced that the Soviet Union controls SWAPO. These right-wing groups have threatened to resist with force any settlement that gives SWAPO an opportunity to form a government.[23] Liberal and progressive opinion in South Africa denies this direct linkage of SWAPO with Moscow but such views have long been disregarded by the Government. South African forces are locked in a deadly combat with SWAPO guerrillas, and it is clear that South Africa finds SWAPO unacceptable and therefore persists in seeking a formula which will give the appearance of democratic election in Namibia but maintains its tributary dependence. They thereby hope to placate Western and African opinion while holding on to their interests.

SWAPO, in the eyes of most informed observers, is the majority-backed party. There is some opposition, but most of it is among the smaller tribal groups such as the Herero. The majority African tribe, the Ovambo, have backed SWAPO since the early 1960s; the South African occupation and repression has only intensified this attitude.

SWAPO began its armed struggle in 1965, and it has continued since then with the aid of Angola and other Front Line African States. Non-military aid has been received in substantial quantity from Sweden, Eastern European states, and Cuba. Fidel Castro has stated that Cuba intends to leave Angola once the South African threat to the MPLA Government is withdrawn and the future of Namibia has been settled.[24] Cuban forces have not been involved in direct support of SWAPO's PLAN (People's Liberation Army of Namibia); but they have been Angola's major protection against South Africa's intrusive military actions. A SWAPO government would not be a Cuban or a Russian surrogate any more than Angola itself has proven to be. Marxist beliefs are heavily diluted with Christian Western values in the leadership, and there would not be a sharp break with existing economic and political ties. However, SWAPO leaders are committed to the control of their own resources and culture, and the change would clearly mean a retention of capital in Namibia for its own development.[25]

South Africans fear that a SWAPO-led Namibia would become a base for the Soviets and the African National Congress (ANC). These fears misunderstood the nature of Namibian nationalism. Whites and "Coloureds" (respectively 12 and 11 percent of the Namibian population) worry about their future. However, SWAPO does not want them to leave, as they contribute to the technical resources and growth of the economy.[26] A SWAPO-formed government would, in all probability, continue the basic tributary relationship, while initiating steps for a new international order of a more equitable system of exchange, and a shift from strategic ties to South Africa toward links with the non-aligned OAU and Front Line states.

The necessary principles of an agreement cannot be resolved by the shuttle diplomacy the Contact Five have employed. A face-to-face meeting of the parties in conflict needs be arranged at a "Geneva-type" conference, as proposed by SWAPO. The attendance of major parties at such a conference would be a sign that they are indeed ready to negotiate. Representation of the other political parties of Namibia can be worked out by the United Nations. There is no way in which the ultimate authority of the United Nations can be by-passed in a peaceful settlement, since under international law it now has full responsibility. While the Contact Five have enormous influence, they cannot replace the United Nations as this would be unacceptable to the Africans. Thus, the United Nations must become the major implementer of whatever basis of agreement emerges from the preliminary negotiations.

TO BREAK THE IMPASSE: HUMAN RIGHTS
AND THE ROLE OF THE UN

The negotiations impasse stems from the underlying realities of the strategic, political, and economic interests of the contending parties described in this chapter. The impasse can be broken in favor of a negotiated settlement, rather than a military solution, only if the Western Contact group adopts a new policy. This policy will have to shift away from a primarily strategic bias to a fully developed human rights priority. What is involved is not a token gesture but a genuine breaking of new ground.

A settlement will not be possible unless it simultaneously recognizes the interests and rights of the parties involved while moving them all to a new relationship. This new relationship must create the prospect for fulfillment of the aspirations of the majority, while protecting the rights and interests of the minorities and the external interested parties. The basic principles derived from a human rights strategy are: (1) majority rule with constitutional protection for minorities; (2) economic justice and development for all; and (3) strategic self-reliance.

The commitment by the outside world to majority rule, as expressed through United Nations and World Court action, is well founded. There is no valid reason to backtrack on this with a complex voting formula. South African fears of the damaging consequences of a SWAPO majority victory are both a reflection of the interests of minority parties, which will probably lose in a free and fair election, and also a projection of anti-Communist paranoia in South Africa. Many conservatives in South Africa have recognized this but have simply been bludgeoned by the far right on this issue. A free and fair election, under Security Council Resolution 435, is the best way to initiate this principle on a majority one-man, one-vote principal, with provision for minority group presentation and protection. This can be written into the Constitution through provision for special seats in the legislature, through an upper house, or through regional government councils, provided they do not destroy majority rule.[27] International guarantee of these rights should be made through a special treaty relationship with South Africa and the creation of an International Commission of Arbitration between the two states. Minority rights in land, resource access, and political liberties need to be given constitutional and legal protection in Namibia, as in all African societies. The lack of such protection has often led to authoritarian repression. The difficulty has been how to guarantee these in the face of majority tendencies to override them. In this case, a special tribunal or ombudsman should be created by treaty between Namibia and South Africa, with the continuing participation of the United Nations,[28] and with the power of arbitration in case of dispute.

The kinds of disputes that would be likely subjects of arbitration are:

1. South African military withdrawal from such areas as the Caprivi Strip and Walvis Bay and the evacuation of foreign military bases.
2. The return of political prisoners and the proper treatment of Namibians in South Africa.
3. Property and political rights of minorities in Namibia.
4. Corporate concessions, taxes, trading rights, and compensation for nationalization.
5. Namibian and South African access to employment, transportation, and port facilities.
6. The long-term status of Walvis Bay.

While the UN Commission for Namibia would not continue after a settlement, the UN Commissioner for Namibia might well be the means for administering an arbitration procedure that would be a legal authority operating according to the rules of international law.

The second major settlement principle is economic justice, which must accept the need for external economic interests to make a greater contribution to the development of Namibia. A majority-based government will require the reinvestment of profits and the retention of taxes in the country. Basic shifts will doubtless be gradual, as in Angola, in either the ownership or trade patterns. But an independent Namibia will follow a NIEO strategy of the African states, and shift from a total dependency on the West and South Africa to a relationship with other regional agencies such as the Southern African Development Coordination Conference (SADCC). African wages obviously cannot remain a fraction of the Poverty Datum Line (PDL). Managerial positions, now almost entirely White or Coloured,[29] must be opened more widely. South Africa cannot continue to drain taxes and multinational corporations must not siphon profits from diamond, copper, and uranium out of the country, with very little payment to Namibia. Unsettled disputes over the nationalization and redirection of resources should be equitably worked out and referred to the arbitration commission. As long as this commission performed its task with judicious equity, it would retain the support of all sides.

The security uncertainty of South Africa and the West is related to continuance of bases and access rights in an independent Namibia. The issue of Cuban presence in Angola is not a long-term concern, once the Namibian conflict is settled and South Africa ends her incursions into Angola and support for anti-government groups. The Cubans are anxious to terminate this costly responsibility and have made no commitment to provide logistic support for the African National Congress (ANC) of South Africa. The Namibians, while sympathetic to the ANC, are no more likely to provide base facilities for an ANC guerrilla army than Botswana or Swaziland has done, and SWAPO has indicated that its intention is the liberation of Namibia, while South Africa is a problem for the South Africans.

A very difficult problem is Walvis Bay, which South Africa has indicated it will retain. The territory clearly belongs to Namibia. However, the Namibians might agree to a short-term solution for the present. In exchange for sovereignty and generous economic concessions, they could give South Africa a ten-year lease under a treaty relationship. Such an agreement would remove a major obstacle in South African thinking about a genuine transfer of authority, and leave to the not-too-distant future the realization of total withdrawal of South African forces. Namibia, under a SWAPO Government, or any representative rule, will opt to move away from South African and Western dominance. Collective self-reliance in association with other African states such as Angola and Zambia is the direction they will take. This will provide minimum security for the new state and help dissuade South Africa from a reoccupation of the country.

CONCLUSION

The violation of human rights in Namibia should be seen as taking place in two stages. The first step is the imposition of Western power interests on South Africa, in order to obtain a nominal independence for Namibia, and thereby prevent the further deterioration of Western interests not only in Namibia, but in the entire South African and Southern African area. The second step is the more complete realization of the right to independence and other freedoms through collective self-reliance and the regional integration of Southern African states through such agencies as the Southern African Development and Cooperation Commission (SADCC).

The global system contains a contradiction of interests between the United States and the other Western powers and South Africa, which is far more than a difference over human rights and racial discrimination. South Africa is essentially a Western surrogate or tributary state which is useful to Western powers only as long as they can assure the continued stability of the region. The occupation of Namibia and warfare with African states, which introduce Soviet and Cuban power into Angola and elsewhere in the region, are viewed with great alarm in Western strategic circles.[30] While there may be a complete agreement on the threat that the increase in Soviet presence presents, there is a sharp, growing difference with South Africa over the best method of dealing with it. Several Western governments believe that South Africa must yield to the insistance of the African states and the United Nations that self-government devolve upon the nationalist representatives, if only because this will end the warfare and provide a basis for the withdrawal of Cuban influence and, indirectly, Soviet power in the region.

It should be recognized that the Contact Five, with great economic interests in the mineral wealth of Namibia, do not see these investments as jeopardized by a SWAPO government. Quite the contrary, the experience of large mineral multinational corporations elsewhere in Southern Africa has been that even socialist governments have provided the stability in which business as usual continues. Like Prime Minister Botha, they would prefer not to have a SWAPO government, but are far more confident of being able to handle Sam Njoma, the head of SWAPO, once the Cuban forces have withdrawn from Angola.

The South African government is deeply divided over how to respond to this Western pressure. The rapid rise of the far right has forced the Botha Government to respond more slowly to the external pressures than would otherwise have been the case.[31] A tributary state is not a colony and has therefore a certain degree of autonomy. The dominant power can only manipulate the environment so as to bring about political change favorable to its policies. In the Namibian case, the Reagan Administration policy of "constructive engagement" has created an illusion of power and independence on the part of the South Africans, which delays the realization of the necessity for accepting the Western power solution. The argument that this gentle persuasion works better than coercion does not appear to be borne out by the increase of militancy within South Africa and the pressure this has exerted on the Government. As Ambassador Donald McHenry has argued, isolation and increased pressure might well be more effective, since it would prick the bubble of illusion of self-sufficiency among Afrikaners.

Western governments, now committed to a course of human rights action under the United Nations, will probably be forced to resort to coercion of South Africa under Article 41 of the UN Charter. Vetoes by the United States and the United Kingdom have prevented such drastic action to date; but this may change.[32] In the long term, the dominant powers will not permit South Africa to continue to prevent their access to the resources of Namibia and to jeopardize their general security positions through a policy that invites chaos. Sanctions may well precipitate an even greater right-wing reaction in South Africa and more intensive repression in Namibia; but the overall effect will be to weaken South Africa's position in Southern Africa and Namibia.

An election under Security Council Resolution 435 of the United Nations is a desirable outcome, if it can be obtained on terms that will provide a fair atmosphere and not prejudice the election results in advance. Such an outcome would be a great triumph for the principles of international order and human rights. However, this reasonable settlement procedure is not likely to take place before the Western nations, as well as the other members of the United Nations, make it unequivocably clear to South Africa that non-compliance will result in severe international penalties. There is a great deal of resistance to such a step in Western business and conservative political circles, which the South Africans have skillfully exploited. However, the system of dominance also has its limits, and it is highly possible that interests combined with morality will force the Western Contact states into taking coercive action. The Reagan Administration's linkage of a Namibian settlement to a Cuban withdrawal from Angola has put the cart before the horse and played into South African hands.

From the standpoint of the Namibians and their aspirations for independence, two key points emerge from this analysis. First, the major elements in their nationalist movement have accepted the necessity of armed struggle to remove South African control. SWAPO has emerged as the major, although not the only, spokesman of this revolutionary strategy. The leaders of SWAPO as well as of other nationalist groups are prepared to accept a settlement with a fair election under the UN framework. Should this fail, certainly SWAPO and probably representatives of the others will intensify their revolutionary opposition, and despite heavy repression, their insurgency will find increased support from Angola, Cuba, and African states. The struggle has already many characteristics of the French and then American involvement in Vietnam, and the cost to South Africa is heavy. If Western sanctions are invoked, the cost will become enormous, at a time when the South African economy is staggering under the impact of the fall in world prices for her mineral exports. Some of the more militant SWAPO leaders are convinced that only an armed struggle can gain them their full body of rights, and they are reluctant to accede to an election process. The controlling Njoma faction believes that the democratic process is the way to at least the first stage on the road to independence, and if this policy is backed by the Western powers, it may prevail. Protracted warfare can only result in increased militancy and perhaps the refusal of important groups to take part in a democratic transition.

Second, in the long term, Namibian self-determination, like other small Southern African states, depends on its ability to develop a form of collective self-reliance that enables it to break with the strategic and economic domination of the West, as well as of South Africa. Government leaders in the area recognize the importance of collective self-reliance, but they are prepared to make progress by stages and to cooperate with such agencies as SADCC and the Front Line states to create the conditions in which full self-determination can be realized. It can be hoped that in South Africa and the West there will emerge a group of leaders prepared to recognize and accept a more just order between the super powers and the new states.

NOTES

1. Emerson summarized it well: "A great era of human history has come to a close—the era of Western domination over the rest of Mankind." Rupert

Emerson, *From Empire to Nation: The Rise of Self-Assertion of Asian and African Peoples* (Cambridge: Harvard University Press, 1960), p. 5.

2. The Western cluster of power is dominated by the United States and is organized around the Organization for Economic Cooperation and Development and the North Atlantic Treaty Organization. Its counterpart is the Communist Economic Council of Nations and the Warsaw Pact, dominated by the Soviet Union. These two clusters have dominance linkages with the new states of the Third World. Johan Galtung outlined this superpower imperialism in "The Structure of Imperialism," *Journal of Peace Research* 8, no. 2 (1971), pp. 81–117.

3. *The Charter of the United Nations Organization*, Article 76.

4. "Legal Consequences for States of the Continued Presence of South Africa in Namibia (South West Africa) Notwithstanding Council Resolution 276," 1971 ICJ 16. In 1966, the United Nations revoked South Africa's mandate by means of General Assembly Resolution 2145.

5. The Council for Namibia of the United Nations has recognized SWAPO. However, the existence of other parties is recognized and accepted by many members of the United Nations. SWAPO was given official Observer Status by General Assembly Resolution 3115 in 1973. The UN Council for Namibia has dealt with other representative groups but has, since early 1970, believed SWAPO to be the most popular and authentic representative.

6. R.F. Botha's letter to Secretary General Kurt Waldheim, February 20, 1979, S/13105.

7. Kenneth Grundy, "Intermediary Power and Global Dependency: The Case of South Africa," *International Studies Quarterly* 20, no. 4 (December 1976), pp. 553–80.

8. Richard V. Green, *From Sudwestafrika to Namibia: The Political Economy of Transition*, Research Report no. 58 (Uppsala: Scandinavian Institute of African Studies, 1981), p. 8.

9. This author stated, during the 1979 negotiations on the United Nations Temporary Assistance Group plan:

> South Africa has called the Western Five's bluff with its recognition that the West wants economic links more than it wants social justice for Namibians. As a South African newspaper put it, "South Africa's strategy has gambled successfully on the fact that the West's bark is worse than its bite, that Vance and Company are not really more than paper tigers, that when the chips are down they will wield their votes against sanctions resolutions put forward at the U.N."

George W. Shepherd, Jr., "No Free and Fair Settlement in Namibia: The Collapse of the Western Five Plan," *Africa Today* 26, no. 2 (1979), pp. 21–22. The theoretical basis for this is amplified in George W. Shepherd, Jr., *Super Powers and New States* (forthcoming).

10. In mining, South Africa owns only forty percent while the United States and European interests control the rest. If all production including farming and fishing is considered, then South Africa owns seventy-five percent of production. *To Be Born a Nation: The Liberation Struggle for Namibia* (London: SWAPO, 1982), pp. 46–48.

11. Ibid., p. 43.

12. South Africa gets huge gains in foreign exchange from Namibia and South African companies like DeBeers that pay only one-half of the taxes in Namibia that they are required to pay in Botswana. Ibid., p. 55.

13. Africans are still forcibly removed from areas to provide for white interests and protection. *Namibia: The Facts* (London: International Defense and Aid Fund for Southern Africa, 1980), p. 22.

14. A confidential document of the U.S. National Security Council proposed a South Atlantic Alliance, including South American countries like Argentina, in order to defend the Cape route. "Reagan Alliance Woos South Africa," *South*, October 1981, p. 24.

15. *Apartheid's Army in Namibia: South Africa's Illegal Military Occupation* (London: International Defense and Aid Fund for Southern Africa, 1982), p. 7.

16. The extensive deployment of the South African Defense Force is outlined in *Apartheid's Army in Namibia*.

17. Ibid., p. 15.

18. *New York Times*, March 24, 1982.

19. "Proposal for a Settlement of the Namibian Situation," *Objective Justice* 10, no. 2 (Summer 1978). Security Council Resolution 431 (July 27, 1978) established the United Nations Temporary Assistance Group.

20. The original idea was that half the members of the Constituent Assembly would be elected on a national basis by proportional representation, half on the basis of single-member constituencies. Each voter was to have two votes, which would enable tribally based candidates as well as a national party to win seats. See "Revised Contact Group Proposal," *Transafrica Forum, Issue Brief* (February 1982).

21. Graham Hovey, "Pretoria Said to Agree to Namibia Plan," *New York Times*, December 28, 1978, p. A3. See also *Update* (African-American Institute), February 10, 1982.

22. *Africa News*, February 22, 1982.

23. Joseph Lelyveld, "South Africa Tied to Abortive Coup," *New York Times*, April 22, 1982, p. A5.

24. "Namibia: A Nation Wronged" (London: British Council of Churches, Division of International Affairs, 1982) reports a belief in Namibia that SWAPO was the *amati* (friends) of the people and that "many SWAPO leaders are Christian."

25. These proposed changes have been published in research reports of the United Nations Institute for Namibia (UNIN) in Lusaka, headed by Hage Geingob. See *UNIN News, UNIN Quarterly*, and other UNIN reports, such as R.H. Green, *Manpower Estimates and Development Implications for Namibia* (1978).

26. There are White and Colored members of SWAPO in Namibia. SWAPO's racial views are similar to those of the Patriotic Front of Zimbabwe, which seeks participation of progressive non-Africans in self-rule.

27. The principle of special seats for minorities is well established in constitutional government. SWAPO is not committed to any formula, but there is no reason to believe that it would not be reasonable. The single-party system

of African governments is not noted for its protection of minority political views. SWAPO is committed to the vanguard party strategy of scientific socialism, which limits opposition of rival groups and parties.

28. For example, the American-Mexican Commission, established in 1868, has handled more than two thousand claims of a similar nature. The famous "Alabama Case" was resolved as a result of the Washington Treaty of 1871. See Gerhard von Vlahn, *Law Among Nations* (New York: Macmillan, 1963), pp. 461–62. The ombudsman idea has emerged in human rights as a product of UN dispute settlement.

29. *To Be Born a Nation*, pp. 77–78. The PDL is a measure of minimum income needed for the average family to survive, and was developed by the International Labor Office in 1977.

30. The Reagan Administration believed that a Namibia settlement would result if the Cubans withdrew from Angola and thereby removed their support for SWAPO. The United States has not attacked SWAPO directly but has backed schemes that would block SWAPO from taking full power upon independence.

31. Alan Cowell, "South African Vote Seen as Rebuff to Ruling Party," *New York Times*, July 20, 1982.

32. The Carter Administration seriously considered abstention from a vote on sanctions by the Security Council. Interview with Ambassador Donald McHenry, March 1977. Other top Carter officials confirmed this. Time may well run out for South Africa in the next American and British administrations. See interview between Ambassador McHenry and Randall Robinson in *Transafrica Forum* 1, no. 1 (1979), p. 1.

CHAPTER TWELVE

The "Right to Development": How Not to Link Human Rights and Development

JACK DONNELLY

As Ronald Meltzer indicated, human rights and development increasingly have come to be seen as complementary concerns and mutually reinforcing practices.[1] Not all human rights, however, are always consistent with all parts of every valid development strategies; *some* trade-offs are certainly going to be necessary.[2] However, recent theory and practice have differed from earlier views of development-rights trade-offs, both in suggesting much more limited and selective trade-offs, and in pressing the case for at least sometimes relinquishing some incremental economic growth in favor of more immediate satisfaction of human rights. All of this can be seen as involving a major conceptual reorientation in which development and human rights are coming to be viewed as complementary rather than competing concerns.

In the last five years, however, another way of linking human rights and development has also become prominent internationally, *viz.*, arguments for a human right to development, the claim that development itself is a basic human right. While the linkage of human rights and development at the level of development planning is an exciting development that is conceptually well-grounded and promises important progress in the realization of human rights in the Third World,[3] I shall argue that the right to development is both conceptually and practically misguided, at best a legally and morally confused notion that is likely to be positively detrimental to the realization of human rights.

Africans have played a leading role in the formulation and advocacy of the right to development. For example, the first serious proposal of an international human right to development was made by the Senegalese jurist Keba M'Baye in 1972.[4] M'Baye, serving as President of the Thirty-third Session of the United Nations Commission on Human Rights in 1977, was also instrumental in securing the first formal international recognition of the right to development, in Commission resolution 4 (XXXIII). Today, the right to development is enshrined as Article 22 of the Banjul Charter, and Africans continue to be among its major advocates. Thus, while I will be discussing the right to development in general, with only occasional explicit reference to Africa, the widespread popularity of the idea in Africa makes my argument an implicit argument against this new, and I believe dangerous, direction in discussions of human rights and development in Africa.

THE RIGHT TO DEVELOPMENT: MORAL AND LEGAL FOUNDATIONS

The document that launched the right to development into international prominence was the 1979 study by the UN Secretary-General on "The International Dimensions of the Right to Development as a Human Right . . . ."[5] *The Secretary-General's Report*, which still is the most comprehensive account of the legal and moral foundations of the right, suggests that "there are a variety of ethical arguments which may be considered to support the existence, in ethical terms, of a right to development" (paragraph 54).[6]

"Development is the condition of all social life and therefore an inherent requirement of every obligation" (paragraph 40). A right to development can also be viewed as arising out of an international duty of solidarity (paragraph 42) and the moral duty of reparation for the underdevelopment caused by colonial and neocolonial exploitation (paragraph 54). Increasing moral interdependence also gives rise to such a right (paragraph 47), and economic interdependence makes it in the interest of all countries (paragraph 48). Furthermore, without protection of the right to development, world peace is endangered, as those whose human rights are denied turn to force as an unfortunate, but understandable and even justified, last resort (paragraphs 50–51).

The Secretary-General's Report also suggests that "there is a very substantial body of principles . . . . which demonstrate the existence of a human right to development in international law" (paragraph 78),[7] including Articles 55 and 56 of the United Nations Charter, Articles 22, 26(2), 28, and 29(1) of the Universal Declaration of Human Rights, and the International Covenant on Economic, Social and Cultural Rights, particularly Articles 1(1), 2(1), and 11. Reference can also be made as well to more specialized human rights conventions, such as those on apartheid and discrimination in education; to regional instruments such as the American Declaration of the Rights of Man and the European Social Charter; and to declarations and resolutions of the General Assembly and other UN organs.

Arguments elsewhere, of which M'Baye's may be taken as typical,[8] are of much the same sort. Admitting that "the association of 'development' and 'right' is somewhat venturesome," M'Baye claims that, nonetheless, "a new right is being fashioned before our very eyes: the right to development." Philosophically, development is a right in the sense that justice demands it. Psychologically, the gross economic disparities between North and South can only be viewed in the Third World as an injustice and a provocation; "this is why development continues to be viewed as an asset and a right." In addition, since poverty and inequality lead to confrontation and even violence, "the desire to safeguard peace is another justification of the right to development."[9]

The actions of the North also give rise to a right to development, according to M'Baye. Trade with, and investment in, the Third World enriches the developed countries, giving rise to correlative obligations which are expressed by the right to development. These obligations are strongly reinforced by an historic responsibility for colonialism, neocolonialism, and forced underdevelopment. In addition, obligations arise from the use of the Third World for strategic bases and the ideological subjugation of developing countries by the manipulation of foreign aid.[10]

But "it is above all solidarity that should be invoked" in justifying the right to development. The "true foundation" of the right "is the obligation of solidarity," which is a legal as well as moral obligation.[11]

This stress on "solidarity" is part of a new wave in international human rights discussions. Along with such rights as the rights to peace, to a healthy and balanced environment and to share in the fruits of the exploitation of the common natural heritage of mankind, the right to development is presented as one of the so-called "third generation" of human rights.[12] It is argued that just as the "first generation" of civil and political rights (based on the idea of "liberty" and providing security against state violations of the individual) proved to be insufficient to protect human dignity and were therefore supplemented by a "second generation" of economic, social, and cultural rights (based on the principle of "equality" and requiring the state to provide social and economic goods, services, and opportunities), so now a "third generation" of "solidarity rights" (based on the idea of "fraternity" at the national and international levels) is required, especially in light of the widespread international inequality which has frustrated the implementation, realization, and enjoyment of the first two generations of human rights, particularly in the Third World.

Multiple rights-holders and duty-bearers of the right to development have been identified. *The Secretary-General's Report* notes that development has been advanced as a right of states, peoples, minorities and individuals (paragraphs 87–93).[13] M'Baye suggests that this is a result of the fact that "development concerns 'all men,' 'every man,' and 'all of man.'"[14] Likewise, the right imposes obligations on the international community, developed countries (singly and collectively), national governments in the developing countries, and individuals, both nationally and internationally (paragraphs 95–110).[15]

This diversity of rights-holders and duty-bearers arises in part from the comprehensiveness of the right. It also seems to reflect a tactical decision to follow a shotgun approach in establishing the right. But it also seems to reflect confusion and disagreement based on conflicting and imprecise conceptualizations of the right.

In particular, the substance of the entitlements and obligations created by the right have been left quite vague; there is not even agreement as to whether the right to development is a new right or whether it is in some way implied by, or the philosophical foundation for, or a synthesis of, older and better recognized human rights.[16] The dominant interpretation is that it is a synthesis of existing rights (paragraph 65), although a dialectical one in which the whole is more than the sum of the parts.[17]

However, such vagueness, while troubling, is of major importance only if we assume that there is a right to development. I shall argue, instead, that there is not. These alleged legal and moral sources do not establish the existence or necessity of a human right to development, and the political consequences of recognizing such a right are highly undesirable from a human rights perspective.

LEGAL SOURCES OF THE RIGHT TO DEVELOPMENT

The promotion of "higher standards of living, full employment, and conditions of economic and social progress and development" and "universal respect for, and observance of, human rights and fundamental freedoms for all without distinction as to race, sex, language or religion" are among the principle objectives of the United Nations specified in the Charter (Article 55). Furthermore, "all Members pledge themselves to take joint and separate action in cooperation with the Organization" to achieve these objectives (Article 56). M'Baye concludes that "the renunciation of the normal attributes of conventional sovereignty" implied by these provisions establishes the existence of a legal right to development.[19]

The renunciation of sovereignty in Articles 55 and 56, however, is extremely limited: states merely accept an obligation to take (unspecified) cooperative action to further (unspecified) human rights; they do not oblige themselves to undertake any particular course of action, let alone to protect or realize any particular human right.[19] The Charter speaks only of human rights in general (enjoyed without discrimination), and development is conceived of as a goal, not a right. Therefore, while it is true that "there certainly is no right to do nothing" with regard to development,[20] the Charter does not recognize *any* particular human rights, let alone a right to development. More promising sources for a right to development are the Universal Declaration of Human Rights and the 1966 International Human Rights Covenants, which specify the "human rights" mentioned in general terms in the Charter.

Article 22 of the Universal Declaration is particularly suggestive:

> Everyone, as a member of society, has the right to social security and is entitled to realization, through national effort and international co-operation and in accordance with the organization and resources of each State, of the economic, social, and cultural rights indispensable for his dignity and the free development of his personality.

However, this article establishes only individual rights, whereas the right to development is at least as much a collective or peoples' right. Furthermore, the only right explicitly mentioned is a right to social security. Finally, and of greatest conceptual significance, individual development is explicitly viewed as the object or consequence of the enjoyment of economic and social rights, not a right in itself.

Not everything that is good or desirable is a right, let alone a human right. We do not even necessarily have a right to everything which some other right aims to realize. Imagine that A establishes a trust fund for B, the purpose of which is to assure B's future financial security. B's right to the proceeds of the trust will in fact contribute to his financial security. However, B does not *ipso facto* have a right to financial security.

Individual development *is* a likely (although not a necessary) consequence of respect for economic, social, and cultural rights. In fact, *all* human rights—civil and political rights as well as economic and social rights—aim at the development of individual personality and the protection of inherent human dignity. The International Human Rights Covenants, for example, present "inherent human dignity" as the source of the rights they enumerate. But this would seem to be precisely why a right to development is *not* recognized—development is one of the primary objectives of all human rights, not a human right itself.

The other promising passage in the Universal Declaration is Article

28: "Everyone is entitled to a social and international order in which the rights and freedoms set forth in this declaration can be fully realized." While one might plausibly extract a derivative human right to development from this, the monumental conflicts between rights-holders seeking to exercise or enjoy their rights to development, and the political problems which this would present, strongly counsel against such a move.

If the right to development is a human right, then it is a universal right, a right held by all. If it is equally a right of individuals, minorities, peoples, and states, it is a right of each and every individual, minority, people, and state. This can only lead to countless intense and refractory conflicts of rights.

In the absence of a priority principle, the only way to salvage the right to development would seem to be to restrict it to a right of peoples or states (rather than individuals), which is how the right appears in the Banjul Charter, or to a right of minimum access to the material necessities for life and ordinary growth (rather than development more comprehensively understood), or even to a doubly restricted right of peoples (or states) to minimum levels of economic development.[21] But such a right is no longer the right its advocates originally advanced.

We would not say that an individual who is simply alive, fed, clothed, and sheltered is developed, nor necessarily even developing. Likewise, a country that is able, through its own efforts, to feed, clothe, and house its people is not necessarily a developed country. While development requires fairly substantial minimum material prerequistives—only the rarest individuals can grow and develop their potentials in the face of gross physical deprivations—an equally important aspect of "development" is growth and development of the mind, which requires freedom of speech and conscience, as well as access to education, knowledge, and culture. Restricted to a right of states or a right to material resources, the right to development is no longer a right to full human development.

It is regularly noted in discussions of the right to development that development, in the relevant sense, means "fulfillment of the human person in harmony with the community" (paragraph 25); "the realization of the potentialities of the human person in harmony with the community should be seen as the central purpose of development" (paragraph 27). Even its advocates admit that it cannot be restricted to a right of peoples or states;[22] it is at least as much a right of individuals.

Likewise, if the right to development is to be not merely the guarantee of animal needs—if we are talking about *human* development and not merely economic development or the satisfaction of physical needs and material interests—it cannot be reduced to economic rights. Rather, it must be a right to development of the *whole* person. However, when serious debate begins, the *economic and social* aspects of development are given nearly exclusive attention, particularly by the advocates of the right to development.

For example, the topic has been discussed in the United Nations almost exclusively under agenda items dealing solely or primarily with economic and social rights in the less developed countries. It first arose in the Commission on Human Rights under the item "Question of the realization in all countries of the economic, social, and cultural rights contained in the [Universal Declaration and Covenants] . . . and study of the special problems which the developing countries face in their efforts to achieve these rights." The most recent agenda item, in a further distortion, adds "(a) problems relating to the right to enjoy an adequate standard of living; the right to development; (b) the effects of the existing unjust international economic order on the economies of the developing countries and the obstacles that this represents for the implementation of human rights and fundamental freedoms." Evolving UN doctrine thus treats the right to development as largely a right not to be economically underdeveloped, transforming human rights concerns related to development into little more than a device to gain economic concessions on largely spurious grounds, or still another way to assert the priority of economic and social rights.[23]

The other sources of a legal right to development are even weaker. Single issue human rights treaties fail to mention the right, while the UN declarations and resolutions that explicitly recognize it (especially Commission on Human Rights resolution 4 (XXXIII) of 1977 and General Assembly Resolutions 34/46 and 36/133) have no binding legal force.[24]

It is of course possible that a legal right to development is emerging; for example, the Commission on Human Rights is at work on a Declaration on the topic. However, such arguments tacitly admit that international law currently does not recognize a human right to development; they are in fact arguments in favor of a *transformation* of international law. The case for such a transformation, though, must be made largely on moral and political grounds.

MORAL ARGUMENTS FOR A RIGHT TO DEVELOPMENT

Probably the most common moral argument infers a right to development from a moral concern for, or obligation to contribute to, development.[25] Such arguments, however, confuse one particular sphere of morality—rights, special entitlements—with moral righteousness in general. Not all moral "oughts" are grounded in rights. It simply is not true that one *has a right* to everything which it would be just or right for one to do or possess. Men do not *have* rights, in the strict and strong sense of titles and claims, to everything which *is* right.[26]

Advocates of the right to development are correct: in a just world, underdevelopment would not be permitted; morality and justice do demand development. But this alone by no means establishes, or even strongly suggests, a moral *right* to development. Demonstrating the existence of a moral (or legal, or other) obligation will not, in itself, establish the existence of a right.[27]

This distinction is not a matter of mere semantics. To have a right to *x* is to be specially *entitled* to *x*, which justifies claims of much greater moral force than other (equally valid) claims to have *x*. *Having* a right to *x* means not merely that it is or would be good, right, or just to be able to have or enjoy *x*, but that one is entitled to *x*, owed *x*, has it as one's due. In addition, rights-holders may press special claims—rights claims—in seeking enjoyment of their rights. A rights-holder is not merely the beneficiary of someone else's obligations, but largely controls the relationship in which he stands to the duty-bearer. And the special force of rights claims makes this control doubly valuable to him.

Clearly this is why establishing a *right* to development is so important to its advocates. They want to be able to press stronger claims for development assistance and to play a more active role in obtaining that assistance than is possible when development is viewed simply as right in the sense of what is right or morally desirable. But grounding the right to development simply on the general moral righteousness of development strips it of its special force *as a right*. Collapsing moral rights into morality in general—i.e., confusing *rights* (in the sense of having a right) with considerations of what *is* right—is not only a serious conceptual error but a self-defeating strategy: the right is emasculated; such a "right" provides no additional force to the claims for development.

The distinction between rights and righteousness—between having a right and being right, between entitlement and obligation—needs to be specially stressed in the African context, because the idea of human rights, as that term is ordinarily understood—namely, as rights/titles/claims held by all individuals simply because they are human beings—is foreign to traditional African society and political culture.[28] However, since the reverse is generally claimed in the contemporary literature—"The African conception of human rights was an essential aspect of African humanism"; "It is not often remembered that traditional African societies supported and practiced human rights."[29]—a brief digression on this topic may be helpful, especially in light of the earlier arguments in this volume by Abdullahi Ahmed El Naiem and Lakshman Marasinghe.

To put it most simply, the evidence advanced for an indigenous African human rights tradition simply fails to establish the claim. For example, Dunstan M. Wai, the author of the second quoted passage above, continues by writing that "traditional African attitudes, beliefs, institutions, and experience sustained the 'view that certain rights should be upheld against alleged necessities of state'."[30] Clearly in this claim he is confusing human rights with limited government. There are many bases on which a government might be limited—divine commandment, human rights, legal rights, and extra-legal checks such as a balance of power, to name a few. Simply having a limited government does not in any way entail that one has human rights.

"There is no point in belaboring the concern for rights, democratic institutions, and rule of law in traditional African politics."[31] But this observation by Asmarom Legesse is particularly pointless in a discussion of human rights, given the form such concerns took in traditional African societies. Even in the many cases where Africans had personal rights vis-à-vis their government, those rights were not based on one's humanity per se but on membership in the community, social status, or some other ascriptive characteristic. Legesse also argues that "many studies have been carried out that suggest that distributive justice, in the economic and political spheres, is the cardinal ethical principle that is shared by most Africans."[32] This is quite true. It is also, once again, irrelevant.

Distributive justice and human rights are quite different concepts. One might base a conception of distributive justice on human rights, but one might as easily base it on some other principle; for example, Plato, Burke, and Bentham all had theories of distributive justice, yet no one would suggest that they thereby advocated human rights. Distributive justice involves giving to each his own, which includes respecting the rights of others. In traditional African societies, however, rights were assigned on the basis of communal membership, family, status, or achievement, and thus were not personal, *human* rights.

There is nothing surprising, let alone disreputable, in this absence of the concept or practice of "human rights." How a society seeks to realize human dignity—and Africans, like all peoples, have always devoted much of their best energies to attempts to realize human *dignity*—is in large part a function of its economic and social organization. In the tightly knit, village-based, and largely autarkic agricultural community common to much of precolonial Africa, the individual is in many ways an anachronistic abstraction. Each person is first and foremost a part of the community. And it is this which gives him his place in the world, protects him against injustice and natural disaster, and provides him with a framework in which to realize his innate human dignity. So long as such a community is functioning smoothly, human rights are sure to remain out of the picture, for there almost certainly will be no such notions as the autonomous individual, universal human nature, and universal rights, concepts without which the concept of human rights is, literally, unthinkable.

Advocates of a traditional African conception of human rights are attempting to establish that the differences with the West lie only in the words used, not the concepts. "Different societies formulate their conception of human rights in diverse cultural idioms."[32] In fact, though, the difference is not simply one of idiom, but one of concept. "Human rights" is a concept foreign to African political culture. Furthermore, the two approaches are radically incompatible: Individual human rights cannot be recognized by a traditional society without disrupting, and probably even destroying, that society; and human rights themselves would be destroyed in attempts to reconceptualize them in traditional African terms.

Syncretism is an often-noted feature of African cultures, and perhaps what we are seeing is the beginnings of a creative synthesis. However, I am very skeptical of such a synthesis' impact on human rights; in any case, if this is really what Africans are up to, let them discuss it as such. The claim to the right to development is of a new human right, and it is that claim that I am arguing is confused or unjustified.

Returning to the right to development in particular, the argument from solidarity, which is generally alleged to be the single most important argument for the existence of a right to development,[33] is merely a variant of this basic conceptual error of confusing rights and duties. By "solidarity" its advocates mean "the fundamental principles of sharing and helping those who are unable to help themselves" (paragraph 42). These principles are undeniably important, and they do establish strong moral obligations to assist those in need. They do not, however, establish a *right* to assistance—as we saw in the examples above—let alone a right to development. "The innate responsibility to help one's fellow men" and "the need for justice, both nationally and internationally,"[34] establish only a moral obligation to act to promote and encourage development, not a right to development itself.

In fact, arguments from solidarity not only misconstrue the conceptual relations between rights and duties, they are incompatible with the very idea of *human* rights. Human rights, as the Covenants put it, "derive from the inherent dignity of the human person." This is equally true of civil, political, economic, social, and cultural rights. But solidarity is a relation *among* persons or groups. It is thus quite a different source of rights. Therefore, to the extent that the "third generation" human rights are based on solidarity, they are not *human* rights—unless "human rights" is not to mean what it has meant up to now. There is not merely a difference in substance—in the object of the right—from the first two "generations" of rights, but a fundamental *qualitative* difference between solidarity rights and all (other) "human rights," based on radically different sources for the rights.[35]

This distinction between rights and obligations also has important implications for the argument that a *right to* development is emerging, or ought to emerge, out of a *law of* development.[36]

> In most cases, before there is an attempt to postulate a "right to . . ." there is the development of a "law of . . . ." In other words, a new body of legal norms or a revision of legal thinking on a given problem provides the conceptual framework for identifying, first, the legal implications of the problem, then the human rights implications, and finally the reformulation of the whole problem in terms of a new human right.[37]

The problem, though, lies in specifying which areas of law make the transition to rights, which do not, and why. Certainly not *all* new issues that are handled through the mechanism of the law will or should give rise to rights; and not even everything that has human rights implications is a human right. Yet Stephen Marks, the author of the passage just quoted, presents as evidence for the case of the right to development little more than some desultory passages from *The Secretary-General's Report* and a few UN resolutions.

Even if we assume, as Hector Gros Espiell argues, that the law of development is "not only . . . a new discipline but also . . . a juridical technique for carrying on the struggle against underdevelopment"[38] it is *not* obvious that a right to development is either necessary or desirable, let alone that a *human* right to development is called for. There may be other possible or preferable means for pursuing the goal of development besides the establishment of an international *right* to development; and even if a right to development is necessary or desirable, such a right might not be best conceived as a human right.

Writers like Marks and Gros Espiell seriously underestimate the gap between "There is a law of *x*" and "There is a right to *x*," or, in broader terms, the gap between obligations and rights. Laws do create or codify obligations—but obligations, even very important obligations, do not establish or necessarily imply rights. Rights *can* be created—the list of human rights is not a divine gift engraved in stone—but the current literature does not provide a clear demonstration, or even a plausibly suggestive argument, that development has or should make the jump.

Other moral arguments are no more successful. For example, interdependence in no way implies a right to development, despite the claims of M'Baye and *The Secretary-General's Report*. Interdependence, as a cooperative joint undertaking, usually does involve conferring rights on the participants in the enterprise. However, these rights are specific to the particular undertaking and are restricted to assuring that everyone performs his role and that the fruits of cooperation are divided equitably. No broad moral rights arise from even very intense interdependence; the scope of the alleged right to development is utterly disproportionate to the collective enterprise. Even if the current international economic order does not equitably distribute the benefits of international trade and financial transactions, this suggests at most a right to a fair share of the proceeds, not a right to *development*, and not a *human* right of any sort.

Another set of arguments attempts to derive a right to development from the instrumental value of development. The most prominent of these rests on the threat to international peace and security posed by underdevelopment. "The desire to safeguard peace is another justification of the right to development."[39] "The interests of world stability and the pursuit of a lasting peace require universal respect for a right to development" (paragraph 51).

The connection between peace, especially international peace, and the right to development is obscure and at best controversial;[40] a cynic might suggest that development merely increases the destructiveness of war rather than fostering peace. But even allowing a significant link between development and peace will not establish a right to development. Disarmament, reductions in international arms sales, the resumption of détente, and the removal of General Khaddafi would all contribute to international peace and stability, but we do not have human rights to these things. That development would be conducive to peace is a fortunate fact about man and the world, but this will not establish the existence of a *right* to development; it simply suggests that development has a certain additional instrumental value.

A formally similar argument suggests that "because of its multitudinous effects and its central characteristic, the question of development could jeopardize human rights as a whole."[41] However, the fact that development is conducive to the realization of human rights in general does not *ipso facto* establish that there is a right to development.

Finally we can consider the claim that "the right to development is in effect the process of the realization of the right to self-determination."[42] Article 1(1) of the International Human Rights Covenants reads: "All peoples have the right to self-determination. By virtue of the right they freely determine their political status and freely pursue their economic, social, and cultural development." But this is a right of peoples only, and thus in no way equivalent to the alleged individual right to development. More important, a right to *pursue* one's development, which is the most that is established by the right to self-determination, is not a right to development—or at least not a right to *be* developed.

Development is ordinarily conceived of as both a process and an end, as is obvious, for example, in our talk of "developing countries" (countries engaged in the process of development) and "developed countries" (countries which have achieved a certain high level of development). A "right to development" conceived of as a *process* would be a right to participate in a process of growth, to strive after self-actualization in conditions of dignity, while a "right to development" conceived of as an *end* would be a right to *be* developed.

A right to be developed would be not only extravagant to the point of absurdity, but destructive of important moral values. Development as an end—true human development of the whole person, the complete unfolding of an individual's nature—is an overarching moral goal; it is achieved but rarely, after much exertion and struggle rather than being something to which each person is entitled simply by virtue of being a human being. There is no more a right to be developed than there is a right to be just or to be holy.

A right to participate in the process of development is neither implausible nor dangerous on its face; in fact, it looks very much like an individual right to self-determination, a right to the removal of impediments to individual development. But this is precisely what is done by *all* human rights—civil, political, economic, social, and cultural alike. As we saw above, development is the ultimate objective of all human rights, a consequence of the implementation and exercise of human rights rather than a human right in itself. Development is a goal rather than a right.

Voijin Dimitrievic speaks of the right to development as a "right to rights."[43] Interpreted in this way, there can be no objection to the right. But such a right is entirely pointless. An entitlement to be entitled to those things recognized or guaranteed by human rights adds nothing of value to the rights-holder, who *already* is entitled to those things as human rights (i.e., simply because he is a human being).

THE POLITICS OF THE RIGHT TO DEVELOPMENT

So far, I have tried to show that the legal and moral arguments advanced in the discussions of the right to development fail to establish the existence of such a right. However, a strong case might be made that it is the political dimensions of the right that are the real concern of its advocates; it certainly is not a coincidence that the vast majority of the literature on the right to development is very closely connected with the United Nations and has a highly politicized air to it.

The political dymanics involved in the emergence of arguments for a right to development in the United Nations are easy to perceive. There is a very strong tactical tendency for issue linkage in the United Nations. With both development and human rights being longstanding central concerns of the organization, it probably was to be expected that they would eventually coalesce into arguments for a human right to development. The general moral force of claims of development made such a linkage especially plausible, as did the fact that decisions concerning priorities among human rights often resemble those made in formulating development strategies. The emergence of the basic human needs strategy of development also seems to have encouraged thinking along these lines, given the often-argued link between rights and needs, while the infusion of the concerns of the New International Economic Order into human rights issues has provided an important ideological impetus. Finally, the ''discovery'' of human rights by the United States, and by Western public opinion in general, made a human right to development an attractive avenue for pursuing long-standing (and long-frustrated) development goals.

Karel Vasak, addressing the Commission on Human Rights as a representative of UNESCO, clearly expressed the real political significance of the right to development: ''The right to development [is] a composite right which, in encompassing a number of already recognized rights, enhanced their value and *made them a true force for the establishment of the new international economic order.*''[44] Therefore, rather than marking ''the penetration of human rights into the field of development,''[45] as it is often presented, the right to development in fact represents the engulfing of human rights by the concerns of development; human rights are transformed into just another political and ideological instrument for seeking progress on the New International Economic Order.

Rather than emphasizing the need to incorporate human rights concerns into development planning, the right to development deflects attention from human rights, development planning, and the possibilities of fruitful linkages between these two vital concerns.

With the right to development viewed as "the synthesis of all human rights,"[46] the sum total of existing human rights, discussion readily shifts from particular rights to the package as a whole. This tends to produce not a broader and more comprehensive view but an increasing detachment from the realities of implementation in particular cases. Talk of this covering right readily lends itself to ignoring particular—and, not incidentally, more embarrassing—human rights questions. While the whole may be more than the sum of its parts, the right to development is too easily used to obscure the fact that progress in realizing that whole must be achieved by the hard work of implementing the "parts," the separate civil, political, economic, social, and cultural human rights that are already recognized internationally.

There is a further danger of a reductionist argument in which economic development per se is treated as respect for human rights. There is no necessity of discussions moving in this direction, but past experience suggests that they will.[47] And since there is little legal or moral justification for the right, such political dangers must carry great weight.

Another troubling facet of recent discussions, especially those in the United Nations, is that one quickly loses track of two simple, yet absolutely essential, political facts: (1) national governments are the major violators of human rights and thus must be the main target of action; and (2) national governments must substantially alter, and in many cases radically rethink, their development strategies if human rights concerns are to be addressed in development planning. The right to development, particularly as it has been discussed in the United Nations and as it appears in the Banjul Charter, instead directs attention to external impediments in the form of the curent international economic order.

Certainly the international economy is an important factor in the human rights performance of many Third World countries. But simply increasing the goods and services available to Third World governments or within Southern economies will increase the enjoyment of human rights only if these resources are equitably distributed. Cases such as Brazil, in which rapid growth has resulted in the growing relative deprivation of the mass of the population, underline the major gap between providing economic and social *goods* in the aggregate and providing economic and social *human rights*. Unless the gains of the New International Economic Order are passed on to the masses of the population, even the enjoyment of economic and social rights will not improve. The connection between development and civil and political rights is even more tenuous.

Economic and social rights involve *assured access* to goods and services. That access is a *political* outcome that is by no means natural or automatic. Goods are translated into the enjoyment of rights through *national* economic and political channels of distribution; national planning and positive action are essential to integrate human rights and development. The right to development conflates rights and development rather than suggesting strategies for integrating these two related, but quite distinct, concerns. Civil and political rights are even more obviously a largely national problem and even less likely to be realized by development alone.

It has been suggested, however, that the right to development, whatever its conceptual flaws, has made a positive contribution to recent discussions of both human rights and development by increasing awareness of the links between the two.[48] Even if this is true, though, the time has come to shift our attention from just any sort of link to the *proper* way to link human rights and development; i.e., away from the right to development and toward the topic of incorporating human rights concerns into the difficult work of national development planning.

Drawing on the discussion here, and in an attempt to point beyond it, let me suggest a few principles and guidelines for thinking about human rights and development.

(1) Where sacrifices of human rights to economic development are required, such trade-offs should be recognized for what they are—distasteful accommodations to harsh and unattractive economic or political realities; they are not essential or desirable parts of any human rights policy.

(2) Trade-offs between human rights and economic development cannot be unidirectional. If alleged trade-offs are genuine adjustments of costs and benefits, and if development and human rights are to be in practice genuinely complementary, then economic growth and development must sometimes give way to human rights considerations. Just as the human rights costs of certain development policies must sometimes be borne, progress on human rights may have economic (and political) costs which are worth accepting.

(3) No class of rights is always antagonistic to economic development, and no particular human right is always justifiably sacrificed to the demands of development. Experience shows that even civil and political rights are often quite compatible with economic development. Defensible trade-offs must rest on an assessment of economic, social, political, and human rights conditions in a particular place at a particular time. Categorical prescriptions for trade-offs are as unjustifiable as categorical priorities between classes of human rights.

(4) In planning for human rights and development, both will best be served by an approach based on true complementarity. The

technical imperatives of rapid development must be constrained by human rights while development planning must be consciously directed toward increasing the enjoyment of human rights by incorporating a concern for the internal distribution of the fruits of development.

(5) Respect for human rights will necessarily bring about *human* development. However, *economic* development (which is the development that, for better or for worse, is discussed in international political circles) has little integral and necessary connection to the realization of human rights. Not only is the enjoyment of human rights largely a contingent feature of particular economic, social, and political systems, but the widespread enjoyment of civil, political, economic, social, and cultural human rights threatens the interests of ruling classes in much of the world and therefore is likely to be vigorously resisted by established elites. The contribution of economic development to the enjoyment of human rights in any actual case must be demonstrated rather than assumed.

(6) Development, in the broad sense of actualizing the potentials of the human person, is the goal of human rights and the likely consequence of their being respected. Thus "development" in some extended sense of the term may be seen as roughly equivalent to respect for, and enjoyment of, human rights. However, this broadly conceived "development" is not instrumental for the realization of human rights. Furthermore, it is quite different from the "development" with which economic and social planners are concerned. These two senses of the term are confused only at great risk to human rights.

Having said all of this, it nonetheless must be admitted that we are likely to see increasing attention paid to and emphasis put on the right to development, particularly in the UN system. Rapid economic development is the overriding political imperative in the United Nations, where the concept of the right to development has come to fruition; economic development is *the* political objective of the developing countries and their allies who control the organization. Efforts to improve the relative economic position of the developing countries have proved largely ineffective, leading to frustration at the international level and to serious domestic political problems, as rising expectations have been disappointed. A right to development provides additional leverage in the pursuit of development, and therefore it will continue to be advocated. That it also deflects attention from national responsibility for the violation of human rights is an added attraction.

This is the political reality underlying arguments for a right to development; the attraction of the really quite bad arguments generally advanced for the right to development cannot be comprehended without attention to this context. However, to understand is not necessarily to justify. The (politically) understandable demands for a right to development threaten vitally important civil, political, economic, social, and cultural human rights, and therefore on human rights grounds must be opposed.

NOTES

I wish to thank Rhoda Howard, Joseph M. Grieco, and Claude Welch for their helpful comments on earlier drafts.

1. See, for example, Irma Adelman, "Economic Development and Political Change in Developing Countries," *Social Research* 47, no. 2 (Summer 1980), pp. 213–34; and Frances Stewart and Paul Streeten, "New Strategies for Development: Poverty, Income Distribution, and Growth," *Oxford Economic Papers* 28 (November 1976), pp. 381–405.

2. See, for example, Robert E. Goodin, "The Development–Rights Trade-off: Some Unwarranted Economic and Political Assumptions," *Universal Human Rights* 1 (April 1979), pp. 31–42; Philip Alston, "Human Rights and the New International Development Strategy," *Bulletin of Peace Proposals* 10 (1979), pp. 281–90; Emanuel de Kadt, "Some Basic Questions on Human Rights and Development," *World Development* 8, no. 2 (February 1980), pp. 97–105; Stephen P. Marks, "The Peace-Human Rights-Development Dialectic," *Bulletin of Peace Proposals* 11 (1980), pp. 339–47; Han S. Park, "The Claim for Development: Right or Cry?" paper presented at the Annual Convention of the International Studies Association, Cincinnati, Ohio, March 1982; and Rhoda Howard, "The 'Full-Belly' Thesis," paper presented at the Annual Convention of the International Studies Association, Mexico City, April 1983.

3. See especially Philip Alston, "Development and the Rule of Law: Prevention versus Cure as a Human Rights Strategy," in International Commission of Jurists, *Development, Human Rights, and the Rule of Law* (Elmsford, N.Y.: Pergamon Press, 1981); and Keith Griffin and Jeffrey James, *The Transition to Egalitarian Development: Economic Policies for Structural Change in the Third World* (New York: St. Martin's Press, 1981).

4. Keba M'Baye, "Le Droit au développment comme un droit de l'homme," *Revue des droits de l'homme* 5 (1972), pp. 505–34. Compare, in the same year, Carrillo Salcedo, "El Derecho al desarrollo como un derecho humano," *Revista Española de derecho international* 25 (1972), pp. 119–25.

5. Report of the Secretary-General, "The International Dimensions of the Right to Development as a Human Right in Relation with Other Human Rights Based on International Cooperation, Including the Right to Peace, Taking into Account the Requirements of the New International Economic Order and Fundamental Human Needs," UN Doc. E/CN.4/1334, 2 January 1979, (Hereafter referred to as *The Secretary-General's Report*).

6. All internal references are to *The Secretary-General's Report* by paragraph number alone.

7. The discussion of legal sources covers pars. 55–78 of *The Secretary-General's Report*. Compare "Report of the Seminar on the Effects of the Existing Unjust International Economic Order on the Economies of the Developing Countries and the Obstacles that These Represent for the Implementation of Human Rights and Fundamental Freedoms, Geneva, 30 June–July 1980," UN Doc. ST/HR/SER.A/8, pars 68, 95. One UNESCO working group of non-governmental organizations has even tried to trace the right back to the American Declaration of Independence and the French Declaration of the Rights of Man and the Citizen! See "The Rights of Solidarity: An Attempt at Conceptual Analysis," UNESCO Doc. SS-80/CONF.806/6, 9 July 1980, par. 36.

8. The most developed version of his argument is "Emergence of the 'Right to Development' as a Human Right in the Context of a New International Economic Order," delivered at the UNESCO Meeting of Experts on Human Rights, Human Needs, and the Establishment of a New International Economic Order, Paris, 19–23 June 1978, UNESCO Doc. SS-78/CONF.630/8, 16 July 1979. See also his remarks as the representative of Senegal to the Commission on Human Rights in UN Doc. E/CN.4/SR.1391, 1398, and 1488.

9. M'Baye, "Right to Development," pp. 1, 5, 8.

10. Ibid., pp. 5–8.

11. Ibid., pp. 9, 13, 12.

12. Karel Vasak is largely responsible for this concept, beginning with his brief article, "Human Rights: A Thirty-Year Struggle," *UNESCO Courier*, November 1977, p. 29. It is now widely accepted in the literature. See, e.g., Hector Gros Espiell, "The Right to Development as a Human Right," *Texas International Law Journal* 16 (Spring 1981), pp. 189–205 at p. 199; Karel de Vey Mestdagh, "The Right to Development," *Netherlands International Law Review* 28 (1981), pp. 30–53 at pp. 33–34; and Stephen P. Marks, "Emerging Human Rights: A New Generation for the 1980s?" *Rutgers Law Review* 33, no. 2 (Winter 1981), pp. 435–52 at p. 441. For an unusual and suggestive attempt to apply this notion to domestic legislation in France, see André Holleaux, "Les Lois de la 'troisième génération des droits de l'homme': ébauche d'étude comparative," *Revue française d'administration publique* 15 (July 1980), pp. 45–73.

13. Compare Gros Espiell, "The Right to Development," p. 198 as well as p. 191, where he adds communities at the national level as rights-holders.

14. M'Baye, "Right to Development," p. 2.

15. Compare Gros Espiell, "The Right to Development," p. 199.

16. For example, serious problems of definition were noted during the 1981 session of the Commission on Human Rights by the delegates of Canada, Greece, Netherlands, Mexico, United States, the United Kingdom, and the Federal Republic of Germany (see UN Doc. E/CN.4/SR.1613, 1614, and 1639). See also Wil Verwey, "The Establishment of a New International Economic Order and the Right to Development and Welfare: A Legal Survey," UN Doc. HR/GENEVA/1980/BP.3, par. 4ff., and Mestdagh, "The Right to Development," p. 49.

17. See, e.g., "Seminar on the Effects," par. 72; UN Doc. E/CN.4/Sub.2/

477, par. 95; Gros Espiell, "The Right to Development," p. 205; and "The Regional and National Dimensions of the Right to Development as a Human Right; Study by the Secretary-General," UN Doc. E/CN.4/1421, 13 November 1980, par. 15(b).

18. M'Baye, "Right to Development," p. 12. Compare *Secretary-General's Report*, pars. 55–57; and International Commission of Jurists, "The Right to Development: Its Scope, Content, and Implementation," January 1982, (mimeographed) par. 22.

19. Compare Article 2(1) of the International Covenant on Economic, Social and Cultural Rights in which each state party pledges "to take steps, individually and through international assistance and co-operation, especially economic and technical, to the maximum of its available resource," to realize progressively the rights recognized in the Covenant. This no more establishes a right to development—which is *not* one of the enumerated rights—than does Article 56 of the Charter. And even if it does, the silence on appropriate implementation machinery leaves the developed countries in a position to plausibly argue that the legal obligation can be discharged by providing official development assistance and encouraging private resource transfers.

20. Verwey, "Establishment of a New International Economic Order," par. 25.

21. See, e.g., *Secretary-General's Report*, par. 62; UN Doc. E/CN.4/SR.1488, par. 18; and "Seminar on the Effects" par. 79.

22. For an interesting discussion of this issue, from a very different perspective, see Verwey, "Establishment of a New International Economic Order," pars. 10–12.

23. Compare Gros Espiell, "The Right to Development," p. 198. *The Secretary-General's Report* (par. 60) claims that "several of the individual rights in that [Economic and Social] Covenant appear, implicitly or explicitly, to be components of the right to development." (Since the right to development is never mentioned there, it is a mystery how these rights could explicitly be held to be part of the right.) To cite just one further example, the 1980 "Report of the Commission on Human Rights" to the Economic and Social Commission, (E/1980/13 [UN Doc. E/CN.4/1408], par. 115), refers to "full realization of economic, social, and cultural rights, including the right to development." On the domination of economic and social rights in UN discussions of human rights, see Jack Donnelly, "Recent UN Human Rights Activity: Description and Polemic," *International Organization* 35, no. 4 (1981), esp. pp. 643–46 and 650–52.

24. The UN Office of Legal Affairs has admitted that even solemn declarations are not legally binding (see *Secretary-General's Report*, par. 58, n. 33). Among the most important recent discussions of the legal status of General Assembly resolutions, see Christopher C. Joyner, "UN General Assembly Resolutions and International Law: Rethinking the Contemporary Dynamics of Norm-Creation," *California Western International Law Review* 11 (Summer 1981), pp. 445–78; Stephen M. Schwebel, "The Effect of Resolutions of the U.N. General Assembly on Customary International Law," *Proceedings of the American Society of International Law* 73 (1979), pp. 301–9; and J. S. Watson, "Instant Custom: Some Serious Questions," paper presented at the Annual

Convention of the International Studies Association, March 25, 1982. For a broader discussion of the creation of legal human rights norms, see J. S. Watson, "Legal Theory, Efficacy, and Validity in the Development of Human Rights Norms in International Law," *University of Illinois Law Forum* (1979), pp. 609–41; and Eric Lane, "Human Rights within the World Legal Order: A Reply to Sonn and McDougal," *Hofstra Law Review* 10 (1982), pp. 747–72.

25. This conceptual error—*viz.*, confusing rights and obligations—is widespread in contemporary discussions of human rights. I have examined it, in somewhat greater detail and in quite different contexts, in "Natural Law and Right in Aquinas' Political Thought," *Western Political Quarterly* 33 (1980), pp. 520–35, and "Human Rights and Human Dignity: An Analytic Critique of Non-Western Human Rights Conceptions," *American Political Science Review* 76 (1982), pp. 303–16. Compare also Martin P. Golding, "The Concept of Rights: an Historical Sketch," in Elise L. Bandman and Bertram Bandman, eds., *Bioethics and Human Rights* (Boston: Little, Brown), 1978, pp. 44–50; A. I. Melden, "Are There Welfare Rights?" in Peter G. Brown, Conrad Johnson, and Paul Vernier, eds., *Income Support: Conceptual and Policy Issues* (Totowa, N.J.: Rowman and Littlefield, 1981), pp. 259–78; and Jack Donnelly, "How Are Rights and Duties Correlative?" *Journal of Value Inquiry* 16 (1982), pp. 287–93.

26. For a more thorough discussion of the correlation of rights and duties, see Donnelly, "How Are Rights and Duties Correlative?" and, with more direct application to human rights, Donnelly, "Human Rights and Human Dignity," pp. 309–10.

27. The following discussion is drawn primarily from Donnelly, "Human Rights and Human Dignity," where this argument and its implications are discussed in much greater detail and with reference to several other non-Western cultures. In order to avoid misunderstanding, let me note that my argument is not intended to single out Africa in particular, or to condemn such an absence; to the best of my knowledge, *all* "premodern" societies, including premodern Europe, lacked the concept of human rights.

28. S. K. B. Asante, "Nation Building and Human Rights in Emergent African Nations," *Cornell International Law Journal* 2 (1969), p. 74; and Dunstan M. Wai, "Human Rights in Sub-Saharan Africa," in Adamantia Pollis and Peter Schwab, eds., *Human Rights: Cultural and Ideological Perspectives* (New York: Praeger, 1980), p. 116.

29. Wai, "Human Rights in Sub-Saharan Africa," p. 116.

30. Ibid., p. 117.

31. Asmarom Legesse, "Human Rights in African Political Culture," in Kenneth W. Thompson, *The Moral Imperatives of Human Rights: A World Survey* (Washington, D.C.: University Press of America, 1980), p. 127.

32. Ibid., p. 124.

33. The current Soviet position, however, seems to be that *all* human rights, not merely the "third generation," are based on solidarity. See, e.g., I. P. Blischenko, UN Doc. HR/GENEVA/1980/BP.4, p. 30. If this were true, though, all "human rights" would be reduced to the weaker claims of moral righteousness, an interpretation consistent with Soviet practice but fatal to human rights, as I suggest in "Human Rights and Human Dignity."

34. UN Doc. E/CN.4/SR.1489, pars. 4, 21. Compare Albert Tévoédjrè, *La Pauvreté: Richesse des peuples* (Paris: Les Éditions ouvrières, 1978), pp. 146–47; *Secretary-General's Report*, par. 40; and M'Baye, "Droit au développement," pp. 523ff.

35. Elsewhere ("Human Rights as Natural Rights," *Human Rights Quarterly* 4 (1982), pp. 391–405) I argue in some detail that the International Bill of Human Rights gives expression to a natural rights conception of human rights, and that such a conception is quite capable of encompassing the full range of internationally recognized civil, political, economic, and social rights. Such arguments also support the distinction drawn here between human rights and solidarity rights.

36. See, e.g., Mestdagh, "The Right to Development," pp. 35ff.; Gros Espiell, "The Right to Development," pp. 190, 192; and Marks, "Emerging Human Rights," pp. 442ff.

37. Marks, "Emerging Human Rights," p. 442.

38. Gros Espiell, "The Right to Development," p. 190, n. 4.

39. M'Baye, "Right to Development," p. 8.

40. The Soviet Union and its allies have argued for a reverse relationship, i.e., that "the right to peace should be recognized as a prerequisite for the enjoyment of the right to development" (UN Doc. E/CN.4/SR.1490, par. 43). "If we wish to observe and develop human rights, to promote social and economic progress, we must first of all secure peace on earth." V. N. Kudryavtsev, "Human Rights, Peace, and Development," UN Doc. HR/NEW YORK/1981/BP.2, p. 20.

Still others have argued for a more organic integration of peace, development and human rights concerns. See Stephen Marks, "Peace–Human Rights–Development Dialectic," and "Report of the Seminar on the Relations That Exist between Human Rights, Peace, and Development, 3–14 August 1981," UN Doc. ST/HR/SER.A/10, especially pars. 91 and 219. Whatever the truth of their claims about the possibility of enjoying the right, should it be shown to exist, these alternative approaches fail to establish the existence of the right to development.

41. UN Doc. E/CN.4/SR.1612, par. 71. Compare *Secretary-General's Report*, par. 43. For a similar argument attempting to establish rights to peace and to a healthy environment, see UNESCO Doc. SS-80/CONF.806/4, pars. 14, 21.

42. Compare *Secretary-General's Report*, par. 59 and Mestdagh, "The Right to Development," pp. 32, 38–40.

43. Voijin Dimitrievic, "Is There a Right to Development?" paper presented at the Annual Convention of the International Studies Association, Cincinnati, March 1982.

44. UN Doc. E/CN.4/SR.1486, par. 5 (emphasis added). Compare UN Doc. E/CN.4/SR.1492, par. 21: "The right to development [is] a result of the solidarity which should exist among the members of the international community and which constitute[s] the means of establishing a new international economic order." See also UN Doc. E/CN.4/Sub.2/459, par. 69.

45. UN Doc. E/CN.4/SR.1486, par. 9.

46. Gros Espiell, "The Right to Development," p. 205. Compare UN Doc. E/CN.4/SR.1486, par. 5; UN Doc. E/CN.4/SR.1612, par. 77; and Mestdagh, "The Right to Development," pp. 47, 49, 53.

47. See Donnelly, "Recent UN Human Rights Activity," esp. pp. 646–48.

48. This was suggested recently by a high official of the UN Division of Human Rights at an international conference. Compare International Commission of Jurists, "The Right to Development," par. 7.

IV

Research Sources

CHAPTER THIRTEEN

Research Problems and Library Resources on Human Rights in Africa

CORINNE NYQUIST

RESEARCH PROBLEMS

Library research on human rights and development in Africa poses significant scholarly problems. Those interested in research materials must labor in areas in which library classification schemes are often inadequate, bibliographic sources are often repetitive, and the materials are difficult to locate. All of these are aspects of what is referred to as the problem of retrievability. The purpose of this chapter is to provide a brief guide, both to library resources that are reasonably accessible, and to research problems that are likely to arise.

First of all, Africanists lack a human rights bibliography such as is available for Europe and Latin America.[1] One must turn to the standard bibliographic tools of the social sciences in general, and of Africana in particular, as well as to the bibliographic tools of law. The few standard human rights bibliographies that exist are a useful place to begin, if one understands their limitations. Human rights concepts have broadened in scope over the years; most bibliographies do not include documents, newspaper articles, and ephemera; and such works are quickly outdated. Further, most bibliographies do not list sources consulted; some do not explain selection principles. Therefore the thorough researcher must repeat much of the work of the original bibliographer.

Governments, international organizations, and non-governmental human rights organizations publish much that is of interest to the human rights researcher on Africa, publications often available only in mimeographed form and limited in distribution. The publications of governments and international organizations are called *documents* and can be identified by becoming familiar with the structure and documentation of the United Nations, regional organizations such as the Organization of African Unity (OAU), and the African governments. Reference works such as directories are the key to identifying non-governmental organizations active in human rights advocacy or investigation, and their publications. Locating these sources is another matter entirely, requiring some knowledge of the collection-building patterns of libraries. Luckily for the researcher, the average university library will own most of the necessary bibliographic tools and reference works.

To use these library tools, one must overcome problems in human rights indexing which contribute to the generally held feeling that such materials are irretrievable. Most academic library card catalogs and reference works follow Library of Congress Subject Headings, which equate human rights with Civil Rights on the national scene and use Civil Rights (International Law) for the world. Efforts at change, particularly of the latter heading, have been initiated by librarians and should be encouraged. As the number of subject headings assigned by the Library of Congress decreases—at present the average is 1.7 per item—the headings themselves become more significant.

More than a change in basic terms is necessary to identify materials relevant to human rights in Africa. The researcher should become acquainted with the "second" and "third generation" of human rights and be able to explain to librarians their implications for social science research. Articles such as Steven P. Marks' "Emerging Human Rights: A New Generation for the 1980's?" *Rutgers Law Review* 33, no. 2 (Winter 1981) pp. 435–52; and Vernon Van Dyke's "The Cultural Rights of Peoples," *Universal Human Rights*, 2, no. 1 (April–June 1980), pp. 1–20, and the working paper by Philip Alston, *Development and the Rule of Law: Prevention versus Cure as a Human Rights Strategy* (The Hague: International Commission of Jurists, 1981) are a beginning. To bridge the understanding gap between the fields of law and the social sciences, where even the same words have different meanings, one might read the review article by John F. McCamant, "Social Science and Human Rights," *International Organization* 35, no. 3 (Summer 1981) pp. 531–52. Another approach to understanding concepts is the bilingual index of—or concordance to—five hundred key words and phrases from the eighteen Declarations and forty-three Conventions that comprise human rights law, by Jean-Bernard Marie, *Glossaire des droits de l'homme: termes fondamentaux dans les instruments universels et régionaux/Glossary of Human Rights: Basic Terms in Universal and Regional Instruments* (Paris: Éditions de la Maison des sciences de l'homme, 1981) A useful exercise would be to equate these key words and phrases with the Library of Congress list of subject headings.

Once identified, the location of materials in libraries is another aspect of the problem of retrievability. Most books and journal articles are easily obtained at one's local academic library or through interlibrary loan. UN documents are deposited for public use at forty-three locations in twenty-eight states and one territory.[2] A number of other research libraries purchase UN documents on paper or microfiche. Categories of UN documents include "General"— available on library deposit or by subscription; "Restricted"—available only to members; and documents with "Limited Distribution" as noted by an "L" somewhere within the symbol, which are not available for distribution or deposit. Limited documents are prized by researchers because of their currency and because some, such as final reports of an ad hoc committee, appear in full only in this provisional form. Limited Documents, like General but unlike Restricted ones, are listed in UN indexes, and piles of them are placed on tables in New York or Geneva UN buildings to be picked up by interested persons. Some individuals and libraries not located in these cities have ingenious methods for obtaining such documents; these collections can be tracked down, with effort.

United States documents are readily available at one or more research libraries in every congressional district, and in the case of congressional hearings, etc., free upon request to one's congressman. However, the location of African regional and country documents presents more of a problem; Africana collections on campuses with law schools, especially those with an international focus, are the place to search for African laws and cases, for example.

Institutions with extensive holdings on Africa can be located by consulting guides by Lee Ash[3] and Peter Duignan.[4] Computer connections through the Research Libraries Information Network (RLIN) link some one hundred and fifty large libraries;[5] through the Online Computer Library Center (OCLC) some two thousand large and small libraries are connected with each other.[6] The MARC (Machine Readable Cataloging) tapes of the Library of Congress, itself a major Africana collection, are loaded into both data bases. Most of the important Africana collections have area bibliographic specialists who will provide terms of direct access on written request. Thirteen institutions contribute records of their Africana acquisitions to the printed *Joint Acquisitions List of Africana* (1963–   ) produced by Northwestern University.[7]

Currently there is no cooperative scheme of Africana acquisitions by which one can be assured that publications from and about each area in Africa have been acquired by at least one library in the United States. Most Africanists have heard of the Farmington Plan, which divided Africa geographically among cooperating institutions agreeing to collect library materials comprehensively from and about an area of the continent. Although the Plan ceased to exist in the early 1970s, an agreement was reached concerning Africana materials that lasted through most of that decade.[8] The most useful cooperative scheme now in operation is the Cooperative Africana Microfilm Project (CAMP). In 1963 Africana librarians created CAMP to bring together in microform a collection of research materials related to Africa for the cooperative use of members of the Center for Research Libraries and non-members on a per-loan fee basis.[9]

Non-governmental organizations provide independent assessments of human rights in various countries; those have been called the "chief antidote to unreliable information in the field of comparative human rights" by Richard Claude ("Reliable Information: The Threshold Problem for Human Rights Research," *Human Rights* 6, no. 2, pp. 169–87 (Winter 1977).[10] Because the non-governmental organizations are so diffuse and their publications considered ephemeral, libraries make little or no effort to collect these materials; those collected are often relegated to the vertical file. Human Rights Internet has assumed the responsibility of systematically collecting non-governmental organizations' materials. Human Rights Internet has also agreed to edit and index this material for a microfiche collection to be published by Inter Documentation of the Netherlands.[11] Under a separate agreement, Inter Documentation has already completed a microfiche collection of Amnesty International's public information. Newspaper clippings, conference papers, dissertations, private papers, and audio-visual materials are often called fugitive materials, indicating how difficult such unpublished work can be to locate.

Representatives of a broad spectrum of organizations and institutions specializing in human rights expressed concern for improving the retrievability of human rights information at meetings in New York City in September 1978; at Chaumontel, France, in April 1979; in Paris in March 1980; and at Strasbourg, France, in February 1981. According to *Human Rights Internet Reporter*, an international expert working group constituted at Chaumontel prepared a memorandum on the establishment of a Human Rights International Documents Service, to be called HURIDOCS, for the purpose of information sharing and networking. At the Strasbourg meeting the group agreed to begin the drafting of a thesaurus for human rights. Members of the HURIDOCS international expert working group are Martin Ennals, chairman, of Amnesty International; Hans Toolen, International Commission of Jurists, Geneva; Asbjorn Eide, Norwegian Peace Research Institute, Oslo; Frederike Knabe, Amnesty International,

London; David Heaps, consultant to the Ford Foundation; and Laurie S. Wiseberg, Human Rights Internet, Washington, D. C. The group gradually will be expanded to include participation from other regions of the world.[12]

That an early project of HURIDOCS should be the compilation of a thesaurus to provide the framework for a subject classification scheme usable in a variety of cultures, is important. However, as retrospective subject analysis of earlier human rights literature cannot be expected for some time, the researcher must have the capability to search the literature as presently organized.

LIBRARY RESOURCES

Effective human rights research on Africa requires a basic knowledge of the literature on international and comparative law, as well as African studies. Beyond this, the researcher faces the extensive publications and the confusing organization of governments and of international organizations.

Guides

There are, however, a number of useful guides to aid the human rights researcher. Thomas H. Reynolds' "Highest Aspirations or Barbarous Acts . . . The Explosion in Human Rights Documentation: A Bibliographic Survey" in *Law Library Journal* (71 (1978) pp. 1–48) is an excellent introduction to the literature. Another effective survey is "Human Rights Documentation" by Myrna S. Feliciano (*International Journal of Law Libraries* 9, no. 3 (June 1981); pp. 95–106). Diana Vincent-Daviss published a three-part series on "Human Rights Law: A Research Guide to the Literature" in the *New York University Journal of International Law and Politics* (14 (1980), pp. 209–319; 14 (1981), pp. 487–573; and 15 (1982), pp. 211–87). Part One covers international law and the United Nations; Part Two covers the international protection of refugees and humanitarian law; Part Three of this very detailed guide covers the human rights activities of the International Labor Organization.[13]

None of the authors cited above discusses the documentation of the Organization of African Unity. The documents librarian of the Ibadan University Library, J. E. Ikem, contributes to this need with his "Documentation of the UN and the OAU" (*International Library Review* 13, no. 3 (July 1981), pp. 287–300).

For the Africanist, there are several guides to the literature. *The Student Africanist's Handbook: A Guide to Resources* by Gerald W. Hartwig and William M. O'Barr (New York: Wiley, 1974) is helpful in finding basic reference works, as is *Sub-Saharan Africa: A Guide to Information Resources* by W. A. E. Skurnik (Detroit: Gale Research, 1977). Because all guides to any field of literature are soon outdated, it is important that the researcher become familiar with a comprehensive, continuously revised reference work such as Eugene P. Sheehy's *Guide to Reference Books*, 9th edition (Chicago: American Library Association, 1976, and its *Supplements* (1980 and 1982), which are available at every college and university library reference desk.

Bibliographies

There are a number of general bibliographies on human rights. Most often recommended is the two-volume, *International Human Rights: A Bibliography* for 1965–69 and 1970–76, compiled by William Miller (Notre Dame, Ind.: Center for Civil Rights, University of Notre Dame Law School, 1976) which is primarily a listing of English language articles published in law journals. The *Checklist of Human Rights Documents*, a highly recommended serial bibliography, was begun at the State University of New York at Buffalo in 1974, moved to Texas in 1976, but discontinued in 1980.[14] The *Checklist* cites under issuing body the documents of the United Nations, the United States and other countries, intergovernmental organizations, and nongovernmental organizations; it lists further reference books, monographs, and journal articles. In the U. S. section, there are detailed references to the *Congressional Record*, for example. Tom Reynolds, law librarian at Berkeley, is preparing an index to the five volumes of the *Checklist*.

Lacking a bibliography on human rights in Africa, what are the Africana sources that will help a scholar build a working bibliography? A beginning is *A World Bibliography of African Bibliographies* by Theodore Besterman, revised and brought up-to-date by J. D. Pearson (Totowa, N.J.: Rowman and Littlefield, 1975). The bibliography is arranged by region and country, subdivided by subject, and indexed by author. Crossroads Press has published complementary works by Yvette Scheven entitled *Bibliographies for African Studies* for 1970–75, 1976–79 (Waltham, Mass.: Crossroads Press, 1977, 1980). Useful topics in Scheven's work are Women, Social Issues, International Relations, and Law and Legislation. Under the last topic was found Jacques Vanderlinden's "African Legal Process and the Individual: Ten Years of Bibliography."[15] Also listed is Vanderlinden's book, *African Law Bibliography/Bibliographie de droit africain 1947–1966* (Brussels: Presses universitaires de Bruxelles, 1972), which continues *African Law Bibliography 1897–1946* and is supplemented by his bibliographies in the *Annual Survey of African Law*.[16]

Winner of the first African Studies Association Helen F. Conover-Dorothy Porter award in 1980 for excellence in Africana bibliography or reference work was Julian W. Witherell, forme. Head of the Africa Section at the Library of Congress. He produced the monumental bibliography, *The United States and Africa: Guide to U. S. Official Documents and Government-Sponsored Publications on Africa, 1785–1975* (Washington, D.C.: Library of Congress, 1978). For additional bibliographies, see the Africana guides listed earlier.

Current Awareness Sources

A general bibliography that deserves recommendation is found in most academic libraries; this is *Current Bibliographical Information (CBI)*, a monthly publication of the UN Dag Hammarskjold Library (UN Doc. ST/LIB/SER.K/1 1971–). CBI is a list of recently received books, publications of governments and of national and international organizations, and of selected periodical articles relating to topics considered by organs of the United Nations. Materials are grouped under broad subject categories, and there are author, title, and geographic subject indexes.[17]

A source of current Africana bibliography is *Africana Journal: a Bibliographic and Review Quarterly*, formerly called *Africana Library Journal*. "The Organization of African Unity: An Annotated Bibliography" by David B. Myers appeared in a 1974 issue (5, no. 4 (1974), pp. 308–32). Another source is *A Current Bibliography on African Affairs*, also a quarterly. Four years ago it included a bibliography by a University of Ife librarian, M. O. Afolabi, with the title, "Select Bibliography of Organization of African Unity Articles Published in English Language Periodicals" (12, no. 4 (1979–80), pp. 454–80). The *Current Bibliography* follows its bibliographic articles with listings of books and articles by subject and by country and geographic area. Another comprehensive listing of books, articles, papers, and documents on Africa is the *International African Bibliography*, which was founded in 1929 by the International African Institute in London as part of its journal *Africa*, and which became a separate journal in 1971. Its listings are arranged geographically by region and country, and tracing of subjects is possible using the Library of Congress headings at the end of each entry; however, there is no subject index.[18]

Other sources of current Africana are sections in the following periodicals: *Africa, Africa News, Africa Today, African Affairs*, and *ASA News* (formerly the *African Studies Newsletter*).

A particularly useful guide to current human rights affairs in Africa is the *Human Rights Internet Reporter* (Washington, D.C.: Human

Rights Internet, 1976–   ), produced five times a year. The *Reporter* summarizes the activities of the United Nations, the work of the non-governmental organizations, and the status of human rights in individual countries. It has annotated listings of recent books, articles on human rights, and longer book reviews. The tables of contents of relevant periodicals are reproduced, and documents are listed along with reports on the activities of the issuing body. The January/February 1982 issue announced on its front page the resignation of Theo van Boven, outspoken director of the UN Division of Human Rights, and the release of the U.S. Department of State's *Country Reports on Human Rights Practices for 1981.* The *Reporter* in its inner pages reprinted portions of van Boven's speech and carried a three-page review of the U.S. document.

For each of its volumes of five issues the *Reporter* produces an index that lists organizations whose activities it has described; conferences, seminars, meetings, symposia, in order of dates;[19] its feature articles, in date and volume order; and book reviews by title. However, it is not a true index since it provides neither an author nor a title index to the tables of contents of the newsletters and periodicals that it reproduces in each issue. The greatest strength of the *Reporter* is that the researcher will find cited there materials not indexed elsewhere. The greatest drawback of the *Reporter* is that it depends on exchanges for its sources and therefore cannot be expected to list every relevant article. Other sources for current materials must be reviewed as well.[20]

Indexes

It should be mentioned that much of the periodical literature, particularly scholarly articles in journals, can be found in the standard legal and social science periodical indexes and abstracts. Before using them, one should ascertain whether important human rights journals are included. Some standard indexes include: *Index to Legal Periodicals, Index to Foreign Legal Periodicals, Current Law Index, Public International Law, Public Affairs Information Service* (PAIS), *P.A.I.S. Foreign Language Index, Social Science Citation Index, Social Sciences Index, International Bibliography of the Social Sciences, International Political Science Abstracts, Internationale Bibliographie der Zeitschriften—Literatur aus allen Gebieten des Wissens, Religion Index* and *Women's Studies Abstracts.* In most cases, subject headings used are those of the Library of Congress; thus there is often no entry for Human Rights and sometimes no cross reference. Then one must search under Civil Rights or Civil Rights (International Law).

Computerized periodical index data bases can help the researcher; they allow for component word access and multiple descriptors. Useful data bases are *Dissertation Abstracts, Legal Resources Index, P.A.I.S. International, Social Scisearch,* and *U.S. Political Science Documents.* On-line reference services, usually on a fee basis, are becoming a standard service of academic libraries. Of course it must be remembered that the computer can supply citations, and sometimes abstracts, but not, as yet, full text.

United Nations Publications

It is difficult to identify UN publications without indexes. The United Nations Bibliographic Information System (UNBIS), an on-line computer-based system, has greatly improved information access to documents received by the Dag Hammarskjold Library. *UNDOC: Current Index; United Nations Document Index* (UN Doc. ST/LIB/SER.M 1979–) is arranged alphabetically by document symbol and contains a full bibliographic description of each document. There are subject, author, and title indexes.

To understand the work of the UN organs in the area of human rights, consult the various yearbooks by or about the United Nations. Examples are the *Annual Review of United Nations Affairs* (Dobbs Ferry, N.Y.: Oceana, 1949–), the *United Nations Secretariat Yearbook on Human Rights* (New York: Nations, 1946–), and the *United Nations Yearbook* (New York: Columbia University Press, in cooperation with the United Nations, 1944/47–). The utility of the last two is lessened by the long delay in publication. For an exhaustive review of UN documentation and human rights, see the articles by Diana Vincent-Daviss cited under "Guides," above.

To follow the activities of the United Nations, consult the *U.N. Monthly Chronicle* (New York, 1965–), which summarizes the proceedings of each UN organ and contains a selective list of recently issued documents. Research into the current status of an international law can be difficult, but a good place to start is the *New York Times Index.* If one has access to the *New York Times Information Bank* or its *Newspaper Index,* so much the better. These indexes provide needed clues—dates, names, places.

Organization of African Unity Publications

The bulk of the documentation by the Organization of African Unity is issued by its Scientific, Technical, and Research Commission (OAU/STRC), which continues the work of the Commission for

Technical Cooperation in Africa South of the Sahara (CCTA) formed in 1950. Publications of these bodies range from mimeographed working papers to official records, from bulletins to research reports. Many of the authors are experts, and subjects treated include diseases, agriculture, oceanography, education, international relations, population, urbanization, economic and social conditions, language, and child welfare.

There is a price list of OAU/STRC publications published by the OAU/STRC Publications Bureau, located in Niamey, Niger Republic. There is, however, no dependable list of other OAU publications.

The basic document of the OAU is the Charter adopted May 25, 1963, in Addis Ababa. The most significant policy-making body of the OAU is the Assembly of Heads of State and Government, which meets annually in various locations, with the chief of state of the host country taking the post of Assembly Chairman until the next meeting. In addition, the OAU Council of Ministers meets twice a year. *Resolutions* and *Declarations* of ordinary and extraordinary sessions of both groups are issued by the OAU General Secretariat in Addis Ababa.

The OAU maintains representatives to the United Nations in both New York City and Geneva. The Executive Secretariat representing the OAU at the United Nations in New York City publishes a newsletter, the *OAU Bulletin*, and sometimes issues other publications as well. Unlike the Organization of American States, the OAU is not a regional agency within the United Nations.

Some of the OAU-organized activities directly relating to human rights are those of its Commission of Mediation, Conciliation, and Arbitration; the Coordinating Committee for Liberation Movements in Africa; and the Bureau for Placement and Education of African Refugees (BPEAR).[21] Documents of major importance are the *Convention Concerning the Specific Aspects of Refugee Problems in Africa*, adopted by the OAU Assembly in 1969 in Addis Ababa, and the *Banjul Charter on Human and Peoples' Rights*, adopted by the Assembly in 1981 in Nairobi. Once the Banjul Charter is ratified by a majority of OAU member states, the African Commission on Human and Peoples' Rights will be established and will issue documents.[22]

The record of U.S. libraries in obtaining complete sets of OAU documents is disappointing. The Library of Congress National Processing and Cataloging Office in Nairobi has the best opportunity to collect such materials and when a second set is available, it is sent to the New York Public Library. As a record of the publications it acquires, the LC office in Nairobi publishes a bimonthly *Accessions List: Eastern Africa*, with an *Annual Serial Supplement* and an *Annual Publisher's Directory* for free distribution to libraries.

Catalogs and Printed Accession Lists

Catalogs in book form, in microform, or as computerized data bases have made it possible for researchers to consult the holdings of major Africana collections without traveling beyond the nearest university library. The current acquisitions of major Africana libraries can be consulted using either the OCLC or RLIN data bases. The following book catalogs or printed accessions lists should be consulted for holdings not on line, both to build a bibliography and to locate materials.

Boston University Libraries, *Catalog of African Government Documents*, 3d ed. rev. and enl., 1 vol. (Boston: Hall, 1976).

University of California at Berkeley, Library, *Author-Title Catalog*, 115 vols. (Boston: Hall, 1973), continued on microfiche.

[Center for Research Libraries,] *CAMP Catalog*, cumulative edition (Chicago: Cooperative Africana Microform Project and CRL, 1977), *Supplement* (1982).

Howard University; *Directory Catalog of the Arthur B. Spingarn Collection of Negro Authors*, 2 vols. (Boston: Hall, 1970).

Howard University, *Catalog of the Jesse E. Moorland Collection of Negro Life and History*, 9 vols. (Boston: Hall, 1970); *1st Supplement*, 3 vols. (1976).

[Library of Congress,] *Accessions List: Eastern Africa* 1-   (January 1968-   ) (Kenya: Library of Congress Office, Nairobi).

[Michigan State University,] *Sahel Bibliographic Bulletin/Bulletin bibliographique* 1-   (1977-   ) (East Lansing, Mich.: Sahel Documentation Center, MSU).

[New York Public Library,] *Dictionary Catalog of the Schomburg Collection of Negro Literature and History*, 9 vols. (Boston: Hall, 1962), *Supplements* for 1967, 1972, 1974, superseded by the following catalog.

[NYPL,] *Dictionary Catalog of the New York Public Library Research Libraries* (New York: NYPL, 1972-   ).

[Northwestern University,] *Africana Conference Papers Index* (Boston: Hall, 1982).

[NU,] *Catalog of the Melville J. Herskovits Library of African Studies, Northwestern University Library, and Africana in Selected Libraries*, 8 vols. (Boston: Hall, 1972); *1st Supplement*, 6 vols. (1978).

[NU, et al.,] *Joint Acquisitions List of Africana* 1-   (1962-   ) (Evanston, Ill.): Melville J. Herskovits Library of African Studies, NU (see Appendix B for list of contributors).

Stanford University, Hoover Institution, *Catalogs of the Western Language Collections* (1969); *Supplement*, 1st (1972); *Supplement*, 2nd (1977).

Conclusion

The bibliography that follows illustrates the materials that can be identified through the use of the library resources discussed in this chapter. It concentrates on books, pamphlets, and periodical articles. The human rights researcher who has exhausted printed bibliographies and library collections should next consider contact with special collections on human rights.[23] The *North American Human Rights Directory, 1980* lists nine university-sponsored centers and programs. It is in a collection such as these that the importance of nongovernmental organizations' materials, press clippings, and collections of fugitive (unpublished) materials can best be understood.

NOTES

1. *Human Rights in Latin America, 1964–1980: A Selective Annotated Bibliography* (Washington, D.C.: Library of Congress, 1982) and Council of Europe, *Bibliography Relating to European Conventions on Human Rights/Bibliographie concernant la Convention européene des droits de l'homme* (Strasbourg: The Council, 1978). Richard Greenfield, Assistant Law Librarian for Foreign and International Law at Harvard Law School, calls them "models for future regional human rights bibliographies" in his article, "The Human Rights Literature of Latin America," *Human Rights Quarterly* 4 no. 2 (Spring 1982), pp. 275–98. This is the fourth in his series of articles that survey professional human rights literature throughout the world. The first three articles appeared in *Human Rights Quarterly*, 3, nos. 2 and 3, and 4, no. 1; they covered Eastern Europe, South Asia, and the Soviet Union, respectively.

2. For a copy of the list of depository libraries, write the United Nations, Public Inquiries Unit, New York, N.Y. 10017.

3. Lee Ash, *Subject Collections: A Guide to Special Book Collections and Subject Emphases as Reported by University, College, Public, and Special Libraries and Museums in the United States and Canada,* 5th ed. rev. and enl. (New York: Bowker, 1978).

4. Peter Duignan, *Handbook of American Resources for African Studies* (Stanford, Calif.: Hoover Institution Press, 1967).

5. Important Africana collections contributing holdings to the RLIN data base are those at Columbia University, Hoover Institution, New York Public Library (NYPL) (including the Schomburg Center for Research in Black Culture), Northwestern University, and Yale University.

6. The following large Africana collections are part of OCLC: Boston University, The Center for Research Libraries (CRL), Howard University, Indiana University, Michigan State University (MSU), Syracuse University, The University of California at both Los Angeles (UCLA) and at Berkeley, University of Florida, University of Houston, University of Illinois at Urbana-Champaign, and the Universities of Virginia, Washington, and Wisconsin.

7. Contributing are Boston, CRL, Columbia, Hoover, Howard, Indiana, Library of Congress, MSU, NYPL and Schomburg, UCLA, Illinois, and of course Northwestern.

8. For information about these Plans, see their journals, now ceased: *Farmington Plan Newsletter*, nos. 1–31, 1949–70, and *Foreign Acquisitions Newsletter*, nos. 32–50, 1970–79.

9. See the *Camp Catalog* 1977 cumulative edition and the 1982 cumulative supplement for a listing of the collection contents and for information on direct access and interlibrary loan.

10. David Weissbrodt, in "The Role of International Non-governmental Organizations in the Implementation of Human Rights," *Texas International Law Journal* 12, nos. 2–3 (Spring–Summer 1977), pp. 293–320, provides an excellent introduction to the work.

11. *Human Rights Internet Reporter* 6, no. 5 (May–June 1981), p. 600.

12. Ibid., no. 3 (January–February 1981), pp. 301–2.

13. Forthcoming in 1983 is a *Bibliography of Human Rights* by Diana Vincent-Daviss to be published by Oceana Publications of Dobbs Ferry, New York. Also in press is *A Research Manual on Human Rights* by Lee Regen and Richard Greenfield, to be published by Human Rights Internet of Washington, D.C.

14. January 1974–January 1976 (Buffalo: Charles B. Sears Law Library, State University of New York at Buffalo); February 1976–April 1980 (Austin: The Tarlton Law Library, University of Texas). After February 1979, the *Checklist* was published by Earl Coleman Enterprises in cooperation with the Tarlton Law Library. Publication ceased with vol. 5, no. 4.

15. In *Legal Process and the Individual: African Source Materials, Including Background Papers, a Bibliography, and Selected Legislation* . . ., edited by Thierry G. Verhelst (Addis Ababa: Centre for African Legal Development, 1971), pp. 376–81.

16. The first supplement covering 1977–80 was published in 1981 in Brussels.

17. Many libraries also receive the *Monthly Bibliography*, a subject compilation of books, documents, and periodicals (but not articles), from the UN library in Geneva.

18. For a compilation of earlier years, see the International African Institute (London), *Cumulative Bibliography of African Studies, Author Catalog*, 2 vols.; and *Classified Catalog*, 3 vols. (Boston: Hall, 1973). For a retrospective approach to journal articles, see Library of Congress, *Africa South of the Sahara: Index to Periodical Literature, 1900–1970*, 4 vols. (Boston: Hall, 1971); and *First Supplement*, 1 vol. (1973).

19. This listing of conferences can be used in conjunction with the *Africana Conference Papers Index* (Boston: Hall, 1982), a listing of over twelve thousand conference papers held at the Northwestern University Library and available through interlibrary loan.

20. Other Internet publications include *Teaching Human Rights* (Washington, D.C.: HRI, 1981), with its useful bibliography, and its directory: *The Human Rights Directory: Latin America; Africa; Asia* (Washington, D.C.:

Human Rights Internet, 1981), covering seventy international organizations and 400 organizations by country.

21. To follow activities of the OAU and events throughout Africa, use *Africa News*, vol. 1–   (1963–   ), a weekly publication published in Durham, N.C., or *Africa Research Bulletin*, vol. 1–   (1963–   ), a monthly publication from Exeter, England, in two series: Economic, Financial, and Technical Series, and Political, Social, and Cultural Series.

22. The text of the Banjul Charter appears in *International Legal Materials* (Washington: American Society of International Law) 21, no. 1 (1982), pp. 59–68, and later in this volume (Appendix 1). The document number is OAU Doc. CAB/LEG/67/3 Rev. 5.

23. Two special collections visited during the preparation of this paper were at universities, and a third at Human Rights Internet in Washington, D.C., where the librarian in charge, Lee Regen, was most helpful. J. Paul Martin, director of the Center for Human Rights at Columbia University, shared his Human Rights Bibliography Classification Scheme with me and discussed the problems of human rights research. David Weissbrodt, director of the International Human Rights Internship Program at the University of Minnesota Law School, arranged for me to browse through his extensive files of fugitive materials.

CHAPTER FOURTEEN

Bibliography

CLAUDE E. WELCH, JR., AND VICKI M. KRAFT

In his bibliographic survey, appropriately subtitled "The Explosion in Human Rights Documentation" and cited below, Thomas Reynolds concludes, "The literature [on human rights] is expanding so rapidly that any effort at a static 'best books' sort of bibliography is assured of almost total inutility within a few years." The pages that follow are presented with that caution. As illustrated in the preceding chapter by Corinne Nyquist, the interested scholar must contend with a torrent of United Nations and a paucity of Organization of African Unity (OAU) documentation, and a bewildering variety of indexes, classification schemes, and sources.

Bibliographic complexity is not confined to human rights. Equally difficult to determine is what should be included in the general areas of "African studies" and "development." The former, at its broadest, includes all works dealing with a vast continent and its associated islands, with more than fifty independent states, and with hundreds, if not thousands, of distinct ethnic groups. Especially when one examines the cultural and philosophical roots of human rights in Africa, a flood of sources could be cited, far beyond the appropriate scope of a concluding bibliography. "Development" offers an analogous range of complexity. The definition of development, including its relationship to industrialization, modernization, or urbanization (to cite three complex, related, and equally ill-defined terms) leads the scholar into dense thickets of verbiage, and a wide variety of published sources.

The citations printed below are illustrative, not exhaustive. They are intended to question the validity of Reynolds' assertion that "there is presently little to be recommended in regarding, as an area for study, the regional or subregional protection of human rights beyond that experienced in Europe and the Western Hemisphere"

(p. 31). A fundamental purpose of this volume, *Human Rights and Development in Africa*, is to illustrate the dynamic, changing character of the subject. Although analysis of the promotion and protection of human rights in Africa certainly remains limited compared with that for Western Europe and the New World, several noteworthy essays have been published. The compilers hope that the items cited below will facilitate further research. They have been grouped into four categories: bibliographies, anthologies, and research guides; general works on the roots and protection of human rights; analyses of human rights in Africa (for the continent as a whole and for regions within it); and studies of development. These headings, it should be obvious, are suggestive rather than conclusive.

We should also point out that this bibliography is selective, not exhaustive. With a few exceptions, all citations are to English-language publications. Few documents emanating from international organizations or non-governmental organizations appear in the following pages. Emphasis has been placed on scholarly analyses, especially from law reviews, academic journals, and specialized books. Journalistic reports and other ephemera, although useful for the study of particular cases, have not been drawn upon. Several sources were consulted in preparing the citations below, most notably, the *Checklist of Human Rights Documents*. Jack Donnelly furnished several hundred suggestions for the section dealing with development—of which, necessarily, a far smaller number appears. The compilers wish to thank him and Corinne Nyquist for their assistance. Citations were verified in the libraries of The State University of New York at Buffalo through June 1982.

BIBLIOGRAPHIC SOURCES AND RESEARCH GUIDES

Afolabi, M.O. "Select Bibliography of Organization of African Unity Articles Published in English Language Periodicals." *Current Bibliography on African Affairs* 12, no. 4 (1979–80), 454–80.

Besterman, Theodore. *A World Bibliography of African Bibliographies*, revised by J.D. Pearson. Totowa, N.J.: Rowman and Littlefield, 1975.

Brownlie, Ian, editor. *Basic Documents on Human Rights*. 2nd ed. Oxford: Clarendon Press, 1981.

Checklist of Human Rights Documents. Pine Plains, N.Y.: Coleman Enterprises, 1974–80.

Current Bibliographical Information. United Nations, Dag Hammarskjold Library, 1971– . UN Document ST/LIB/SER.K/1 1971– .

Dryden, P.K. "Annotated Bibliography of Political Rights of African Women." *African Law Studies* 7 (December 1972), 27–61.

Feliciano, Myrna S. "Human Rights Documentation." *International Journal of Law Libraries* 9, no. 3 (June 1981), 95–106.

Hafkin, Nancy. *Women and Development in Africa: An Annotated Bibliography.* Addis Ababa: Economic Commission for Africa, 1977.

Human Rights Internet Reporter. Washington, D.C.: Human Rights Internet, 1976– .

Ikem, J.E. "Documentation of the UN and the OAU." *International Library Review* 13 (1981), 287–300.

Joyce, James Avery. *Human Rights: International Documents.* Dobbs Ferry, N.Y.: Oceana Publications, 1982.

Laqueur, Walter, and Rubin, Barry, editors. *The Human Rights Reader.* New York: Meridian, 1979.

Miller, William, editor. *International Human Rights: A Bibliography, 1965–1969,* and *International Human Rights: A Bibliography, 1970–1976.* Notre Dame, Ind.: Center for Civil Rights, University of Notre Dame Law School, 1976.

Myers, David B. "The Organization of African Unity: An Annotated Bibliography." *Africana Library Journal* 5, no. 4 (1975), 308–32.

O'Connor, Barry, and Scanlan, John A., editors. *International Human Rights: A Bibliography, 1970–1975.* Notre Dame, Ind.: University of Notre Dame Press, 1981.

Reynolds, Thomas H. "Highest Aspirations or Barbarous Acts . . . The Explosion in Human Rights Documentation: A Bibliographic Survey." *Law Library Journal* 71 (1978), 1–48.

Scheven, Yvette. *Bibliographies for African Studies 1970–1975; 1976–1979.* Waltham, Mass.: Crossroads Press, 1977, 1980.

Vanderlinden, Jacques. *African Law Bibliography/Bibliographie de droit africain 1947–1966.* Brussels: Presses universitaires de Bruxelles, 1972.

Vanderlinden, Jacques. "African Legal Process and the Individual: Ten Years of Bibliography." In Thierry G. Verhelst, editor, *Legal Process and the Individual: African Source Materials, Including Background Papers, a Bibliography, and Selected Legislation . . . ,* pp. 376–81. Addis Ababa: Centre for African Legal Development, 1971.

Vincent-Daviss, Diana. *A Bibliography of Human Rights.* Dobbs Ferry, N.Y.: Oceana Publications, 1983.

Vincent-Daviss, Diana. "Human Rights Law: A Research Guide to the Literature." *New York University Journal of International Law and Politics* 14 (1980–81), 209–319, 487–573, 15 (1982), 211–87.

Witherell, Julian W. *The United States and Africa: Guide to U.S. Official Documents and Government-Sponsored Publications on Africa, 1785–1975.* Washington: Library of Congress, 1978.

GENERAL WORKS ON HUMAN RIGHTS

Abdul Rauf, Muhammad. *The Islamic View of Women and the Family.* New York: Speller, 1977.

Alexander, Yonah, and Friedlander, Robert A., editors. *Self-Determination: National, Regional, and Global Dimensions.* Boulder, Colo.: Westview Press, 1980.

Bay, Christian. "Universal Human Rights Priorities: Toward a Rational Order." In Jack L. Nelson and Vera M. Green, editors, *International Human Rights: Contemporary Issues*, pp. 5–27. Stanfordville, N.Y.: Human Rights Publishing Group, 1980.

Bayley, David H. *Public Liberties in the New States.* Chicago: Rand McNally, 1964.

Bilder, Richard B. "Rethinking International Human Rights: Some Basic Questions." *Human Rights Journal* 2, no. 4 (1969), 186–213.

Bissell, Richard E. *Apartheid and International Organizations.* Boulder, Colo.: Westview Press, 1977.

Braham, Randolf L., editor. *Human Rights: Contemporary Domestic and International Issues and Conflicts.* New York: Irvington Publishers, 1980.

Brown, Peter G., and MacLean, Douglas, editors. *Human Rights and U.S. Foreign Policy.* Lexington, Mass.: Lexington Books, 1979.

Buergenthal, Thomas. "The American Convention on Human Rights: Illusions and Hopes." *Buffalo Law Review* 21, no. 1 (Fall 1971), 121–36.

Buergenthal, Thomas. "International and Regional Human Rights Law and Institutions: Some Examples of Their Interaction." *Texas International Law Journal* 12, nos. 2–3 (Spring–Summer 1977), 321–30.

Buergenthal, Thomas, and Torney, Judith V. "Expanding the International Human Rights Research Agenda." *International Studies Quarterly* 23, no. 2 (June 1979), 321–34.

Carey, John. *UN Protection of Civil and Political Rights.* Syracuse: Syracuse University Press, 1970.

Chossudovsky, Michel. "The Political Economy of Human Rights." *Bulletin of Peace Proposals* 10, no. 2 (1979), 172–8.

Claude, Richard P., editor. *Comparative Human Rights.* Baltimore: Johns Hopkins University Press, 1976.

Claude, Richard. "Reliable Information: The Threshold Problem for Human Rights Research." *Human Rights* 6, no. 2 (Winter 1977), 169–87.

Del Russo, A. Luihi. *International Protection of Human Rights.* Washington, D.C.: Lerner Law Book Co., 1970.

Department of State, *Country Reports on Human Rights Practices, Report Submitted to the Committee on Foreign Affairs, U.S. House of Representatives, and Committee on Foreign Relations, U.S. Senate, by U.S. Department of State.* Washington, D.C.: U.S. Government Printing Office, annual.

Dinstein, Yoram. "Collective Human Rights of Peoples and Minorities." *International and Comparative Law Quarterly* 25, no. 1 (January 1976), 102–20.

Dominguez, Jorge I.; Rodley, Nigel S.; Wood, Bryce; and Falk, Richard. *Enhancing Global Human Rights.* New York: McGraw-Hill, 1979.

Donnelly, Jack. "Human Rights and Human Dignity: An Analytic Critique of Non-Western Conceptions of Human Rights." *American Political Science Review* 76, no. 2 (June 1982), 303–16.

Donnelly, Jack. "Recent Trends in UN Human Rights Activity: Description and Polemic." *International Organization* 35, no. 4 (Autumn 1981), 633–55.

Emerson, Rupert. "The Fate of Human Rights in the Third World." *World Politics* 27, no. 2 (January 1975), 201–26.

Falk, Richard. "Comparative Protection of Human Rights in Capitalist and Socialist Third World Countries." *Universal Human Rights* 1, no. 2 (April–June 1979), 3–29.

Falk, Richard A. *Human Rights and State Sovereignty*. New York: Holmes and Meier, 1981.

Falk, Richard A. "Militarization and Human Rights in the Third World." *Bulletin of Peace Proposals* 8, no. 3 (1977), 220–32.

Forsythe, David P., and Wiseberg, Laurie S. "Human Rights Protection: A Research Agenda." *Universal Human Rights* 1, no. 4 (October–December 1979), 1–24.

Franck, Thomas M. *Human Rights in Third World Perspective*. Dobbs Ferry, N.Y.: Oceana Publications, 1982.

Franck, Thomas M., and Hoffman, Paul. "The Right of Self-Determination in Very Small Places." *New York University Journal of International Law and Politics* 8, no. 3 (Winter 1976), 331–86.

Gastil, Raymond D., editor. *Freedom in the World: Political Rights and Civil Liberties*. New York: Freedom House, annual.

Haas, Ernst B. *Human Rights and International Action: The Case of Freedom of Association*. Stanford, Calif.: Stanford University Press, 1970.

Henderson, Conway W. "Underdevelopment and Political Rights: A Revisionist Challenge." *Government and Opposition* 12, no. 3 (Summer 1977), 276–92.

Henkin, Louis, editor. *The International Bill of Rights: The Covenant on Civil and Political Rights*. New York: Columbia University Press, 1981.

Henkin, Louis. *The Rights of Man Today*. Boulder, Colo.: Westview Press, 1978.

Hevener, Natalie Kaufman, editor. *The Dynamics of Human Rights in United States Foreign Policy*. New Brunswick, N.J.: Transaction Books, 1981.

Hosken, Fran P., guest editor. Issue on "Women and International Human Rights." *Human Rights Quarterly* 3, no. 2 (Spring 1981), 1–135.

Joyce, James Avery. *The New Politics of Human Rights*. New York: St. Martin's Press, 1979.

Kamenka, Eugene, and Tay, Alice Ehr-Soon, editors. *Human Rights, Ideas and Ideologies*. New York: St. Martin's Press, 1978.

Kommers, Donald P., and Loescher, D. Gilburt. *Human Rights and American Foreign Policy*. Notre Dame, Ind.: University of Notre Dame Press, 1979.

Kuper, Leo. *Genocide: Its Political Use in the Twentieth Century*. New Haven: Yale University Press, 1981.

Lauterpacht, Hersh. *International Law and Human Rights*. Hamden, Conn.: Shoestring Press, 1968.

Lawson, Ruth C. *International Regional Organizations: Constitutional Foundations*. New York: Praeger, 1962.

Lillich, Richard B., and Newman, Frank C. *International Human Rights: Problems of Law and Policy*. Boston: Little, Brown, 1979.

Luard, Evan. *Human Rights and Foreign Policy*. Oxford: Pergamon Press, 1981.

Luard, Evan, editor. *International Protection of Human Rights*. New York: Praeger, 1967.

McCamant, John F. "Social Science and Human Rights." *International Organization*, 35, no. 3 (Summer 1981), 531-52.

Macdonald, Ronald St. John; Johnodon, Douglas M.; and Morris, Gerlad L., editors. *The International Law and Policy of Human Welfare*. The Hague: Sijthoof and Noordhoff, 1978.

McDougal, Myres S. "Human Rights and World Public Order: Principles of Content and Procedures for Clarifying General Community Policies." *Virginia Journal of International Law* 14, no. 3 (Spring 1974), 387-421.

McDougal, Myres S.; Lasswell, Harold D.; and Chen, Lung-cho. "The Protection of Respect and Human Rights: Freedom of Choice and World Public Order." *American University Law Review* 24 (Summer 1975), 919-1086.

McDougal, Myres S; Lasswell, Harold D.; and Chen, Lung-cho. "The Right to Religious Freedom and World Public Order: The Emerging Norm of Nondiscrimination." *Michigan Law Review* 74 (April 1976), 865-93.

Mower, A. Glenn, Jr. *The United States, The United Nations, and Human Rights: The Eleanor Roosevelt and Jimmy Carter Eras*. Westport, Conn.: Greenwood Press, 1979.

Newberg, Paula R., editor. *The Politics of Human Rights*. New York: New York University Press, 1980.

Newman, Frank C.; Buergenthal, Thomas; and Vendrell, Francis. "U.N. Human Rights Covenants Become Law: So What?" *American Society of International Law: Proceedings (1976)*, 97-105.

Ramcharan, B. G. *Human Rights, Thirty Years after the Universal Declaration*. The Hague: Martinus Nijhoff, 1979.

Ramcharan, B. G. *The International Law Commission: Its Approach to the Codification and Progressive Development of International Law*. The Hague: Martinus Nijhoff, 1977.

Robertson, Arthur Henry *Human Rights in National and International Law*. Dobbs Ferry, N.Y.: Oceana Publications, 1968.

Robertson, Arthur Henry. *Human Rights in the World*. Manchester: Manchester University Press, 1972.

Rogers, Barbara. *The Domestication of Women: Discrimination in Developing Societies*. New York: St. Martin's Press, 1980.

Rubin, Barry M., and Spiro, Elizabeth, editors. *Human Rights and U.S. Foreign Policy*. Boulder, Colo.: Westview Press, 1979.

Said, Abdul Aziz, editor. *Human Rights and World Order*. New York: Praeger, 1978.

Said, Abdul Aziz. "Precept and Practice of Human Rights in Islam." *Universal Human Rights* 1, no. 1 (January–March 1979), 63-79.

Schoultz, Lars. *Human Rights and United States Policy toward Latin America*. Princeton, N.J.: Princeton University Press, 1981.

Schreiber, Anna P. *The Inter-American Commission on Human Rights*. Leiden: Sijthoff, 1970.

Schwelb, Egon. *Human Rights and the International Community: The Roots and Growth of the Universal Declaration of Human Rights, 1948-1963*. Chicago: Quadrangle Books, 1964.

Schwelb, Egon. "The International Convention on the Elimination of All Forms of Racial Discrimination." *International and Comparative Law Quarterly* 15 (October 1966), 996–1068.

Schwelb, Egon. "The International Court of Justice and the Human Rights Clauses of the Charter." *American Journal of International Law* 66 (1972), 337–51.

Scoble, Harry M., and Wiseberg, Laurie S. "Problems of Comparative Research on Human Rights." In Ved P. Nanda, James R. Scarritt, and George W. Shepherd, Jr., editors, *Global Human Rights: Public Policies, Comparative Measures and NGO Strategies*, pp. 147–71. Boulder, Colo.: Westview Press, 1981.

Sinha, S. Prakash. "The Anthropocentric Theory of International Law as a Basis for Human Rights." *Case Western Reserve Journal of International Law* 10 (Summer 1978), 469–502.

Sohn, Louis B., and Buergenthal, Thomas, editors. *International Protection of Human Rights*. Indianapolis: Bobbs-Merrill, 1973.

Van Boven, Theo C. "Some Remarks on Special Problems Relating to Human Rights in Developing Countries." *Human Rights Journal* 3, no. 3 (1970), 383–95.

Van Boven, Theo C. "The United Nations and Human Rights: A Critical Appraisal." *Bulletin of Peace Proposals* 8, no. 3 (1977), 198–208.

Van Dyke, Vernon. "The Cultural Rights of Peoples." *Universal Human Rights* 2, no. 1 (April–June 1980), 1–20.

Van Dyke, Vernon. *Human Rights, the United States, and the World Community*. New York: Oxford University Press, 1970.

Vogelsang, Sandy. *American Dream, Global Nightmare: The Dilemma of U.S. Human Rights Policy*. New York: Norton, 1980.

Weissbrodt, David "The Role of International Non-governmental Organizations in the Implementation of Human Rights." *Texas International Law Journal* 12, nos. 2–3 (Spring–Summer 1977), 293–320.

Whyte, Martin King. *The Status of Women in Pre-Industrial Societies*. Princeton, N.J. Princeton University Press, 1978.

HUMAN RIGHTS IN AFRICA

General

Adegbite, Latif O. "African Attitudes to the International Protection of Human Rights." In Asbjorn Eide and August Schou, editors, *International Protection of Human Rights*, pp. 69–81. New York: Interscience Publishers, 1968.

Aiboni, Sam Amaize. *Protection of Refugees in Africa*. Uppsala: Scandinavian Institute of African Studies, 1978.

Akinyemi, A. Bolaji. "The O.A.U. and the Concept of Non-interference in Internal Affairs of Member States." *British Yearbook of International Law* 46 (1972–73), 393–400.

Aluko, Olajide. "The Organization of African Unity and Human Rights." *Round Table* 283 (July 1981), 234–42.

Asante, S.K.B. "Nation Building and Human Rights in Emergent African Nations." *Cornell International Law Journal* 2 (Spring 1969), 72–107.

Ault, David E., and Rutman, Gilbert L. "The Development of Individual Rights to Property in Tribal Africa." *Journal of Law and Economics* 22, no. 1 (April 1979), 163–82.

Bello, Emmanuel G. "Human Rights: The Rule of Law in Africa." *International and Comparative Law Quarterly* 30 (July 1981), 628–37.

Bozeman, Adda B. *Conflict in Africa: Concepts and Realities*. Princeton, N.J.: Princeton University Press, 1976.

Bretton, Henry L. "Human Rights in Africa: Further Thoughts and an Agenda for Action." Paper presented at the annual meeting of the Latin American Studies Association and the African Studies Association, Houston, Texas, 1977.

Commission to Study the Organization of Peace. "Regional Protection and Promotion of Human Rights in Africa." New York: The Commission, 1980.

Ebiasah, John K. "Protecting the Human Rights of Political Detainees: The Contradictions and Paradoxes in the African Experience." *Howard Law Journal* 22, no. 3 (1979), 249–81.

El-Ayouty, Yassin, editor. *Africa and International Organisation*. The Hague: Martinus Nijhoff, 1974.

El-Ayouty, Yassin, editor. *The Organization of African Unity after Ten Years: Comparative Perspectives*. New York: Praeger, 1975.

Elias, T.O. *Africa and the Development of International Law*. Dobbs Ferry, N.Y.: Oceana Publications, 1972.

Esiemokhai, Emmanuel O. "Towards Adequate Defence of Human Rights in Africa." *Quarterly Journal of Administration* 24, no. 4 (July 1980), 451–61.

Eze, Osita C. "Prospects for International Protection of Human Rights in Africa." *African Review* 4, no. 1 (1974), 79–90.

Gower, Laurence Cecil Bartlett. *Independent Africa: The Challenge to the Legal Profession*. Cambridge, Mass. Harvard University Press, 1967.

Hannum, Hurst. "The Butare Colloquium on Human Rights and Economic Development in Francophone Africa: A Summary and Analysis." *Universal Human Rights* 1, no. 2 (April–June 1979), 63–87.

Harvey, William B. *Law and Social Change in Ghana*. Princeton, N.J.: Princeton University Press, 1966.

Howard, Rhoda. "The Dilemma of Human Rights in Sub-Saharan Africa." *International Journal* 35, no. 4 (Autumn 1980), 724–47.

Human Rights in Africa. Hearing before the Subcommittees on Africa and on International Organizations of the Committee on Foreign Affairs, U.S. House of Representatives, Ninety-Sixth Congress, October 31, 1979. Washington, D.C.: U.S. Government Printing Office, 1980.

International Commission of Jurists. *Human Rights in a One-Party State*. London: Search Press, for the ICJ, 1978.

Jinadu, L. Adele. *Human Rights and U.S.-African Policy under President Carter.* Lagos: Nigerian Institute of International Affairs, 1980.

Jose, Alhaji Babatunde. "Press Freedom in Africa." *African Affairs* 74, no. 296 (July 1975), 255–62.

Kunnert, Dirk. "Carter, the Tradition of American Foreign Policy, and Africa." *South Africa International* 8, no. 2 (October 1977), 65–78 and 99–105.

Legesse, Asmarom. "Human Rights in African Political Culture." In Kenneth W. Thompson, editor, *The Moral Imperatives of Human Rights: A World Survey*, pp. 81–108. Washington, D.C.: University Press of America for the Council on Religion and International Affairs, 1980.

Mangin, Gilbert. "Les droits de l'homme dans les pays de l'Afrique francophone." *Human Rights Journal* 1, no. 3 (September 1968), 453–70.

Mazrui, Ali A. "Academic Freedom in Africa: The Dual Tyranny." *African Affairs* 74, no. 297 (October 1975), 393–400.

Mazrui, Ali A. *Towards a Pax Africana.* Chicago: University of Chicago Press, 1967.

M'Baye, Keba. "Les réalités du monde noir et les droits de l'homme." *Human Rights Journal* 2, no. 3 (September 1969), 382–94.

Melander, Goran, and Nobel, Peter. *African Refugees and the Law.* Uppsala: Scandinavian Institute of African Studies, 1978.

Menkiti, Ifeanyi A. "Person and Community in African Traditional Thought." In Richard A. Wright, editor, *African Philosophy: An Introduction.* 2nd ed., pp. 157–68. Washington, D.C.: University Press of America, 1979.

Miers, Suzanne, and Kopytoff, Igor, editors. *Slavery in Africa: Historical and Anthropological Perspectives.* Madison: University of Wisconsin Press, 1977.

Mojekwu, Chris C. "International Human Rights: The African Perspective." In Jack L. Nelson and Vera M. Green, editors, *International Human Rights: Contemporary Issues*, pp. 85–95. Stanfordville, N.Y.: Human Rights Group, 1980.

Mower, A. Glenn, Jr. "Human Rights in Black Africa: A Double Standard?" *Human Rights Journal* 9, no. 1 (1976), 39–70.

Nwabueze, B.O. *Constitutionalism in the Emergent States.* Rutherford, N.J.: Fairleigh Dickinson University Press, 1973.

Nwabueze, B.O. *Judicialism in Commonwealth Africa: The Role of the Courts in Government.* New York: St. Martin's Press, 1977.

Ogwurike, Chijioke. *The Concept of Law in English-speaking Africa.* New York: Nok Publishers, 1979.

Okoth-Ogendo, H.W.O. "National Implementation of International Responsibility: Some Thoughts on Human Rights in Africa." *East African Law Journal* 10 (1974), 1–16.

Paul, James C.N. "Human Rights and Legal Development: Observations on Some African Experiences." In James C. Tuttle, editor, *International Human Rights: Law and Practice*, pp. 23–37. Philadelphia: International Printing, 1978.

Paul, James C.N. "Some Observations on Constitutionalism, Judicial Review, and the Rule of Law in Africa." *Ohio State Law Journal* 35, no. 4 (1974), 851–69.

Ramcharan, B.G. "Human Rights in Africa: Whither Now?" *University of Ghana Law Journal* 12 (1975), 88–105.

Robertson, A.H. "African Legal Process and the Individual." *Human Rights Journal* 5, nos. 2–3 (1979), 465–78.

Seidman, Robert B. "Administrative Law and Legitimacy in Anglophonic Africa." *Law and Society Review* 5, no. 2 (November 1970), 161–204.

Seidman, Robert B. "Judicial Review and Fundamental Freedoms in Anglophonic Independent Africa." *Ohio State Law Journal* 35 (1974), 820–50.

Shepherd, George W., Jr. "Humanitarian Assistance to Liberation Movements." *Africa Today* 21, no. 4 (Fall 1974), 75–87.

Sohn, Louis B., compiler. *Basic Documents of African Regional Organizations: Constitutional Foundations.* Dobbs Ferry, N.Y.: Oceana Publications, 1971–72.

Umozurike, U.O. "The Domestic Jurisdiction Clause in the OAU Charter." *African Affairs* 78, no. 311 (April 1979), 197–209.

Wai, Dunstan. "Human Rights in Sub-Saharan Africa." In Adamantia Pollis and Peter Schwab, editors, *Human Rights: Cultural and Ideological Perspectives*, pp. 115–44. New York: Praeger, 1979.

Weinstein, Warren. "African Perspectives on Human Rights." Washington, D.C.: Council for Policy and Social Research, 1980.

Weinstein, Warren. "Africa's Approach to Human Rights at the United Nations." *Issue* 6, no. 4 (Winter 1976), 14–21.

Weinstein, Warren. "Human Rights in Africa: A Long-Awaited Voice." *Current History* 78, no. 455 (March 1980), 97–101, 130–2.

Weis, Paul. "The Convention of the Organization of African Unity Governing the Specific Aspects of Refugee Problems in Africa." *Human Rights Journal* 3, no. 2 (September 1970), 449–64.

Welch, Claude E., Jr. "The OAU and Human Rights: Towards a New Definition." *Journal of Modern African Studies* 19, no. 3 (September 1981), 401–20.

Welch, Claude E., Jr. "The Right of Association in Ghana and Tanzania." *Journal of Modern African Studies* 16, no. 4 (December 1978), 639–56.

Wiseberg, Laurie W. "Human Rights in Africa: Toward a Definition of the Problem of a Double Standard." *Issue* 6, no. 4 (Winter 1976), 3–13.

North and East Africa

Amnesty International. "Human Rights Violations in Ethiopia." London: Amnesty International, 1978.

Conboy, Kevin. "Note: Detention without Trial in Kenya." *Georgia Journal of Comparative and International Law* 8, no. 2 (1978), 441–61.

Don Nanjira, Daniel D. *The Status of Asians in East Africa: Asians and Europeans in Tanzania, Uganda, and Kenya.* New York: Praeger, 1976.

Ghai, Y.P., and McAuslan, J.P.W.B. *Public Law and Political Change in Kenya: A Study of the Legal Framework of Government from Colonial Times to the Present.* Nairobi: Oxford University Press, 1970.

International Commission of Jurists. *Uganda and Human Rights: Reports to the United Nations Commission on Human Rights.* Geneva: ICJ, 1977.

Maina, Rose; Machai, V.W.; and Gatto, S.B.O. "Law and the Status of Women in Kenya." *Columbia Human Rights Law Review* 8, no. 1 (Spring-Summer 1976), 185-206.

Martin, Robert. *Personal Freedom and the Law in Tanzania: A Study of Socialist State Administration.* Nairobi: Oxford University Press, 1974.

Okeyo, Achola Pala. "Daughters of the Lakes and Rivers: Colonization and the Land Rights of Luo Woman." In Mona Etienne and Eleanor Leacock, editors, *Women and Colonization*, pp. 186-213. New York: Praeger, 1980.

Pfeiffer, Steven B. "The Judiciary in the Constitutional Systems of East Africa." *Journal of Modern African Studies* 16, no. 1 (March 1978), 33-66.

Plender, Richard. "The Exodus of Asians from East and Central Africa: Some Comparative and International Law Aspects." *American Journal of Comparative Law* 19, no. 2 (1971), 287-324.

Schwab, Peter. "Human Rights in Ethiopia." *Journal of Modern African Studies* 14, no. 1 (March 1976), 155-60.

Sharma, Vishnu D., and Woolridge, F. "Some Legal Questions Arising from the Expulsion of the Ugandan Asians." *International and Comparative Law Quarterly* 23, no. 2 (April 1974), 397-425.

Ullman, Richard H. "Human Rights and Economic Power: The United States versus Idi Amin." *Foreign Affairs* 56 (April 1978), 529-43.

Southern Africa

Abernathy, David B. "Assessing Human Rights Violations: A Comparison of the Contemporary South African and Ugandan Regimes." In Lee C. MacDonald, editor, *Human Rights and Educational Responsibility*, pp. 179-214. Santa Barbara, Calif.: American Bibliographic Center-CLIO, 1979.

Adelman, Kenneth L. "The Black Man's Burden." *Foreign Affairs* 28 (Fall 1977), 86-109.

Amnesty International. "Political Imprisonment in South Africa." London: Amnesty International, 1978.

Bernstein, Hilda. *For Their Triumphs and for Their Tears: Conditions and Resistance of Women in Apartheid South Africa.* London: International Defence and Aid Fund, 1978.

Clark, Roger S. "The International League for Human Rights and South West Africa, 1947-1957: The Human Rights NGO as Catalyst in the International Legal Process." *Human Rights Quarterly* 3, no. 4 (Fall 1981), 101-36.

Dugard, John. *Human Rights and the South African Legal Order.* Princeton, N.J.: Princeton University Press, 1978.

Forsyth, C.F., and Schiller, J.E. *Human Rights: The Cape Town Conference: Proceedings of the First International Conference on Human Rights in South Africa, 22–26 January 1979.* Cape Town: Juta, 1979.

International Commission of Jurists. *South Africa and the Rule of Law.* Geneva: ICJ, 1960.

Jespersen, Rob Rand. "The Jurisprudential Problem of Apartheid." *Texas Southern University Law Review* 4 (Summer 1977), 323–41.

Mathews, Anthony S. *Law, Order, and Liberty in South Africa.* Cape Town: Juta, 1971.

Ojo, Michael Adeleye. "U.N. and Freedom for Portuguese Colonies." *Africa Quarterly* 16, no. 1 (July 1976), 5–28.

Okolie, Charles Chukwuma. "Human Rights in Southern Africa in the Context of Public International Law." *Glendale Law Review* 2, no. 3 (1978), 219–72.

Pollock, A.J. "The South West Africa Cases and the Jurisprudence of International Law." *International Organization* 23, no. 4 (Autumn 1969), 767–87.

Richardson, Henry J., III. "Self-Determination, International Law, and the South African Bantustan Policy." *Columbia Journal of Transnational Law* 2 (1978), 185–219.

Scarritt, James R. "The External Pressures on Human Rights in South Africa: Problems of Research and Design." Paper presented at the Annual Meeting of the African Studies Association, Baltimore, 1978.

Shepherd, George W., Jr. *Anti-Apartheid: Transnational Conflict and Western Policy in the Liberation of South Africa.* Westport, Conn.: Greenwood Press, 1977.

Stokke, O., and Widstrand, C., editors. *The UN-OAU Conference on Southern Africa.* Uppsala: Scandinavian Institute of African Studies, 1973.

Weisfelder, Richard F. "The Decline of Human Rights in Lesotho: An Evaluation of Domestic and External Determinants." *Issue* 6, n. 4 (Winter 1976), 22–33.

West Africa

Adegbite, Latif O. "Human Rights in Nigeria." In Elias, T.O., editor, *Law and Social Change in Nigeria,* pp. 223–53. Ibadan and London: University of Lagos and Evans Bros., 1972.

Akpan, Moses E. "The 1979 Nigerian Constitution and Human Rights." *Universal Human Rights* 2, no. 2 (April–June 1980), 23–41.

Bukh, Jette. *The Village Woman in Ghana.* Uppsala: Scandinavian Institute of African Studies, 1979.

Carter, Marshall, and Marenin, Otwin. "Human Rights in the Nigerian Context: A Case Study and Discussion of the Nigerian Police." *Universal Human Rights* 1, no. 2 (April–June 1979), 43–61.

Fegley, Randall. "The UN Human Rights Commission: The Equatorial Guinea Case." *Human Rights Quarterly* 3, no. 1 (February 1981), 34–47.

Luckham, Yaa. "Law and the Status of Women in Ghana." *Columbia Human Rights Law Review* 8, no. 1 (Spring–Summer 1976), 69–94.

Nwosu, Humphrey N. "The Concepts of Nationalism and Right to Self-Determination: Cameroon as a Case Study." *Africa Quarterly* 16, no. 2 (October 1976), 1–26.

Okonkwo, R. Chude. "The Legal Basis of Freedom of Expression in Nigeria." *California Western International Law Journal* 8, no. 2 (Spring 1978), 256–73.

Peil, Margaret. "The Expulsion of West African Aliens." *Journal of Modern African Studies* 9, no. 2 (August 1971), 205–29.

Proehl, Paul O. *Fundamental Rights under the Nigerian Constitution, 1960–1965.* U.C.L.A. African Studies Center, Occasional Paper no. 8. Los Angeles: Center, 1970.

Wiseberg, Laurie S. "Humanitarian Intervention: Lessons from the Nigerian Civil War." *Human Rights Journal* 17, no. 1 (1974), 61–98.

HUMAN RIGHTS AND DEVELOPMENT

Adelman, Irma. "Economic Development and Political Change in Developing Countries." *Social Research* 47, no. 2 (Summer 1980), 213–34.

Adelman, Irma, and Morris, Cynthia Taft. *Economic Growth and Social Equity in Developing Countries.* Stanford: Stanford University Press, 1973.

Ahluwalia, Montek, A. "Inequality, Poverty and Development." *Journal of Development Economics* 3, no. 4 (December 1976), 307–42.

Ahluwalia, Montek S.; Carter, Nicholas G.; and Chenery, Hollis B. "Growth and Poverty in Developing Countries." *Journal of Development Economics* 6, no. 3 (September 1979), 299–342.

Ahluwalia, Montek S.; Duloy, John H.; Pyatt, Graham; and Srinivisan, T.N. "Who Benefits from Economic Development?" *American Economic Review* 70 (March 1980), 242–48.

Ajami, Fouad. *Human Rights and World Order Politics.* Institute for World Order Working Paper no. 4. New York: Institute, 1978.

Alston, Philip. "Development and the Rule of Law: Prevention versus Cure as a Human Rights Strategy." In International Commission of Jurists, *Development, Human Rights, and the Rule of Law.* Oxford: Pergamon Press, 1981.

Beitz, Charles R. "Economic Rights and Distributive Justice in Developing Societies." *World Politics* 33, no. 3 (April (1981), 321–46.

Boserup, Ester. *Woman's Role in Economic Development.* New York: St. Martin's Press, 1970.

Brietzke, Paul H. *Law, Development, and the Ethiopian Revolution.* Lewisburg, Pa.: Bucknell University Press, 1982.

Burki, Shahid Jaued. "The Prospects for the Developing World: A Review of Recent Forecasts." *Finance and Development* 18, no. 1 (March 1981), pp. 20–24.

Chenery, Hollis B.; Ahluwalia, Montek K.; Bell, C.L.A.; Duloy, John; and Jolly, Richard. *Redistribution with Growth.* Oxford: Oxford University Press, 1974.

Chichilnisky, Graciela, and Cole, H.S.D. "Human Rights and Basic Needs in a North-South Context." In Paula S. Newberg, editor, *The Politics of Human Rights*, pp. 113–42. New York: New York University Press, 1980.

Cline, William R. "Distribution and Development: A Survey of the Literature." *Journal of Development Economics* 1, no. 4 (February 1975), 359–400.

Curry, Robert L., Jr., and Rothchild, Donald. "The Fiscal Costs of a Basic Human Needs Strategy." *Journal of Modern African Studies* 18, no. 1 (March 1980), 143–50.

de Kadt, Emanuel. "Some Basic Questions on Human Rights and Development." *World Development* 8, no. 2 (February 1980), 97–105.

Dell, Sidney. "Basic Needs or Comprehensive Development: Should the UNDP Have a Development Strategy?" *World Development* 7, no. 3 (March 1979), 291–308.

Dias, C.J., and Paul, J.C.N. "Lawyers, Legal Professions, Modernization, and Development." In Dias, C.J.; Luckham, R.; Lynch, D.O.; and Paul, J.C.N., editors, *Lawyers in the Third World: Comparative and Developmental Perspectives*, pp. 11–25. Uppsala: Scandinavian Institute of African Studies and International Center for Law in Development, 1981.

Faaland, Just. "Growth, Employment, and Equity: Lessons of the Employment Strategy Mission to the Sudan." *International Labour Review* 114, no. 1 (July–August 1976), 1–10.

Fields, Gary S. *Poverty, Inequality, and Development.* Cambridge: Cambridge University Press, 1980.

Galtung, Johan, and Wirak, Helge Anders. "Human Needs and Human Rights—A Theoretical Approach." *Bulletin of Peace Proposals* 8, no. 3 (1977), 251–60.

Garnick, Laura, and Twitchett, Carol Cosgrove. "Human Rights and a Successor to the Lomé Convention." *International Relations* 6, no. 3 (May 1979), 540–57.

Goodin, Robert E. "The Development–Rights Trade-off: Some Unwarranted Economic and Political Assumptions." *Universal Human Rights* 1 (April 1979), 31–42.

Griffin, Keith, and James, Jeffrey. *The Transition to Egalitarian Development: Economic Policies for Structural Change in the Third World.* New York: St. Martin's Press, 1981.

Hewlett, Sylvia Ann. "Human Rights and Economic Realities: Trade-offs in Historical Perspective." *Political Science Quarterly* 94 (Fall 1979), 453–73.

Hicks, Norman, and Streeten, Paul. "Indicators of Development: The Search for a Basic Needs Yardstick." *World Development* 7, no. 6 (June 1979), 567–80.

International Labour Organization. *Employment Growth and Basic Needs.* Geneva: ILO, 1976.

Lee, Eddy. "Export-led Rural Development: The Ivory Coast." *Development and Change* 11, no. 4 (October 1980), 607–42.

Marks, Stephen P. "Development and Human Rights: Some Reflections on the Study of Development, Human Rights, and Peace." *Bulletin of Peace Proposals* 8, no. 3 (1977), 236–46.

Marks, Stephen P. "Emerging Human Rights: A New Generation for the 1980s?" *Rutgers Law Review* 33, no. 2 (Winter 1981), 435–52.

Marks, Stephen P. "The Peace–Human Rights–Development Dialectic." *Bulletin of Peace Proposals* 11 (1980), 339–47.

M'Baye, Keba. "Le Droit au développement comme un droit de l'homme." *Revue des droits de l'homme* 5 (1972), 505–34.

M'Baye, Keba. "Emergence of the 'Right to Development' as a Human Right in the Context of a New International Economic Order." UNESCO Document SS–78/CONF.630/8, 16 July 1979.

Merryman, John Henry. "Comparative Law and Social Change: On the Origins, Style, Decline, and Revival of the Law and Development Movement." *American Journal of Comparative Law* 25 (1977), 457–89.

Nayar, M.G. Kaladharan. "Human Rights and Economic Development: The Legal Foundations." *Universal Human Rights* 2, no. 3 (July–September 1980), 55–81.

Nelson, Nici. *African Women in the Development Process.* London: Frank Cass, 1981.

Okolie, Charles Chukwuma. *International Law Perspectives of the Developing Countries: The Relationship of Law and Economic Development to Human Rights.* New York: Nok Publishers, 1978.

Paul, J.C.N. "Development, Human Rights, and Public Law: Some General Observations Drawn from Comparative Experience." Unpublished paper, Lagos, 1981.

Richardson, Malcolm. *Human Rights, Human Needs, and Developing Nations: A Bellagio Conference, June 26–30, 1980.* New York: Rockefeller Foundation, 1980.

Rimmer, Douglas. "Basic Needs and the Origins of the Development Ethos." *Journal of Developing Areas* 15, no. 2 (January 1981), 215–37.

Rousseau-Mukenge, Ida. "Conceptualizations of African Women's Role in Development: A Search for New Directions." *Journal of International Affairs* 30, no. 2 (Fall–Winter 1976/77), 261–8.

Sheehan, Glen, and Hopkins, Mike. "Meeting Basic Needs: An Examination of the World Situation in 1970." *International Labour Review* 117, no. 5 (September–October 1978), 523–42.

Streeten, Paul. "Basic Needs and Human Rights." *World Development* 8, no. 2 (February 1980), 107–11.

United Nations. "Report of the Seminar on the Effects of the Existing Unjust International Economic Order on the Economies of the Developing Countries and the Obstacles That These Represent for the Implementation of Human Rights and Fundamental Freedoms, 30 June–11 July 1980." UN Document ST/HR/SER.A/8.

United Nations. "Report of the Seminar on the Relations that Exist between Human Rights, Peace, and Development, 3–14 August 1981." UN Document ST/HR/SER.A/10., New York, August 1981.

United Nations Commission on Human Rights. *Report of the Secretary-General.* "The International Dimensions of the Right to Development as a Human Right in Relation with Other Human Rights Based on International

Cooperation, Including the Right to Peace, Taking into Account the Requirements of the New International Economic Order and Fundamental Human Needs.'' UN Document E/CN.4/1334 (1979).

Wright, Charles L. ''Income Inequality and Economic Growth: Examining the Evidence.'' *Journal of Developing Areas* 13, no. 1 (October 1978), 47–66.

Young-Awanaty, Amy. ''Human Rights and the ACP-EEC Lomé II Convention: Business as Usual at the EEC.'' *New York University Journal of International Law and Politics* 13, no. 1 (Spring 1980), 63–98.

The African Charter on Human and Peoples' Rights

PREAMBLE

The African States members of the Organization of African Unity, parties to the present convention entitled "African Charter on Human and Peoples' Rights,"

Recalling Decision 115 (XVI) of the Assembly of Heads of State and Government at its Sixteenth Ordinary Session held in Monrovia, Liberia, from 17 to 20 July 1979 on the preparation of a "preliminary draft on an African Charter on Human and Peoples' Rights providing *inter alia* for the establishment of bodies to promote and protect human and peoples' rights";

Considering the Charter of the Organization of African Unity, which stipulates that "freedom, equality, justice, and dignity are essential objectives for the achievement of the legitimate aspirations of the African peoples";

Reaffirming the pledge they solemnly made in Article 2 of the said Charter to eradicate all forms of colonialism from Africa, to coordinate and intensify their cooperation and efforts to achieve a better life for the peoples of Africa, and to promote international cooperation having due regard to the Charter of the United Nations and the Universal Declaration of Human Rights;

Taking into consideration the virtues of their historical tradition and the values of African civilization which should inspire and characterize their reflection on the concept of human and peoples' rights;

Recognizing on the one hand, that fundamental human rights stem from the attributes of human beings, which justifies their national and international protection, and on the other hand that the reality and respect of peoples' rights should necessarily guarantee human rights;

Considering that the enjoyment of rights and freedoms also implies the performance of duties on the part of everyone;

Convinced that it is henceforth essential to pay a particular attention to the right to development and that civil and political rights cannot be dissociated from economic, social, and cultural rights in their conception as well as universality, and that the satisfaction of economic, social, and cultural rights is a guarantee for the enjoyment of civil and political rights;

Conscious of their duty to achieve the total liberation of Africa, the peoples of which are still struggling for their dignity and genuine independence, and undertaking to eliminate colonialism, neo-colonialism, apartheid, zionism, and to dismantle aggressive foreign military bases and all forms of discrimination, particularly those based on race, ethnic group, color, sex, language, religion, or political opinions;

Reaffirming their adherence to the principles of human and peoples' rights and freedoms contained in the declarations, conventions, and other instruments adopted by the Organization of African Unity, the Movement of Non-Aligned Countries, and the United Nations;

Firmly convinced of their duty to promote and protect human and peoples' rights and freedoms, taking into account the importance traditionally attached to these rights and freedoms in Africa;

have agreed as follows:

PART II: *RIGHTS AND DUTIES*

CHAPTER I. HUMAN AND PEOPLES' RIGHTS

ARTICLE 1 The Member States of the Organization of African Unity parties to the present Charter shall recognize the rights, duties, and freedoms enshrined in this Charter and shall undertake to adopt legislative or other measures to give effect to them.

ARTICLE 2 Every individual shall be entitled to the enjoyment of the rights and freedoms recognized and guaranteed in the present Charter without distinction of any kind, such as race, ethnic group, color, sex, language, religion, political or any other opinion, national and social origin, fortune, birth, or other status.

ARTICLE 3
  1.   Every individual shall be equal before the law.
  2.   Every individual shall be entitled to equal protection of the law.

ARTICLE 4 Human beings are inviolable. Every human being shall be entitled to respect for his life and the integrity of his person. No one may be arbitrarily deprived of this right.

ARTICLE 5 Every individual shall have the right to the respect of the dignity inherent in a human being and to the recognition of his legal status. All forms of exploitation and degradation of man, particularly slavery, slave trade, torture, cruel, inhuman or degrading punishment and treatment, shall be prohibited.

ARTICLE 6 Every individual shall have the right to liberty and to the security of his person. No one may be deprived of his freedom except for reasons and conditions previously laid down by law. In particular, no one may be arbitrarily arrested or detained.

ARTICLE 7
1. Every individual shall have the right to have his cause heard. This comprises:
   (a) the right to an appeal to competent national organs against acts of violating his fundamental rights as recognized and guaranteed by conventions, laws, regulations, and customs in force;
   (b) the right to be presumed innocent until proved guilty by a competent court or tribunal;
   (c) the right to defence, including the right to be defended by counsel of his choice;
   (d) the right to be tried within a reasonable time by an impartial court or tribunal.
2. No one may be condemned for an act or omission which did not constitute a legally punishable offence at the time it was committed. No penalty may be inflicted for an offence for which no provision was made at the time it was committed. Punishment is personal and can be imposed only on the offender.

ARTICLE 8 Freedom of conscience, the profession and free practice of religion shall be guaranteed. No one may, subject to law and order, be submitted to measures restricting the exercise of these freedoms.

ARTICLE 9
1. Every individual shall have the right to receive information.
2. Every individual shall have the right to express and disseminate his opinions within the law.

ARTICLE 10
1. Every individual shall have the right to free association provided that he abides by the law.
2. Subject to the obligation of solidarity provided for in Article 29, no one may be compelled to join an association.

ARTICLE 11 Every individual shall have the right to assemble freely with others. The exercise of this right shall be subject only to necessary restrictions provided for by law, in particular those enacted in the interest of national security, the safety, health, ethics, and rights and freedoms of others.

ARTICLE 12
1. Every individual shall have the right to freedom of movement and residence within the borders of a State provided he abides by the law.
2. Every individual shall have the right to leave any country including his own, and to return to his country. This right may only be subject to restrictions, provided for by law, for the protection of national security, law and order, public health or morality.

3. Every individual shall have the right, when persecuted, to seek and obtain asylum in other countries in accordance with laws of those countries and international conventions.
4. A non-national legally admitted in a territory of a State Party to the present Charter, may only be expelled from it by virtue of a decision taken in accordance with the law.
5. The mass explusion of non-nationals shall be prohibited. Mass expulsion shall be that which is aimed at national, racial, ethnic, or religious groups.

ARTICLE 13
1. Every citizen shall have the right to participate freely in the government of his country, either directly or through freely chosen representatives in accordance with the provisions of the law.
2. Every citizen shall have the right of equal access to the public service of his country.
3. Every individual shall have the right of access to public property and services in strict equality of all persons before the law.

ARTICLE 14 The right to property shall be guaranteed. It may only be encroached upon in the interest of public need or in the general interest of the community and in accordance with the provisions of appropriate laws.

ARTICLE 15 Every individual shall have the right to work under equitable and satisfactory conditions, and shall receive equal pay for equal work.

ARTICLE 16
1. Every individual shall have the right to enjoy the best attainable state of physical and mental health.
2. States parties to the present Charter shall take the necessary measures to protect the health of their people and to ensure that they receive medical attention when they are sick.

ARTICLE 17
1. Every individual shall have the right to education.
2. Every individual may freely take part in the cultural life of his community.
3. The promotion and protection of morals and traditional values recognized by the community shall be the duty of the State.

ARTICLE 18
1. The family shall be the natural unit and basis of society. It shall be protected by the State, which shall take care of its physical and moral health.
2. The State shall have the duty to assist the family, which is the custodian of morals and traditional values recognized by the community.
3. The State shall ensure the elimination of every discrimination against women and also ensure the protection of the rights of the woman and

the child as stipulated in international declarations and conventions.
4.   The aged and the disabled shall also have the right to special measures of protection in keeping with their physical or moral needs.

ARTICLE 19 All peoples shall be equal; they shall enjoy the same respect and shall have the same rights. Nothing shall justify the domination of a people by another.

ARTICLE 20
1.   All peoples shall have the right to existence. They shall have the unquestionable and inalienable right to self-determination. They shall freely determine their political status and shall pursue their economic and social development according to the policy they have freely chosen.
2.   Colonized or oppressed peoples shall have the right to free themselves from the bonds of domination by resorting to any means recognized by the international community.
3.   All peoples shall have the right to the assistance of the States parties to the present Charter in their liberation struggle against foreign domination, be it political, economic, or cultural.

ARTICLE 21
1.   All peoples shall freely dispose of their wealth and natural resources. This right shall be exercised in the exclusive interest of the people. In no case shall a people be deprived of it.
2.   In case of spoliation the dispossessed people shall have the right to the lawful recovery of its property as well as to an adequate compensation.
3.   The free disposal of wealth and natural resources shall be exercised without prejudice to the obligation of promoting international economic cooperation based on mutual respect, equitable exchange, and the principles of international law.
4.   States parties to the present Charter shall individually and collectively exercise the right to free disposal of their wealth and natural resources with a view to strengthening African unity and solidarity.
5.   States parties to the present Charter shall undertake to eliminate all forms of foreign economic exploitation, particularly that practiced by international monopolies, so as to enable their peoples to fully benefit from the advantages derived from their national resources.

ARTICLE 22
1.   All peoples shall have the right to their economic, social, and cultural development, with due regard to their freedom and identity and in the equal enjoyment of the common heritage of mankind.
2.   States shall have the duty, individually or collectively, to ensure the exercise of the right to development.

ARTICLE 23
1. All peoples shall have the right to national and international peace and security. The principles of solidarity and friendly relations implicitly affirmed by the Charter of the United Nations and reaffirmed by that of the Organization of African Unity shall govern relations between States.
2. For the purpose of strengthening peace, solidarity, and friendly relations, States parties to the present Charter shall ensure that:
   (a) any individual enjoying the right of asylum under Article 12 of the present Charter shall not engage in subversive activities against his country of origin or any other State party to the present Charter;
   (b) their territories shall not be used as bases for subversive or terrorist activities against the people of any other State party to the present Charter.

ARTICLE 24 All peoples shall have the right to a general satisfactory environment favorable to their development.

ARTICLE 25 States parties to the present Charter shall have the duty to promote and ensure through teaching, education, and publication, the respect of the rights and freedoms contained in the present Charter and to see to it that these freedoms and rights as well as corresponding obligations and duties are understood.

ARTICLE 26 States parties to the present Charter shall have the duty to guarantee the independence of the Courts and shall allow the establishment and improvement of appropriate national institutions entrusted with the promotion and protection of the rights and freedoms guaranteed by the present Charter.

CHAPTER II. DUTIES

ARTICLE 27
1. Every individual shall have duties towards his family and society, the State and other legally recognized communities, and the international community.
2. The rights and freedoms of each individual shall be exercised with due regard to the rights of others, collective security, morality, and common interest.

ARTICLE 28 Every individual shall have the duty to respect and consider his fellow being without discrimination, and to maintain relations aimed at promoting, safeguarding, and reinforcing mutual respect and tolerance.

ARTICLE 29 The individual shall also have the duty:
1. To preserve the harmonious development of the family and to work

for the cohesion and respect of the family; to respect his parents at all times, to maintain them in case of need;

2. To serve his national community by placing his physical and intellectual abilities at its service;
3. Not to compromise the security of the State whose national or resident he is;
4. To preserve and strengthen social and national solidarity, particularly when the latter is threatened;
5. To preserve and strengthen the national independence and the territorial integrity of his country and to contribute to its defence in accordance with the law;
6. To work to the best of his abilities and competence, and to pay taxes imposed by law in the interest of the society;
7. To preserve and strengthen positive African cultural values in his relations with other members of the society, in the spirit of tolerance, dialogue, and consultation, and, in general, to contribute to the promotion of the moral well-being of society;
8. To contribute to the best of his abilities, at all times and at all levels, to the promotion and achievement of African unity.

PART II: MEASURES OF SAFEGUARD

CHAPTER I. ESTABLISHMENT AND ORGANIZATION OF THE AFRICAN COMMISSION ON HUMAN AND PEOPLES' RIGHTS

ARTICLE 30 An African Commission on Human and Peoples' Rights, hereinafter called "the Commission," shall be established within the Organization of African Unity to promote human and peoples' rights and ensure their protection in Africa.

ARTICLE 31
1. The Commission shall consist of eleven members chosen from amongst African personalities of the highest reputation, known for their high morality, integrity, impartiality, and competence in matters of human and peoples' rights, particular consideration being given to persons having legal experience.
2. The members of the Commission shall serve in their personal capacity.

ARTICLE 32 The Commission shall not include more than one national of the same State.

ARTICLE 33 The members of the Commission shall be elected by secret ballot by the Assembly of Heads of State and Government, from a list of persons nominated by the States parties to the present Charter.

ARTICLE 34 Each State party to the present Charter may not nominate more than two candidates. The candidates must have the nationality of one of the States parties to the present Charter. When two candidates are nominated by a State, one of them may not be a national of that State.

ARTICLE 35
1. The Secretary-General of the Organization of African Unity shall invite States parties to the present Charter at least four months before the elections to nominate candidates;
2. The Secretary-General of the Organization of African Unity shall make an alphabetical list of the persons thus nominated and communicate it to the Heads of State and Government at least one month before the elections.

ARTICLE 36 The members of the Commission shall be elected for a six-year period and shall be eligible for re-election. However, the term of office of four of the members elected at the first election shall terminate after two years and the term of office of the three others, at the end of four years.

ARTICLE 37 Immediately after the first election, the Chairman of the Assembly of Heads of State and Government of the Organization of African Unity shall draw lots to decide the names of those members referred to in Article 36.

ARTICLE 38 After their election, the members of the Commission shall make a solemn declaration to discharge their duties impartially and faithfully.

ARTICLE 39
1. In case of death or resignation of a member of the Commission, the Chairman of the Commission shall immediately inform the Secretary-General of the Organization of African Unity, who shall declare the seat vacant from the date of death or from the date on which the resignation takes effect.
2. If, in the unanimous opinion of other members of the Commission, a member has stopped discharging his duties for any reason other than a temporary absence, the Chairman of the Commission shall inform the Secretary-General of the Organization of African Unity, who shall then declare the seat vacant.
3. In each of the cases anticipated above, the Assembly of Heads of State and Government shall replace the member whose seat became vacant for the remaining period of his term unless the period is less than six months.

ARTICLE 40 Every member of the Commission shall be in office until the date his successor assumes office.

ARTICLE 41 The Secretary-General of the Organization of African Unity shall appoint the Secretary of the Commission. He shall also provide the staff and services necessary for the effective discharge of the duties of the Commission. The Organization of African Unity shall bear the costs of the staff and services.

ARTICLE 42

1. The Commission shall elect its Chairman and Vice Chairman for a two-year period. They shall be eligible for re-election.
2. The Commission shall lay down its rules of procedure.
3. Seven members shall form a quorum.
4. In case of an equality of votes, the Chairman shall have a casting vote.
5. The Secretary-General may attend the meetings of the Commission. He shall neither participate in deliberations nor shall he be entitled to vote. The Chairman of the Commission may, however, invite him to speak.

ARTICLE 43 In discharging their duties, members of the Commission shall enjoy diplomatic privileges and immunities provided for in the General Convention on the Privileges and Immunities of the Organization of African Unity.

ARTICLE 44 Provision shall be made for the emoluments and allowances of the members of the Commission in the Regular Budget of the Organization of African Unity.

CHAPTER II. MANDATE OF THE COMMISSION

ARTICLE 45 The functions of the Commission shall be:

1. To promote Human and Peoples' Rights and in particular:
   (a) to collect documents, undertake studies and researches on African problems in the field of human and peoples' rights, organize seminars, symposia, and conferences, disseminate information, encourage national and local institutions concerned with human and peoples' rights, and should the case arise, give its views or make recommendations to Governments.
   (b) to formulate and lay down principles and rules aimed at solving legal problems relating to human and peoples' rights and fundamental freedoms, upon which African Governments may base their legislations.
   (c) to co-operate with other African and international institutions concerned with the promotion and protection of human and peoples' rights.
2. Ensure the protection of human and peoples' rights under conditions laid down by the present Charter.
3. Interpret all the provisions of the present Charter at the request of a State party, an institution of the OAU, or an African Organization recognized by the OAU.
4. Perform any other tasks which may be entrusted to it by the Assembly of Heads of State and Government.

CHAPTER III. PROCEDURE OF THE COMMISSION

ARTICLE 46 The Commission may resort to any appropriate method of investigation; it may hear from the Secretary-General of the Organization of African Unity or any other person capable of enlightening it.

COMMUNICATION FROM STATES

ARTICLE 47 If a State party to the present Charter has good reasons to believe that another State party to this Charter has violated the provisions of the Charter, it may draw, by written communication, the attention of that State to the matter. This communication shall also be addressed to the Secretary-General of the OAU and to the Chairman of the Commission. Within three months of the receipt of the communication, the State to which the communication is addressed shall give the enquiring State written explanation or statement elucidating the matter. This should include as much as possible relevant information relating to the laws and rules of procedure applied and applicable, and the redress already given or course of action available.

ARTICLE 48 If within three months from the date on which the original communication is received by the State to which it is addressed the issue is not settled to the satisfaction of the two States involved through bilateral negotiation or by any other peaceful procedure, either State shall have the right to submit the matter to the Commission through the Chairman, and shall notify the other States involved.

ARTICLE 49 Notwithstanding the provisions of Article 47, if a State party to the present Charter considers that another State party has violated the provisions of the Charter, it may refer the matter directly to the Commission by addressing a communication to the Chairman, to the Secretary-General of the Organization of African Unity, and the State concerned.

ARTICLE 50 The Commission can only deal with a matter submitted to it after making sure that all local remedies, if they exist, have been exhausted, unless it is obvious to the Commission that the procedure of achieving these remedies would be unduly prolonged.

ARTICLE 51
1. The Commission may ask the States concerned to provide it with all relevant information.
2. When the Commission is considering the matter, States concerned may be represented before it and submit written or oral representation.

ARTICLE 52 After having obtained from the States concerned and from other sources all the information it deems necessary and after having tried all appropriate means to reach an amicable solution based on the respect of Human and Peoples' Rights, the Commission shall prepare, within a reasonable period of time from the notification referred to in Article 48, a report stating the facts and its findings. This report shall be sent to the States concerned and communicated to the Assembly of Heads of State and Government.

ARTICLE 53 While transmitting its report, the Commission may make to the Assembly of Heads of State and Government such recommendations as it deems useful.

ARTICLE 54 The Commission shall submit to each ordinary Session of the Assembly of Heads of State and Government a report on its activities.

OTHER COMMUNICATIONS

ARTICLE 55
1. Before each Session, the Secretary of the Commission shall make a list of the communications other than those of States parties to the present Charter and transmit them to the members of the Commission, who shall indicate which communications should be considered by the Commission.
2. A communication shall be considered by the Commission if a simple majority of its members so decide.

ARTICLE 56 Communications relating to human and peoples' rights referred to in Article 55 received by the Commission shall be considered if they:
1. Indicate their authors even if the latter request anonymity,
2. Are compatible with the Charter of the Organization of African Unity or with the present Charter,
3. Are not written in disparaging or insulting language directed against the State concerned and its institutions or to the Organization of African Unity,
4. Are not based exclusively on news disseminated through the mass media,
5. Are sent after exhausting local remedies, if any, unless it is obvious that this procedure is unduly prolonged,
6. Are submitted within a reasonable period from the time local remedies are exhausted or from the date the Commission is seized of the matter, and
7. Do not deal with cases which have been settled by these States involved in accordance with the principles of the Charter of the United Nations, or the Charter of the Organization of African Unity, or the provisions of the present Charter.

ARTICLE 57 Prior to any substantive consideration, all communications shall be brought to the knowledge of the State concerned by the Chairman of the Commission.

ARTICLE 58
1. When it appears after deliberations of the Commission that one or more communications apparently relate to special cases which reveal the existence of a series of serious or massive violations of human and

peoples' rights, the Commission shall draw the attention of the Assembly of Heads of State and Government to these special cases.

2. The Assembly of Heads of State and Government may then request the Commission to undertake an in-depth study of these cases and make a factual report, accompanied by its findings and recommendations.

3. A case of emergency duly noticed by the Commission shall be submitted by the latter to the Chairman of the Assembly of Heads of State and Government, who may request an in-depth study.

ARTICLE 59

1. All measures taken within the provisions of the present Chapter shall remain confidential until such a time as the Assembly of Heads of State and Government shall otherwise decide.

2. However, the report shall be published by the Chairman of the Commission upon the decision of the Assembly of Heads of State and Government.

3. The report on the activities of the Commission shall be published by its Chairman after it has been considered by the Assembly of Heads of State and Government.

CHAPTER IV. APPLICABLE PRINCIPLES

ARTICLE 60 The Commission shall draw inspiration from international law on human and peoples' rights, particularly from the provisions of various African instruments on human and peoples' rights, the Charter of the United Nations, the Charter of the Organization of African Unity, the Universal Declaration of Human Rights, other instruments adopted by the United Nations and by African countries in the field of human and peoples' rights, as well as from the provisions of various instruments adopted within the Specialized Agencies of the United Nations of which the parties to the present Charter are members.

ARTICLE 61 The Commission shall also take into consideration, as subsidiary measures to determine the principles of law, other general or special international conventions, laying down rules expressly recognized by member states of the Organization of African Unity, African practices consistent with international norms on human and peoples' rights, customs generally accepted as law, general principles of law recognized by African states, as well as legal precedents and doctrine.

ARTICLE 62 Each state party shall undertake to submit every two years, from the date the present Charter comes into force, a report on the legislative or other measures taken with a view to giving effect to the rights and freedoms recognized and guaranteed by the present Charter.

ARTICLE 63
1. The present Charter shall be open to signature, ratification, or adherence of the member states of the Organization of African Unity.
2. The instruments of ratification or adherence to the present Charter shall be deposited with the Secretary-General of the Organization of African Unity.
3. The present Charter shall come into force three months after the reception by the Secretary-General of the instruments of ratification or adherence of a simple majority of the member states of the Organization of African Unity.

PART III: GENERAL PROVISIONS

ARTICLE 64
1. After the coming into force of the present Charter, members of the Commission shall be elected in accordance with the relevant Articles of the present Charter.
2. The Secretary-General of the Organization of African Unity shall convene the first meeting of the Commission at the Headquarters of the Organization within three months of the constitution of the Commission. Thereafter, the Commission shall be convened by its Chairman whenever necessary but at least once a year.

ARTICLE 65 For each of the States that will ratify or adhere to the present Charter after its coming into force, the Charter shall take effect three months after the date of the deposit by that State of its instrument of ratification or adherence.

ARTICLE 66 Special protocols or agreements may, if necessary, supplement the provisions of the present Charter.

ARTICLE 67 The Secretary-General of the Organization of African Unity shall inform member states of the Organization of the deposit of each instrument of ratification or adherence.

ARTICLE 68 The present Charter may be amended if a State party makes a written request to that effect to the Secretary-General of the Organization of African Unity. The Assembly of Heads of State and Government may only consider the draft amendment after all the States parties have been duly informed of it and the Commission has given its opinion on it at the request of the sponsoring State. The amendment shall be approved by a simple majority of the States parties. It shall come into force for each State which has accepted it in accordance with its constitutional procedure three months after the Secretary-General has received notice of the acceptance.

Concordance of Basic Human Rights Guaranteed in the Banjul Charter and Other Major Human Rights Treaties

ROBERT C. WIGTON

Concordance of Basic Human Rights Guaranteed in the Banjul Charter and Other Major Human Rights Treaties

Right Guaranteed ARTICLES	Banjul Charter	European Convention	American Convention	UN Universal Declaration	UN Covenant on Civil and Political Rights	UN Covenant on Economic, Social and Cultural Rights
I. Civil and Political Rights of Individuals						
Right to enjoy other rights without discrimination (a)	2	14	1	2	2(1), 3, 27	2(2), 3
Rights to equality before the law and to equal protection thereunder	3	—	24	7	26	—
Right to life	4	2(1)	4	1, 3	6	—
Right to personal dignity and recognition of legal status (b)	5	3, 4	3, 5, 6, 11	4, 5, 6, 12	7, 8, 16, 17	—
Right to liberty and security of person (c)	6	5(1)	7	3, 9	9	—
Right to a fair trial (d)	7	5, 6, 7, 13	7, 8, 9, 25	8, 10, 11	9, 14, 15	—
Freedom of conscience and religion (e)	8	9	12	18	18	—
Freedom of information and expression (f)	9	10	13	19	19	—
Freedom of association	10(1)	11	16	20(1), 23(4)	22	8
Freedom from compulsory association (g)	10(2)	—	—	20(2)	—	—
Freedom of assembly	11	11	15	20(1)	21	—
Right of legally admitted non-nationals to reside	12(4)	—	22(6)	—	13	—

Freedom of movement and residence (h)	12	—	22	13	12	—
Right to asylum	12(3)	—	22(7)	14	—	—
Right to participate in government (i)	13(1)	—	23	21	25	—
Right to equal access to public property and services	13(3)	—	23(1)	21(2)	25	—
II. Economic, Social and Cultural Rights of Individuals						
Right to property (j)	14	—	21	17	—	—
Right to equitable and satisfactory work conditions and to equal pay for equal work	15	—	—	23, 24	—	6, 7
Right to a better standard of living (k)	16(1)	—	—	25(1)	—	12
Right to education (1)	17(1)	—	—	26	—	13
Right to partake in nation's cultural life (m)	17(2)	—	—	27	—	15
Special rights of women and children (n)	18(3)	—	—	25(2)	23(4), 24	10(2), (3)
Rights of the family (o)	—	12	17	16, 25(2)	23, 24	10(1)
Right of the aged and disabled to special protection	18(4)	—	—	—	—	—
III. Duties of States Parties						
Duty of States to recognize other rights in Charter and to adopt legislation to implement those rights	1	1	1, 2	—	2	2
Duty of States to protect the health of their people	16(2)	—	—	—	—	12(2)

Right Guaranteed ARTICLES	Banjul Charter	European Convention	American Convention	UN Universal Declaration	UN Covenant on Civil and Political Rights	UN Covenant on Economic, Social and Cultural Rights
Duty of States to protect the morals and traditional values of society	17(3)	—	—	—	—	—
Duty of States to assist and protect the family	18(1),(2)	—	17(4), 19	16(3), 25(2)	23(1), (4), 24(1)	10
Duty of States to dispose of their natural resources with a view to strengthening African unity	21(4)	—	—	—	—	—
Duty of States to eliminate foreign economic exploitation in order to enable their people to fully benefit from natural resources	21(5)	—	—	—	—	—
Duty of States to ensure exercise of the right to development	22(2)	—	26	—	2(2)	2(1), 11
Duty of States to prevent those whom they grant asylum from engaging in subversive activities against other States, and to not allow their country to become a base for subversive activities against another member State	23(2)	—	—	—	—	—
Duty of States to promote and ensure respect or the rights in this Charter	25	—	—	Preamble	—	—
Duty of States to guarantee the independence of the courts and other institutions protecting the rights in this Charter	26	—	25(2)	—	—	—

IV. Rights of Peoples

Freedom of non-nationals from mass expulsion (p)	12(5)	—	22(8), (9)	—	13	—
All peoples' right to equality and to enjoy the same rights; no people shall have domination over another people	19	—	—	—	—	—
All peoples' right to existence, self-determination, and free choice of social and economic development	20(1)	—	—	—	1	1
Rights of colonized or oppressed peoples to any means for freeing themselves and to the assistance of signatory States	20(2), (3)	—	—	—	—	—
Peoples' right to full benefit from their natural resources (q)	21	—	—	—	1(2)	1(2), 25
Peoples' right to economic, social, and cultural development (r)	22(1)	—	—	—	—	11
Peoples' right to national and international peace and security (s)	23(1)	—	—	28	—	—
Peoples' right to a satisfactory environment for development	24	—	—	22	—	—

V. Duties of the Individual

Individual duties and limitations on personal rights	27	—	32	29	—	—
Duty of the Individual to respect others without discrimination / to promote mutual respect and tolerance	28	—	—	—	—	—
Specified Duties of the individual (t)	29	—	—	—	—	—

(a) All six of the treaties compared here guarantee enjoyment of other rights and freedoms without discrimination on the basis of race, color, sex, language, religion, "political or (any) other opinion," birth, or "any other status." In addition, the Banjul Charter guarantees its enumerated rights without distinction on the basis of "ethnic group." This has no analogous wording in the other agreements; however, the European Convention does guarantee other rights without discrimination on the grounds of an individual's "association with a national minority." The Banjul Charter also proscribes discrimination on the basis of one's "fortune." This is paralleled in the American Charter by a guarantee of non-discrimination on grounds of "economic status" and in the four other treaties by prohibition of discrimination on basis of "property."

(b) The Right to Personal Dignity entails prohibition of slavery, torture, and inhuman or degrading punishment.

(c) The Right to Liberty includes the freedom from arbitrary arrest or detention.

(d) The Right to a Fair Trial includes the following basic guarantees: right of appeal to a higher court, a presumption of innocence, right to a speedy and impartial trial, right to counsel, and freedom from *ex post facto* laws. The European Convention and the Universal Declaration do not expressly grant a right of appeal. Only the Banjul Charter (Art. 7(2)) expressly provides that punishment shall be personal and imposed only on the offender.

(e) The Banjul Charter guarantees "the profession and free practice of religion." The European Convention, the Universal Declaration, and the American Convention guarantee a right to change one's religion and to observe it in community with others either privately or publicly. The American Convention includes the right to profess or disseminate one's religious beliefs; the European Convention and Universal Declaration guarantee a right to "teach" one's religion.

(f) Each of the treaties containing a right of expression and information guarantees a right to receive and to impart information. In addition, the American Convention, the Universal Declaration, and the Covenant on Civil and Political Rights also guarantee a right to "seek" information. The American Convention (Art. 14) grants a Right of Reply to inaccurate or offensive statements. The Universal Declaration and the Covenant on Civil and Political Rights guarantee a right to "hold opinions" as well as a freedom of expression.

(g) The Banjul Charter may limit this right by the imposition of duties on the individual in Art. 29.

(h) The Right of Movement and Residence includes the freedom of movement within one's own state as well as the freedom to leave and reenter one's country.

(i) The four treaties guaranteeing a Right to Freely Participate in Government all specify that this may be either directly or through freely chosen representatives. The American Convention, the Universal Declaration and Covenant on Civil and Political Rights also grant a right to "vote and be elected" that is absent from the other treaties.

(j) Only the American Convention mentions a right to compensation for property that has been confiscated.

(k) The Banjul Charter guarantees a right to enjoy the "best attainable" physical and mental health, the Universal Declaration grants a right to an "adequate" living standard, and the Covenant on Economic, Social and Cultural Rights recognizes a right to enjoy the "highest attainable" standard of living.

(l) The Banjul Charter does not provide for compulsory primary education as do the other two treaties establishing this right.

(m) The Banjul Charter imposes on the states the duty to promote and protect morals and traditional values of the community (Art. 17 (3)).

(n) The Banjul Charter imposes a duty on states to eliminate discrimination against women and to ensure the protection of the rights of children. The Universal Declaration states that motherhood and childhood are entitled to special protection. The Covenant on Civil and Political Rights lists specific rights of the child only. The Covenant on Economic, Social and Cultural Rights grants special protection to pregnant women and children.

(o) The Banjul Charter does not grant any specific rights to the family as such aside from State protection and assistance (Art. 18 (1), (1)). The Universal Declaration, and the Covenant on Civil and Political Rights, however, guarantee the following additional rights: a general right to marry and found a family, the necessity of the full and free consent of both spouses to any marriage, a right of both spouses to equality in marriage and in the dissolution of marriage, and the equal rights and treatment of children born out of wedlock with other children. The European Convention grants only the right to marry and found a family. The Covenant on Economic, Social and Cultural Rights only guarantees that both parties must fully and freely agree to any marriage.

(p) The Banjul Charter defines "mass expulsion" as that directed towards "national, racial, ethnic, or religious groups." The American Convention prohibits the "collective expulsion of aliens," and the deportation of an alien to a country where his life or freedom would be violated because of his "race, nationality, religion, social status, or political opinions."

(q) The Banjul Charter's provisions concerning natural resources include: the use of such resources in the exclusive interest of the people, and to strengthen African unity, a right to compensation and the goal of eliminating all forms of foreign economic exploitation.

(r) Whereas the Banjul Charter speaks in terms of "peoples'" rights, the Covenant on Economic, Social and Cultural Rights recognizes the "right of everyone" to an adequate living standard and to the "continuous improvement of living standards."

(s) The Universal Declaration states that everyone is entitled to an international order in which the rights in that instrument can be fully realized.

(t) The Banjul Charter imposes the following duties on the individual: to preserve harmonious family development, to respect parents, and provide for their support if necessary; to serve the national community; not to compromise state security; to preserve and strengthen social and national solidarity, independence, and national integrity; to work to the best of one's ability and pay taxes; to preserve African cultural values and contribute to the achievement of African unity.

Major African Conferences on Human Rights, 1961–81 (Locations, Dates, and Sources)

Lagos, Nigeria, January 3–7, 1961. "African Conference on the Rule of Law, Lagos, Nigeria, January 3–7, 1961: A Report of the Proceedings of the Conference." Geneva: International Commission of Jurists, 1961.

Dakar, Senegal, February 8–22, 1966. "Seminar on Human Rights in Developing Countries." UN Document ST/TAO/HR/25.

Cairo, Egypt, September 2–15, 1969. "Seminar on the Establishment of Regional Commissions on Human Rights with Special Reference to Africa." UN Document ST/TAO/HR/38.

Addis Ababa, Ethiopia, April 19–23, 1971. "Report of the Conference of African Jurists on the African Legal Process and the Individual." UN Document E/CN/14/521, 5 July 1971.

Dar-es-Salaam, Tanzania, October 23-November 5, 1973. "Seminar on the Study of New Ways and Means for Promoting Human Rights with Special Attention to the Problems and Needs of Africa." UN Document ST/TAO/HR/48.

Khartoum, Sudan, February 16–22, 1975. "Structures of Injustice: A Report of a Consultation on Violations of Human Rights." Nairobi: All Africa Council of Churches/World Council of Churches. Also see "Factors Responsible for the Violations of Human Rights in Africa," *ISSUE* 6, no. 4 (Winter 1976), pp. 44–46.

Dar-es-Salaam, Tanzania, September 23–28, 1976. *Human Rights in a One-Party State*. London: Search Press, for the International Commission of Jurists, 1978.

Butare, Rwanda, July 3–7, 1978. Hurst Hannum, "The Butare Colloquium on Human Rights and Economic Development in Francophone Africa: A Summary and Analysis," *Universal Human Rights* 1, no. 2 (April–June 1979), 63–87.

Freetown, Sierra Leone, August 1–5, 1978. Third biennial conference of the African Bar Association, "Human Rights in Africa." *Africa Research Bulletin* 15, no. 8 (September 1978), cols. 4973–74; *West Africa* August 14, 1978, 1588–90 and August 21, 1978, 1628 and 1668.

Cape Town, South Africa, January 22–26, 1979. First international conference on human rights in South Africa. C.F. Forsyth and J.E. Schiller, *Human Rights: The Cape Town Conference*. Cape Town: Juta, 1979.

Arusha, Tanzania, May 7–17, 1979. Conference on refugees in Africa, sponsored by the OAU, the United Nations High Commission on Refugees, and the World Council of Churches.

Kigale, Rwanda, May 21–2, 1979. Conference of French-speaking African countries, at which a six-nation commission to investigate human rights violations in the Central African Empire was established.

Monrovia, Liberia, July 17–21, 1979. OAU summit meeting, at which a Senegal-Gambia resolution was passed calling for experts to draft an African Charter of Human Rights. OAU Document AHG/115 (XVI).

Monrovia, Liberia, September 10–21, 1979. "Seminar on the Establishment of Regional Commissions on Human Rights with Special Reference to Africa." UN Document ST/HR/SER.A/4.

Dakar, Senegal, November 25–December 2, 1979. "African Charter of Human and Peoples' Rights" (Dakar Draft). OAU Document CAB/LEG/67/3/Rev.1.

Banjul, the Gambia, June 8–15, 1980. Conference of ministers of justice and legal experts to work on the proposed charter; 11 articles finished.

Banjul, the Gambia, January 7–19, 1981. "African Charter of Human and Peoples' Rights" (Banjul Charter). OAU Document CAB/LEG/67/3/Rev.5. (For complete text, see Appendix 1 to this book.)

Nairobi, Kenya, June 24–28, 1981. OAU summit meeting, at which the Banjul Charter was adopted for ratification by a simple majority of member states.

About the Authors

Jack Donnelly, Assistant Professor of Political Science at The College of the Holy Cross, has published numerous articles on human rights in such journals as *The American Political Science Review, Human Rights Quarterly, International Organization*, and *World Politics*. His degrees are from Georgetown University (B.S.F.S. and M.A.) and the University of California at Berkeley (Ph.D.).

Richard Gittleman, Research Associate at the International Human Rights Law Group in Washington, D.C., received his J.D. degree from American University. He was a Peace Corps volunteer from 1977 to 1979 in Zaire, where he taught English at the high school level and conducted workshops in the Equateur and Bas-Zaire regions. He was an official observer at the 1981 OAU summit meeting at which the Banjul Charter was adopted.

Rhoda Howard, Associate Professor of Sociology at McMaster University, Hamilton, Ontario, received her undergraduate and graduate degrees at McGill University. Her publications include *Colonialization and Underdevelopment in Ghana* and articles dealing with African refugees, African human rights, and social stratification.

Edward Kannyo has been Project Director for Africa at the International League for Human Rights, where he has focused upon the effectiveness of human rights organizations now functioning in Africa. He received his M.A. and Ph.D. degrees from Yale University after completing his B.A. at Makerere College. His publications include articles on Uganda and Zaire.

Vicki Kraft has an M.A. degree in Political Science from Northern Illinois University and a J.D. degree from the State University of New York at Buffalo. She is currently a Ph.D. student in Political Science at SUNY/Buffalo.

Lakshman Marasinghe, recipient of the LL.B., LL.M. and Ph.D. degrees from the University of London, is Professor in the Faculty of Law at the University of Windsor, Ontario. A barrister and solicitor in the Province of Ontario and Barrister-at-Law of the English Bar, he has published extensively in law journals on the subjects of comparative jurisprudence, civil law, and conflicts of laws in developing countries. He is editor of *Third World Legal Studies*, and has taught in Kenya, Nigeria, and the Sudan.

Ronald I. Meltzer, Associate Professor of Political Science at the State University of New York at Buffalo, received his degrees at Ohio University (B.A.) and Columbia University (M. Phil. and Ph.D.). He has written numerous articles and chapters on international trade matters, North-South relations, and international economic institutions. He co-authored *U.S. International Economic Policy in Action*.

Abdullahi Ahmed El Naiem is Lecturer and Head of the Department of Public Law at the University of Khartoum. He has published works on the role of the Sudanese magistrate and on discovery in criminal cases in English and Sudanese journals. He holds his Ph.D. from the University of Edinburgh, his LL.B. from Cambridge University and the University of Khartoum, and his Diploma in Criminology from Cambridge University. In 1981 he was named a Rockefeller Fellow in Human Rights at Columbia University.

Corinne Nyquist, Associate Librarian at the State University College in New Paltz, N.Y., received her M.A. from the University of Minnesota. Her major specialities are human rights and African studies. She has co-edited the New York African Studies Association *Newsletter* and published *Human Rights and Citizenship* through the State Education Department of New York.

Harry M. Scoble, Executive Vice Chairman of Human Rights Internet, formerly taught at the University of North Carolina, Boston University, University of Wisconsin, University of California at Los Angeles, and the University of Illinois at Chicago Circle. He has published close to fifty professional papers and chapters on American domestic politics and international human rights. He co-edits the *Human Rights Internet Newsletter*.

Timothy M. Shaw, Associate Professor of Political Science at Dalhousie University in Halifax, Nova Scotia, has written numerous books and monographs on African politics. He holds degrees from the University of Sussex, the University of East Africa, and Princeton University. His many articles in journals and books cover African politics, Canadian policy toward Africa, and the impact of international economic conditions on Africa, among other topics.

George W. Shepherd, Jr., Professor of International and African Studies at the Graduate School of International Studies, University of Denver, has edited *Africa Today* since 1965. His books include *Global Human Rights, Anti-Apartheid*, and *The Politics of African Nationalism*. In summer 1982, he was awarded a National Endowment for the Humanities grant to lead a seminar on human rights and third world issues.

Richard Weisfelder, Associate Professor of Political Science at the University of Toledo, received his B.A. at Amherst, his M.A. and Ph.D. at Harvard. He was awarded a Fulbright-Hayes Lectureship for 1979–1981, spent at the University College of Botswana, and has published on human rights and political issues in the states of Southern Africa.

Claude E. Welch, Jr., Professor of Political Science, State University of New York at Buffalo, received his baccalaureate and doctoral degrees at Harvard and Oxford, respectively. He has authored three books and edited five on political change, African politics, and the political roles of armed forces. Fifteen chapters by Welch have appeared in books by other authors. His numerous journal articles have focused on human rights, civil-military relations, and political change in Africa.

Robert C. Wigton is a Ph.D. student in Political Science at the State University of New York at Buffalo, where he previously earned his M.A. and J.D. degrees.

Index